C# 3.0:
A Beginner's Guide

Herbert Schildt

New York Chicago San Francisco
Lisbon London Madrid Mexico City
Milan New Delhi San Juan
Seoul Singapore Sydney Toronto

Cataloging-in-Publication Data is on file with the Library of Congress

McGraw-Hill books are available at special quantity discounts to use as premiums and sales promotions, or for use in corporate training programs. To contact a special sales representative, please visit the Contact Us page at www.mhprofessional.com.

C# 3.0: A Beginner's Guide

1234567890 DOC DOC 0198

ISBN 978-0-07-158830-0
MHID   0-07-158830-2

Sponsoring Editor   Jane Brownlow
Editorial Supervisor   Patty Mon
Project Manager   Vasundhara Sawhney, International Typesetting and Composition
Acquisitions Coordinator   Jennifer Housh
Technical Editor   Eric Lippert
Copy Editor   Lisa McCoy
Proofreader   Laura Bowman
Indexer   Sheryl Schildt
Production Supervisor   Jean Bodeaux
Composition   International Typesetting and Composition
Illustration   International Typesetting and Composition
Cover Designer   Jeff Weeks

About the Author

Herb Schildt is a leading authority on C#, Java, C, and C++. His programming books have sold more than 3.5 million copies worldwide and have been translated into all major foreign languages. His acclaimed books include *C#: The Complete Reference, Java: The Complete Reference, Java: A Beginner's Guide, C++: The Complete Reference*, and *C++: A Beginner's Guide*. Although interested in all facets of computing, his primary focus is computer languages, including compilers, interpreters, and robotic control languages. He also has an active interest in the standardization of languages. Schildt holds both graduate and undergraduate degrees from the University of Illinois. He can be reached at his consulting office at (217) 586-4683. His website is **www.HerbSchildt.com**.

About the Tech Editor

Eric Lippert is a senior developer on the Microsoft C# compiler development team.

Contents

Preface

In an age in which "the network is the computer," the .NET Framework has become a leading environment for which code is created. The premier language for .NET development is C#. Therefore, if .NET programming is in your future, you have chosen the right language to learn.

Beyond its use for .NET programming, C# is important for another reason. Its innovative features are reshaping the programming world, changing the way code is written, and enabling solutions to be framed in new ways. Thus, C# is helping to define the future direction of programming. As a result, fluency in C# is no longer an option for the professional programmer. It has become a necessity.

The purpose of this book is to teach you the fundamentals of C# programming. It uses a step-by-step approach complete with numerous examples and self tests. It assumes no previous programming experience. The book starts with the basics, such as how to compile and run a C# program. It then discusses the keywords, features, and constructs that comprise the C# language. By the time you finish, you will have a firm grasp of the essentials of C# programming.

As all programmers know, nothing stands still very long in the world of programming. C# is no exception. Since its creation in 2000, C# has undergone two major revisions, with each revision adding significant new features. At the time of this writing, the current version of C# is 3.0, and this is the version of C# described by this book. Therefore, this book includes coverage of C#'s newest features, including Language Integrated Query (LINQ) and lambda expressions.

Of course, this beginner's guide is just a starting point. C# is a very large language and involves more than just the keywords and syntax that define it. It also involves the use of a sophisticated set of libraries called the .NET Framework Class Library. This library is very large, and a complete discussion would require a book of its own. Although several of the classes defined by this library are discussed in this book, because of space limitations, most are not. To be a top-notch C# programmer implies mastery of this library, too. After completing this book, you will have the knowledge to explore this library and all other aspects of C#.

How This Book Is Organized

This book presents an evenly paced tutorial in which each section builds upon the previous one. It contains 15 chapters, each discussing an aspect of C#. This book is unique because it includes several special elements that help organize and reinforce what you are learning.

Key Skills and Concepts

Each chapter begins with a list of the key skills and concepts that are taught in the chapter.

Self Test

Each chapter concludes with a Self Test, which lets you test your knowledge. The answers are in the Appendix.

Ask the Expert

Sprinkled throughout the book are special "Ask the Expert" boxes. These contain additional information or interesting commentary about a topic. They use a question/answer format.

Try This

Each chapter contains one or more Try This sections. They present step-by-step examples that show you how to apply what you are learning.

No Previous Programming Experience Required

This book assumes no previous programming experience. Thus, if you have never programmed before, you can use this book. Of course, in this day and age, most readers will have at least a little prior programming experience. For many, this previous experience will be in C++ or Java. As you will learn, C# is related to both of these languages. Therefore, if you already know C++ or Java, then you will be able to learn C# easily.

Required Software

To compile and run the programs in this book, you will need a version of Visual Studio 2008 (or later) that supports C#. Visual C# 2008 Express Edition is a good choice because it is available free of charge from Microsoft. All code in this book was tested using that compiler. Of course, the .NET Framework must be installed on your computer.

Don't Forget: Code on the Web

The source code for all of the examples and projects in this book is available free of charge on the Web at **www.mhprofessional.com**.

More from Herbert Schildt

C# 3.0: A Beginner's Guide is just one of Herb's many programming books. Here are some others that you will find of interest.

To continue your study of C#, we suggest:

C# 3.0: The Complete Reference

To learn about Java, we recommend:

Java: The Complete Reference

Java: A Beginner's Guide

The Art of Java

Swing: A Beginner's Guide

Herb Schildt's Java Programming Cookbook

To learn about C++, you will find these books especially helpful:

C++: The Complete Reference

C++: A Beginner's Guide

C++ from the Ground Up

STL Programming from the Ground Up

The Art of C++

Herb Schildt's C++ Programming Cookbook

If you want to learn about the C language, then the following title will be of interest:

C: The Complete Reference

When you need solid answers fast, turn to Herbert Schildt, the recognized authority on programming.

Chapter 1

C# Fundamentals

Key Skills & Concepts

- The history behind C#

- How C# relates to and uses the .NET Framework

- The three principles of object-oriented programming

- Create, compile, and run C# programs

- Variables

- The **if** and **for** statements

- Code blocks

- The C# keywords

The quest for the perfect programming language is as old as the discipline of programming itself. In this quest, C# is the current standard bearer. Created by Microsoft to support development for its .NET Framework, C# leverages time-tested features with cutting-edge innovations and provides a highly usable, efficient way to write programs for the modern enterprise computing environment. In the course of this book, you will learn to program using it.

The purpose of this chapter is to introduce C#, including the forces that drove its creation, its design philosophy, and several of its most important features. By far, the hardest thing about learning a programming language is the fact that no element exists in isolation. Instead, the components of the language work together. It is this interrelatedness that makes it difficult to discuss one aspect of C# without involving others. To overcome this problem, this chapter provides a brief overview of several C# features, including the general form of a C# program, two control statements, and several operators. It does not go into too many details, but rather concentrates on the general concepts common to any C# program.

At this time, version 3.0 is the current release of C#, and this is the version taught in this book. Of course, much of the information presented here applies to all versions of C#.

C#'s Family Tree

Computer languages do not exist in a void. Rather, they relate to one another, with each new language influenced in one form or another by the ones that came before. In a process akin to cross-pollination, features from one language are adapted by another, a new innovation is integrated into an existing context, or an older construct is removed. In this way, languages evolve and the art of programming advances. C# is no exception.

C# inherits a rich programming legacy. It is directly descended from two of the world's most successful computer languages: C and C++. It is closely related to another: Java. Understanding the nature of these relationships is critical to understanding C#. Thus, we begin our examination of C# by placing it in the historical context of these three languages.

C: The Beginning of the Modern Age of Programming

The creation of C marks the beginning of the modern age of programming. C was invented by Dennis Ritchie in the 1970s on a DEC PDP-11 that used the UNIX operating system. While some earlier languages, most notably Pascal, had achieved significant success, it was C that established the paradigm that still charts the course of programming today.

C grew out of the *structured programming* revolution of the 1960s. Structured languages are defined by their rich set of well-designed control statements, subroutines with local variables, code blocks, and other improvements that make it easier to organize and maintain a program. Although other languages at the time had similar features, C implemented these elements using a terse yet easy-to-use syntax. It also embodied a philosophy that put the programmer (not the language) at the center of the development process. As a result, C quickly won many converts. It became the dominant structured programming language of the late 1970s and 1980s, and it remains so to this day.

The Creation of OOP and C++

As useful as C is, by the late 1970s, the size of many projects was near or at the limits of what structured programming methodologies and the C language could handle. Programs were simply becoming too large. To address this problem, a new way to program began to emerge. This method is called *object-oriented programming* (OOP for short). Using OOP, a programmer could handle much larger programs. The trouble was that C, the most popular language at the time, did not support object-oriented programming. The desire for an object-oriented version of C ultimately led to the creation of C++.

C++ was invented by Bjarne Stroustrup, beginning in 1979, at Bell Laboratories in Murray Hill, New Jersey. He initially called the new language "C with Classes." However, in 1983, the name was changed to "C++." C++ contains the entire C language. Thus, C is the foundation upon which C++ is built. Most of the additions that Stroustrup made to C were designed to support object-oriented programming. In essence, C++ is the object-oriented version of C.

By building upon the foundation of C, Stroustrup provided a smooth migration path to OOP. Instead of having to learn an entirely new language, a C programmer needed to learn only a few new features before reaping the benefits of the object-oriented methodology. This made it easy for legions of programmers to make the shift from structured programming to object-oriented programming. As a result, by the second half of the 1990s, C++ became the preeminent language for the development of high-performance code.

It is critical to understand that the invention of C++ was not an attempt to create a new programming language. Instead, it was an enhancement to an already highly successful language. This approach to language development—beginning with an existing language and moving it forward—established a trend that continues today.

The Internet and Java Emerge

The next major advance in programming languages was Java. Work on Java, which was originally called Oak, began in 1991 at Sun Microsystems. The main driving force behind Java's design was James Gosling. Patrick Naughton, Chris Warth, Ed Frank, and Mike Sheridan also played a role.

Java is a structured, object-oriented language with a syntax and philosophy derived from C++. The innovative aspects of Java were driven not so much by advances in the art of programming (although some certainly were), but rather by changes in the computing environment. Prior to the mainstreaming of the Internet, most programs were written, compiled, and targeted for a specific CPU and a specific operating system. While it has always been true that programmers like to reuse their code, the ability to easily port a program from one environment to another took a backseat to more pressing problems. However, with the rise of the Internet, in which many different types of CPUs and operating systems are connected, the old problem of portability became substantially more important. To solve this problem, a new language was needed, and this new language was Java.

Java achieved portability by translating a program's source code into an intermediate language called *bytecode*. This bytecode was then executed by the Java Virtual Machine (JVM). Therefore, a Java program could run in any environment for which a JVM was available. Also, since the JVM is relatively easy to implement, it was readily available for a large number of environments.

In addition to the need for portability, there was a second fundamental problem that needed to be solved before Internet-based programming could become a reality. This problem was security. As all Internet users know, computer viruses constitute a serious and on-going potential threat. What good would portable programs be if no one could trust them? Who would want to risk executing a program delivered via the Internet? It might contain malicious code. Fortunately, the solution to the security problem is also found in the JVM and bytecode. Because the JVM executes the bytecode, it has full control of the program and can prevent a Java program from doing something that it shouldn't. Thus, the JVM and bytecode solved both the issues of portability and security.

It is key to understand that Java's use of bytecode differed radically from both C and C++, which were nearly always compiled to executable machine code. Machine code is tied to a specific CPU and operating system. Thus, if you wanted to run a C/C++ program on a different system, it needed to be recompiled to machine code specifically for that environment. To create a C/C++ program that would run in a variety of environments, several different executable versions of the program were needed. Not only was this impractical, it was also expensive. Java's use of an intermediate language was an elegant and cost-effective solution. It was also a solution that C# would adapt for its own purposes.

As mentioned, Java is descended from C and C++. Its syntax is based on C, and its object model is evolved from C++. Although Java code is neither upwardly nor downwardly compatible with C or C++, its syntax is sufficiently similar that the large pool of existing C/C++ programmers could move to Java with very little effort. Furthermore, because Java built upon and improved an existing paradigm, Gosling, et al., were free to focus their attentions on the new and innovative features. Just as Stroustrup did not need to "reinvent the wheel" when creating C++, Gosling did not need to create an entirely new language when developing Java.

Moreover, with the creation of Java, C and C++ became an accepted substrata upon which to build a new computer language.

The Creation of C#

While Java has successfully addressed many of the issues surrounding portability and security in the Internet environment, there are still features that it lacks. One is *cross-language interoperability,* also called *mixed-language programming.* This is the ability for the code produced by one language to work easily with the code produced by another. Cross-language interoperability is crucial for the creation of large, distributed software systems. It is also desirable for programming software components, because the most valuable component is one that can be used by the widest variety of computer languages in the greatest number of operating environments.

Another feature lacking in Java is full integration with the Windows platform. Although Java programs can be executed in a Windows environment (assuming that the Java Virtual Machine has been installed), Java and Windows are not closely coupled. Since Windows is the mostly widely used operating system in the world, lack of direct support for Windows is a drawback to Java.

To answer these and other needs, Microsoft developed C#. C# was created at Microsoft late in the 1990s and was part of Microsoft's overall .NET strategy. It was first released in its alpha version in the middle of 2000. C#'s chief architect was Anders Hejlsberg.

C# is directly related to C, C++, and Java. This is not by accident. These are three of the most widely used—and most widely liked—programming languages in the world. Furthermore, nearly all professional programmers today know C, C++, or Java. By building C# upon a solid, well-understood foundation, C# offers an easy migration path from these languages. Since it was neither necessary nor desirable for Hejlsberg to "reinvent the wheel," he was free to focus on specific improvements and innovations.

The family tree for C# is shown in Figure 1-1. The grandfather of C# is C. From C, C# derives its syntax, many of its keywords, and operators. C# builds upon and improves the object model defined by C++. If you know C or C++, you will feel at home with C#.

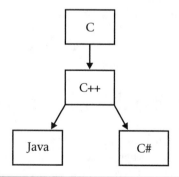

Figure 1-1   The C# family tree

C# and Java have a bit more complicated relationship. As explained, Java is also descended from C and C++. It, too, shares the C/C++ syntax and object model. Like Java, C# is designed to produce portable code, and C# programs execute in a secure controlled runtime environment. However, C# is not descended from Java. Instead, C# and Java are more like cousins, sharing a common ancestry, but differing in many important ways. The good news, though, is that if you know Java, many C# concepts will be familiar. Conversely, if in the future you need to learn Java, many of the things you learn about C# will carry over.

C# contains many innovative features that we will examine at length throughout the course of this book, but some of its most important features relate to its built-in support for software components. In fact, C# has been characterized as being a component-oriented language because it contains integral support for the writing of software components. For example, C# includes features that directly support constituents of components, such as properties, methods, and events. However, C#'s ability to work in a secure, mixed-language environment is perhaps its most important component-oriented feature.

The Evolution of C#

Since its original 1.0 release, C# has been evolving at a rapid pace. Not long after C# 1.0, Microsoft released version 1.1. It contained many minor tweaks, but added no major features. However, the situation was much different with the release of C# 2.0. This was a watershed event in the lifecycle of C# because version 2.0 added many new features, such as generics, partial types, and anonymous methods, that fundamentally expanded the scope, power, and range of the language. Version 2.0 firmly put C# at the forefront of computer language development. It also demonstrated Microsoft's long-term commitment to the language.

The next major release of C# was 3.0, and (at the time of this writing) this is the current version of C#. Because of the many new features added by C# 2.0, one might have expected the development of C# to slow a bit, just to let programmers catch up, but this was not the case. With version 3.0, Microsoft once again put C# on the cutting edge of language design, this time adding a set of innovative features that redefined the programming landscape.

Perhaps the two most exciting new features in C# 3.0 are language-integrated query (LINQ) and lambda expressions. LINQ enables you to write database queries using C# programming elements. Lambda expressions are often used in LINQ expressions. Together they add an entirely new dimension to C# programming. Other innovations include implicitly typed variables and extension methods. Because this book is based on C# 3.0, these important advances are covered.

How C# Relates to the .NET Framework

Although C# is a computer language that can be studied on its own, it has a special relationship to its runtime environment, the .NET Framework. The reason for this is twofold. First, C# was initially designed by Microsoft to create code for the .NET Framework. Second, the libraries used by C# are the ones defined by the .NET Framework. Thus, even though it is possible to separate the C# language from the .NET environment, the two are closely linked.

Because of this, it is important to have a general understanding of the .NET Framework and why it is important to C#.

What Is the .NET Framework?

In a sentence, the .NET Framework defines an environment that supports the development and execution of highly distributed, component-based applications. It enables different computer languages to work together and provides for security, program portability, and a common programming model for the Windows platform.

As it relates to C#, the .NET Framework defines two very important entities. The first is the *Common Language Runtime.* This is the system that manages the execution of your program. Along with other benefits, the Common Language Runtime is the part of the .NET Framework that enables programs to be portable, supports mixed-language programming, and provides for security.

The second entity is the .NET *class library.* This library gives your program access to the runtime environment. For example, if you want to perform I/O, such as displaying something on the screen, you will use the .NET class library to do it. If you are new to programming, the term *class* may be new. Although it will be explained in detail a bit later, briefly, a class is an object-oriented construct that helps organize programs. As long as your program restricts itself to the features defined by the .NET class library, your programs can run anywhere that the .NET runtime system is supported. Since C# automatically uses the .NET class library, C# programs are automatically portable to all .NET environments.

How the Common Language Runtime Works

The Common Language Runtime (CLR) manages the execution of .NET code. Here is how it works. When you compile a C# program, the output of the compiler is not executable code. Instead, it is a file that contains a special type of pseudocode called *Microsoft Intermediate Language*, or MSIL for short. MSIL defines a set of portable instructions that are independent of any specific CPU. In essence, MSIL defines a portable assembly language. One other point: Although MSIL is similar in concept to Java's bytecode, the two are not the same.

It is the job of the CLR to translate the intermediate code into executable code when a program is run. Thus, any program compiled to MSIL can be run in any environment for which the CLR is implemented. This is part of how the .NET Framework achieves portability.

Microsoft Intermediate Language is turned into executable code using a *JIT* compiler. JIT stands for "just in time." The process works like this: When a .NET program is executed, the CLR activates the JIT compiler. The JIT compiler converts MSIL into native code on a demand basis, as each part of your program is needed. Thus, your C# program actually executes as native code, even though it was initially compiled into MSIL. This means that your program runs nearly as fast as it would if it had been compiled to native code in the first place, but it gains the portability and security benefits of MSIL.

In addition to MSIL, one other thing is output when you compile a C# program: *metadata.* Metadata describes the data used by your program and enables your code to interact with other code. The metadata is contained in the same file as the MSIL.

Fortunately, for the purposes of this book, and for the majority of programming tasks, it is not necessary to know any more about the CLR, MSIL, or metadata. C# handles the details for you.

Managed vs. Unmanaged Code

In general, when you write a C# program, you are creating what is called *managed code*. Managed code is executed under the control of the Common Language Runtime, as just described. Because it is running under the control of the CLR, managed code is subject to certain constraints—and derives several benefits. The constraints are easily described and met: The compiler must produce an MSIL file targeted for the CLR (which C# does) and use the .NET Framework library (which C# does). The benefits of managed code are many, including modern memory management, the ability to mix languages, better security, support for version control, and a clean way for software components to interact.

The opposite of managed code is *unmanaged* code. Unmanaged code does not execute under the Common Language Runtime. Thus, all Windows programs prior to the creation of the .NET Framework use unmanaged code. It is possible for managed code and unmanaged code to work together, so the fact that C# generates managed code does not restrict its ability to operate in conjunction with preexisting programs.

The Common Language Specification

Although all managed code gains the benefits provided by the CLR, if your code will be used by other programs written in different languages, for maximum usability, it should adhere to the Common Language Specification (CLS). The CLS describes a set of features, such as data types, that different languages have in common. CLS compliance is especially important when creating software components that will be used by other languages. Although we won't need to worry about the CLS for the purposes of this book, it is something you will want to look into when you begin writing commercial code.

Ask the Expert

Q: To address the issues of portability, security, and mixed-language programming, why was it necessary to create a new computer language such as C#? Couldn't a language like C++ be adapted to support the .NET Framework?

A: Yes, it is possible to adapt C++ so that it produces .NET-compatible code that runs under the CLR. In fact, Microsoft did just that. Initially, Microsoft added what are called the *managed extensions* to C++. However, this approach has been rendered obsolete and is replaced by a set of extended keywords and syntax defined by the Ecma C++/CLI Standard. (CLI stands for Common Language Infrastructure.) Although C++/CLI make it possible to port existing code to the .NET Framework, new .NET development is much easier in C# because it was originally designed with .NET in mind.

Object-Oriented Programming

At the center of C# is object-oriented programming (OOP). The object-oriented methodology is inseparable from C#, and all C# programs are, at least to some extent, object-oriented. Because of its importance to C#, it is useful to understand OOP's basic principles before you write even a simple C# program.

OOP is a powerful way to approach the job of programming. Programming methodologies have changed dramatically since the invention of the computer, primarily to accommodate the increasing complexity of programs. For example, when computers were first invented, programming was done by toggling in the binary machine instructions using the computer's front panel. As long as programs were just a few hundred instructions long, this approach worked. As programs grew, assembly language was invented so that a programmer could deal with larger, increasingly complex programs, using symbolic representations of the machine instructions. As programs continued to grow, high-level languages, such as FORTRAN and COBOL, were introduced that gave the programmer more tools with which to handle complexity. When these early languages began to reach their breaking point, structured programming was invented.

Consider this: At each milestone in the development of programming, techniques and tools were created to allow the programmer to deal with increasingly greater complexity. Each step of the way, the new approach took the best elements of the previous methods and moved forward. The same is true of object-oriented programming. Prior to OOP, many projects were nearing (or exceeding) the point where the structured approach no longer worked. A better way to handle complexity was needed, and object-oriented programming was the solution.

Object-oriented programming took the best ideas of structured programming and combined them with several new concepts. The result was a different and better way of organizing a program. In the most general sense, a program can be organized in one of two ways: around its code (what is happening) or around its data (what is being affected). Using only structured programming techniques, programs are typically organized around code. This approach can be thought of as "code acting on data."

Object-oriented programs work the other way around. They are organized around data, with the key principle being "data controlling access to code." In an object-oriented language, you define the data and the routines that are permitted to act on that data. Thus, a data type defines precisely what sort of operations can be applied to that data.

To support the principles of object-oriented programming, all OOP languages, including C#, have three traits in common: encapsulation, polymorphism, and inheritance. Let's examine each.

Encapsulation

Encapsulation is a programming mechanism that binds together code and the data it manipulates, and keeps both safe from outside interference and misuse. In an object-oriented language, code and data can be bound together in such a way that a self-contained *black box* is created. Within the box are all necessary data and code. When code and data are linked together in this fashion, an object is created. In other words, an object is the device that supports encapsulation.

Within an object, code, data, or both may be *private* to that object or *public*. Private code or data is known to and accessible by only another part of the object. That is, private code or data cannot be accessed by a piece of the program that exists outside the object. When code or data is public, other parts of your program can access it, even though it is defined within an object. Typically, the public parts of an object are used to provide a controlled interface to the private elements of the object.

C#'s basic unit of encapsulation is the *class*. A class defines the form of an object. It specifies both the data and the code that will operate on that data. C# uses a class specification to construct *objects*. Objects are instances of a class. Thus, a class is essentially a set of plans that specify how to build an object.

The code and data that constitute a class are called *members* of the class. Specifically, the data defined by the class is referred to as *member variables* or *instance variables*. The code that operates on that data is referred to as *member methods* or just *methods*. "Method" is C#'s term for a subroutine. If you are familiar with C/C++, it may help to know that what a C# programmer calls a *method*, a C/C++ programmer calls a *function*. Because C# is a direct descendent of C++, the term "function" is also sometimes used when referring to a C# method.

Polymorphism

Polymorphism (from Greek, meaning "many forms") is the quality that allows one interface to access a general class of actions. A simple example of polymorphism is found in the steering wheel of an automobile. The steering wheel (the interface) is the same, no matter what type of actual steering mechanism is used. That is, the steering wheel works the same whether your car has manual steering, power steering, or rack-and-pinion steering. Thus, turning the steering wheel left causes the car to go left no matter what type of steering is used. The benefit of the uniform interface is, of course, that once you know how to operate the steering wheel, you can drive any type of car.

The same principle can also apply to programming. For example, consider a stack (which is a first-in, last-out list). You might have a program that requires three different types of stacks. One stack is used for integer values, one for floating-point values, and one for characters. In this case, the algorithm that implements each stack is the same, even though the data being stored differs. In a non–object-oriented language, you would be required to create three different sets of stack routines, with each set using different names. However, because of polymorphism, in C#, you can specify the general form of a stack once and then use it for all three specific situations. This way, if you know how to use one stack, you can use them all.

More generally, the concept of polymorphism is often expressed by the phrase "one interface, multiple methods." This means that it is possible to design a generic interface to a group of related activities. Polymorphism helps reduce complexity by allowing the same interface to be used to specify a *general class of action*. It is the compiler's job to select the *specific action* (that is, method) as it applies to each situation. You, the programmer, don't need to do this selection manually. You need only remember and utilize the general interface.

Inheritance

Inheritance is the process by which one object can acquire the properties of another object. This is important because it supports the concept of hierarchical classification. If you think about it, most knowledge is made manageable by hierarchical (that is, top-down) classifications.

Ask the Expert

Q: You state that object-oriented programming is an effective way to manage large programs. However, it seems that OOP might add substantial overhead to relatively small programs. Since you say that all C# programs are, to some extent, object-oriented, does this impose a penalty for smaller programs?

A: No. As you will see, for small programs, C#'s object-oriented features are nearly transparent. Although it is true that C# follows a strict object model, you have wide latitude as to the degree to which you employ it. For smaller programs, their "object-orientedness" is barely perceptible. As your programs grow, you will integrate more object-oriented features effortlessly.

For example, a Red Delicious apple is part of the classification *apple,* which, in turn, is part of the *fruit* class, which is under the larger class *food.* That is, the *food* class possesses certain qualities (edible, nutritious, and so on) that also, logically, apply to its subclass, *fruit.* In addition to these qualities, the *fruit* class has specific characteristics (juicy, sweet, and so forth) that distinguish it from other food. The *apple* class defines those qualities specific to an apple (grows on trees, not tropical, and so on). A Red Delicious apple would, in turn, inherit all the qualities of all preceding classes and would define only those qualities that make it unique.

Without the use of hierarchies, each object would have to explicitly define all of its characteristics. Using inheritance, an object need only define those qualities that make it unique within its class. It can inherit its general attributes from its parent. Thus, it is the inheritance mechanism that makes it possible for one object to be a specific instance of a more general case.

Creating, Compiling, and Running Your First C# Program

It is now time to learn how to create, compile, and run a C# program. Since this is a "hands-on" guide to C# programming, being able to successfully complete these tasks is a necessary first step. Here is the program we will use:

```
/*
   This is a simple C# program.

   Call this program Example.cs.
*/

using System;

class Example {
```

```
// A C# program begins with a call to Main().
static void Main() {
  Console.WriteLine("C# gives you programming power.");
}
}
```

Although quite short, this program does contain several key features that are common to all C# programs. Once you have learned how to compile and run it, we will examine it in detail.

Obtain a C# 3.0 Compiler

To create, compile, and run a C# program, you will need a copy of Microsoft's Visual C#. This book uses Visual C# 2008, which is the compiler that supports C# 3.0. Although many of the programs in this book can be compiled by an earlier version of C#, you will need Visual C# 2008 to handle the newer features.

If you do not currently have Visual C# 2008, you will need to acquire it. Microsoft supplies Visual C# 2008 in a variety of forms, including its commercial offerings, which can be purchased. However, at the time of this writing, you can also obtain a copy free of charge by downloading an Express edition. Visual C# Express edition contains a full-featured compiler that supports all of C# 3.0 and is, therefore, able to compile all of the code in this book. It also includes Visual Studio, which is Microsoft's integrated development environment (IDE). Although the Express edition does not supply all of the tools that a commercial developer will want, it is perfect for learning C#. At the time of this writing, Visual C# 2008 Express can be downloaded from **www.microsoft.com/express**. All of the code in this book has been tested against this compiler.

Using Visual C#, there are two general approaches you can take to creating, compiling, and running a C# program. First, you can use the Visual Studio IDE. Second, you can use the command-line compiler, **csc.exe**. Both methods are described here.

Using the Visual Studio IDE

As mentioned, Visual Studio is Microsoft's integrated programming environment. It lets you edit, compile, run, and debug a C# program, all without leaving its well thought-out environment. Visual Studio offers convenience and helps manage your programs. It is most effective for larger projects, but it can be used to great success with smaller programs, such as those that constitute the examples in this book.

The steps required to edit, compile, and run a C# program using the Visual Studio 2008 IDE are shown here. These steps assume that you are using the IDE provided by Visual C# Express 2008. Slight differences may exist with other versions of Visual Studio 2008.

1. Create a new, empty C# project by selecting File | New Project. Next, select Empty Project.

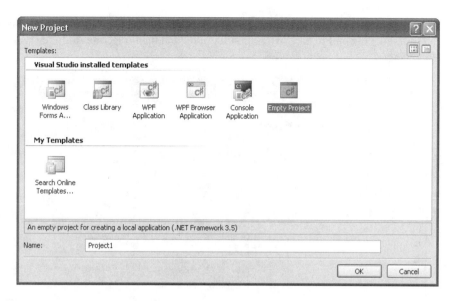

Then, press OK to create the project.

2. Once the new project is created, the Visual Studio IDE will look like this:

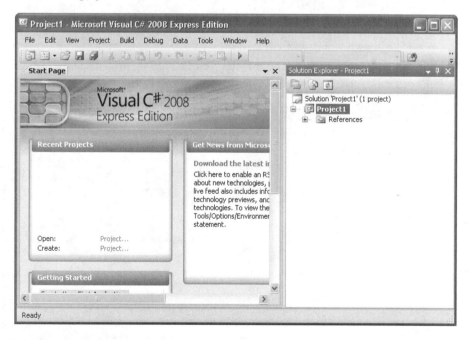

If, for some reason, you do not see the Solution Explorer window, activate it by selecting Solution Explorer from the View menu.

3. At this point, the project is empty and you will need to add a C# source file to it. Do this by right-clicking on Project1 in Solution Explorer and then selecting Add. You will see the following:

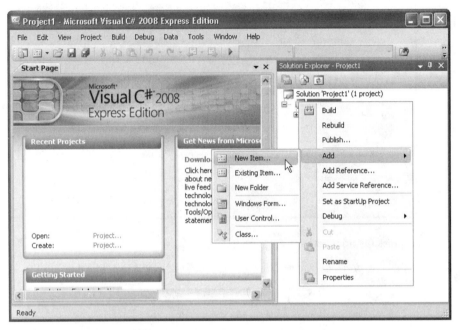

4. Next, select New Item. This causes the Add New Item dialog to be displayed. Select Code File and then change the name to **Example.cs**, as shown here:

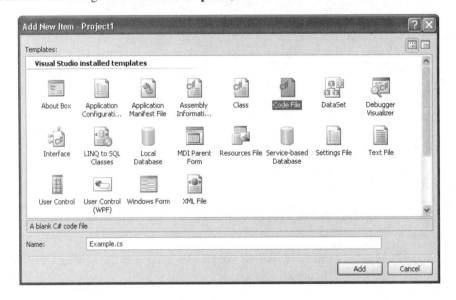

5. Next, add the file to the project by pressing Add. Your screen will now look like this:

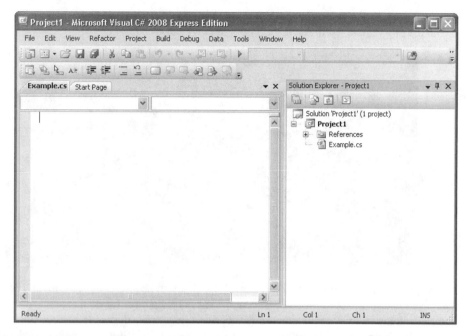

6. Next, type the example program into the Example.cs window and then save the file. (You can download the source code to the programs in this book from **www.mhprofessional.com** so you won't have to manually type each example.) When done, your screen will look like this:

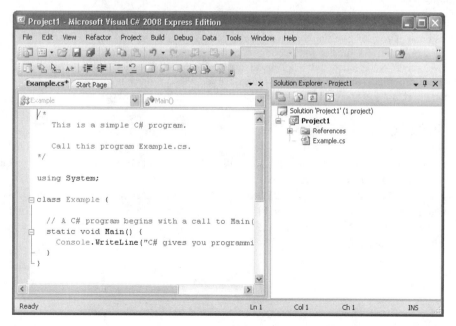

7. Compile the program by selecting Build Solution from the Build menu.

8. Run the program by selecting Start Without Debugging from the Debug menu. When you run the program, you will see the window shown here:

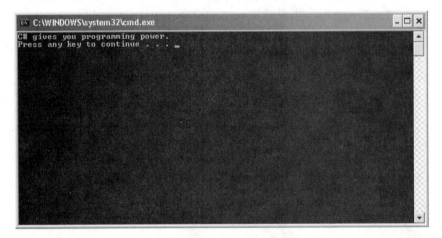

As the preceding instructions show, compiling short sample programs using the IDE involves a number of steps. However, you don't need to create a new project for each example program in this book. Instead, you can use the same C# project. Just delete the current source file and add the new file. Then, recompile and run. This approach greatly simplifies the process. Understand, however, that for real-world applications, each program will use its own project.

TIP

Although the preceding instructions are sufficient to compile and run the programs in this book, if you will be using the Visual Studio IDE for your main work environment, you should become familiar with all of its capabilities and features. It is a very powerful development environment that helps make large projects manageable. It also provides a way of organizing the files and resources associated with a project. It is worth the time and effort that you spend to become proficient at running Visual Studio.

Using csc.exe, the C# Command-Line Compiler

Although the Visual Studio IDE is what you will probably be using for your commercial projects, some readers will find the C# command-line compiler more convenient, especially for compiling and running the sample programs shown in this book. The reason is that you don't have to create a project for the program. You can simply create the program, then compile it, and run it—all from the command line. Therefore, if you know how to use the Command Prompt window and its command-line interface, using the command-line compiler will be faster and easier than using the IDE.

CAUTION

If you are not familiar with the Command Prompt window, it is probably better to use the Visual Studio IDE. Although its commands are not difficult to learn, trying to learn both the Command Prompt and C# at the same time will be a challenging experience.

To create and run programs using the C# command-line compiler, follow these three steps:

1. Enter the program using a text editor.

2. Compile the program using **csc.exe**.

3. Run the program.

Entering the Program

As mentioned, the programs shown in this book are available from Mcgraw-Hill's website: **www.mhprofessional.com**. However, if you want to enter the programs by hand, you are free to do so. In this case, you must enter the program into your computer using a text editor, such as Notepad. Remember, you must create text-only files, not formatted word-processing files, because the format information in a word processor file will confuse the C# compiler. When entering the program, call the file **Example.cs**.

Compiling the Program

To compile the program, execute the C# compiler, **csc.exe**, specifying the name of the source file on the command line, as shown here:

```
C:\>csc Example.cs
```

The **csc** compiler creates a file called **Example.exe** that contains the MSIL version of the program. Although MSIL is not executable code, it is still contained in an **exe** file. The Common Language Runtime automatically invokes the JIT compiler when you attempt to execute **Example.exe**. Be aware, however, that if you try to execute **Example.exe** (or any other **exe** file that contains MSIL) on a computer for which the .NET Framework is not installed, the program will not execute, because the CLR will be missing.

NOTE

Prior to running **csc.exe**, you will need to open a Command Prompt window that is configured for Visual Studio. The easiest way to do this is to select "Visual Studio 2008 Command Prompt" under Visual Studio Tools in the Start menu. Alternatively, you can start an unconfigured Command Prompt window and then run the batch file **vsvars32 .bat**, which is provided by Visual Studio. You may, however, encounter a problem with the command-line approach. At the time of this writing, Visual C# 2008 Express edition does not provide the Visual Studio Tools menu or the **vsvars32.bat** file. Therefore, if you are using Visual C# Express, you may not be able to automatically configure a Command Prompt window. In this case, use the Visual Studio IDE instead. However, Visual C++ 2008 Express edition does supply both **vsvars32.bat** and the "Visual Studio 2008 Command Prompt" menu selection. Therefore, if you also install Visual C++ 2008 Express Edition, you will be able to start a properly configured Command Prompt window that will also work for C#.

Running the Program

To actually run the program, just type its name on the command line, as shown here:

```
C:\>Example
```

When the program runs, the following output is displayed:

```
C# gives you programming power.
```

The First Example Program Line by Line

Although **Example.cs** is quite short, it includes several key features that are common to all C# programs. Since this is your first C# program, it warrants close examination. We will begin with its name.

The name of a C# program can be chosen arbitrarily. Unlike some computer languages (most notably, Java) in which the name of a program file is very important, this is not the case for C#. You were told to call the sample program **Example.cs** so that the instructions for compiling and running the program would apply, but as far as C# is concerned, you could have called the file by another name. For example, the preceding sample program could have been called **Sample.cs**, **Test.cs**, or even **MyProg.cs**.

By convention, C# programs use the **.cs** file extension, and this is a convention that you should follow. Also, many programmers call a file by the name of the principal class defined within the file. This is why the filename **Example.cs** was chosen. Since the names of C# programs are arbitrary, names won't be specified for most of the sample programs in this book. Just use names of your own choosing.

The program begins with the following lines:

```
/*
   This is a simple C# program.

   Call this program Example.cs.
*/
```

This is a *comment*. Like most other programming languages, C# lets you enter remarks into a program's source file. The contents of a comment are ignored by the compiler. Instead, a comment describes or explains the operation of the program to anyone who is reading its source code. In this case, the comment describes the program and reminds you to call the source file **Example.cs**. Of course, in real applications, comments generally explain how some part of the program works or what a specific feature does.

C# supports three styles of comments. The one shown at the top of the program is called a *multiline comment*. This type of comment must begin with /* and end with */. Anything between these two comment symbols is ignored by the compiler. As the name suggests, a multiline comment can be several lines long.

The next line in the program is

```
using System;
```

This line indicates that the program is using the **System** namespace. In C#, a *namespace* defines a declarative region. Although we will look at the namespaces in detail later, a brief description is useful now. A namespace provides a way to keep one set of names separate from another. In essence, names declared in one namespace will not conflict with the same names declared in another. The namespace used by the program is **System**, which is the namespace reserved for items associated with the .NET Framework class library, which is the library used by C#. The **using** keyword states that the program is using the names in the given namespace.

The next line of code in the program is shown here:

```
class Example {
```

This line uses the keyword **class** to declare that a new class is being defined. As mentioned, the class is C#'s basic unit of encapsulation. **Example** is the name of the class. The class definition begins with the opening curly brace ({) and ends with the closing curly brace (}). The elements between the two braces are members of the class. For the moment, don't worry too much about the details of a class, except to note that program activity occurs within one.

The next line in the program is a *single-line comment,* shown here:

```
// A C# program begins with a call to Main().
```

This is the second type of comment supported by C#. A *single-line comment* begins with a *//* and ends at the end of the line. As a general rule, programmers use multiline comments for longer remarks and single-line comments for brief, line-by-line descriptions.

The next line of code is shown here:

```
static void Main() {
```

This line begins the **Main( )** method. As mentioned earlier, in C#, a subroutine is called a method. As the comment preceding it suggests, this is the line at which the program will begin executing. All C# applications begin execution by calling **Main( )**. The complete meaning of each part of this line cannot be given now, since it involves a detailed understanding of several other C# features. However, since many of the examples in this book will use this line of code, a brief explanation is warranted.

The line begins with the keyword **static**. A method that is modified by **static** can be called before an object of its class has been created. This is necessary because **Main( )** is called at program startup. The keyword **void** indicates that **Main( )** does not return a value. As you will see, methods can also return values. The empty parentheses that follow **Main** indicate that no information is passed to **Main( )**. As you will also see, it is possible to pass information into **Main( )** or into any other method. The last character on the line is the {. This signals the start of **Main( )**'s body. All of the code that comprises a method will occur between the method's opening curly brace and its closing curly brace.

The next line of code is shown here. Notice that it occurs inside **Main( )**.

```
Console.WriteLine("C# gives you programming power.");
```

Ask the Expert

Q: You said that C# supports three types of comments, but you only mentioned two. What is the third?

A: The third type of comment supported by C# is a *documentation comment,* also called an *XML comment.* A documentation comment uses XML tags to help you create self-documenting code.

This line outputs the string "C# gives you programming power." followed by a new line on the screen. Output is actually accomplished by the built-in method **WriteLine( )**. In this case, **WriteLine( )** displays the string that is passed to it. Information that is passed to a method is called an *argument.* In addition to strings, **WriteLine( )** can be used to display other types of information, such as numeric data. The line begins with **Console**, which is the name of a predefined class that supports console I/O. By connecting **Console** with **WriteLine( )**, you are telling the compiler that **WriteLine( )** is a member of the **Console** class. The fact that C# uses an object to define console output is further evidence of its object-oriented nature.

Notice that the **WriteLine( )** statement ends with a semicolon, as does the **using System** statement earlier in the program. In general, all statements in C# end with a semicolon. The exception to this rule is the *block,* which begins with { and ends with }. A block does not end with a semicolon. This is why lines ending with } are not followed by a semicolon. Blocks provide a mechanism for grouping statements. They are examined in detail later in this chapter.

The first } in the program ends **Main( )**, and the last } ends the **Example** class definition.

One last point: C# is case-sensitive. Forgetting this can cause serious problems. For example, if you accidentally type **main** instead of **Main**, or **writeline** instead of **WriteLine**, the preceding program will be incorrect. Furthermore, although the C# compiler *will* compile classes that do not contain a **Main( )** method, there is no way to use one as an entry point for executing your program. So, if you had mistyped **Main**, the compiler would still compile your program. However, you would also see an error message that states that **Example.exe** does not have an entry point defined.

Handling Syntax Errors

If you have not yet done so, enter, compile, and run the preceding program. As you may know from your previous programming experience, it is quite easy to accidentally type something incorrectly when entering code into your computer. If this happens, the compiler will report a *syntax error* when it tries to compile it. The message displayed will contain the line number and character position at which the error is found and a description of the error.

Although the syntax errors reported by the compiler are, obviously, helpful, they are also sometimes misleading. The C# compiler attempts to make sense out of your source code no matter what you have written. For this reason, the error that is reported may not always reflect the actual cause of the problem. In the preceding program, for example, an accidental omission of the opening curly brace after the **Main( )** method generates the following sequence of errors when compiled by the **csc** command-line compiler (Similar errors are generated when compiling using the IDE.):

```
EX1.CS(12,21): error CS1002: ; expected
EX1.CS(13,22): error CS1519: Invalid token '(' in class, struct, or
interface member declaration
EX1.CS(15,1): error CS1022: Type or namespace definition, or
end-of-file expected
```

Clearly, the first error message is completely wrong, because what is missing is not a semicolon, but a curly brace. The second two messages are equally confusing.

The point of this discussion is that when your program contains a syntax error, don't necessarily take the compiler's messages at face value. They may be misleading. You may need to "second guess" an error message in order to find the problem. Also, look at the last few lines of code immediately preceding the one in which the error was reported. Sometimes an error will not be reported until several lines after the point at which the error really occurred.

A Small Variation

Although all of the programs in this book will use it, the statement

```
using System;
```

at the start of the first example program is not technically needed. It is, however, a valuable convenience. The reason it's not necessary is that in C# you can always *fully qualify* a name with the namespace to which it belongs. For example, the line

```
Console.WriteLine("A simple C# program.");
```

can be rewritten as

```
System.Console.WriteLine("A simple C# program.");
```

You will occasionally see C# code that uses this approach, but it's not common. Most C# programmers include the **using System** statement at the top of their programs, as do all of the programs in this book. Doing so avoids the tedium of always having to specify the **System** namespace whenever a member of that namespace is used. It is important to understand, however, that you can explicitly qualify a name with its namespace if needed.

Using a Variable

Perhaps no other construct is as important to a programming language as the variable. A *variable* is a named memory location that can be assigned a value. It is called a variable because its value can be changed during the execution of a program. In other words, the contents of a variable are changeable, not fixed.

Let's begin with an example. The following program creates three variables called **length**, **width**, and **area**. It uses these variables to compute and display the area of a rectangle that has the dimensions 9 by 7.

```
// This program introduces variables.

using System;

class UseVars {
  static void Main() {
    int length; // this declares a variable
    int width;  // this declares another variable      ◄──── Declare variables
    int area;   // this is a third variable

    // Assign length the value 9.
    length = 9;  ◄─────────────────────── This assigns 9 to length.

    // This displays the current value of length.
    Console.WriteLine("length contains " + length);

    // Assign width the value 7.
    width = 7;  ◄─────────────────────── This assigns 7 to width.

    // This displays the current value of width.
    Console.WriteLine("width contains " + width);

    // Assign to area the product of length and width.
    area = length * width;  ◄─────── Multiply length by width
                                     and assign area the result.
    // Display the result.
    Console.Write("area contains length * width: ");
    Console.WriteLine(area);
  }
}
```

When you run this program, you will see the following output:

```
length contains 9
width contains 7
area contains length * width: 63
```

This program introduces several new concepts. First, the statement

```
int length; // this declares a variable
```

declares a variable called **length** of type integer. In C#, all variables must be declared before they are used. Further, the kind of values that the variable can hold must also be specified. This is called the *type* of the variable. In this case, **length** can hold integer values. These are whole numbers. In C#, to declare a variable to be of type integer, precede its name with the keyword **int**. Thus, the preceding statement declares a variable called **length** of type **int**.

The next two lines declare two more **int** variables, called **width** and **area**:

```
int width;   // this declares another variable
int area;    // this is a third variable
```

Notice that each uses the same format as the first, except that the name of the variable is different.

In general, to declare a variable, you will use a statement like this:

type var-name;

Here, *type* specifies the type of variable being declared, and *var-name* is the name of the variable. In addition to **int**, C# supports several other data types, such as **double**, **char**, and **string**.

The following line of code assigns **length** the value 9:

```
length = 9;
```

In C#, the assignment operator is the single equal sign. It copies the value on its right side into the variable on its left.

The next line of code outputs the value of **length** preceded by the string "length contains."

```
Console.WriteLine("length contains " + length);
```

In this statement, the plus sign causes the value of **length** to be displayed after the string that precedes it. This approach can be generalized. Using the + operator, you can chain together as many items as you want within a single **WriteLine( )** statement.

Next, the value of **width** is set to 7 and displayed, using the same type of statements just described. Then, the following line of code assigns **area** the value of **length** times **width**.

```
area = length * width;
```

This line multiplies the value in **length** (which is 9) by the value in **width** (which is 7), and then stores that result in **area**. Thus, after the line executes, **area** will contain the value 63. The values of **length** and **width** will be unchanged.

Like most other computer languages, C# supports a complete set of arithmetic operators, including those shown here:

+	Addition
−	Subtraction
*	Multiplication
/	Division

These can be used with any type of numeric data.

Ask the Expert

Q: You say that all variables must be declared before they are used, and that all variables have a type. However, you mention that C# 3.0 includes a new feature called an *implicitly typed variable*. What is this, and does it circumvent the need to declare variables?

A: As you will learn in Chapter 2, implicitly typed variables are variables whose type is automatically determined by the compiler. Understand, however, that an implicitly typed variable still needs to be declared. Instead of using a type name, such as **int**, an implicitly typed variable is declared using the **var** keyword. Implicitly typed variables are very useful in several specialized situations (especially those involving LINQ), but they are not intended to replace explicitly typed variables in general. Normally, when you declare a variable, you give it an explicit type.

Here are the next two lines in the program:

```
Console.Write("area contains length * width: ");
Console.WriteLine(area);
```

Two new things are occurring here. First, the built-in method **Write( )** is used to display the string "area contains length * width:". This string is *not* followed by a new line. This means that when the next output is generated, it will start on the same line. The **Write( )** method is just like **WriteLine( )**, except that it does not output a new line after each call. Second, in the call to **WriteLine( )**, notice that **area** is used by itself. Both **Write( )** and **WriteLine( )** can be used to output values of any of C#'s built-in types.

One more point about declaring variables before we move on: It is possible to declare two or more variables using the same declaration statement. Just separate their names by commas. For example, **length** and **width** could have been declared like this:

```
int length, width; // both length and width declared using one statement
```

The double Data Type

In the preceding program, a variable of type **int** was used. However, a variable of type **int** can hold only whole numbers. Thus, it cannot be used when a fractional component is required. For example, an **int** variable can hold the value 18, but not the value 18.3. Fortunately, **int** is only one of several data types defined by C#. To allow numbers with fractional components, C# defines two floating-point types: **float** and **double**, which represent single- and double-precision values, respectively. Of the two, **double** is the most commonly used.

To declare a variable of type **double**, use a statement similar to that shown here:

```
double result;
```

Here, **result** is the name of the variable, which is of type **double**. Because **result** has a floating-point type, it can hold values such as 122.23, 0.034, and –19.0.

To better understand the difference between **int** and **double**, try the following program:

```
/*
   This program illustrates the differences
   between int and double.
*/

using System;

class IntVsDouble {
  static void Main() {
    int ivar;     // this declares an int variable
    double dvar;  // this declares a floating-point variable

    // Assign ivar the value 10.
    ivar = 10;

    // Assign dvar the value 10.0.
    dvar = 10.0;

    Console.WriteLine("Original value of ivar: " + ivar);
    Console.WriteLine("Original value of dvar: " + dvar);

    Console.WriteLine(); // print a blank line

    // Now, divide both by 4.
    ivar = ivar / 4;
    dvar = dvar / 4.0;
    Console.WriteLine("ivar after division: " + ivar);
    Console.WriteLine("dvar after division: " + dvar);
  }
}
```

ivar is of type **int**.

dvar is of type **double**.

Output a blank line.

This is a whole-number division.

This division preserves the fractional component.

The output from this program is shown here:

```
Original value of ivar: 10
Original value of dvar: 10

ivar after division: 2
dvar after division: 2.5
```

As you can see, when **ivar** is divided by 4, a whole-number division is performed and the outcome is 2—the fractional component is lost. However, when **dvar** is divided by 4.0, the fractional component is preserved and the outcome is 2.5.

Ask the Expert

Q: Why does C# have different data types for integers and floating-point values? That is, why aren't all numeric values just the same type?

A: C# supplies different data types so that you can write efficient programs. For example, integer arithmetic is faster than floating-point calculations. Thus, if you don't need fractional values, you don't need to incur the overhead associated with types **float** or **double**. Secondly, the amount of memory required for one type of data might be less than that required for another. By supplying different types, C# enables you to make the best use of system resources. Finally, some algorithms require (or at least benefit from) the use of a specific type of data. C# supplies a number of built-in types to give you the greatest flexibility.

As the program shows, when you want to specify a floating-point value in a program, it must include a decimal point. If you don't, it will be interpreted as an integer. For example, in C#, the value 100 is an integer, but the value 100.0 is a floating-point value.

There is one other new thing to notice in the program. To print a blank line, simply call **WriteLine( )** without any arguments.

Try This Convert Fahrenheit to Celsius

Although the preceding sample programs illustrate several important features of the C# language, they are not very useful. Even though you do not know much about C# at this point, you can still put what you have learned to work to create a practical program. Here you will create a program that converts Fahrenheit to Celsius.

The program declares two **double** variables. One will hold the number of the degrees in Fahrenheit, and the second will hold the number of degrees in Celsius after the conversion. The formula for converting Fahrenheit to Celsius is

$$C = 5/9 * (F - 32)$$

where C is the temperature in degrees Celsius and F is the temperature in degrees Fahrenheit.

Step by Step

1. Create a new C# file called **FtoC.cs**. (If you are using the Visual Studio IDE rather than the command-line compiler, you will need to add this file to a C# project, as described earlier.)

2. Enter the following program into the file:

```
/*
    This program converts Fahrenheit to Celsius.
```

```
    Call this program FtoC.cs.
*/

using System;

class FtoC {
  static void Main() {
    double f; // holds the temperature in Fahrenheit
    double c; // holds the temperature in Celsius

    // Begin with 59 degrees Fahrenheit
    f = 59.0;

    // convert to Celsius
    c = 5.0 / 9.0 * (f - 32.0);

    Console.Write(f + " degrees Fahrenheit is ");
    Console.WriteLine(c + " degrees Celsius.");
  }
}
```

3. Compile the program using the Visual Studio IDE (using the instructions shown earlier in this chapter) or by using the following command line:

```
C>csc FtoC.cs
```

4. Run the program. You will see this output:

```
59 degrees Fahrenheit is 15 degrees Celsius.
```

5. As it stands, this program converts 59 degrees Fahrenheit to Celsius. However, by changing the value assigned to **f**, you can have the program convert a different temperature. Notice that the variables **f** and **c** are of type **double**. This is necessary because the fractional component of the operations is needed to ensure an accurate conversion.

Two Control Statements

Inside a method, execution proceeds from one statement to the next, top to bottom. However, it is possible to alter this flow through the use of the various program control statements supported by C#. Although we will look closely at control statements in Chapter 3, two are briefly introduced here because we will be using them to write sample programs.

The if Statement

You can selectively execute part of a program through the use of C#'s conditional statement: the **if**. The **if** statement works in C# much like the IF statement in any other language. For example, it is syntactically similar to the **if** statements in C, C++, and Java. Its simplest form is shown here:

if(*condition*) *statement*;

Here, *condition* is a Boolean (that is, true or false) expression. If *condition* is true, then the statement is executed. If *condition* is false, then the statement is bypassed. Here is an example:

```
if(10 < 11) Console.WriteLine("10 is less than 11");
```

In this case, since 10 is less than 11, the conditional expression is true, and **WriteLine( )** will execute. However, consider the following:

```
if(10 < 9) Console.WriteLine("this won't be displayed");
```

In this case, 10 is not less than 9. Thus, the call to **WriteLine( )** will not take place.

C# defines a full complement of relational operators that can be used in a conditional expression. They are shown here:

Operator	Meaning
<	Less than
<=	Less than or equal to
>	Greater than
>=	Greater than or equal to
= =	Equal to
!=	Not equal to

Notice that the test for equality is the double equal sign.

Here is a program that illustrates the **if** statement and the relational operators.

```
// Demonstrate the if.

using System;

class IfDemo {
  static void Main() {
    int a, b, c;

    a = 2;
    b = 3;

    // This if statement succeeds because a is less than b.
    if(a < b) Console.WriteLine("a is less than b");
```

The **WriteLine( )** statement is executed only when the condition is true.

This is the condition tested by the **if**.

```
    // This won't display anything because a does not equal b.
    if(a == b) Console.WriteLine("you won't see this");

    // This if succeeds because a contains the value 2.
    if(a == 2) Console.WriteLine("a contains the value 2");

    // This if fails because a does not contain the value 19.
    if(a == 19) Console.WriteLine("you won't see this");

    // This if will succeed because a will be equal to b - 1.
    if(a == b-1) Console.WriteLine("a equals b - 1");

    Console.WriteLine();

    c = a - b; // c contains -1

    Console.WriteLine("c contains -1");
    if(c >= 0) Console.WriteLine("c is non-negative");
    if(c < 0) Console.WriteLine("c is negative");

    Console.WriteLine();

    c = b - a; // c now contains 1

    Console.WriteLine("c now contains 1");
    if(c >= 0) Console.WriteLine("c is non-negative");
    if(c < 0) Console.WriteLine("c is negative");

    Console.WriteLine();
  }
}
```

The output generated by this program is shown here:

```
a is less than b
a contains the value 2
a equals b - 1

c contains -1
c is negative

c now contains 1
c is non-negative
```

Notice one other thing in this program. The line

```
int a, b, c;
```

declares three variables, **a**, **b**, and **c**, by use of a comma-separated list. As mentioned earlier, when you need two or more variables of the same type, they can be declared in one statement. Just separate the variable names by commas.

The for Loop

You can repeatedly execute a sequence of code by creating a *loop*. C# supplies a powerful assortment of loop constructs. The one we will look at here is the **for** loop. If you are familiar with C, C++, or Java, you will be pleased to know that the **for** loop in C# works the same way it does in those languages. The simplest form of the **for** loop is shown here:

for(*initialization*; *condition*; *iteration*) *statement*;

In its most common form, the *initialization* portion of the loop sets a loop control variable to an initial value. The *condition* is a Boolean expression that tests the loop control variable. If the outcome of that test is true, the **for** loop continues to iterate. If it is false, the loop terminates. The *iteration* expression determines how the loop control variable is changed each time the loop iterates. Here is a short program that illustrates the **for** loop:

```
// Demonstrate the for loop.

using System;

class ForDemo {
  static void Main() {
    int count;

    Console.WriteLine("Counting from 0 to 4:");

    for(count = 0; count < 5; count = count+1)
      Console.WriteLine("   count is " + count);

    Console.WriteLine("Done!");
  }
}
```

Initialize **count** to zero.

If **count** is less than 5, execute the **WriteLine( )** statement.

Increase **count** by 1 each time through the loop.

The output generated by the program is shown here:

```
Counting from 0 to 4:
   count is 0
   count is 1
   count is 2
   count is 3
   count is 4
Done!
```

In this example, **count** is the loop control variable. It is set to zero in the initialization portion of the **for**. At the start of each iteration (including the first one), the conditional test **count < 5** is performed. If the outcome of this test is true, the **WriteLine( )** statement is executed, and then the iteration portion of the loop is executed. This process continues until the conditional test is false, at which point execution picks up at the bottom of the loop.

As a point of interest, in professionally written C# programs, you will almost never see the iteration portion of the loop written as shown in the preceding program. That is, you will seldom see statements like this:

```
count = count + 1;
```

The reason is that C# includes a special increment operator that performs this operation more compactly. The increment operator is **++** (two consecutive plus signs). The increment operator increases its operand by one. By use of the increment operator, the preceding statement can be written like this:

```
count++;
```

Thus, the **for** in the preceding program will usually be written like this:

```
for(count = 0; count < 5; count++)
```

You might want to try this. As you will see, the loop still runs exactly the same as it did before.

C# also provides a decrement operator, which is specified as − − (two consecutive minus signs). This operator decreases its operand by one.

Using Blocks of Code

Another key element of C# is the *code block*. A code block is a grouping of statements. A code block is created by enclosing the statements between opening and closing curly braces. Once a block of code has been created, it becomes a logical unit that can be used any place that a single statement can. For example, a block can be a target for **if** and **for** statements. Consider this **if** statement:

```
if(counter < max) {
  usercount = counter;
  delaytime = 0;
}
```

Here, if **counter** is less than **max**, both statements inside the block will be executed. Thus, the two statements inside the block form a logical unit, and one statement cannot execute without the other also executing. The key point here is that whenever you need to logically link two or more statements, you do so by creating a block. Code blocks allow many algorithms to be implemented with greater clarity and efficiency. Here is a program that uses a block of code to prevent a division by zero:

```
// Demonstrate a block of code.

using System;
```

```
class BlockDemo {
  static void Main() {
    double i, j, d;

    i = 5.0;
    j = 10.0;

    // The target of this if is a block.
    if(i != 0) {
      Console.WriteLine("i does not equal zero");
      d = j / i;
      Console.WriteLine("j / i is " + d);
    }
  }
}
```

The target of the **if** is the entire block.

The output generated by this program is shown here:

```
i does not equal zero
j / i is 2
```

In this case, the target of the **if** statement is a block of code and not just a single statement. If the condition controlling the **if** is true (as it is in this case), the three statements inside the block will be executed. Try setting **i** to zero and observe the result.

As you will see later in this book, blocks of code have additional properties and uses. However, the main reason for their existence is to create logically inseparable units of code.

Semicolons and Positioning

In C#, the semicolon signals the end of a statement. That is, each individual statement must end with a semicolon.

As you know, a block is a set of logically connected statements that are surrounded by opening and closing braces. A block is *not* terminated with a semicolon. Since a block is a group of statements, it makes sense that a block is not terminated by a semicolon; instead, the end of the block is indicated by the closing brace.

Ask the Expert

Q: Does the use of a code block introduce any runtime inefficiencies? In other words, do the { and } consume any extra time during the execution of my program?

A: No. Code blocks do not add any overhead whatsoever. In fact, because of their ability to simplify the coding of certain algorithms, their use generally increases speed and efficiency.

C# does not recognize the end of the line as the end of a statement—only a semicolon terminates a statement. For this reason, it does not matter where on a line you put a statement. For example, to C#,

```
x = y;
y = y + 1;
Console.WriteLine(x + " " + y);
```

is the same as

```
x = y;   y = y + 1;   Console.WriteLine(x + " " + y);
```

Furthermore, the individual elements of a statement can also be put on separate lines. For example, the following is perfectly acceptable:

```
Console.WriteLine("This is a long line of output" +
                  x + y + z +
                  "more output");
```

Breaking long lines in this fashion is often used to make programs more readable. It can also help prevent excessively long lines from wrapping.

Indentation Practices

You may have noticed in the previous examples that certain statements were indented. C# is a free-form language, meaning that it does not matter where you place statements relative to each other on a line. However, over the years, a common and accepted indentation style has developed that allows for very readable programs. This book follows that style, and it is recommended that you do so as well. Using this style, you indent one level after each opening brace, and move back out one level after each closing brace. There are certain statements that encourage some additional indenting; these will be covered later.

Try This Improve the Temperature Conversion Program

You can use the **for** loop, the **if** statement, and code blocks to create an improved version of the Fahrenheit-to-Celsius converter that you developed in the first Try This example. This new version will print a table of conversions, beginning with 0 degrees Fahrenheit and ending with 99. After every 10 degrees, a blank line will be output. This is accomplished through the use of a variable called **counter** that counts the number of lines that have been output. Pay special attention to its use.

(continued)

Step by Step

1. Create a new file called **FtoCTable.cs**.

2. Enter the following program into the file:

```
/*
    This program displays a conversion
    table of Fahrenheit to Celsius.

    Call this program FtoCTable.cs.
*/

using System;

class FtoCTable {
  static void Main() {
    double f, c;
    int counter;

    counter = 0;
    for(f = 0.0; f < 100.0; f++) {

      // Convert to Celsius
      c = 5.0 / 9.0 * (f - 32.0);

      Console.WriteLine(f + " degrees Fahrenheit is " +
                         c + " degrees Celsius.");

      counter++;

      // Every 10th line, print a blank line.
      if(counter == 10) {
        Console.WriteLine();
        counter = 0; // reset the line counter
      }
    }
  }
}
```

3. Compile the program as described earlier.

4. Run the program. Here is a portion of the output that you will see. Notice how a blank line is output every tenth line. As mentioned, this is controlled by the **counter** variable, which is initially set to zero. Each time through the **for** loop, **counter** is incremented. When **counter** equals 10, a blank line is output and then **counter** is reset to zero. This process causes the output to be grouped into lines of ten units.

```
0 degrees Fahrenheit is -17.7777777777778 degrees Celsius.
1 degrees Fahrenheit is -17.2222222222222 degrees Celsius.
```

```
 2 degrees Fahrenheit is -16.6666666666667 degrees Celsius.
 3 degrees Fahrenheit is -16.1111111111111 degrees Celsius.
 4 degrees Fahrenheit is -15.5555555555556 degrees Celsius.
 5 degrees Fahrenheit is -15 degrees Celsius.
 6 degrees Fahrenheit is -14.4444444444444 degrees Celsius.
 7 degrees Fahrenheit is -13.8888888888889 degrees Celsius.
 8 degrees Fahrenheit is -13.3333333333333 degrees Celsius.
 9 degrees Fahrenheit is -12.7777777777778 degrees Celsius.

10 degrees Fahrenheit is -12.2222222222222 degrees Celsius.
11 degrees Fahrenheit is -11.6666666666667 degrees Celsius.
12 degrees Fahrenheit is -11.1111111111111 degrees Celsius.
13 degrees Fahrenheit is -10.5555555555556 degrees Celsius.
14 degrees Fahrenheit is -10 degrees Celsius.
15 degrees Fahrenheit is -9.44444444444444 degrees Celsius.
16 degrees Fahrenheit is -8.88888888888889 degrees Celsius.
17 degrees Fahrenheit is -8.33333333333333 degrees Celsius.
18 degrees Fahrenheit is -7.77777777777778 degrees Celsius.
19 degrees Fahrenheit is -7.22222222222222 degrees Celsius.
```

The C# Keywords

At its foundation, a computer language is defined by its keywords, and C# provides a rich and diverse set. Furthermore, C# defines two general types of keywords: *reserved* and *contextual*. The reserved keywords cannot be used as names for variables, classes, or methods. They can be used only as keywords. This is why they are called *reserved*. The terms *reserved words* or *reserved identifiers* are also sometimes used. There are currently 77 reserved keywords defined by version 3.0 of the C# language. They are shown in Table 1-1.

C# 3.0 defines 13 contextual keywords that have a special meaning in certain contexts. In those contexts, they act as keywords. Outside their context, they can be used as names for other program elements, such as variable names. Thus, they are not technically reserved. As a general rule, however, you should consider the contextual keywords reserved and avoid using them for any other purpose. Using a contextual keyword as a name for some other program element can be confusing and is considered bad practice by many programmers. The contextual keywords are shown in Table 1-2.

Identifiers

In C#, an identifier is a name assigned to a method, a variable, or any other user-defined item. Identifiers can be from one to several characters long. Variable names may start with any letter of the alphabet or with an underscore. Next may be a letter, a digit, or an underscore. The underscore can be used to enhance the readability of a variable name, as in **line_count**.

abstract	as	base	bool	break
byte	case	catch	char	checked
class	const	continue	decimal	default
delegate	do	double	else	enum
event	explicit	extern	false	finally
fixed	float	for	foreach	goto
if	implicit	in	int	interface
internal	is	lock	long	namespace
new	null	object	operator	out
override	params	private	protected	public
readonly	ref	return	sbyte	sealed
short	sizeof	stackalloc	static	string
struct	switch	this	throw	true
try	typeof	uint	ulong	unchecked
unsafe	ushort	using	virtual	void
volatile	while			

Table 1-1 The C# Reserved Keywords

Uppercase and lowercase are different; that is, to C#, **myvar** and **MyVar** are separate names. Here are some examples of acceptable identifiers:

Test	x	y2	MaxLoad
up	_top	my_var	sample23

Remember that you can't start an identifier with a digit. Thus, **12x** is invalid, for example. Good programming practice dictates that you use identifier names that reflect the meaning or usage of the items being named.

Although you cannot use any of the C# keywords as identifiers, C# does allow you to precede a keyword with an @, allowing it to be a legal identifier. For example, **@for** is a valid identifier. In this case, the identifier is actually **for** and the @ is ignored. Frankly, using @-qualified keywords for identifiers is not recommended, except for special purposes. Also, the @ can precede any identifier, but this is considered bad practice.

from	get	group	into	join
let	orderby	partial	select	set
value	where	yield		

Table 1-2 The C# Contextual Keywords

The C# Class Library

The sample programs shown in this chapter make use of two of C#'s built-in methods: **WriteLine( )** and **Write( )**. As mentioned, these methods are members of the **Console** class, which is part of the **System** namespace, which is defined by the .NET Framework's class library. As explained earlier in this chapter, the C# environment relies on the .NET Framework class library to provide support for such things as I/O, string handling, networking, and GUIs. Thus, C# as a totality is a combination of the C# language itself, plus the .NET standard classes. As you will see, the class library provides much of the functionality that is part of any C# program. Indeed, part of becoming a C# programmer is learning to use the standard library. Throughout this book, various elements of the .NET library classes and methods are described. However, the .NET library is quite large, and it is something you will also want to explore more on your own.

Chapter 1 Self Test

1. What is the MSIL and why is it important to C#?

2. What is the Common Language Runtime?

3. What are the three main principles of object-oriented programming?

4. Where do C# programs begin execution?

5. What is a variable? What is a namespace?

6. Which of the following variable names is invalid?

   A. count

   B. $count

   C. count27

   D. 67count

   E. @if

7. How do you create a single-line comment? How do you create a multiline comment?

8. Show the general form of the **if** statement. Show the general form of the **for** loop.

9. How do you create a block of code?

10. Is it necessary to start each C# program with the following statement?

```
using System;
```

11. The moon's gravity is about 17 percent that of Earth's. Write a program that computes your effective weight on the moon.

12. Adapt the FtoCTable program in "Try This: Improve the Temperature Conversion Program" so that it prints a conversion table of inches to meters. Display 12 feet of conversions, inch by inch. Output a blank line every 12 inches. (One meter equals approximately 39.37 inches.)

Chapter 2

Introducing Data Types
and Operators

Key Skills & Concepts

- C#'s basic types
- Format output
- Literals
- Initialize variables
- The scope rules of a method
- Type conversion and casting
- The arithmetic operators
- The relational and logical operators
- The assignment operator
- Expressions

At the foundation of any programming language are its data types and operators, and C# is no exception. These elements define the limits of a language and determine the kinds of tasks to which it can be applied. As you might expect, C# supports a rich assortment of both data types and operators, making it suitable for a wide range of programming.

Data types and operators are a large subject. We will begin here with an examination of C#'s foundational data types and its most commonly used operators. We will also take a closer look at variables and examine the expression.

Why Data Types Are Important

Data types are especially important in C# because it is a strongly typed language. This means that all operations are type-checked by the compiler for type compatibility. Illegal operations will not be compiled. Thus, strong type-checking helps prevent errors and enhances reliability. To enable strong type-checking, all variables, expressions, and values have a type. There is no concept of a "typeless" variable, for example. Furthermore, the type of a value determines what operations are allowed on it. An operation allowed on one type might not be allowed on another.

C#'s Value Types

C# contains two general categories of built-in data types: *value types* and *reference types*. The difference between the two types is what a variable contains. For a value type, a variable holds an actual value, such 101 or 98.6. For a reference type, a variable holds a reference to the value.

The most commonly used reference type is the class, and a discussion of classes and reference types is deferred until later. The value types are described here.

At the core of C# are the 13 value types shown in Table 2-1. Collectively, these are referred to as the *simple types*. They are called simple types because they consist of a single value. (In other words, they are not a composite of two or more values.) They form the foundation of C#'s type system, providing the basic, low-level data elements upon which a program operates. The simple types are also sometimes referred to as *primitive types*.

C# strictly specifies a range and behavior for each simple type. Because of portability requirements and to support mixed-language programming, C# is uncompromising on this account. For example, an **int** is the same in all execution environments. There is no need to rewrite code to fit a specific platform. While strictly specifying the size of the simple types may cause a small loss of performance in some environments, it is necessary in order to achieve portability.

NOTE

In addition to the simple types, C# defines three other categories of value types. These are enumerations, structures, and nullable types, all of which are described later in this book.

Integers

C# defines nine integer types: **char**, **byte**, **sbyte**, **short**, **ushort**, **int**, **uint**, **long**, and **ulong**. However, the **char** type is primarily used for representing characters, and it is discussed later

Type	Meaning
bool	Represents true/false values
byte	8-bit unsigned integer
char	Character
decimal	Numeric type for financial calculations
double	Double-precision floating point
float	Single-precision floating point
int	Integer
long	Long integer
sbyte	8-bit signed integer
short	Short integer
uint	Unsigned integer
ulong	Unsigned long integer
ushort	Unsigned short integer

Table 2-1 The C# Simple Types

in this chapter. The remaining eight integer types are used for numeric calculations. Their bit-width and ranges are shown here:

Type	Width in Bits	Range
byte	8	0 to 255
sbyte	8	−128 to 127
short	16	−32,768 to 32,767
ushort	16	0 to 65,535
int	32	−2,147,483,648 to 2,147,483,647
uint	32	0 to 4,294,967,295
long	64	−9,223,372,036,854,775,808 to 9,223,372,036,854,775,807
ulong	64	0 to 18,446,744,073,709,551,615

As the table shows, C# defines both signed and unsigned versions of the various integer types. The difference between signed and unsigned integers is in the way the high-order bit of the integer is interpreted. If a signed integer is specified, the C# compiler will generate code that assumes the high-order bit of an integer is to be used as a *sign flag*. If the sign flag is 0, the number is positive; if it is 1, the number is negative. Negative numbers are almost always represented using the *two's complement* approach. In this method, all bits in the number are reversed, and then 1 is added to this number.

Signed integers are important for a great many algorithms, but they have only half the absolute magnitude of their unsigned relatives. For example, as a **short**, here is 32,767:

```
0 1 1 1 1 1 1 1   1 1 1 1 1 1 1 1
```

For a signed value, if the high-order bit were set to 1, the number would then be interpreted as −1 (assuming the two's complement format). However, if you declared this to be a **ushort**, then when the high-order bit was set to 1, the number would become 65,535.

Probably the most commonly used integer type is **int**. Variables of type **int** are often employed to control loops, to index arrays, and for general-purpose integer math. When you need an integer that has a range greater than **int**, you have many options. If the value you want to store is unsigned, you can use **uint**. For large signed values, use **long**. For large unsigned values, use **ulong**.

Here is a program that computes the number of cubic inches contained in a cube that is 1 mile long on each side. Because this value is so large, the program uses a **long** variable to hold it.

```
// Compute the number of cubic inches in 1 cubic mile.

using System;

class Inches {
  static void Main() {
```

```
    long ci;
    long im;        ←———— Declare two long variables.

    im = 5280 * 12;

    ci = im * im * im;

    Console.WriteLine("There are " + ci +
                      " cubic inches in cubic mile.");
  }
}
```

Here is the output from the program:

```
There are 254358061056000 cubic inches in cubic mile.
```

Clearly, the result could not have been held in an **int** or **uint** variable.

The smallest integer types are **byte** and **sbyte**. The **byte** type is an unsigned value between 0 and 255. Variables of type **byte** are especially useful when working with raw binary data, such as a byte stream produced by some device. For small signed integers, use **sbyte**. Here is an example that uses a variable of type **byte** to control a **for** loop that produces the summation of the number 100:

```
// Use byte.

using System;

class Use_byte {
  static void Main() {
    byte x;
    int sum;

    sum = 0;
    for(x = 1; x <= 100; x++)  ←——— Use a byte variable
      sum = sum + x;                  to control a for loop.

    Console.WriteLine("Summation of 100 is " + sum);
  }
}
```

The output from the program is shown here:

```
Summation of 100 is 5050
```

Since the **for** loop runs only from 0 to 100, which is well within the range of a **byte**, there is no need to use a larger type variable to control it. Of course, **byte** could not have been used to hold the result of the summation because 5050 is far outside its range. This is why **sum** is an **int**.

When you need an integer that is larger than a **byte** or **sbyte** but smaller than an **int** or **uint**, use **short** or **ushort**.

Floating-Point Types

As explained in Chapter 1, the floating-point types can represent numbers that have fractional components. There are two kinds of floating-point types, **float** and **double**, which represent single- and double-precision numbers, respectively. The type **float** is 32 bits wide and has a range of 1.5E–45 to 3.4E+38. The **double** type is 64 bits wide and has a range of 5E–324 to 1.7E+308.

Of the two, **double** is the most commonly used. One reason for this is that many of the math functions in C#'s class library (which is the .NET Framework library) use **double** values. For example, the **Sqrt( )** method (which is defined by the **System.Math** class) returns a **double** value that is the square root of its **double** argument. Here, **Sqrt( )** is used to compute the length of the hypotenuse given the lengths of the two opposing sides:

```
/*
    Use the Pythagorean theorem to find the length of the hypotenuse
    given the lengths of the two opposing sides.
*/

using System;

class Hypot {
    static void Main() {
        double x, y, z;

        x = 3;
        y = 4;

        z = Math.Sqrt(x*x + y*y);

        Console.WriteLine("Hypotenuse is " + z);
    }
}
```

Notice how **Sqrt( )** is called. It is preceded by the name of the class of which it is a member.

The output from the program is shown here:

```
Hypotenuse is 5
```

Here's another point about the preceding example. As mentioned, **Sqrt( )** is a member of the **Math** class. Notice how **Sqrt( )** is called; it is preceded by the name **Math**. This is similar to the way **Console** precedes **WriteLine( )**. Although not all standard methods are called by specifying their class name first, several are.

The decimal Type

Perhaps the most interesting C# numeric type is **decimal**, which is intended for use in monetary calculations. The **decimal** type utilizes 128 bits to represent values within the range 1E–28 to 7.9E+28. As you may know, normal floating-point arithmetic is subject to a variety of rounding errors when it is applied to decimal values. The **decimal** type eliminates these errors and can accurately represent up to 28 decimal places (or 29 places, in some cases). This ability to represent decimal values without rounding errors makes it especially useful for computations that involve money.

Here is a program that uses the **decimal** type in a financial calculation. The program computes a balance after interest has been applied.

```
// Use the decimal type in a financial calculation.

using System;

class UseDecimal {
  static void Main() {
    decimal balance;
    decimal rate;

    // Compute new balance.
    balance = 1000.10m;          ◄──── decimal values must be
    rate = 0.1m;                        followed by an m or M.
    balance = balance * rate + balance;

    Console.WriteLine("New balance: $" + balance);
  }
}
```

The output from this program is shown here:

```
New balance: $1100.110
```

In the program, notice that the decimal constants are followed by the **m** or **M** suffix. This is necessary because without the suffix, these values would be interpreted as standard floating-point constants, which are not compatible with the **decimal** data type. (We will look more closely at how to specify numeric constants later in this chapter.)

Ask the Expert

Q: The other computer languages that I have worked with do not have a decimal data type. Is it unique to C#?

A: The **decimal** type is not supported by C, C++, or Java as a built-in type. Thus, within its direct line of descent, it is unique.

Characters

In C#, characters are not 8-bit quantities like they are in many other computer languages, such as C++. Instead, C# uses Unicode. *Unicode* defines a character set that can represent all of the characters found in all human languages. Thus, in C#, **char** is an unsigned 16-bit type having a range of 0 to 65,535. The standard 8-bit ASCII character set is a subset of Unicode and ranges from 0 to 127. Thus, the ASCII characters are still valid C# characters.

A character variable can be assigned a value by enclosing the character inside single quotes. For example, this assigns X to the variable **ch**:

```
char ch;
ch = 'X';
```

You can output a **char** value using a **WriteLine( )** statement. For example, this line outputs the value in **ch**:

```
Console.WriteLine("This is ch: " + ch);
```

Although **char** is defined by C# as an integer type, it cannot be freely mixed with integers in all cases. This is because there is no automatic type conversion from integer to **char**. For example, the following fragment is invalid:

```
char ch;

ch = 10; // error, won't work
```

The reason the preceding code will not work is that 10 is an integer value and it won't automatically convert to a **char**. Thus, the assignment involves incompatible types. If you attempt to compile this code, you will see an error message. Later in this chapter you will see a way around this restriction.

Ask the Expert

Q: Why does C# use Unicode?

A: C# was designed to allow programs to be written for worldwide use. Thus, it needs to use a character set that can represent all of the world's languages. Unicode is the standard character set designed expressly for this purpose. Of course, the use of Unicode is inefficient for languages such as English, German, Spanish, or French, whose characters can be contained within 8 bits. But such is the price of global portability.

The bool Type

The **bool** type represents true/false values. C# defines the values true and false using the reserved words **true** and **false**. Thus, a variable or expression of type **bool** will be one of these two values. Furthermore, there is no conversion defined between **bool** and integer values. For example, 1 does not convert to true, and 0 does not convert to false.

Here is a program that demonstrates the **bool** type:

```
// Demonstrate bool values.

using System;

class BoolDemo {
  static void Main() {
    bool b;

    b = false;
    Console.WriteLine("b is " + b);
    b = true;
    Console.WriteLine("b is now " + b);

    // A bool value can control the if statement.
    if(b) Console.WriteLine("This is executed.");

    b = false;
    if(b) Console.WriteLine("This is not executed.");

    // The outcome of a relational operator is a bool value.
    Console.WriteLine("88 > 17 is " + (88 > 17));
  }
}
```

A single **bool** value can control an **if** statement.

The output generated by this program is shown here:

```
b is False
b is now True
This is executed.
88 > 17 is True
```

There are three interesting things to notice about this program. First, as you can see, when a **bool** value is output by **WriteLine( )**, "True" or "False" is displayed. Second, the value of a **bool** variable is sufficient, by itself, to control the **if** statement. There is no need to write an **if** statement like this:

```
if(b == true) ...
```

Third, the outcome of a relational operator, such as **<**, is a **bool** value. This is why the expression **88 > 17** displays the value "True." Further, the extra set of parentheses around **88 > 17** is necessary because the **+** operator has a higher precedence than the **>** operator.

Some Output Options

Before continuing our examination of data types and operators, a small digression will be useful. Up to this point, when outputting lists of data, you have been separating each part of the list with a plus sign, as shown here:

```
Console.WriteLine("You ordered " + 2 + " items at $" + 3 + " each.");
```

Although very convenient, outputting numeric information in this way does not give you any control over how that information appears. For example, for a floating-point value, you can't control the number of decimal places displayed. Consider the following statement:

```
Console.WriteLine("Here is 10/3: " + 10.0/3.0);
```

It generates this output:

```
Here is 10/3: 3.33333333333333
```

While this might be fine for some purposes, displaying so many decimal places could be inappropriate for others. For example, in financial calculations, you will usually want to display two decimal places.

To control how numeric data is formatted, you will need to use a second form of **WriteLine( )**, shown here, which allows you to embed formatting information:

WriteLine(*"format string"*, *arg0, arg1, ... , argN*)

In this version, the arguments to **WriteLine( )** are separated by commas and not plus signs. The *format string* contains two items: regular, printing characters that are displayed as-is and format specifiers. Format specifiers take this general form:

{*argnum, width: fmt*}

Here, *argnum* specifies the number of the argument (starting from zero) to display. The minimum width of the field is specified by *width,* and the format is specified by *fmt.*

During execution, when a format specifier is encountered in the format string, the corresponding argument, as specified by *argnum,* is substituted and displayed. Thus, it is the position of a format specification within the format string that determines where its matching data will be displayed. Both *width* and *fmt* are optional. Thus, in its simplest form, a format specifier simply indicates which argument to display. For example, **{0}** indicates *arg0,* **{1}** specifies *arg1,* and so on.

Let's begin with a simple example. The statement

```
Console.WriteLine("February has {0} or {1} days.", 28, 29);
```

produces the following output:

```
February has 28 or 29 days.
```

As you can see, the value 28 is substituted for {0}, and 29 is substituted for {1}. Thus, the format specifiers identify the location at which the subsequent arguments—in this case,

28 and 29—are displayed within the string. Furthermore, notice that the additional values are separated by commas, not plus signs.

Here is a variation of the preceding statement that specifies minimum field widths:

```
Console.WriteLine("February has {0,10} or {1,5} days.", 28, 29);
```

It produces the following output:

```
February has         28 or     29 days.
```

As you can see, spaces have been added to fill out the unused portions of the fields. Remember, a minimum field width is just that: the *minimum* width. Output can exceed that width if needed.

In the preceding examples, no formatting was applied to the values themselves. Of course, the value of using format specifiers is to control the way the data looks. The types of data most commonly formatted are floating-point and decimal values. One of the easiest ways to specify a format is to describe a template that **WriteLine( )** will use. To do this, show an example of the format that you want, using #s to mark the digit positions. For instance, here is a better way to display 10 divided by 3:

```
Console.WriteLine("Here is 10/3: {0:#.##}", 10.0/3.0);
```

The output from this statement is shown here:

```
Here is 10/3: 3.33
```

In this example, the template is #.##, which tells **WriteLine( )** to display two decimal places. It is important to understand, however, that **WriteLine( )** will display more than one digit to the left of the decimal point if necessary so as not to misrepresent the value.

If you want to display monetary values, use the **C** format specifier. For example,

```
decimal balance;

balance = 12323.09m;
Console.WriteLine("Current balance is {0:C}", balance);
```

The output from this sequence is shown here (in U.S. dollar format):

```
Current balance is $12,323.09
```

Try This   Talk to Mars

At its closest point to Earth, Mars is approximately 34 million miles away. Assuming there is someone on Mars you want to talk with, what is the delay between the time a radio signal leaves Earth and the time it arrives on Mars? This program supplies the answer. Recall that light travels approximately 186,000 miles per second. Thus, to compute the delay, you will need to divide the distance by the speed of light. Display the delay in terms of seconds and minutes.

(continued)

Step by Step

1. Create a new file called **Mars.cs**.

2. To compute the delay, you will need to use floating-point values. Why? Because the time interval will have a fractional component. Here are the variables used by the program:

```
double distance;
double lightspeed;
double delay;
double delay_in_min;
```

3. Give **distance** and **lightspeed** these values:

```
distance = 34000000; // 34,000,000 miles
lightspeed = 186000; // 186,000 miles per second
```

4. To compute the delay, divide **distance** by **lightspeed**. This yields the delay in seconds. Assign this value to **delay** and display the results. These steps are shown here:

```
delay = distance / lightspeed;

Console.WriteLine("Time delay when talking to Mars: " +
                   delay + " seconds.");
```

5. Divide the number of seconds in **delay** by 60 to obtain the delay in minutes; display that result using these lines of code:

```
delay_in_min = delay / 60;

Console.WriteLine("This is " + delay_in_min +
                   " minutes.");
```

Here is the entire **Mars.cs** program listing:

```
// Talk to Mars

using System;

class Mars {
  static void Main() {
    double distance;
    double lightspeed;
    double delay;
    double delay_in_min;

    distance = 34000000; // 34,000,000 miles
    lightspeed = 186000; // 186,000 miles per second

    delay = distance / lightspeed;
```

```
Console.WriteLine("Time delay when talking to Mars: " +
                  delay + " seconds.");

delay_in_min = delay / 60;

Console.WriteLine("This is " + delay_in_min +
                  " minutes.");
    }
}
```

6. Compile and run the program. The following result is displayed:

```
Time delay when talking to Mars: 182.795698924731 seconds.
This is 3.04659498207885 minutes.
```

7. For most people, the program displays too many decimal places. To improve the readability of the program, substitute the following **WriteLine( )** statements for the ones shown in the program:

```
Console.WriteLine("Time delay when talking to Mars: {0:#.###} seconds",
                  delay);

Console.WriteLine("This is about {0:#.###} minutes", delay_in_min);
```

8. Recompile and run the program. When you do, you will see this output:

```
Time delay when talking to Mars: 182.796 seconds
This is about 3.047 minutes
```

Now, only three decimal places are displayed.

Literals

In C#, *literals* refer to fixed values that are represented in their human-readable form. For example, the number 100 is a literal. For the most part, literals and their usage are so intuitive that they have been used in one form or another by all the preceding sample programs. Now the time has come to explain them formally.

C# literals can be of any of the value types. The way each literal is represented depends upon its type. As explained earlier, character literals are enclosed between single quotes. For example 'a' and '%' are both character literals.

Integer literals are specified as numbers without fractional components. For example, 10 and –100 are integer literals. Floating-point literals require the use of the decimal point followed by the number's fractional component. For example, 11.123 is a floating-point literal. C# also allows you to use scientific notation for floating-point numbers.

Since C# is a strongly typed language, literals, too, have a type. Naturally, this raises the following question: What is the type of a numeric literal? For example, what is the type of 12, 123987, or 0.23? Fortunately, C# specifies some easy-to-follow rules that answer these questions.

First, for integer literals, the type of the literal is the smallest integer type that will hold it, beginning with **int**. Thus, an integer literal is of type **int**, **uint**, **long**, or **ulong**, depending upon its value. Second, floating-point literals are of type **double**.

If C#'s default type is not what you want for a literal, you can explicitly specify its type by including a suffix. To specify a **long** literal, append an *l* or an *L*. For example, 12 is an **int**, but 12L is a **long**. To specify an unsigned integer value, append a *u* or *U*. Thus, 100 is an **int**, but 100U is a **uint**. To specify an unsigned, long integer, use *ul* or *UL*. For example, 984375UL is of type **ulong**.

To specify a **float** literal, append an *F* or *f*. For example, 10.19F is of type **float**. Although redundant, you can specify a **double** literal by appending a **D** or **d**. (As just mentioned, floating-point literals are **double** by default.)

To specify a **decimal** literal, follow its value with an *m* or *M*. For example, 9.95M is a **decimal** literal.

Although integer literals create an **int**, **uint**, **long**, or **ulong** value by default, they can still be assigned to variables of type **byte**, **sbyte**, **short**, or **ushort** as long as the value being assigned can be represented by the target type.

Hexadecimal Literals

In programming, it is sometimes easier to use a number system based on 16 instead of 10. The base 16 number system is called *hexadecimal* and uses the digits 0 through 9, plus the letters A through F, which stand for 10, 11, 12, 13, 14, and 15. For example, the hexadecimal number 10 is 16 in decimal. Because of the frequency with which hexadecimal numbers are used, C# allows you to specify integer literals in hexadecimal format. A hexadecimal literal must begin with 0x (a zero followed by an *x*). Here are some examples:

```
count = 0xFF; // 255 in decimal
incr = 0x1a;  // 26 in decimal
```

Character Escape Sequences

Enclosing character constants in single quotes works for most printing characters, but a few characters, such as the carriage return, pose a special problem when a text editor is used. In addition, certain other characters, such as single and double quotes, have special meaning in C#, so you cannot use them directly. For these reasons, C# provides special *escape sequences,* shown in Table 2-2. These sequences are used in place of the characters that they represent.

For example, this assigns **ch** the tab character:

```
ch = '\t';
```

The next example assigns a single quote to **ch**:

```
ch = '\'';
```

Escape Sequence	Description
\a	Alert (bell)
\b	Backspace
\f	Form feed
\n	Newline (linefeed)
\r	Carriage return
\t	Horizontal tab
\v	Vertical tab
\0	Null
\'	Single quote
\"	Double quote
\\	Backslash

Table 2-2   Character Escape Sequences

String Literals

C# supports another type of literal: the string. A string literal is a set of characters enclosed by double quotes. For example,

```
"this is a test"
```

is a string. You have seen examples of strings in many of the **WriteLine( )** statements in the preceding sample programs.

In addition to normal characters, a string literal can also contain one or more of the escape sequences just described. For example, consider the following program. It uses the **\n** and **\t** escape sequences.

Ask the Expert

Q: I know that C++ allows integer literals to be specified in octal (a number system based on 8). Does C# allow octal literals?

A: No. C# allows integer literals to be specified only in decimal or hexadecimal form. Octal is seldom used in today's modern programming environments.

```
// Demonstrate escape sequences in strings.

using System;

class StrDemo {
    static void Main() {
        Console.WriteLine("First line\nSecond line");
        Console.WriteLine("A\tB\tC");
        Console.WriteLine("D\tE\tF");
    }
}
```

Use \n to generate a new line.

Use tabs to align output.

The output is shown here:

```
First line
Second line
A      B      C
D      E      F
```

Notice how the **\n** escape sequence is used to generate a new line. You don't need to use multiple **WriteLine( )** statements to get multiline output. Just embed **\n** within a longer string at the points at which you want the newlines to occur.

In addition to the form of string literal just described, you can specify a *verbatim string literal*. A verbatim string literal begins with an @, which is followed by a quoted string. The contents of the quoted string are accepted without modification and can span two or more lines. Thus, you can include newlines, tabs, and so on, but you don't need to use the escape sequences. The only exception is that to obtain a double quote ("), you must use two double quotes in a row (""). Here is a program that demonstrates verbatim string literals:

```
// Demonstrate verbatim literal strings.

using System;

class Verbatim {
    static void Main() {
        Console.WriteLine(@"This is a verbatim
string literal
that spans several lines.
");
        Console.WriteLine(@"Here is some tabbed output:
1      2      3      4
5      6      7      8
");
        Console.WriteLine(@"Programmers say, ""I like C#.""");
    }
}
```

This verbatim quote contains embedded newlines.

This one contains embedded tabs, too.

The output from this program is shown here:

```
This is a verbatim
string literal
that spans several lines.

Here is some tabbed output:
1       2       3       4
5       6       7       8

Programmers say, "I like C#."
```

The important point to notice about the preceding program is that the verbatim string literals are displayed precisely as they are entered into the program.

The advantage of verbatim string literals is that you can specify output in your program exactly as it will appear on the screen. However, in the case of multiline strings, the wrapping will cause the indentation of your program to be obscured. For this reason, the programs in this book will make only limited use of verbatim string literals. That said, they are still a wonderful benefit for many formatting situations.

A Closer Look at Variables

Variables were introduced in Chapter 1. As you learned, variables are declared using this form of statement:

type var-name;

where *type* is the data type of the variable and *var-name* is its name. You can declare a variable of any valid type, including the value types just described. It is important to understand that the capabilities of the variable are determined by its type. For example, a variable of type **bool** cannot be used to store floating-point values. Furthermore, the type of a variable cannot change during its lifetime. An **int** variable cannot turn into a **char** variable, for example.

All variables in C# must be declared. This is necessary because the compiler must know what type of data a variable contains before it can properly compile any statement that uses the variable. It also enables C# to perform strict type-checking.

C# defines several different kinds of variables. The kinds that we have been using are called *local variables* because they are declared within a method.

Ask the Expert

Q: Is a string consisting of a single character the same as a character literal? For example, is "k" the same as 'k'?

A: No. You must not confuse strings with characters. A character literal represents a single letter of type **char**. A string containing only one letter is still a string. Although strings consist of characters, they are not the same type.

Initializing a Variable

One way to give a variable a value is through an assignment statement, as you have already seen. Another way is by giving it an initial value when it is declared. To do this, follow the variable's name with an equal sign and the value being assigned. The general form of initialization is shown here:

type var-name = value;

Here, *value* is the value that is given to *var-name* when *var-name* is created. The value must be compatible with the specified type.

Here are some examples:

```
int count = 10; // give count an initial value of 10
char ch = 'X';  // initialize ch with the letter X
float f = 1.2F; // f is initialized with 1.2
```

When declaring two or more variables of the same type using a comma-separated list, you can give one or more of those variables an initial value. For example:

```
int a, b = 8, c = 19, d; // b and c have initializations
```

In this case, only **b** and **c** are initialized.

Dynamic Initialization

Although the preceding examples have used only constants as initializers, C# allows variables to be initialized dynamically, using any expression valid at the point at which the variable is declared. For example, here is a short program that computes the volume of a cylinder given the radius of its base and its height:

```
// Demonstrate dynamic initialization.

using System;

class DynInit {
    static void Main() {                          volume is dynamically
        double radius = 4, height = 5;            initialized at runtime.

        // Dynamically initialize volume.
        double volume = 3.1416 * radius * radius * height;

        Console.WriteLine("Volume is " + volume);
    }
}
```

Here, three local variables—**radius**, **height**, and **volume**—are declared. The first two, **radius** and **height**, are initialized by constants. However, **volume** is initialized dynamically to the volume of the cylinder. The key point here is that the initialization expression can use any element valid at the point of the initialization, including calls to methods, other variables, or literals.

Implicitly Typed Variables

As explained, in C# all variables must be declared. Normally, a declaration includes the type of the variable, such as **int** or **bool**, followed by the name of the variable. However, beginning with C# 3.0, it is possible to let the compiler determine the type of a variable based on the value used to initialize it. This is called an *implicitly typed variable*.

An implicitly typed variable is declared using the keyword **var**, and it must be initialized. The compiler uses the type of the initializer to determine the type of the variable. Here is an example:

```
var pi = 3.1416;
```

Because **pi** is initialized with a floating-point literal (whose type is **double** by default), the type of **pi** is **double**. Had **pi** been declared like this:

```
var pi = 3.1416M;
```

then **pi** would have the type **decimal** instead.

The following program demonstrates implicitly typed variables:

```
// Demonstrate implicitly typed variables.

using System;

class ImpTypedVar {
  static void Main() {

    // These are implicitly typed variables.
    var pi = 3.1416; // pi is a double
    var radius = 10; // radius is an int

    // Both msg and msg2 are string types.
    var msg = "Radius: ";
    var msg2 = "Area: ";

    // Explicitly declare area as a double.
    double area;

    Console.WriteLine(msg2 + radius);
    area = pi * radius * radius;
    Console.WriteLine(msg + area);

    Console.WriteLine();

    radius = radius + 2;

    Console.WriteLine(msg2 + radius);
    area = pi * radius * radius;
```

Implicitly typed variables.

```
      Console.WriteLine(msg + area);

      // The following statement will not compile because
      // radius is an int and cannot be assigned a floating-
      // point value.
//       radius = 12.2;  // Error!
    }
}
```

The output is shown here:

```
Area: 10
Radius: 314.16

Area: 12
Radius: 452.3904
```

It is important to emphasize that an implicitly typed variable is still a strongly typed variable. Notice this commented-out line in the program:

```
//     radius = 12.2;  // Error!
```

This assignment is invalid because **radius** is of type **int**. Thus, it cannot be assigned a floating-point value. The only difference between an implicitly typed variable and a "normal" explicitly typed variable is how the type is determined. Once that type has been determined, the variable has a type, and this type is fixed throughout the lifetime of the variable. Thus, the type of **radius** cannot be changed during the execution of the program.

Implicitly typed variables were added to C# to handle some special-case situations, the most important of which relate to LINQ (language-integrated query), which is described later in this book. For the majority of variables, you should use explicitly typed variables because they make your code easier to read and easier to understand. Implicitly typed variables should be used only when necessary. They are not intended to replace normal variable declarations in general. In essence, use, but don't abuse, this new C# feature.

One last point: Only one implicitly typed variable can be declared at any one time. Therefore, the following declaration

```
var count = 10, max = 20; // Error!
```

is wrong and won't compile because it attempts to declare both **count** and **max** at the same time.

The Scope and Lifetime of Variables

So far, all of the variables that we have been using are declared at the start of the **Main( )** method. However, C# allows a local variable to be declared within any block. As explained in Chapter 1, a block is begun with an opening curly brace and ended with a closing curly brace. A block defines a *scope*. Thus, each time you start a new block, you are creating a new scope. A scope determines what names are visible to other parts of your program. It also determines the lifetime of local variables.

The most important scopes in C# are those defined by a class and those defined by a method. A discussion of class scope (and variables declared within it) is deferred until later in this book, when classes are described. For now, we will examine only the scopes defined by or within a method.

The scope defined by a method begins with its opening curly brace and ends with its closing curly brace. However, if that method has parameters, they, too, are included within the scope defined by the method.

As a general rule, local variables declared inside a scope are not visible to code that is defined outside that scope. Thus, when you declare a variable within a scope, you are preventing it from being accessed or modified by code outside the scope. Indeed, the scope rules provide the foundation for encapsulation.

Scopes can be nested. For example, each time you create a block of code, you are creating a new, nested scope. When this occurs, the outer scope encloses the inner scope. This means that local variables declared in the outer scope will be visible to code within the inner scope. However, the reverse is not true. Local variables declared within the inner scope will not be visible outside it.

To understand the effect of nested scopes, consider the following program:

```
// Demonstrate block scope.

using System;

class ScopeDemo {
  static void Main() {
    int x; // known to all code within Main()

    x = 10;
    if(x == 10) { // start new scope
      int y = 20; // known only to this block

      // x and y both known here.
      Console.WriteLine("x and y: " + x + " " + y);
      x = y * 2;
    }
    // y = 100; // Error! y not known here   ◄─────── Here, y is outside its scope.

    // x is still known here.
    Console.WriteLine("x is " + x);
  }
}
```

As the comments indicate, the variable **x** is declared at the start of **Main( )**'s scope and is accessible to all subsequent code within **Main( )**. Within the **if** block, **y** is declared. Since a block defines a scope, **y** is visible only to other code within its block. This is why outside of its block, the line **y = 100;** is commented out. If you remove the leading comment symbol, a compile-time error will occur because **y** is not visible outside of its block. Within the **if** block, **x** can be used because code within a block (that is, a nested scope) has access to variables declared by an enclosing scope.

Within a block, local variables can be declared at any point, but are valid only after they are declared. Thus, if you define a variable at the start of a method, it is available to all of the code within that method. Conversely, if you declare a variable at the end of a block, it is effectively useless, because no code will have access to it.

If a variable declaration includes an initializer, that variable will be reinitialized each time the block in which it is declared is entered. For example, consider this program:

```
// Demonstrate the lifetime of a variable.

using System;

class VarInitDemo {
  static void Main() {
    int x;

    for(x = 0; x < 3; x++) {
      int y = -1; // y is initialized each time block is entered
      Console.WriteLine("y is: " + y); // this always prints -1
      y = 100;
      Console.WriteLine("y is now: " + y);
    }
  }
}
```

The output generated by this program is shown here:

```
y is: -1
y is now: 100
y is: -1
y is now: 100
y is: -1
y is now: 100
```

As you can see, **y** is always reinitialized to –1 each time the **for** block is entered. Even though it is subsequently assigned the value 100, this value is lost.

There is one quirk to C#'s scope rules that may surprise you: Although blocks can be nested, no variable declared within an inner scope can have the same name as a variable declared by an enclosing scope. For example, the following program, which tries to declare two separate variables with the same name, will not compile:

```
/*
   This program attempts to declare a variable
   in an inner scope with the same name as one
   defined in an outer scope.

   *** This program will not compile. ***
*/

using System;
```

```
class NestVar {
  static void Main() {
    int count;

    for(count = 0; count < 10; count = count+1) {
      Console.WriteLine("This is count: " + count);

      // Illegal!!! This conflicts with the previous count.
      int count;  ◄——————— Can't declare count again because it's already declared by Main( ).

      for(count = 0; count < 2; count++)
        Console.WriteLine("This program is in error!");
    }
  }
}
```

If you come from a C/C++ background, you know that there is no restriction on the names that you give variables declared in an inner scope. Thus, in C/C++, the declaration of **count** within the block of the outer **for** loop is completely valid. However, in C/C++, such a declaration hides the outer **count**. The designers of C# felt that this type of *name hiding* could easily lead to programming errors and disallowed it.

Operators

C# provides a rich operator environment. An operator is a symbol that tells the compiler to perform a specific mathematical or logical manipulation. C# has four general classes of operators: *arithmetic, bitwise, relational,* and *logical.* C# also has several other operators that handle certain special situations. This chapter will examine the arithmetic, relational, and logical operators. It also examines the assignment operator. The bitwise and other special operators are examined later.

Arithmetic Operators

C# defines the following arithmetic operators:

Operator	Meaning
+	Addition
−	Subtraction (also unary minus)
*	Multiplication
/	Division
%	Modulus
++	Increment
− −	Decrement

The operators +, −, *, and / all work in the expected way. These can be applied to any built-in numeric data type.

Although the actions of the basic arithmetic operators are well known to all readers, the % warrants some explanation. First, remember that when / is applied to an integer, any remainder will be truncated; for example, 10/3 will equal 3 in integer division. You can obtain the remainder of this division by using the modulus operator %. It works in C# the way that it does in other languages: It yields the remainder of an integer division. For example, 10 % 3 is 1. In C#, the % can be applied to both integer and floating-point types. Thus, 10.0 % 3.0 is also 1. (This differs from C/C++, which allow modulus operations only on integer types.) The following program demonstrates the modulus operator:

```
// Demonstrate the % operator.

using System;

class ModDemo {
  static void Main() {
    int iresult, irem;
    double dresult, drem;

    iresult = 10 / 3;
    irem = 10 % 3;                    ◄──────┐
                                             ├── Use the modulus operator.
    dresult = 10.0 / 3.0;                    │
    drem = 10.0 % 3.0;  ◄────────────────────┘

    Console.WriteLine("Result and remainder of 10 / 3: " +
                      iresult + " " + irem);
    Console.WriteLine("Result and remainder of 10.0 / 3.0: " +
                      dresult + " " + drem);
  }
}
```

The output from the program is shown here:

```
Result and remainder of 10 / 3: 3 1
Result and remainder of 10.0 / 3.0: 3.33333333333333 1
```

As you can see, the % yields a remainder of 1 for both integer and floating-point operations.

Increment and Decrement

Introduced in Chapter 1, the ++ and the − − are the increment and decrement operators, respectively. As you will see, they have some special properties that make them quite interesting. Let's begin by reviewing precisely what the increment and decrement operators do.

The increment operator adds 1 to its operand, and the decrement operator subtracts 1. Therefore:

```
x = x + 1;
```

is the same as

```
x++;
```

and

```
x = x - 1;
```

is the same as

```
--x;
```

Both the increment and decrement operators can either precede (*prefix*) or follow (*postfix*) the operand. For example:

```
x = x + 1;
```

can be written as

```
++x; // prefix form
```

or as

```
x++; // postfix form
```

In the foregoing example, there is no difference whether the increment is applied as a prefix or a postfix. However, when an increment or decrement is used as part of a larger expression, there is an important difference. In this case, when the operator *precedes* its operand, the result of the operation is the value of the operand *after* the increment or decrement. If the operator *follows* its operand, the result of the operation is the value of the operand *before* the increment or decrement. Consider the following:

```
x = 10;
y = ++x;
```

In this case, **y** will be set to 11. This is because **x** is first incremented and then its value is obtained. However, if the code is written as

```
x = 10;
y = x++;
```

then **y** will be set to 10. In this case, the value of **x** is first obtained, **x** is incremented, and then the original value of **x** is returned. In both cases, **x** is still set to 11; the difference is what is returned by the operator.

Here is a bit more complicated example:

```
x = 10;
y = 2;
z = x++ - (x * y);
```

This gives **z** the value –12. The reason is that when **x++** is evaluated, it sets **x** to 11, but yields the value 10 (**x**'s original value). This means that **z** is assigned 10 – (11 * 2), which is –12. However, written like this:

```
z = ++x - (x * y);
```

The result is –11. This is because the **x** is first incremented and then its value is obtained. Thus, **z** is assigned 11 – (11 * 2), which is –11. As this example hints at, there can be significant advantages in being able to control when the increment or decrement operation takes place.

Relational and Logical Operators

In the terms *relational operator* and *logical operator*, *relational* refers to the relationships that values can have with one another, and *logical* refers to the ways in which true and false values can be connected together. Since the relational operators produce true or false results, they often work with the logical operators. For this reason, they will be discussed together here.

The relational operators are shown here:

Operator	Meaning
==	Equal to
!=	Not equal to
>	Greater than
<	Less than
>=	Greater than or equal to
<=	Less than or equal to

The logical operators are shown next:

Operator	Meaning
&	AND
|	OR
^	XOR (exclusive OR)
||	Short-circuit OR
&&	Short-circuit AND
!	NOT

The outcome of the relational and logical operators is a **bool** value.

In general, objects can be compared for equality or inequality using == and !=. However, the comparison operators, <, >, <=, or >=, can be applied only to those types that support an ordering relationship. Therefore, all of the relational operators can be applied to all numeric types. However, values of type **bool** can only be compared for equality or inequality, since the **true** and **false** values are not ordered. For example, **true > false** has no meaning in C#.

For the logical operators, the operands must be of type **bool**, and the result of a logical operation is of type **bool**. The logical operators, **&**, **|**, **^**, and **!**, support the basic logical operations AND, OR, XOR, and NOT, according to the following truth table:

p	q	p & q	p | q	p ^ q	!p
False	False	False	False	False	True
True	False	False	True	True	False
False	True	False	True	True	True
True	True	True	True	False	False

As the table shows, the outcome of an exclusive OR operation is true only when exactly one operand is true.

Here is a program that demonstrates several of the relational and logical operators:

```
// Demonstrate the relational and logical operators.

using System;

class RelLogOps {
  static void Main() {
    int i, j;
    bool b1, b2;

    i = 10;
    j = 11;
    if(i < j) Console.WriteLine("i < j");
    if(i <= j) Console.WriteLine("i <= j");
    if(i != j) Console.WriteLine("i != j");
    if(i == j) Console.WriteLine("this won't execute");
    if(i >= j) Console.WriteLine("this won't execute");
    if(i > j) Console.WriteLine("this won't execute");

    b1 = true;
    b2 = false;
    if(b1 & b2) Console.WriteLine("this won't execute");
    if(!(b1 & b2)) Console.WriteLine("!(b1 & b2) is true");
    if(b1 | b2) Console.WriteLine("b1 | b2 is true");
    if(b1 ^ b2) Console.WriteLine("b1 ^ b2 is true");
  }
}
```

The output from the program is shown here:

```
i < j
i <= j
i != j
!(b1 & b2) is true
b1 | b2 is true
b1 ^ b2 is true
```

Short-Circuit Logical Operators

C# supplies special *short-circuit* versions of its AND and OR logical operators that can be used to produce more efficient code. To understand why, consider the following. In an AND operation, if the first operand is false, the outcome is false, no matter what value the second operand has. In an OR operation, if the first operand is true, the outcome of the operation is true, no matter what the value of the second operand. Thus, in these two cases, there is no need to evaluate the second operand. By not evaluating the second operand, time is saved and more efficient code is produced.

The short-circuit AND operator is **&&**, and the short-circuit OR operator is **||**. As described earlier, their normal counterparts are **&** and **|**. The only difference between the normal and short-circuit versions is that the normal operands will always evaluate each operand, but short-circuit versions will evaluate the second operand only when necessary.

Here is a program that demonstrates the short-circuit AND operator. The program determines if the value in **d** is a factor of **n**. It does this by performing a modulus operation. If the remainder of **n / d** is zero, then **d** is a factor. However, since the modulus operation involves a division, the short-circuit form of the AND is used to prevent a divide-by-zero error.

```
// Demonstrate the short-circuit operators.

using System;

class SCops {
  static void Main() {
    int n, d;

    n = 10;
    d = 2;

    // Here, d is 2, so the modulus operation takes place.
    if(d != 0 && (n % d) == 0)
      Console.WriteLine(d + " is a factor of " + n);

    d = 0; // now, set d to zero

    // Since d is zero, the second operand is not evaluated.
    if(d != 0 && (n % d) == 0)  ◄——— The short-circuit operator prevents a division by zero.
      Console.WriteLine(d + " is a factor of " + n);

    // Now, try same thing without short-circuit operator.
    // This will cause a divide-by-zero error.   Now, both expressions are evaluated,
    if(d != 0 & (n % d) == 0)  ◄——————————— allowing a division by zero to occur.
      Console.WriteLine(d + " is a factor of " + n);
  }
}
```

To prevent a divide-by-zero error, the **if** statement first checks to see if **d** is equal to zero. If it is, the short-circuit AND stops at that point and does not perform the modulus division.

Thus, in the first test, **d** is 2 and the modulus operation is performed. Next, **d** is set to zero. This causes the second test to fail, and the modulus operation is skipped, avoiding a divide-by-zero error. Finally, the normal AND operator is tried. This causes both operands to be evaluated, which leads to a runtime error when the division-by-zero occurs.

One other point: The short-circuit AND is also known as the *conditional AND,* and the short-circuit OR is also called the *conditional OR.*

Try This Display a Truth Table for the Logical Operators

Here you will create a program that displays the truth table for C#'s logical operators. This program makes use of several features covered in this chapter, including one of C#'s character escape sequences and the logical operators. It also illustrates the differences in the precedence between the arithmetic + operator and the logical operators.

Step by Step

1. Create a new file called **LogicalOpTable.cs**.

2. To ensure that the columns line up, use the **\t** escape sequence to embed tabs into each output string. For example, this **WriteLine( )** statement displays the header for the table:

```
Console.WriteLine("P\tQ\tAND\tOR\tXOR\tNOT");
```

3. For each subsequent line in the table, use tabs to properly position the outcome of each operation under its proper heading.

4. Here is the entire **LogicalOpTable.cs** program listing. Enter it at this time.

```
// Print a truth table for the logical operators.

using System;

class LogicalOpTable {
  static void Main() {

    bool p, q;

    Console.WriteLine("P\tQ\tAND\tOR\tXOR\tNOT");

    p = true; q = true;
    Console.Write(p + "\t" + q +"\t");
    Console.Write((p&q) + "\t" + (p|q) + "\t");
    Console.WriteLine((p^q) + "\t" + (!p));

    p = true; q = false;
    Console.Write(p + "\t" + q +"\t");
    Console.Write((p&q) + "\t" + (p|q) + "\t");
    Console.WriteLine((p^q) + "\t" + (!p));
```

(continued)

```
        p = false; q = true;
        Console.Write(p + "\t" + q +"\t");
        Console.Write((p&q) + "\t" + (p|q) + "\t");
        Console.WriteLine((p^q) + "\t" + (!p));

        p = false; q = false;
        Console.Write(p + "\t" + q +"\t");
        Console.Write((p&q) + "\t" + (p|q) + "\t");
        Console.WriteLine((p^q) + "\t" + (!p));
    }
}
```

5. Compile and run the program. The following table is displayed:

P	Q	AND	OR	XOR	NOT
true	true	true	true	false	false
true	false	false	true	true	false
false	true	false	true	true	true
false	false	false	false	false	true

6. Notice the parentheses surrounding the logical operations inside the **Write( )** and **WriteLine( )** statements. They are necessary because of the precedence of C#'s operators. The **+** operator is higher than the logical operators.

7. On your own, try modifying the program so that it uses and displays 1's and 0's, rather than true and false.

Ask the Expert

Q: Since the short-circuit operators are, in some cases, more efficient than their normal counterparts, why does C# still offer the normal AND and OR operators?

A: In some cases, you will want both operands of an AND or OR operation to be evaluated because of the side effects produced. Consider the following:

```
// Side effects can be important.

using System;

class SideEffects {
  static void Main() {
    int i;

    i = 0;

    // Here, i is incremented even though the if statement fails.
```

```
    if(false & (++i < 100))
        Console.WriteLine("this won't be displayed");
    Console.WriteLine("if statement executed: " + i); // displays 1

    // In this case, i is not incremented because the short-circuit
    // operator skips the increment.
    if(false && (++i < 100))
        Console.WriteLine("this won't be displayed");
    Console.WriteLine("if statement executed: " + i); // still 1 !!
  }
}
```

As the comments indicate, in the first **if** statement, **i** is incremented whether the **if** succeeds or not. However, when the short-circuit operator is used, the variable **i** is not incremented when the first operand is false. The lesson here is that if your code expects the right-hand operand of an AND or OR operation to be evaluated, you must use the normal forms of these operations.

The Assignment Operator

You have been using the assignment operator since Chapter 1. Now it is time to take a formal look at it. The *assignment operator* is the single equal sign, **=**. The assignment operator works in C# much as it does in other computer languages. It has this general form:

var = expression;

Here, the type of *var* must be compatible with the type of *expression*.

The assignment operator does have one interesting attribute with which you may not be familiar: It allows you to create a chain of assignments. For example, consider this fragment:

```
int x, y, z;

x = y = z = 100; // set x, y, and z to 100
```

This fragment sets the variables **x**, **y**, and **z** to 100 using a single statement. This works because the **=** is an operator that yields the assigned value. Thus, the value of **z = 100** is 100, which is then assigned to **y**, which, in turn, is assigned to **x**. Using a "chain of assignment" is an easy way to set a group of variables to a common value.

Compound Assignments

C# provides special *compound assignment* operators that simplify the coding of certain assignment statements. Let's begin with an example. The assignment statement shown here:

```
x = x + 10;
```

can be written using a compound assignment, such as

```
x += 10;
```

The operator pair **+=** tells the compiler to assign to **x** the value of **x** plus 10.

Here is another example. The statement

```
x = x - 100;
```

is the same as

```
x -= 100;
```

Both statements assign to **x** the value of **x** minus 100.

There are compound assignment operators for many of the binary operators (that is, those that require two operands). The general form of the shorthand is

variable op = expression;

Thus, the arithmetic and logical assignment operators are

+=	-=	*=	/=
%=	&=	|=	^=

Because the compound assignment statements are shorter than their noncompound equivalents, the compound assignment operators are also sometimes called the *shorthand assignment* operators.

The compound assignment operators provide two benefits. First, they are more compact than their "longhand" equivalents. Second, they can result in more efficient executable code (because the left-hand operand is evaluated only once). For these reasons, you will often see the compound assignment operators used in professionally written C# programs.

Type Conversion in Assignments

In programming, it is common to assign a value of one type to a variable of another type. For example, you might want to assign an **int** value to a **float** variable, as shown here:

```
int i;
float f;

i = 10;
f = i; // assign an int to a float
```

When compatible types are mixed in an assignment, the value of the right side is automatically converted to the type of the left side. Thus, in the preceding fragment, the value in **i** is converted into a **float** and then assigned to **f**. However, because of C#'s strict type-checking, not all types are compatible, and thus, not all type conversions are implicitly allowed. For example, **bool** and **int** are not compatible.

When one type of data is assigned to another type of variable, an *implicit* type conversion will take place automatically, if:

- The two types are compatible.

- The destination type is larger than the source type.

When these two conditions are met, a *widening conversion* takes place. For example, the **int** type is always large enough to hold all valid **byte** values, and both **int** and **byte** are integer types, so an implicit conversion can be applied.

For widening conversions, the numeric types, including integer and floating-point types, are compatible with each other. For example, the following program is perfectly valid, since **long** to **double** is a widening conversion that is automatically performed:

```
// Demonstrate implicit conversion from long to double.

using System;

class LtoD {
  static void Main() {
    long L;
    double D;

    L = 100123285L;
    D = L;  ◄———————————— Automatic conversion
                         from long to double.

    Console.WriteLine("L and D: " + L + " " + D);
  }
}
```

Although there is an implicit conversion from **long** to **double**, there is no implicit conversion from **double** to **long**, since this is not a widening conversion. Thus, the following version of the preceding program is invalid:

```
// *** This program will not compile. ***

using System;

class LtoD {
  static void Main() {
    long L;
    double D;

    D = 100123285.0;
    L = D; // Illegal!!! ◄——————— No automatic conversion
                                  from double to long.

    Console.WriteLine("L and D: " + L + " " + D);

  }
}
```

In addition to the restrictions just described, there are no implicit conversions between **decimal** and **float** or **double**, or from the numeric types to **char** or **bool**. Also, **char** and **bool** are not compatible with each other.

Casting Incompatible Types

Although the implicit type conversions are helpful, they will not fulfill all programming needs because they apply only to widening conversions between compatible types. For all other cases, you must employ a cast. A *cast* is an instruction to the compiler to convert an expression into a specified type. Thus, it requests an explicit type conversion. A cast has this general form:

(*target-type*) *expression*

Here, *target-type* specifies the desired type to convert the specified expression to. For example, if you want the type of the expression **x/y** to be **int**, you can write

```
double x, y;
// ...
(int) (x / y)
```

Here, even though **x** and **y** are of type **double**, the cast converts the outcome of the expression to **int**. The parentheses surrounding **x / y** are necessary. Otherwise, the cast to **int** would apply only to the **x**, and not to the outcome of the division. The cast is necessary here because there is no implicit conversion from **double** to **int**.

When a cast involves a *narrowing conversion,* information might be lost. For example, when casting a **long** into an **int**, information will be lost if the **long**'s value is greater than the range of an **int** because its high-order bits are removed. When a floating-point value is cast to an integer type, the fractional component will also be lost due to truncation. For example, if the value 1.23 is assigned to an integer, the resulting value will simply be 1. The 0.23 is lost.

The following program demonstrates some type conversions that require casts:

```
// Demonstrate casting.

using System;

class CastDemo {
  static void Main() {
    double x, y;
    byte b;
    int i;
    char ch;

    x = 10.0;
    y = 3.0;

    i = (int) (x / y);   ◀——— Truncation will occur in this conversion.
    Console.WriteLine("Integer outcome of x / y: " + i);
```

```
    i = 100;
    b = (byte) i;  ◄————————— No loss of info here. A byte can hold the value 100.
    Console.WriteLine("Value of b: " + b);

    i = 257;
    b = (byte) i;  ◄————————— Information loss this time. A byte cannot hold the value 257.
    Console.WriteLine("Value of b: " + b);

    b = 88; // ASCII code for X
    ch = (char) b;  ◄————————— Cast required between incompatible types.
    Console.WriteLine("ch: " + ch);
  }
}
```

The output from the program is shown here:

```
Integer outcome of x / y: 3
Value of b: 100
Value of b: 1
ch: X
```

In the program, the cast of (**x / y**) to **int** results in the truncation of the fractional component and information is lost. Next, no loss of information occurs when **b** is assigned the value 100 because a **byte** can hold the value 100. However, when the attempt is made to assign **b** the value 257, information loss occurs because 257 exceeds a **byte**'s range. This results in **b** having the value 1 because only the 1 bit is set in the low-order 8 bits of the binary representation of 257. Finally, no information is lost, but a cast is needed when assigning a **byte** value to a **char**.

Operator Precedence

Table 2-3 shows the order of precedence for all C# operators, from highest to lowest. This table includes several operators that will be discussed later in this book.

Type Conversion in Expressions

Within an expression, it is possible to mix two or more different types of data, as long as they are compatible with each other. For example, you can mix **short** and **long** within an expression because they are both numeric types. When different types of data are mixed within an expression, they are converted to the same type on an operation-by-operation basis.

The conversions are accomplished through the use of C#'s *type promotion rules*. Here is the algorithm that the rules define for binary operations:

IF one operand is **decimal**, THEN the other operand is promoted to **decimal**
    (unless it is of type **float** or **double**, in which case an error results).

ELSE IF one of the operands is **double**, the second is promoted to **double**.

Highest					
()	[]	.	++(postfix)	--(postfix)	
	checked	new	sizeof	typeof	unchecked
!	~	(cast)	+(unary)	-(unary)	++(prefix)	--(prefix)
*	/	%			
+	-				
<<	>>				
<	>	<=	>=	is	
==	!=				
&					
^					
|					
&&					
||					
??					
?:					
=	*op=*	=>			
Lowest					

Table 2-3 The Precedence of the C# Operators

ELSE IF one operand is a **float** operand, the second is promoted to **float**.

ELSE IF one operand is a **ulong**, the second is promoted to **ulong** (unless it is of type **sbyte**, **short**, **int**, or **long**, in which case an error results).

ELSE IF one operand is a **long**, the second is promoted to **long**.

ELSE IF one operand is a **uint** and the second is of type **sbyte**, **short**, or **int**, both are promoted to **long**.

ELSE IF one operand is a **uint**, the second is promoted to **uint**.

ELSE both operands are promoted to **int**.

There are a couple of important points to be made about the type promotion rules. First, not all types can be mixed in an expression. Specifically, there is no implicit conversion from **float** or **double** to **decimal**, and it is not possible to mix **ulong** with any signed integer type. To mix these types requires the use of an explicit cast.

Second, pay special attention to the last rule. It states that if none of the preceding rules applies, then all other operands are promoted to **int**. Therefore, in an expression, all **char, sbyte, byte, ushort,** and **short** values are promoted to **int** for the purposes of calculation. This is called *integer promotion*. It also means that the outcome of all arithmetic operations will be no smaller than **int**.

It is important to understand that type promotions apply to the values operated upon only when an expression is evaluated. For example, if the value of a **byte** variable is promoted to **int** inside an expression, outside the expression, the variable is still a **byte**. Type promotion only affects the evaluation of an expression.

Type promotion can, however, lead to somewhat unexpected results. For example, when an arithmetic operation involves two **byte** values, the following sequence occurs: First, the **byte** operands are promoted to **int**. Then the operation takes place, yielding an **int** result. Thus, the outcome of an operation involving two **byte** values will be an **int**. This is not what you might intuitively expect. Consider the following program:

```
// A type promotion surprise!

using System;

class PromDemo {
  static void Main() {
    byte b;
    int i;

    b = 10;
    i = b * b; // OK, no cast needed

    b = 10;
    b = (byte) (b * b); // cast needed!!

    Console.WriteLine("i and b: " + i + " " + b);
  }
}
```

No cast needed because result is already evaluated to **int**.

Cast is needed here to assign an **int** to a **byte**.

Somewhat counterintuitively, no cast is needed when assigning **b * b** to **i**, because **b** is promoted to **int** when the expression is evaluated. Thus, the result type of **b * b** is **int**. However, when you try to assign **b * b** to **b**, you do need a cast—back to **byte**! Keep this in mind if you get unexpected type-incompatibility error messages on expressions that would otherwise seem perfectly okay.

This same sort of situation also occurs when performing operations on **char**s. For example, in the following fragment, the cast back to **char** is needed because of the promotion of **ch1** and **ch2** to **int** within the expression:

```
char ch1 = 'a', ch2 = 'b';

ch1 = (char) (ch1 + ch2);
```

Without the cast, the result of adding **ch1** to **ch2** would be **int**, which can't be assigned to a **char**.

Casts are not only useful when converting between types in an assignment. They can be used within an expression. For example, consider the following program. It uses a cast to **double** to obtain a fractional component from an otherwise integer division.

```
// Using a cast.

using System;

class UseCast {
  static void Main() {
    int i;

    for(i = 1; i < 5; i++) {
      Console.WriteLine(i + " / 3: " + i / 3);
      Console.WriteLine(i + " / 3 with fractions: {0:#.##}",
                        (double) i / 3);
      Console.WriteLine();
    }
  }
}
```

In the expression:

```
(double) i / 3
```

the cast to **double** causes **i** to be converted to **double**, which ensures that the fractional component of the division by 3 is preserved. The output from the program is shown here:

```
1 / 3: 0
1 / 3 with fractions: .33

2 / 3: 0
2 / 3 with fractions: .67

3 / 3: 1
3 / 3 with fractions: 1

4 / 3: 1
4 / 3 with fractions: 1.33
```

Ask the Expert

Q: Do type promotions occur when a unary operation, such as the unary –, takes place?

A: Yes. For the unary operations, operands smaller than **int** (**byte**, **sbyte**, **short**, and **ushort**) are promoted to **int**. Also, a **char** operand is converted to **int**. Furthermore, if a **uint** value is negated, it is promoted to **long**.

Spacing and Parentheses

An expression in C# can have tabs and spaces in it to make it more readable. For example, the following two expressions are the same, but the second is easier to read:

```
x=10/y*(127-x);

x = 10 / y * (127 - x);
```

Parentheses can be used to group subexpressions, thereby effectively increasing the precedence of the operations contained within them, just like in algebra. Use of redundant or additional parentheses will not cause errors or slow down the execution of the expression. You are encouraged to use parentheses to make clear how an expression is evaluated, both for yourself and for others who may have to maintain your program later. For example, which of the following two expressions is easier to read?

```
x = y/3-34*temp+127;

x = (y/3) - (34*temp) + 127;
```

Try This Compute the Regular Payments on a Loan

As mentioned earlier, the **decimal** type is especially well suited for calculations that involve money. This program demonstrates its use in this capacity. The program computes the regular payments on a loan, such as a car loan. Given the principal, the length of time, number of payments per year, and the interest rate, the program will compute the payment. Since this is a financial calculation, it makes sense to use the **decimal** type to represent the data. This program also demonstrates casting and another of C#'s library methods.

To compute the payments, you will use the following formula:

$$\text{Payment} = \frac{\text{IntRate} * (\text{Principal} / \text{PayPerYear})}{1 - ((\text{IntRate} / \text{PayPerYear}) + 1)^{-\text{PayPerYear} * \text{NumYears}}}$$

where IntRate specifies the interest rate, Principal contains the starting balance, PayPerYear specifies the number of payments per year, and NumYears specifies the length of the loan in years.

Notice that in the denominator of the formula, you must raise one value to the power of another. To do this, you will use the C# math method **Math.Pow( )**. Here is how you will call it:

result = Math.Pow(*base*, *exp*);

Pow( ) returns the value of *base* raised to the *exp* power. The arguments to **Pow( )** must be of type **double**, and it returns a value of type **double**. This means that you will need to use a cast to convert between **double** and **decimal**.

(continued)

Step by Step

1. Create a new file called **RegPay.cs**.

2. Here are the variables that will be used by the program:

```
decimal Principal;        // original principal
decimal IntRate;          // interest rate as a decimal, such as 0.075
decimal PayPerYear;       // number of payments per year
decimal NumYears;         // number of years
decimal Payment;          // the regular payment
decimal numer, denom;     // temporary work variables
double b, e;              // base and exponent for call to Pow()
```

Since most of the calculation will be done using the **decimal** data type, most of the variables are of type **decimal**.

Notice how each variable declaration is followed by a comment that describes its use. This helps anyone reading your program understand the purpose of each variable. Although we won't include such detailed comments for most of the short programs in this book, it is a good practice to follow as your programs become longer and more complicated.

3. Add the following lines of code, which specify the loan information. In this case, the principal is $10,000, the interest rate is 7.5 percent, the number of payments per year is 12, and the length of the loan is 5 years.

```
Principal = 10000.00m;
IntRate = 0.075m;
PayPerYear = 12.0m;
NumYears = 5.0m;
```

4. Add the lines that perform the financial calculation:

```
numer = IntRate * Principal / PayPerYear;

e = (double) -(PayPerYear * NumYears);
b = (double) (IntRate / PayPerYear) + 1;

denom = 1 - (decimal) Math.Pow(b, e);

Payment = numer / denom;
```

Notice how casts must be used to pass values to **Pow( )** and to convert the return value. Remember, there are no implicit conversions between **decimal** and **double** in C#.

5. Finish the program by outputting the regular payment, as shown here:

```
Console.WriteLine("Payment is {0:C}", Payment);
```

6. Here is the entire **RegPay.cs** program listing:

```
// Compute the regular payments for a loan.
```

```
using System;

class RegPay {
  static void Main() {
    decimal Principal;     // original principal
    decimal IntRate;       // interest rate as a decimal, such as 0.075
    decimal PayPerYear;    // number of payments per year
    decimal NumYears;      // number of years
    decimal Payment;       // the regular payment
    decimal numer, denom;  // temporary work variables
    double b, e;           // base and exponent for call to Pow()

    Principal = 10000.00m;
    IntRate = 0.075m;
    PayPerYear = 12.0m;
    NumYears = 5.0m;

    numer = IntRate * Principal / PayPerYear;

    e = (double) -(PayPerYear * NumYears);
    b = (double) (IntRate / PayPerYear) + 1;

    denom = 1 - (decimal) Math.Pow(b, e);

    Payment = numer / denom;

    Console.WriteLine("Payment is {0:C}", Payment);
  }
}
```

Here is the output from the program:

```
Payment is $200.38
```

Before moving on, you might want to try having the program compute the regular payments for differing amounts, periods, and interest rates.

Chapter 2 Self Test

1. Why does C# strictly specify the range and behavior of its simple types?

2. What is C#'s character type, and how does it differ from the character type used by some other programming languages?

3. A **bool** value can have any value you like because any nonzero value is true. True or false?

4. Given this output:

```
One
Two
Three
```

Use a single string and escape sequences to show the **WriteLine( )** statement that produced it.

5. What is wrong with this fragment?

```
for(i = 0; i < 10; i++) {
   int sum;

   sum = sum + i;
}
Console.WriteLine("Sum is: " + sum);
```

6. Explain the difference between the prefix and postfix forms of the increment operator.

7. Show how a short-circuit AND can be used to prevent a divide-by-zero error.

8. In an expression, what type are **byte** and **short** promoted to?

9. Which of the following types cannot be mixed in an expression with a **decimal** value?

    A. float

    B. int

    C. uint

    D. byte

10. In general, when is a cast needed?

11. Write a program that finds all of the prime numbers between 2 and 100.

12. On your own, rewrite the truth table program in *Try This: Display a Truth Table for the Logical Operators* so that it uses verbatim string literals with embedded tab and newline characters rather escape sequences.

Chapter 3

Program Control Statements

Key Skills & Concepts

- Input characters from the keyboard
- **if** and **for**
- **switch**
- **while**
- **do-while**
- **break**
- **continue**
- **goto**

This chapter describes the statements that control a program's flow of execution. There are three categories of program control statements: *selection* statements, which include **if** and **switch**; *iteration* statements, which include the **for**, **while**, **do-while**, and **foreach** loops; and *jump* statements, which include **break**, **continue**, **goto**, **return**, and **throw**. Except for **return**, **foreach**, and **throw**, which are discussed later in this book, the remaining control statements are examined in detail here.

Inputting Characters from the Keyboard

Before examining C#'s control statements, we will make a short digression that will allow you to begin writing interactive programs. Up to this point, the sample programs in this book have displayed information *to* the user, but they have not received information *from* the user. Thus, you have been using console output, but not console (that is, keyboard) input. Here, you will begin to use input by reading characters that are typed at the keyboard.

To read a character from the keyboard, call **Console.Read( )**. This method waits until the user presses a key and then returns the key. The character is returned as an integer, so it must be cast to **char** to assign it to a **char** variable. By default, console input is line-buffered, so you must press ENTER before any character that you type will be sent to your program. Here is a program that reads a character from the keyboard:

```
// Read a character from the keyboard.

using System;

class KbIn {
  static void Main() {
    char ch;
```

```
    Console.Write("Press a key followed by ENTER: ");

    // Read a key from the keyboard.
    ch = (char) Console.Read();  ◄─────────── Read a character from the keyboard.

    Console.WriteLine("Your key is: " + ch);
  }
}
```

Here is a sample run:

```
Press a key followed by ENTER: t
Your key is: t
```

The fact that **Read( )** is line-buffered is a source of annoyance at times. When you press ENTER, a carriage-return, linefeed sequence is entered into the input stream. Furthermore, these characters are left pending in the input buffer until you read them. Thus, for some applications, you may need to remove them (by reading them) before the next input operation. You will see an example of this later in this chapter.

The if Statement

Chapter 1 introduced the **if** statement. It is examined in detail here. The complete form of the **if** statement is

if(*condition*) *statement*;
else *statement*;

where the targets of the **if** and **else** are single statements. The **else** clause is optional. Because a block of statements can be used wherever a single statement is legal, the targets of both the **if** and **else** can be blocks of statements. Therefore, the general form of the **if** using blocks of statements is

if(*condition*)
{
  statement sequence
}
else
{
  statement sequence
}

If the conditional expression is true, the target of the **if** will be executed; otherwise, if it exists, the target of the **else** will be executed. At no time will both of them be executed. The conditional expression controlling the **if** must produce a **bool** result.

To demonstrate the **if**, we will evolve a simple computerized guessing game that would be suitable for small children. In the first version of the game, the program asks the player for a letter between A and Z. If the player presses the right letter on the keyboard, the program responds by printing the message **** Right ****. The program is shown here:

```
// Guess the letter game.

using System;

class Guess {
  static void Main() {
    char ch, answer = 'K';

    Console.WriteLine("I'm thinking of a letter between A and Z.");
    Console.Write("Can you guess it: ");

    ch = (char) Console.Read(); // get the user's guess

    if(ch == answer) Console.WriteLine("** Right **");
  }
}
```

This program prompts the player and then reads a character from the keyboard. Using an **if** statement, it then checks that character against the answer, which is K in this case. If K was entered, the message is displayed. When you try this program, remember that the K must be entered in uppercase.

Taking the guessing game further, the next version uses the **else** to print a message when the wrong letter is picked.

```
// Guess the letter game, 2nd version.

using System;

class Guess2 {
  static void Main() {
    char ch, answer = 'K';

    Console.WriteLine("I'm thinking of a letter between A and Z.");
    Console.Write("Can you guess it: ");

    ch = (char) Console.Read(); // get the user's guess

    if(ch == answer) Console.WriteLine("** Right **");
    else Console.WriteLine("...Sorry, you're wrong.");
  }
}
```

Nested ifs

A *nested if* is an **if** statement that is the target of another **if** or **else**. Nested **if**s are very common in programming. The main thing to remember about nested **if**s in C# is that an **else** clause is always associated with the nearest **if** statement that is within the same block as the **else** and not already associated with an **else**. Here is an example:

```
if(i == 10) {          ───── This if goes with this else.
  if(j < 20) a = b;
  if(k > 100) c = d;   ─────────────────────── This if goes with this else.
  else a = c; // this else refers to if(k > 100)
}
else a = d; // this else refers to if(i == 10)
```

As the comments indicate, the final **else** is not associated with **if(j<20)**, because it is not in the same block (even though it is the nearest **if** without an **else**). Rather, the final **else** is associated with **if(i==10)**. The inner **else** refers to **if(k>100)**, because it is the closest **if** within the same block.

You can use a nested **if** to add a further improvement to the guessing game. This addition provides the player with feedback about a wrong guess.

```
// Guess the letter game, 3rd version.

using System;

class Guess3 {
  static void Main() {
    char ch, answer = 'K';

    Console.WriteLine("I'm thinking of a letter between A and Z.");
    Console.Write("Can you guess it: ");

    ch = (char) Console.Read(); // get the user's guess

    if(ch == answer) Console.WriteLine("** Right **");
    else {
      Console.Write("...Sorry, you're ");

                                              ───── A nested if.
      // A nested if.
      if(ch < answer) Console.WriteLine("too low");
      else Console.WriteLine("too high");
    }
  }
}
```

A sample run is shown here:

```
I'm thinking of a letter between A and Z.
Can you guess it: Z
...Sorry, you're too high
```

The if-else-if Ladder

A common programming construct that is based upon the nested **if** is the *if-else-if ladder*. It looks like this:

if(*condition*)
  statement;
else if(*condition*)
  statement;
else if(*condition*)
  statement;
.
.
.
else
  statement;

The conditional expressions are evaluated from the top down. As soon as a true condition is found, the statement associated with it is executed, and the rest of the ladder is bypassed. If none of the conditions are true, the final **else** clause will be executed. The final **else** often acts as a default condition; that is, if all other conditional tests fail, the last **else** clause is executed. If there is no final **else** and all other conditions are false, no action will take place.

The following program demonstrates the **if-else-if** ladder:

```
// Demonstrate an if-else-if ladder.

using System;

class Ladder {
  static void Main() {
    int x;

    for(x=0; x<6; x++) {
      if(x==1)
        Console.WriteLine("x is one");
      else if(x==2)
        Console.WriteLine("x is two");
      else if(x==3)
        Console.WriteLine("x is three");
      else if(x==4)
        Console.WriteLine("x is four");
      else
        Console.WriteLine("x is not between 1 and 4");
    }
  }
}
```

This is the default statement.

The program produces the following output:

```
x is not between 1 and 4
x is one
x is two
x is three
x is four
x is not between 1 and 4
```

As you can see, the final **else** is executed only if none of the preceding **if** statements succeed.

The switch Statement

The second of C#'s selection statements is the **switch**. The **switch** provides for a multiway branch. Thus, it enables a program to select among several alternatives. Although a series of nested **if** statements can perform multiway tests, for many situations, the **switch** is a more efficient approach. It works like this: The value of an expression is successively tested against a list of constants. When a match is found, the statement sequence associated with that match is executed. The general form of the **switch** statement is

```
switch(expression) {
  case constant1:
    statement sequence
    break;
  case constant2:
    statement sequence
    break;
  case constant3:
    statement sequence
    break;
  .
  .
  .
  default:
    statement sequence
    break;
}
```

The **switch** expression must be an integral type, such as **char**, **byte**, **short**, or **int**; an enumeration type; or type **string**. (Enumerations and the **string** type are described later in this book.) Thus, floating-point expressions, for example, are not allowed. Frequently, the expression controlling the **switch** is simply a variable. The **case** constants must be of a type compatible with the expression. No two **case** constants in the same **switch** can have identical values.

The **default** sequence is executed if no **case** constant matches the expression. The **default** is optional; if it is not present, no action takes place if all matches fail. When a match is found, the statements associated with that **case** are executed until the **break** is encountered.

The following program demonstrates the **switch**:

```
// Demonstrate the switch.

using System;

class SwitchDemo {
  static void Main() {
    int i;

    for(i=0; i < 10; i++)
      switch(i) {
        case 0:
          Console.WriteLine("i is zero");
          break;
        case 1:
          Console.WriteLine("i is one");
          break;
        case 2:
          Console.WriteLine("i is two");
          break;
        case 3:
          Console.WriteLine("i is three");
          break;
        case 4:
          Console.WriteLine("i is four");
          break;
        default:
          Console.WriteLine("i is five or more");
          break;
      }

  }
}
```

The value of **i** determines which **case** statement executes.

The output produced by this program is shown here:

```
i is zero
i is one
i is two
i is three
i is four
i is five or more
i is five or more
i is five or more
i is five or more
i is five or more
```

As you can see, each time through the loop, the statements associated with the **case** constant that matches **i** are executed. All others are bypassed. When **i** is five or greater, no **case** constants match, so the statements associated with the **default** case are executed.

In the preceding example, the **switch** was controlled by an **int** variable. As explained, you can control a **switch** with any integral type, including **char**. Here is an example that uses a **char** expression and **char** case constants:

```
// Use a char to control the switch.

using System;

class SwitchDemo2 {
  static void Main() {
    char ch;

    for(ch='A'; ch <= 'E'; ch++)
      switch(ch) {
        case 'A':
          Console.WriteLine("ch is A");
          break;
        case 'B':
          Console.WriteLine("ch is B");
          break;
        case 'C':
          Console.WriteLine("ch is C");
          break;
        case 'D':
          Console.WriteLine("ch is D");
          break;
        case 'E':
          Console.WriteLine("ch is E");
          break;
      }
  }
}
```

The output from this program is shown here:

```
ch is A
ch is B
ch is C
ch is D
ch is E
```

Notice that this example does not include the **default** case. Remember, the **default** is optional. When not needed, it can be left out.

In C#, it is an error for the statement sequence associated with one **case** to continue on into the next **case**. This is called the *no fall-through rule*. This is why **case** sequences end with **break**.

(You can avoid fall-through in other ways, but **break** is by far the most commonly used approach.) When encountered within the statement sequence of a **case**, **break** causes program flow to exit from the entire **switch** statement and resume at the next statement outside the **switch**. One other point: The **default** sequence must also not "fall through," and it, too, usually ends with a **break**.

Although you cannot allow one **case** sequence to fall through into another, you can have two or more **case** labels for the same code sequence, as shown in this example:

```
switch(i) {
  case 1:            These cases refer to the same code sequence.
  case 2:
  case 3: Console.WriteLine("i is 1, 2 or 3");
     break;
  case 4: Console.WriteLine("i is 4");
     break;
}
```

In this fragment, if **i** has the value 1, 2, or 3, the first **WriteLine( )** statement executes. If it is 4, the second **WriteLine( )** statement executes. The *stacking* of **cases** does not violate the no fall-through rule because the **case** statements all use the same statement sequence.

Stacking **case** labels is a commonly employed technique when several **case**s share common code. For example, here it is used to categorize lowercase letters of the alphabet into vowels and consonants:

```
// Categorize lowercase letters into vowels and consonants.

using System;

class VowelsAndConsonants {
  static void Main() {
    char ch;

    Console.Write("Enter a letter: ");
    ch = (char) Console.Read();
    switch(ch) {
        case 'a':
        case 'e':
        case 'i':
        case 'o':
        case 'u':
        case 'y':
          Console.WriteLine("Letter is a vowel.");
          break;
        default:
          Console.WriteLine("Letter is a consonant.");
          break;
      }
    }
  }
}
```

Ask the Expert

Q: **Under what conditions should I use an** if-else-if **ladder rather than a** switch **when coding a multiway branch?**

A: In general, use an **if-else-if** ladder when the conditions controlling the selection process do not rely upon a single value. For example, consider the following **if-else-if** sequence:

```
if(x == 10) // ...
else if(ch == 'a') // ...
else if(done == true) // ...
```

This sequence cannot be recoded into a **switch** because all three conditions involve different variables—and differing types. What variable would control the **switch**? Also, you will need to use an **if-else-if** ladder when testing floating-point values or when testing other objects that are not of types valid for use in a **switch** expression. Finally, the **switch** can only test for equality. If you will be testing for some other relationship, such as less than or not equal, you must use an **if-else-if** ladder. For example,

```
if(x < 10) // ...
else if(y >= 0) // ...
else if(z != -1) // ...
```

This sequence cannot be represented in a **switch**.

If this example were written without **case** stacking, the same **WriteLine( )** statement would have been duplicated six times. The stacking of **case**s prevents this redundant duplication.

Nested switch Statements

It is possible to have a **switch** as part of the statement sequence of an outer **switch**. This is called a *nested switch*. The **case** constants of the inner and outer **switch** can contain common values, and no conflicts will arise. For example, the following code fragment is perfectly acceptable:

```
switch(ch1) {
  case 'A': Console.WriteLine("This A is part of outer switch.");
    switch(ch2) {  ◀─────────── A nested switch.
      case 'A':
        Console.WriteLine("This A is part of inner switch");
        break;
      case 'B': // ...
    } // end of inner switch
    break;
  case 'B': // ...
```

Ask the Expert

Q: In C, C++, and Java, one case **may continue on (that is, fall through) into the next** case. **Why is this not allowed by C#?**

A: There are two reasons that C# instituted the no fall-through rule for **case**s. First, it allows the order of the cases to be rearranged. Such a rearrangement would not be possible if one **case** could flow into the next. Second, requiring each **case** to explicitly end prevents a programmer from accidentally allowing one **case** to flow into the next.

Try This Start Building a C# Help System

Here you will start building a simple help system that displays the syntax for the C# control statements. This help system will be enhanced throughout the course of this chapter. This first version displays a menu containing the control statements and then waits for you to choose one. After one is chosen, the syntax of the statement is shown. In this first version of the program, help is available only for the **if** and **switch** statements. The other control statements are added later in subsequent Try This sections.

Step by Step

1. Create a file called **Help.cs**.

2. The program begins by displaying the following menu:

```
Help on:
  1. if
  2. switch
Choose one:
```

To accomplish this, you will use the statement sequence shown here:

```
Console.WriteLine("Help on:");
Console.WriteLine("  1. if");
Console.WriteLine("  2. switch");
Console.Write("Choose one: ");
```

3. The program obtains the user's selection by calling **Console.Read( )**, as shown here:

```
choice = (char) Console.Read();
```

4. Once the selection has been obtained, the program uses the **switch** statement shown here to display the syntax for the selected statement:

```
switch(choice) {
  case '1':
    Console.WriteLine("The if:\n");
```

```
      Console.WriteLine("if(condition) statement;");
      Console.WriteLine("else statement;");
      break;
    case '2':
      Console.WriteLine("The switch:\n");
      Console.WriteLine("switch(expression) {");
      Console.WriteLine("  case constant:");
      Console.WriteLine("    statement sequence");
      Console.WriteLine("    break;");
      Console.WriteLine("  // ...");
      Console.WriteLine("}");
      break;
    default:
      Console.Write("Selection not found.");
      break;
  }
}
```

Notice how the **default** clause catches invalid choices. For example, if the user enters 3, no **case** constants will match, causing the **default** sequence to execute.

5. Here is the entire **Help.cs** program listing:

```
// A simple help system.

using System;

class Help {
  static void Main() {
    char choice;

    Console.WriteLine("Help on:");
    Console.WriteLine("  1. if");
    Console.WriteLine("  2. switch");
    Console.Write("Choose one: ");
    choice = (char) Console.Read();

    Console.WriteLine("\n");

    switch(choice) {
      case '1':
        Console.WriteLine("The if:\n");
        Console.WriteLine("if(condition) statement;");
        Console.WriteLine("else statement;");
        break;
      case '2':
        Console.WriteLine("The switch:\n");
        Console.WriteLine("switch(expression) {");
        Console.WriteLine("  case constant:");
        Console.WriteLine("    statement sequence");
```

(continued)

```
      Console.WriteLine("     break;");
      Console.WriteLine("  // ...");
      Console.WriteLine("}");
      break;
    default:
      Console.Write("Selection not found.");
      break;
  }
 }
}
```

Here is a sample run:

```
Help on:
  1. if
  2. switch
Choose one: 1

The if:

if(condition) statement;
else statement;
```

The for Loop

You have been using a simple form of the **for** loop since Chapter 1. You might be surprised at just how powerful and flexible the **for** loop is. Let's begin by reviewing the basics, starting with the most traditional forms of the **for**.

The general form of the **for** loop for repeating a single statement is

for(*initialization*; *condition*; *iteration*) *statement*;

For repeating a block, the general form is

for(*initialization*; *condition*; *iteration*)
{
  statement sequence
}

The *initialization* is usually an assignment statement that sets the initial value of the *loop control variable,* which acts as the counter that controls the loop. The *condition* is a Boolean expression that determines whether the loop will repeat. The *iteration* expression defines the amount by which the loop control variable will change each time the loop is repeated. Notice that these three major sections of the loop must be separated by semicolons. The **for** loop will continue to execute as long as the condition tests true. Once the condition becomes false, the loop will exit, and program execution will resume on the statement following the **for**.

The following program uses a **for** loop to print the square roots of the numbers between 1 and 99. It also displays the rounding error present for each square root.

```
// Show square roots of 1 to 99 and the rounding error.

using System;

class SqrRoot {
  static void Main() {
    double num, sroot, rerr;

    for(num = 1.0; num < 100.0; num++) {
      sroot = Math.Sqrt(num);
      Console.WriteLine("Square root of " + num +
                        " is " + sroot);

      // Compute rounding error.
      rerr = num - (sroot * sroot);
      Console.WriteLine("Rounding error is " + rerr);
      Console.WriteLine();
    }
  }
}
```

Notice that the rounding error is computed by squaring the square root of each number. This result is then subtracted from the original number, thus yielding the rounding error. Of course, in some cases, rounding errors occur when the square root is squared, so sometimes the rounding error, itself, is rounded! This example illustrates the fact that floating-point calculations are not always as precise as we sometimes think they should be!

The **for** loop can proceed in a positive or negative fashion, and it can change the loop control variable by any amount. For example, the following loop prints the numbers 100 to −100, in decrements of 5:

```
// A negatively running for loop.
for(x = 100; x > -100; x -= 5)
  Console.WriteLine(x);
}
```

An important point about **for** loops is that the conditional expression is always tested at the top of the loop. This means that the code inside the loop may not be executed at all if the condition is false to begin with. Here is an example:

```
for(count=10; count < 5; count++)
  x += count; // this statement will not execute
```

This loop will never execute because its control variable, **count**, is greater than five when the loop is first entered. This makes the conditional expression, **count<5**, false from the outset; thus, not even one iteration of the loop will occur.

Some Variations on the for Loop

The **for** is one of the most versatile statements in the C# language because it allows a wide range of variations. For example, multiple loop control variables can be used. Consider the following program:

```
// Use commas in a for statement.

using System;

class Comma {
  static void Main() {
    int i, j;

    for(i=0, j=10; i < j; i++, j--)
      Console.WriteLine("i and j: " + i + " " + j);
  }
}
```

Notice the two loop control variables.

The output from the program is shown here:

```
i and j: 0 10
i and j: 1 9
i and j: 2 8
i and j: 3 7
i and j: 4 6
```

Here, commas separate the two initialization statements and the two iteration expressions. When the loop begins, both **i** and **j** are initialized. Each time the loop repeats, **i** is incremented and **j** is decremented. Multiple loop control variables are often convenient and can simplify certain algorithms. You can have any number of initialization and iteration statements, but in practice, more than two make the **for** loop unwieldy.

The condition controlling the loop can be any valid expression that produces a **bool** result. It does not need to involve the loop control variable. In the next example, the loop continues to execute until the user types **S** at the keyboard.

```
// Loop until an S is typed.

using System;

class ForTest {
  static void Main() {
    int i;

    Console.WriteLine("Press S to stop.");

    for(i = 0; (char) Console.Read() != 'S'; i++)
      Console.WriteLine("Pass #" + i);
  }
}
```

Missing Pieces

Some interesting **for** loop variations are created by leaving pieces of the loop definition empty. In C#, it is possible for any or all of the initialization, condition, or iteration portions of the **for** loop to be blank. For example, consider the following program:

```
// Parts of the for can be empty.

using System;

class Empty {
  static void Main() {
    int i;

    for(i = 0; i < 10; ) {          The iteration expression is missing.
      Console.WriteLine("Pass #" + i);
      i++; // increment loop control variable
    }
  }
}
```

Here, the iteration expression of the **for** is empty. Instead, the loop control variable **i** is incremented inside the body of the loop. This means that each time the loop repeats, **i** is tested to see whether it equals 10, but no further action takes place. Of course, since **i** is incremented within the body of the loop, the loop runs normally, displaying the following output:

```
Pass #0
Pass #1
Pass #2
Pass #3
Pass #4
Pass #5
Pass #6
Pass #7
Pass #8
Pass #9
```

In the next example, the initialization portion is also moved out of the **for**.

```
// Move more out of the for loop.

using System;

class Empty2 {
  static void Main() {
    int i;

    i = 0; // move initialization out of loop
    for(; i < 10; ) {          The initialization expression
                               is moved out of the loop.
```

```
        Console.WriteLine("Pass #" + i);
        i++; // increment loop control var
      }
    }
}
```

In this version, **i** is initialized before the loop begins, rather than as part of the **for**. Normally, you will want to initialize the loop control variable inside the **for**. Placing the initialization outside of the loop is generally done only when the initial value is derived through a complex process that does not lend itself to containment inside the **for** statement.

The Infinite Loop

You can create an *infinite loop* (a loop that never terminates) using the **for** by leaving the conditional expression empty. For example, the following fragment shows the way many C# programmers create an infinite loop:

```
for(;;) // intentionally infinite loop
{
   //...
}
```

This loop will run forever. Although there are some programming tasks that require an infinite loop, such as operating-system command processors, most "infinite loops" are really just loops with special termination requirements. Near the end of this chapter you will see how to halt a loop of this type. (Hint: It's done using the **break** statement.)

Loops with No Body

In C#, the body associated with a **for** loop (or any other loop) can be empty. This is because an empty statement is syntactically valid. Body-less loops are often useful. For example, the following program uses one to sum the numbers 1 through 5:

```
// The body of a loop can be empty.

using System;

class Empty3 {
  static void Main() {
    int i;
    int sum = 0;

    // Sum the numbers through 5.
    for(i = 1; i <= 5; sum += i++) ;          ◄———————— No body in this loop!

    Console.WriteLine("Sum is " + sum);
  }
}
```

The output from the program is shown here:

```
Sum is 15
```

Notice that the summation process is handled entirely within the **for** statement and no body is needed. Pay special attention to the iteration expression:

```
sum += i++
```

Don't be intimidated by statements like this. They are common in professionally written C# programs and are easy to understand if you break them down into their parts. In words, this statement says "add to **sum** the value of **sum** plus **i**, then increment **i**." Thus, it is the same as this sequence of statements:

```
sum = sum + i;
i++;
```

Declaring Loop Control Variables Inside the for Loop

Often, the variable that controls a **for** loop is needed only for the purposes of the loop and is not used elsewhere. When this is the case, it is possible to declare the variable inside the initialization portion of the **for**. For example, the following program computes both the summation and the factorial of the numbers 1 through 5. It declares its loop control variable **i** inside the **for**:

```
// Declare loop control variable inside the for.

using System;

class ForVar {
  static void Main() {
    int sum = 0;
    int fact = 1;

    // Compute the factorial of the numbers through 5.
    for(int i = 1; i <= 5; i++) {          Notice that i is declared
      sum += i;  // i is known throughout the loop    inside the loop.
      fact *= i;
    }

    // Here, i is not known.

    Console.WriteLine("Sum is " + sum);
    Console.WriteLine("Factorial is " + fact);
  }
}
```

When you declare a variable inside a **for** loop, there is one important point to remember: The scope of that variable ends when the **for** statement does. (That is, the scope of the variable is limited to the **for** loop.) Outside the **for** loop, the variable will cease to exist. Thus, in the preceding example, **i** is not accessible outside the **for** loop. If you need to use the loop control variable elsewhere in your program, you will not be able to declare it inside the **for** loop.

Before moving on, you might want to experiment with your own variations on the **for** loop. As you will find, it is a fascinating loop.

The while Loop

Another of C#'s loops is the **while**. The general form of the **while** loop is

while(*condition*) *statement*;

where *statement* can be a single statement or a block of statements, and *condition* defines the condition that controls the loop and may be any valid Boolean expression. The statement is performed while the condition is true. When the condition becomes false, program control passes to the line immediately following the loop.

Here is a simple example in which a **while** is used to print the alphabet:

```
// Demonstrate the while loop.

using System;

class WhileDemo {
  static void Main() {
    char ch;

    // Print the alphabet using a while loop.
    ch = 'a';
    while(ch <= 'z') {          ◄──────  Loop while ch is less
      Console.Write(ch);                 than or equal to 'z'.
      ch++;
    }
  }
}
```

Here, **ch** is initialized to the letter *a*. Each time through the loop, **ch** is output and then incremented. This process continues until **ch** is greater than z.

As with the **for** loop, the **while** checks the conditional expression at the top of the loop, which means that the loop code may not execute at all. This often eliminates the need for performing a separate test before the loop. The following program illustrates this characteristic of the **while** loop. It computes the integer powers of 2 from 0 to 9.

```
// Compute integer powers of 2.

using System;

class Power {
  static void Main() {
```

```
   int e;
   int result;

   for(int i=0; i < 10; i++) {
     result = 1;
     e = i;
     while(e > 0) {
       result *= 2;              This won't execute when
       e--;                      e is zero or negative.
     }

     Console.WriteLine("2 to the " + i +
                         " power is " + result);
   }
  }
}
```

The output from the program is shown here:

```
2 to the 0 power is 1
2 to the 1 power is 2
2 to the 2 power is 4
2 to the 3 power is 8
2 to the 4 power is 16
2 to the 5 power is 32
2 to the 6 power is 64
2 to the 7 power is 128
2 to the 8 power is 256
2 to the 9 power is 512
```

Notice that the **while** loop executes only when **e** is greater than 0. Thus, when **e** is zero, as it is in the first iteration of the **for** loop, the **while** loop is skipped.

Ask the Expert

Q: Given the flexibility inherent in all of C#'s loops, what criteria should I use when selecting a loop? That is, how do I choose the right loop for a specific job?

A: Use a **for** loop when performing a known number of iterations. Use the **do-while** when you need a loop that will always perform at least one iteration. The **while** is best used when the loop will repeat an unknown number of times.

The do-while Loop

The next loop is the **do-while**. Unlike the **for** and the **while** loops, in which the condition is tested at the top of the loop, the **do-while** loop checks its condition at the bottom of the loop. This means that a **do-while** loop will always execute at least once. The general form of the **do-while** loop is

```
do {
   statements;
} while(condition);
```

Although the braces are not necessary when only one statement is present, they are often used to improve readability of the **do-while** construct, thus preventing confusion with the **while**. The **do-while** loop executes as long as the conditional expression is true.

The following program loops until the user enters the letter **q**:

```
// Demonstrate the do-while loop.

using System;

class DWDemo {
  static void Main() {
    char ch;

    do {
      Console.Write("Press a key followed by ENTER: ");
      ch = (char) Console.Read(); // read a keypress
    } while(ch != 'q');                              Loop while ch does
  }                                                   not equal 'q'.
}
```

Using a **do-while** loop, we can further improve the guessing game program from earlier in this chapter. This time, the program loops until you guess the letter.

```
// Guess the letter game, 4th version.

using System;

class Guess4 {
  static void Main() {
    char ch, answer = 'K';

    do {
      Console.WriteLine("I'm thinking of a letter between A and Z.");
      Console.Write("Can you guess it: ");

      // Read a letter, but skip cr/lf.
```

```
do {
  ch = (char) Console.Read();
} while(ch == '\n' | ch == '\r');

if(ch == answer) Console.WriteLine("** Right **");
else {
  Console.Write("...Sorry, you're ");
  if(ch < answer) Console.WriteLine("too low");
  else Console.WriteLine("too high");
  Console.WriteLine("Try again!\n");
}
    } while(answer != ch);
  }
}
```

Here is a sample run:

```
I'm thinking of a letter between A and Z.
Can you guess it: A
...Sorry, you're too low
Try again!

I'm thinking of a letter between A and Z.
Can you guess it: Z
...Sorry, you're too high
Try again!

I'm thinking of a letter between A and Z.
Can you guess it: K
** Right **
```

Notice one other thing of interest in this program. The **do-while** loop shown here obtains the next character, skipping over any carriage-return and linefeed characters that might be in the input stream:

```
// read a letter, but skip cr/lf
do {
  ch = (char) Console.Read(); // get a char
} while(ch == '\n' | ch == '\r');
```

Here is why this loop is needed. As explained earlier, console input is line-buffered—you have to press ENTER before characters are sent. Pressing ENTER causes a carriage-return and a linefeed character to be generated. These characters are left pending in the input buffer. This loop discards those characters by continuing to read input until neither is present.

Try This   Improve the C# Help System

This program expands on the C# help system that was begun in the previous Try This section. This version adds the syntax for the **for**, **while**, and **do-while** loops. It also checks the user's menu selection, looping until a valid response is entered.

Step by Step

1. Copy **Help.cs** to a new file called **Help2.cs**.

2. Change the portion of the program that displays the choices so that it uses the loop shown here:

```
do {
  Console.WriteLine("Help on:");
  Console.WriteLine("  1. if");
  Console.WriteLine("  2. switch");
  Console.WriteLine("  3. for");
  Console.WriteLine("  4. while");
  Console.WriteLine("  5. do-while\n");
  Console.Write("Choose one: ");
  do {
    choice = (char) Console.Read();
  } while(choice == '\n' | choice == '\r');
} while( choice < '1' | choice > '5');
```

Notice that a nested **do-while** loop is used to discard any spurious carriage-return or linefeed characters that may be present in the input stream. After making this change, the program will loop, displaying the menu until the user enters a response that is between 1 and 5.

3. Expand the **switch** statement to include the **for**, **while**, and **do-while** loops, as shown here:

```
switch(choice) {
  case '1':
    Console.WriteLine("The if:\n");
    Console.WriteLine("if(condition) statement;");
    Console.WriteLine("else statement;");
    break;
  case '2':
    Console.WriteLine("The switch:\n");
    Console.WriteLine("switch(expression) {");
    Console.WriteLine("  case constant:");
    Console.WriteLine("    statement sequence");
    Console.WriteLine("    break;");
    Console.WriteLine("  // ...");
    Console.WriteLine("}");
    break;
  case '3':
    Console.WriteLine("The for:\n");
    Console.Write("for(init; condition; iteration)");
```

```
      Console.WriteLine(" statement;");
      break;
    case '4':
      Console.WriteLine("The while:\n");
      Console.WriteLine("while(condition) statement;");
      break;
    case '5':
      Console.WriteLine("The do-while:\n");
      Console.WriteLine("do {");
      Console.WriteLine("  statement;");
      Console.WriteLine("} while (condition);");
      break;
  }
```

Notice that no **default** is present in this version of the **switch**. Since the menu loop ensures that a valid response will be entered, it is no longer necessary to include a **default** sequence to handle an invalid choice.

4. Here is the entire **Help2.cs** program listing:

```
/*
   An improved Help system that uses a
   do-while to process a menu selection.
*/

using System;

class Help2 {
  static void Main() {
    char choice;

    do {
      Console.WriteLine("Help on:");
      Console.WriteLine("  1. if");
      Console.WriteLine("  2. switch");
      Console.WriteLine("  3. for");
      Console.WriteLine("  4. while");
      Console.WriteLine("  5. do-while\n");
      Console.Write("Choose one: ");
      do {
        choice = (char) Console.Read();
      } while(choice == '\n' | choice == '\r');
    } while( choice < '1' | choice > '5');

    Console.WriteLine("\n");

    switch(choice) {
      case '1':
        Console.WriteLine("The if:\n");
```

(continued)

```
      Console.WriteLine("if(condition) statement;");
      Console.WriteLine("else statement;");
      break;
    case '2':
      Console.WriteLine("The switch:\n");
      Console.WriteLine("switch(expression) {");
      Console.WriteLine("  case constant:");
      Console.WriteLine("    statement sequence");
      Console.WriteLine("    break;");
      Console.WriteLine("  // ...");
      Console.WriteLine("}");
      break;
    case '3':
      Console.WriteLine("The for:\n");
      Console.Write("for(init; condition; iteration)");
      Console.WriteLine(" statement;");
      break;
    case '4':
      Console.WriteLine("The while:\n");
      Console.WriteLine("while(condition) statement;");
      break;
    case '5':
      Console.WriteLine("The do-while:\n");
      Console.WriteLine("do {");
      Console.WriteLine("  statement;");
      Console.WriteLine("} while (condition);");
      break;
    }
  }
}
```

Use break to Exit a Loop

It is possible to force an immediate exit from a loop, bypassing any code remaining in the body of the loop and the loop's conditional test, by using the **break** statement. When a **break** statement is encountered inside a loop, the loop is terminated and program control resumes at the next statement following the loop. Here is a simple example:

```
// Using break to exit a loop.

using System;

class BreakDemo {
  static void Main() {
    int num;
```

```
   num = 100;

   // Loop while i squared is less than num.
   for(int i=0; i < num; i++) {

      // Terminate loop if i*i >= 100.
      if(i*i >= num) break;  ◄———————— Use break to terminate the loop.

      Console.Write(i + " ");
   }
   Console.WriteLine("Loop complete.");
   }
}
```

This program generates the following output:

```
0 1 2 3 4 5 6 7 8 9 Loop complete.
```

As you can see, although the **for** loop is designed to run from 0 to **num** (which, in this case, is 100), the **break** statement causes it to terminate early, when **i** squared is greater than or equal to **num**.

The **break** statement can be used with any of C#'s loops, including intentionally infinite loops. For example, the following program simply reads input until the user presses **q**:

```
// Read input until a q is received.

using System;

class Break2 {
  static void Main() {
    char ch;

    for( ; ; ) {  ◄
      ch = (char) Console.Read();     ├— This infinite loop is terminated by break.
      if(ch == 'q') break;  ◄
    }
    Console.WriteLine("You pressed q!");
  }
}
```

When used inside a set of nested loops, the **break** statement will break out of only the innermost loop. For example:

```
// Using break with nested loops.

using System;

class Break3 {
  static void Main() {
```

```
for(int i=0; i<3; i++) {
  Console.WriteLine("Outer loop count: " + i);
  Console.Write("    Inner loop count: ");

  int t = 0;
  while(t < 100) {
    if(t == 10) break;  ◄──────── Break out of the inner loop.
    Console.Write(t + " ");
    t++;
  }
  Console.WriteLine();
}
Console.WriteLine("Loops complete.");
}
}
```

This program generates the following output:

```
Outer loop count: 0
    Inner loop count: 0 1 2 3 4 5 6 7 8 9
Outer loop count: 1
    Inner loop count: 0 1 2 3 4 5 6 7 8 9
Outer loop count: 2
    Inner loop count: 0 1 2 3 4 5 6 7 8 9
Loops complete.
```

As you can see, the **break** statement in the inner loop causes only the termination of that loop. The outer loop is unaffected.

Here are two other points to remember about **break**. First, more than one **break** statement may appear in a loop, but be careful. Too many **break** statements have the tendency to destructure your code. Second, the **break** that exits a **switch** statement affects only that **switch** statement and not any enclosing loops.

Ask the Expert

Q: I know that in Java, the break and continue **statements can be used with a label. Does C# support the same feature?**

A: No. The designers of C# did not give **break** or **continue** that capability. Instead, **break** and **continue** work the same in C# as they do in C and C++. One reason that C# did not follow Java's lead on this issue is that Java does not support the **goto** statement, but C# does. Thus, Java needs to give **break** and **continue** extra power to make up for the lack of the **goto**.

Use continue

It is possible to force an early iteration of a loop, bypassing the loop's normal control structure. This is accomplished using **continue**. The **continue** statement forces the next iteration of the loop to take place, skipping any code in between. Thus, **continue** is essentially the complement of **break**. For example, the following program uses **continue** to help print the even numbers between 0 and 100:

```
// Use continue.

using System;

class ContDemo {
  static void Main() {
    int i;

    // Print even numbers between 0 and 100.
    for(i = 0; i<=100; i++) {

      // Iterate if i is odd.
      if((i%2) != 0) continue;   ◄────── Iterate the loop if i is odd.

      Console.WriteLine(i);
    }
  }
}
```

Only even numbers are printed, because an odd one will cause the loop to iterate early, bypassing the call to **WriteLine( )**.

In **while** and **do-while** loops, a **continue** statement will cause control to go directly to the conditional expression. In the case of the **for**, the iteration expression of the loop is evaluated and then the conditional expression is executed.

Good uses of **continue** are rare. One reason is that C# provides a rich set of loop statements that fit most applications. However, for those special circumstances in which early iteration is needed, the **continue** statement provides a structured way to accomplish it.

The goto

The **goto** is C#'s unconditional jump statement. When encountered, program flow jumps to the location specified by the **goto**. The statement fell out of favor with programmers many years ago because it encouraged the creation of "spaghetti code," a tangled mess of unconditional jumps that resulted in hard-to-follow code. However, the **goto** is still occasionally—and sometimes effectively—used. This book will not make a judgment regarding its validity as a form of program control. It should be stated, however, that there are no programming situations that require the use of the **goto** statement—it is not an item necessary for making the language complete. Rather, it is a convenience, which, if used wisely, can be of benefit in certain programming situations. As such, the **goto** is not used in this book outside of this section. The chief concern most programmers have about the **goto** is its tendency to clutter a program and render it nearly unreadable. However, there are times when the use of the **goto** can clarify program flow rather than confuse it.

The **goto** requires a label for operation. A *label* is a valid C# identifier followed by a colon. Furthermore, the label must be in the same method as the **goto** that uses it. For example, a loop from 1 to 100 could be written using a **goto** and a label, as shown here:

```
x = 1;
loop1:
   x++;
   if(x < 100) goto loop1;     Execution jumps to loop1.
```

One good use for the **goto** is to exit from a deeply nested routine. Here is a simple example:

```
// Demonstrate the goto.

using System;

class Use_goto {
  static void Main() {
    int i=0, j=0, k=0;

    for(i=0; i < 10; i++) {
      for(j=0; j < 10; j++ ) {
        for(k=0; k < 10; k++) {
          Console.WriteLine("i, j, k: " + i + " " + j + " " + k);
          if(k == 3) goto stop;
        }
      }
    }

stop:
    Console.WriteLine("Stopped! i, j, k: " + i + ", " + j + ", " + k);

  }
}
```

The output from the program is shown here.

```
i, j, k: 0 0 0
i, j, k: 0 0 1
i, j, k: 0 0 2
i, j, k: 0 0 3
Stopped! i, j, k: 0, 0, 3
```

Eliminating the **goto** would force the use of three **if** and **break** statements. In this case, the **goto** simplifies the code. While this is a contrived example used for illustration, you can imagine real-world situations in which a **goto** might be beneficial.

The **goto** does have one important restriction: You cannot jump into a block. Of course, you can jump out of a block, as the preceding example shows.

In addition to working with "normal" labels, the **goto** can be used to jump to a **case** or **default** label within a **switch**. For example, this is a valid **switch** statement:

```
switch(x) {
  case 1: // ...
    goto default;
  case 2: // ...
    goto case 1;
  default: // ...
    break;
}
```

The **goto default** jumps to the **default** label. The **goto case 1** jumps to **case 1**. Because of the restriction stated above, you cannot jump into the middle of a **switch** from code outside the **switch** because a **switch** defines a block. Therefore, these types of **goto** statements must be executed from within the **switch**.

Try This Finish the C# Help System

Here you will put the finishing touches on the C# help system. This version adds the syntax for **break**, **continue**, and **goto**. It also allows the user to request the syntax for more than one statement. It does this by adding an outer loop that runs until the user enters a **q** as a menu selection.

Step by Step

1. Copy **Help2.cs** to a new file called **Help3.cs**.

2. Surround all of the program code with an infinite **for** loop. Break out of this loop, using **break**, when a **q** is entered. Since this loop surrounds all of the program code, breaking out of this loop causes the program to terminate.

3. Change the menu loop, as shown here:

```
do {
  Console.WriteLine("Help on:");
  Console.WriteLine("  1. if");
  Console.WriteLine("  2. switch");
  Console.WriteLine("  3. for");
  Console.WriteLine("  4. while");
  Console.WriteLine("  5. do-while");
  Console.WriteLine("  6. break");
  Console.WriteLine("  7. continue");
  Console.WriteLine("  8. goto\n");
  Console.Write("Choose one (q to quit): ");
  do {
    choice = (char) Console.Read();
  } while(choice == '\n' | choice == '\r');
} while( choice < '1' | choice > '8' & choice != 'q');
```

(continued)

Notice that this loop now includes the **break, continue,** and **goto** statements. It also accepts a **q** as a valid choice.

4. Expand the **switch** statement to include the **break, continue,** and **goto** statements, as shown here:

```
case '6':
  Console.WriteLine("The break:\n");
  Console.WriteLine("break;");
  break;
case '7':
  Console.WriteLine("The continue:\n");
  Console.WriteLine("continue;");
  break;
case '8':
  Console.WriteLine("The goto:\n");
  Console.WriteLine("goto label;");
  break;
```

5. Here is the entire **Help3.cs** program listing:

```
/*
    The finished C# statement help system
    that processes multiple requests.
*/

using System;

class Help3 {
  static void Main() {
    char choice;

    for(;;) {
      do {
        Console.WriteLine("Help on:");
        Console.WriteLine("  1. if");
        Console.WriteLine("  2. switch");
        Console.WriteLine("  3. for");
        Console.WriteLine("  4. while");
        Console.WriteLine("  5. do-while");
        Console.WriteLine("  6. break");
        Console.WriteLine("  7. continue");
        Console.WriteLine("  8. goto\n");
        Console.Write("Choose one (q to quit): ");
        do {
          choice = (char) Console.Read();
        } while(choice == '\n' | choice == '\r');
      } while( choice < '1' | choice > '8' & choice != 'q');

      if(choice == 'q') break;
```

```
    Console.WriteLine("\n");

    switch(choice) {
      case '1':
        Console.WriteLine("The if:\n");
        Console.WriteLine("if(condition) statement;");
        Console.WriteLine("else statement;");
        break;
      case '2':
        Console.WriteLine("The switch:\n");
        Console.WriteLine("switch(expression) {");
        Console.WriteLine("  case constant:");
        Console.WriteLine("    statement sequence");
        Console.WriteLine("    break;");
        Console.WriteLine("  // ...");
        Console.WriteLine("}");
        break;
      case '3':
        Console.WriteLine("The for:\n");
        Console.Write("for(init; condition; iteration)");
        Console.WriteLine(" statement;");
        break;
      case '4':
        Console.WriteLine("The while:\n");
        Console.WriteLine("while(condition) statement;");
        break;
      case '5':
        Console.WriteLine("The do-while:\n");
        Console.WriteLine("do {");
        Console.WriteLine("  statement;");
        Console.WriteLine("} while (condition);");
        break;
      case '6':
        Console.WriteLine("The break:\n");
        Console.WriteLine("break;");
        break;
      case '7':
        Console.WriteLine("The continue:\n");
        Console.WriteLine("continue;");
        break;
      case '8':
        Console.WriteLine("The goto:\n");
        Console.WriteLine("goto label;");
        break;
    }
    Console.WriteLine();
  }
 }
}
```

(continued)

Here is a sample run:

```
Help on:
  1. if
  2. switch
  3. for
  4. while
  5. do-while
  6. break
  7. continue
  8. goto

Choose one (q to quit): 1

The if:

if(condition) statement;
else statement;

Help on:
  1. if
  2. switch
  3. for
  4. while
  5. do-while
  6. break
  7. continue
  8. goto

Choose one (q to quit): 6

The break:

break;

Help on:
  1. if
  2. switch
  3. for
  4. while
  5. do-while
  6. break
  7. continue
  8. goto

Choose one (q to quit): q
```

Nested Loops

As you have seen in some of the preceding examples, one loop can be nested inside another. Nested loops are used to solve a wide variety of programming problems and are an essential part of programming. So, before leaving the topic of C#'s loop statements, let's look at one more nested loop example. The following program uses a nested **for** loop to find the factors of the numbers from 2 to 100:

```
// Use nested loops to find factors of numbers between 2 and 100.

using System;

class FindFac {
  static void Main() {

    for(int i=2; i <= 100; i++) {
      Console.Write("Factors of " + i + ": ");
      for(int j = 2; j <= i/2; j++)
        if((i%j) == 0) Console.Write(j + " ");
      Console.WriteLine();
    }
  }
}
```

Here is a portion of the output produced by the program:

```
Factors of 2:
Factors of 3:
Factors of 4: 2
Factors of 5:
Factors of 6: 2 3
Factors of 7:
Factors of 8: 2 4
Factors of 9: 3
Factors of 10: 2 5
Factors of 11:
Factors of 12: 2 3 4 6
Factors of 13:
Factors of 14: 2 7
Factors of 15: 3 5
Factors of 16: 2 4 8
Factors of 17:
Factors of 18: 2 3 6 9
Factors of 19:
Factors of 20: 2 4 5 10
```

In the program, the outer loop runs **i** from 2 through 100. The inner loop successively tests all numbers from 2 up to **i**, printing those that evenly divide **i**.

Chapter 3 Self Test

1. Write a program that reads characters from the keyboard until a period is received. Have the program count the number of spaces. Report the total at the end of the program.

2. In the **switch**, can the code sequence from one **case** run into the next?

3. Show the general form of the **if-else-if** ladder.

4. Given

```
if(x < 10)
   if(y > 100) {
      if(!done) x = z;
      else y = z;
   }
   else Console.WriteLine("error"); // what if?
```

   with what **if** does the last **else** associate?

5. Show the **for** statement for a loop that counts from 1,000 to 0 by –2.

6. Is the following fragment valid?

```
for(int i = 0; i < num; i++)
   sum += i;

count = i;
```

7. Explain what **break** does.

8. In the following fragment, after the **break** statement executes, what is displayed?

```
for(i = 0; i < 10; i++) {
   while(running) {
      if(x<y) break;
      // ...
   }
   Console.WriteLine("after while");
}
Console.WriteLine("After for");
```

9. What does the following fragment print?

```
for(int i = 0; i<10; i++) {
   Console.Write(i + " ");
   if((i%2) == 0) continue;
   Console.WriteLine();
}
```

10. The iteration expression in a **for** loop need not always alter the loop control variable by a fixed amount. Instead, the loop control variable can change in any arbitrary way. Using this concept, write a program that uses a **for** loop to generate and display the progression 1, 2, 4, 8, 16, 32, and so on.

11. The ASCII lowercase letters are separated from the uppercase letters by 32. Thus, to convert a lowercase letter to uppercase, subtract 32 from it. Use this information to write a program that reads characters from the keyboard. Have it convert all lowercase letters to uppercase, and all uppercase letters to lowercase, displaying the result. Make no changes to any other character. Have the program stop when the user presses the period key. At the end, have the program display the number of case changes that have taken place.

Chapter 4

Introducing Classes, Objects, and Methods

Key Skills & Concepts

- Class fundamentals
- Instantiate an object
- Method basics
- Method parameters
- Return a value from a method
- Constructors
- **new**
- Garbage collection
- Destructors
- The **this** keyword

Before you can go much further in your study of C#, you need to learn about the class. The class is the essence of C# because it defines the nature of an object. As such, the class forms the basis for object-oriented programming in C#. Within a class are defined data and the code that acts upon that data. The code is contained in methods. Because classes, objects, and methods are fundamental to C#, they are introduced in this chapter. Having a basic understanding of these features will allow you to write more sophisticated programs and to better understand certain key C# elements described in Chapter 5.

Class Fundamentals

We have been using classes since the start of this book. Of course, only extremely simple classes have been used, and we have not taken advantage of the majority of their features. As you will see, classes are substantially more powerful than the limited ones presented so far.

Let's begin by reviewing the basics. A class is a template that defines the form of an object. It typically specifies both code and data, with the code acting on the data. C# uses a class specification to construct *objects*. Objects are *instances* of a class. Thus, a class is essentially a set of plans that specify how to build an object. It is important to be clear on one issue: A class is a logical abstraction. It is not until an object of that class has been created that a physical representation of that class exists in memory.

One other point: Recall that the methods and variables that constitute a class are called *members* of the class.

The General Form of a Class

When you define a class, you declare the data that it contains and the code that operates on it. While very simple classes might contain only code or only data, most real-world classes contain both.

In general terms, data is contained in instance variables defined by the class, and code is contained in methods. It is important to state at the outset, however, that C# defines several specific flavors of members, which include instance variables, static variables, constants, methods, constructors, destructors, indexers, events, operators, and properties. For now, we will limit our discussion of the class to its essential elements: instance variables and methods. Later in this chapter, constructors and destructors are discussed. The other types of members are described in later chapters.

A class is created by using the keyword **class**. The general form of a **class** definition that contains only instance variables and methods is shown here:

```
class classname {
    // Declare instance variables.
    access type var1;
    access type var2;
    // ...
    access type varN;

    // Declare methods.
    access ret-type method1(parameters) {
        // body of method
    }
    access ret-type method2(parameters) {
        // body of method
    }
        // ...
    access ret-type methodN(parameters) {
        // body of method
    }
}
```

Notice that each variable and method is preceded with *access*. Here, *access* is an access specifier, such as **public**, which specifies how the member can be accessed. As mentioned in Chapter 1, class members can be private to a class or more accessible. The access specifier determines what type of access is allowed. The access specifier is optional and, if absent, the member is private to the class. Members with private access can be used only by other members of their class. For the examples in this chapter, all members (except for the **Main( )** method) will be specified as **public**. This means they can be used by all other code—even code defined outside the class. (The **Main( )** method will continue to use the default access because this is the currently recommended approach.) We will return to the topic of access specifiers in a later chapter, after you have learned the fundamentals of the class.

Although there is no syntactic rule that enforces it, a well-designed class should define one and only one logical entity. For example, a class that stores names and telephone numbers will not normally also store information about the stock market, average rainfall, sunspot cycles, or other unrelated information. The point here is that a well-designed class groups logically connected information. Putting unrelated information into the same class will quickly destructure your code!

Up to this point, the classes that we have been using have had only one method: **Main( )**. Soon you will see how to create others. However, notice that the general form of a class does not specify a **Main( )** method. A **Main( )** method is required only if that class is the starting point for your program.

Define a Class

To illustrate classes, we will evolve a class that encapsulates information about vehicles, such as cars, vans, and trucks. This class is called **Vehicle**, and it will store three items of information about a vehicle: the number of passengers that it can carry, its fuel capacity, and its average fuel consumption (in miles per gallon).

The first version of **Vehicle** is shown here. It defines three instance variables: **Passengers**, **FuelCap**, and **Mpg**. Notice that **Vehicle** does not contain any methods. Thus, it is currently a data-only class. (Subsequent sections will add methods to it.)

```
class Vehicle {
  public int Passengers; // number of passengers
  public int FuelCap;    // fuel capacity in gallons
  public int Mpg;        // fuel consumption in miles per gallon
}
```

The instance variables defined by **Vehicle** illustrate the way that instance variables are declared in general. The general form for declaring an instance variable is shown here:

access type var-name;

Here, *access* specifies the access, *type* specifies the type of variable, and *var-name* is the variable's name. Thus, aside from the access specifier, you declare an instance variable in the same way that you declare local variables. For **Vehicle**, the variables are preceded by the **public** access modifier. As explained, this allows them to be accessed by code outside of **Vehicle**.

A **class** definition creates a new data type. In this case, the new data type is called **Vehicle**. You will use this name to declare objects of type **Vehicle**. Remember that a **class** declaration is only a type description; it does not create an actual object. Thus, the preceding code does not cause any objects of type **Vehicle** to come into existence.

To actually create a **Vehicle** object, you will use a statement like the following:

```
Vehicle minivan = new Vehicle(); // create a Vehicle object called minivan
```

After this statement executes, **minivan** will be an instance of **Vehicle**. Thus, it will have "physical" reality. For the moment, don't worry about the details of this statement.

Each time you create an instance of a class, you are creating an object that contains its own copy of each instance variable defined by the class. Thus, every **Vehicle** object will contain its own copies of the instance variables **Passengers**, **FuelCap**, and **Mpg**. To access these variables, you will use the member access operator, which is a period. It is commonly referred to as the *dot operator*. The dot operator links the name of an object with the name of a member. The general form of the dot operator is shown here:

object.member

Thus, the object is specified on the left, and the member is put on the right. For example, to assign the **FuelCap** variable of **minivan** the value 16, use the following statement:

```
minivan.FuelCap = 16;
```

In general, you can use the dot operator to access both instance variables and methods.

Here is a complete program that uses the **Vehicle** class:

```
/* A program that uses the Vehicle class.

   Call this file UseVehicle.cs
*/

using System;

// A class that encapsulates information about vehicles.
class Vehicle {
  public int Passengers; // number of passengers
  public int FuelCap;    // fuel capacity in gallons
  public int Mpg;        // fuel consumption in miles per gallon
}

// This class declares an object of type Vehicle.
class VehicleDemo {
  static void Main() {
    Vehicle minivan = new Vehicle();     ← Create an instance of Vehicle
    int range;                             called minivan.

    // Assign values to fields in minivan.
    minivan.Passengers = 7;
    minivan.FuelCap = 16;      ←          Notice the use of the dot operator
    minivan.Mpg = 21;                      to access a member.

    // Compute the range assuming a full tank of gas.
    range = minivan.FuelCap * minivan.Mpg;

    Console.WriteLine("Minivan can carry " + minivan.Passengers +
                " with a range of " + range);
  }
}
```

This program consists of two classes: **Vehicle** and **VehicleDemo**. Inside **VehicleDemo**, the **Main( )** method creates an instance of **Vehicle** called **minivan**. Then the code within **Main( )** accesses the instance variables associated with **minivan**, assigning them values and using those values. It is important to understand that **Vehicle** and **VehicleDemo** are two separate classes. The only relationship they have to each other is that one class creates an instance of the other. Although they are separate classes, code inside **VehicleDemo** can access the members of **Vehicle** because they are declared **public**. If they had not been given the **public** access specifier, their access would have been limited to the **Vehicle** class, and **VehicleDemo** would not have been able to use them.

Assuming that you call the preceding file **UseVehicle.cs**, compiling this program creates a file called **UseVehicle.exe**. Both the **Vehicle** and **VehicleDemo** classes are automatically part of the executable file. The program displays the following output:

```
Minivan can carry 7 with a range of 336
```

It is not necessary for both the **Vehicle** and the **VehicleDemo** classes to actually be in the same source file. You could put each class in its own file, called **Vehicle.cs** and **VehicleDemo.cs**, for example. Just tell the C# compiler to compile both files and link them together. For example, you could use this command line to compile the program if you split it into two pieces as just described:

```
csc Vehicle.cs VehicleDemo.cs
```

This will create **VehicleDemo.exe** because that is the class that contains the **Main( )** method. If you are using the Visual Studio IDE, you will need to add both files to your project and then build.

Before moving on, let's review a fundamental principle: Each object has its own copies of the instance variables defined by its class. Thus, the contents of the variables in one object can differ from the contents of the variables in another. There is no connection between the two objects, except for the fact that they are both objects of the same type. For example, if you have two **Vehicle** objects, each has its own copy of **Passengers**, **FuelCap**, and **Mpg**, and the contents of these can differ between the two objects. The following program demonstrates this fact:

```
// This program creates two Vehicle objects.

using System;

// A class that encapsulates information about vehicles.
class Vehicle {
  public int Passengers; // number of passengers
  public int FuelCap;    // fuel capacity in gallons
  public int Mpg;        // fuel consumption in miles per gallon
}

// This class declares two objects of type Vehicle.
class TwoVehicles {
```

```
static void Main() {
    Vehicle minivan = new Vehicle();
    Vehicle sportscar = new Vehicle();

    int range1, range2;

    // Assign values to fields in minivan.
    minivan.Passengers = 7;
    minivan.FuelCap = 16;
    minivan.Mpg = 21;

    // Assign values to fields in sportscar.
    sportscar.Passengers = 2;
    sportscar.FuelCap = 14;
    sportscar.Mpg = 12;

    // Compute the ranges assuming a full tank of gas.
    range1 = minivan.FuelCap * minivan.Mpg;
    range2 = sportscar.FuelCap * sportscar.Mpg;

    Console.WriteLine("Minivan can carry " + minivan.Passengers +
                      " with a range of " + range1);

    Console.WriteLine("Sportscar can carry " + sportscar.Passengers +
                      " with a range of " + range2);
    }
}
```

Remember, **minivan** and **sportscar** refer to separate objects.

The output produced by this program is shown here:

```
Minivan can carry 7 with a range of 336
Sportscar can carry 2 with a range of 168
```

As you can see, **minivan**'s data is completely separate from the data contained in **sportscar**. Figure 4-1 depicts this situation.

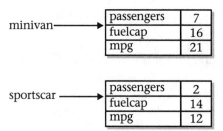

Figure 4-1 One object's instance variables are separate from another's.

How Objects Are Created

In the preceding programs, the following line was used to create an object of type **Vehicle**:

```
Vehicle minivan = new Vehicle();
```

This declaration performs three functions. First, it declares a variable called **minivan** of the class type **Vehicle**. This variable is not, itself, an object. Instead, it is simply a variable that can *refer to* an object. Second, the declaration creates an actual, physical instance of the object. This is done by using the **new** operator. Finally, it assigns to **minivan** a reference to that object. Thus, after the line executes, **minivan** refers to an object of type **Vehicle**.

The **new** operator *dynamically allocates* (that is, allocates at runtime) memory for an object and returns a reference to it. This reference is then stored in a variable. Thus, in C#, all class objects must be dynamically allocated.

As you might expect, it is possible to separate the declaration of **minivan** from the creation of the object to which it will refer, as shown here:

```
Vehicle minivan; // declare a reference to an object
minivan = new Vehicle(); // allocate a Vehicle object
```

The first line declares **minivan** as a reference to an object of type **Vehicle**. Thus, **minivan** is a variable that can refer to an object, but it is not an object itself. The next line creates a new **Vehicle** object and assigns a reference to it to **minivan**. Now, **minivan** is linked with an object.

The fact that class objects are accessed through a reference explains why classes are called *reference types*. The key difference between value types and reference types is what a variable of each type means. For a variable of a value type, the variable itself contains the value. For example, given

```
int x;
x = 10;
```

x contains the value 10 because **x** is a variable of type **int**, which is a value type. However, in the case of

```
Vehicle minivan = new Vehicle();
```

minivan does not, itself, contain the object. Instead, it contains a reference to the object.

Reference Variables and Assignment

In an assignment operation, reference variables act differently than do variables of a value type, such as **int**. When you assign one value type variable to another, the situation is straightforward. The variable on the left receives a *copy* of the *value* of the variable on the right. When you assign one object reference variable to another, the situation is a bit more complicated because you are causing the variable on the left to refer to the object referred to by the variable on the right. The effect of this difference can cause some counterintuitive results. For example, consider the following fragment:

```
Vehicle car1 = new Vehicle();
Vehicle car2 = car1;
```

At first glance, it is easy to think that **car1** and **car2** refer to different objects, but this is not the case. Instead, **car1** and **car2** will both refer to the *same* object. The assignment of **car1** to **car2** simply makes **car2** refer to the same object as does **car1**. Thus, the object can be acted upon by either **car1** or **car2**. For example, after this assignment executes,

```
car1.Mpg = 26;
```

both of these **WriteLine( )** statements display the same value, 26:

```
Console.WriteLine(car1.Mpg);
Console.WriteLine(car2.Mpg);
```

Although **car1** and **car2** both refer to the same object, they are not linked in any other way. For example, a subsequent assignment to **car2** simply changes what object **car2** refers to. For example:

```
Vehicle car1 = new Vehicle();
Vehicle car2 = car1;
Vehicle car3 = new Vehicle();

car2 = car3; // now car2 and car3 refer to the same object.
```

After this sequence executes, **car2** refers to the same object as **car3**. Of course, **car1** continues to refer to its original object.

Methods

As explained, instance variables and methods are two of the primary constituents of classes. So far, the **Vehicle** class contains data, but no methods. Although data-only classes are perfectly valid, most classes will have methods. Methods are subroutines that manipulate the data defined by the class and, in many cases, provide access to that data. Typically, other parts of your program will interact with a class through its methods.

A method contains one or more statements. In well-written C# code, each method performs only one task. Each method has a name, and this name is used to call the method. In general, you can name a method using any valid identifier that you please. However, remember that **Main( )** is reserved for the method that begins execution of your program. Also, don't use C#'s keywords for method names.

When denoting methods in text, this book has used and will continue to use a convention that has become common when writing about C#. A method will have parentheses after its name. For example, if a method's name is **GetVal**, it will be written **GetVal( )** when its name is used in a sentence. This notation will help you distinguish variable names from method names in this book.

The general form of a method is shown here:

access ret-type name(parameter-list) {
    // body of method
}

Here, *access* is an access modifier that governs what other parts of your program can call the method. As explained earlier, the access modifier is optional. If not present, the method is private to the class in which it is declared. For now, we will declare methods **public** so that they can be called by any other code in the program. The *ret-type* specifies the type of data returned by the method. This can be any valid type, including class types that you create. If the method does not return a value, its return type must be **void**. The name of the method is specified by *name*. This can be any legal identifier other than those which would cause conflicts within the current declaration space. The *parameter-list* is a sequence of type and identifier pairs separated by commas. Parameters are essentially variables that receive the value of the *arguments* passed to the method when it is called. If the method has no parameters, the parameter list will be empty.

Add a Method to the Vehicle Class

As just explained, the methods of a class typically manipulate and provide access to the data of the class. With this in mind, recall that **Main( )** in the preceding examples computed the range of a vehicle by multiplying its fuel consumption rate by its fuel capacity. While technically correct, this is not the best way to handle this computation. The calculation of a vehicle's range is something that is best handled by the **Vehicle** class itself. The reason for this conclusion is easy to understand: The range of a vehicle is dependent upon the capacity of the fuel tank and the rate of fuel consumption, and both of these quantities are encapsulated by **Vehicle**. By adding a method to **Vehicle** that computes the range, you are enhancing its object-oriented structure.

To add a method to **Vehicle**, specify it within **Vehicle**'s declaration. For example, the following version of **Vehicle** contains a method called **Range( )** that displays the range of the vehicle:

```
// Add range to Vehicle.

using System;

// A class that encapsulates information about vehicles.
class Vehicle {
  public int Passengers;  // number of passengers
  public int FuelCap;     // fuel capacity in gallons
  public int Mpg;         // fuel consumption in miles per gallon

  // Display the range.
  public void Range() {
    Console.WriteLine("Range is " + FuelCap * Mpg);
  }
}
```

The **Range( )** method is contained within the **Vehicle** class.

Notice that **FuelCap** and **Mpg** are used directly, without the dot operator.

```
class AddMeth {
  static void Main() {
    Vehicle minivan = new Vehicle();
    Vehicle sportscar = new Vehicle();

    // Assign values to fields in minivan.
    minivan.Passengers = 7;
    minivan.FuelCap = 16;
    minivan.Mpg = 21;

    // Assign values to fields in sportscar.
    sportscar.Passengers = 2;
    sportscar.FuelCap = 14;
    sportscar.Mpg = 12;


    Console.Write("Minivan can carry " + minivan.Passengers +
                  ". ");

    minivan.Range(); // display range of minivan

    Console.Write("Sportscar can carry " + sportscar.Passengers +
                  ". ");

    sportscar.Range(); // display range of sportscar.
  }
}
```

This program generates the following output:

```
Minivan can carry 7. Range is 336
Sportscar can carry 2. Range is 168
```

Let's look at the key elements of this program, beginning with the **Range( )** method itself. The first line of **Range( )** is

```
public void Range() {
```

This line declares a method called **Range** that has no parameters. It is specified as **public,** so it can be used by all other parts of the program. Its return type is **void**. Thus, **Range( )** does not return a value to the caller. The line ends with the opening curly brace of the method body.

The body of **Range( )** consists solely of this line:

```
Console.WriteLine("Range is " + FuelCap * Mpg);
```

This statement displays the range of the vehicle by multiplying **FuelCap** by **Mpg**. Since each object of type **Vehicle** has its own copy of **FuelCap** and **Mpg**, when **Range( )** is called, the range computation uses the calling object's copies of those variables.

The **Range( )** method ends when its closing curly brace is encountered. This causes program control to transfer back to the caller.

Next, look closely at this line of code from inside **Main( )**:

```
minivan.Range();
```

This statement invokes the **Range( )** method on **minivan**. That is, it calls **Range( )** relative to the object referred to by **minivan**, by use of the dot operator. When a method is called, program control is transferred to the method. When the method terminates, control is transferred back to the caller, and execution resumes with the line of code following the call.

In this case, the call to **minivan.Range( )** displays the range of the vehicle defined by **minivan**. In a similar fashion, the call to **sportscar.Range( )** displays the range of the vehicle defined by **sportscar**. Each time **Range( )** is invoked, it displays the range for the specified object.

There is something very important to notice inside the **Range( )** method: The instance variables **FuelCap** and **Mpg** are referred to directly, without use of the dot operator. When a method uses an instance variable that is defined by its class, it does so directly, without explicit reference to an object and without use of the dot operator. This is easy to understand if you think about it. A method is always invoked relative to some object of its class. Once this invocation has occurred, the object is known. Thus, within a method, there is no need to specify the object a second time. This means that **FuelCap** and **Mpg** inside **Range( )** implicitly refer to the copies of those variables found in the object that invokes **Range( )**.

Return from a Method

In general, there are two conditions that cause a method to return. The first, as the **Range( )** method in the preceding example shows, occurs when the method's closing curly brace is encountered. The second is when a **return** statement is executed. There are two forms of **return**: one for use in **void** methods (those that do not return a value) and one for returning values. The first form is examined here. The next section explains how to return values.

In a **void** method, you can cause the immediate termination of a method by using this form of **return**:

```
return ;
```

When this statement executes, program control returns to the caller, skipping any remaining code in the method. For example, consider this method:

```
public void MyMeth() {
  int i;

  for(i=0; i<10; i++) {
    if(i == 5) return; // stop at 5
    Console.WriteLine(i);
  }
}
```

Here, the **for** loop will only run from 0 to 5, because once **i** equals 5, the method returns.

It is permissible to have multiple return statements in a method, especially when there are two or more routes out of it. For example,

```
public void MyMeth() {
  // ...
  if(done) return;
  // ...
  if(error) return;
}
```

Here, the method returns if it is done or if an error occurs. Be careful, however, because having too many exit points in a method can destructure your code, so avoid using them casually.

To review: A **void** method can return in one of two ways: its closing curly brace is reached, or a **return** statement is executed.

Return a Value

Although methods with a return type of **void** are not rare, most methods will return a value. In fact, the ability to return a value is one of the most useful features of a method. You have already seen an example of a return value: when we used **Math.Sqrt( )** to obtain a square root in chapters 2 and 3.

Return values are used for a variety of purposes in programming. In some cases, such as with **Math.Sqrt( )**, the return value contains the outcome of some calculation. In other cases, the return value may simply indicate success or failure. In still others, it may contain a status code. Whatever the purpose, using method return values is an integral part of C# programming.

Methods return a value to the calling routine using this form of **return**:

return *value*;

Here, *value* is the value returned.

You can use a return value to improve the implementation of **Range( )**. Instead of displaying the range, a better approach is to have **Range( )** compute the range and return this value. Among the advantages to this approach is that you can use the value for other calculations. The following example modifies **Range( )** to return the range rather than displaying it:

```
// Use a return value.

using System;

// A class that encapsulates information about vehicles.
class Vehicle {
  public int Passengers; // number of passengers
  public int FuelCap;    // fuel capacity in gallons
  public int Mpg;        // fuel consumption in miles per gallon
```

```
     // Return the range.
     public int Range() {
       return Mpg * FuelCap;        ◄─────── Now Range( ) returns a value.
     }
   }

   class RetMeth {
     static void Main() {
       Vehicle minivan = new Vehicle();
       Vehicle sportscar = new Vehicle();

       int range1, range2;

       // Assign values to fields in minivan.
       minivan.Passengers = 7;
       minivan.FuelCap = 16;
       minivan.Mpg = 21;

       // Assign values to fields in sportscar.
       sportscar.Passengers = 2;
       sportscar.FuelCap = 14;
       sportscar.Mpg = 12;

       // Get the ranges.
       range1 = minivan.Range();        ◄──────  Assign the value returned
       range2 = sportscar.Range();              by Range( ) to a variable.

       Console.WriteLine("Minivan can carry " + minivan.Passengers +
                         " with range of " + range1 + " miles.");

       Console.WriteLine("Sportscar can carry " + sportscar.Passengers +
                         " with range of " + range2 + " miles.");
     }
   }
```

The output is shown here:

```
Minivan can carry 7 with range of 336 miles.
Sportscar can carry 2 with range of 168 miles.
```

In the program, notice that when **Range( )** is called, it is put on the right side of an assignment statement. On the left is a variable that will receive the value returned by **Range( )**. Thus, after this line executes,

```
range1 = minivan.Range();
```

the range of the **minivan** object is stored in **range1**.

Notice that **Range( )** now has a return type of **int**. This means that it will return an integer value to the caller. The return type of a method is important because the type of data returned by a method must be compatible with the return type specified by the method. Thus, if you want a method to return data of type **double**, its return type must be type **double**.

Although the preceding program is correct, it is not written as efficiently as it could be. Specifically, there is no need for the **range1** or **range2** variables. A call to **Range( )** can be used in the **WriteLine( )** statement directly, as shown here:

```
Console.WriteLine("Minivan can carry " + minivan.Passengers +
                    " with range of " + minivan.Range() + " Miles");
```

In this case, when **WriteLine( )** is executed, **minivan.Range( )** is called automatically and its value will be passed to **WriteLine( )**. Furthermore, you can use a call to **Range( )** whenever the range of a **Vehicle** object is needed. For example, this statement compares the ranges of two vehicles:

```
if(v1.Range() > v2.Range()) Console.WriteLine("v1 has greater range");
```

Ask the Expert

Q: I have heard that C# detects "unreachable code." What does this mean?

A: You heard correctly. The C# compiler will issue a warning message if you create a method that contains code that no path of execution will ever reach. Consider this example:

```
public void m() {
  char a, b;

  // ...

  if(a==b) {
    Console.WriteLine("equal");
    return;
  } else {
    Console.WriteLine("not equal");
    return;
  }
  Console.WriteLine("this is unreachable");
}
```

Here, the method **m( )** will always return before the final **WriteLine( )** statement is executed. If you try to compile this method, you will receive a warning. In general, unreachable code constitutes a mistake on your part, so it is a good idea to take unreachable code warnings seriously!

Use Parameters

It is possible to pass one or more values to a method when the method is called. As explained, a value passed to a method is called an *argument*. Inside the method, the variable that receives the argument is called a *formal parameter*, or just *parameter*, for short. Parameters are declared inside the parentheses that follow the method's name. The parameter declaration syntax is the same as that used for variables. The scope of a parameter is the body of its method. Aside from its special task of receiving an argument, it acts like any other local variable.

Here is a simple example that uses a parameter. Inside the **ChkNum** class, the method **IsEven( )** returns **true** if the value that it is passed is even. It returns **false** otherwise. Therefore, **IsEven( )** has a return type of **bool**.

```
// A simple example that uses a parameter.

using System;

// This class contains the method isEven that takes a parameter.
class ChkNum {
  // Return true if x is even.
  public bool IsEven(int x) {          Here, x is an integer parameter of IsEven( ).
    if((x%2) == 0) return true;
    else return false;
  }
}

class ParmDemo {
  static void Main() {
    ChkNum e = new ChkNum();
                                    Pass an argument to IsEven( ).
    if(e.IsEven(10)) Console.WriteLine("10 is even.");

    if(e.IsEven(9)) Console.WriteLine("9 is even.");

    if(e.IsEven(8)) Console.WriteLine("8 is even.");

  }
}
```

Here is the output produced by the program:

```
10 is even.
8 is even.
```

In the program, **IsEven( )** is called three times, and each time, a different value is passed. Let's look at this process closely. First, notice how **IsEven( )** is called. The argument is specified between the parentheses. When **IsEven( )** is called the first time, it is passed the value 10. Thus, when **IsEven( )** begins executing, the parameter **x** receives the value 10. In the second call, 9 is the argument and **x** then has the value 9. In the third call, the argument is 8, which is the value that **x** receives. The point is that the value passed as an argument when **IsEven( )** is called is the value received by its parameter, **x**.

A method can have more than one parameter. Simply declare each parameter, separating one from the next with a comma. For example, the **Factor** class defines a method called **IsFactor(( )** that determines if the first parameter is a factor of the second.

```
using System;

class Factor {
  // Determine if x is a factor of y.
  public bool IsFactor(int x, int y) {  ←———————— This method has two parameters.
    if( (y % x) == 0) return true;
    else return false;
  }
}

class IsFact {
  static void Main() {
    Factor x = new Factor();

    if(x.IsFactor(2, 20)) Console.WriteLine("2 is factor");
    if(x.IsFactor(3, 20)) Console.WriteLine("this won't be displayed");

  }
}
```

Notice that when **IsFactor( )** is called, the arguments are also separated by commas.

When using multiple parameters, each parameter specifies its own type, which can differ from the others. For example, this is perfectly valid:

```
int MyMeth(int a, double b, float c) {
 // ...
```

Add a Parameterized Method to Vehicle

You can use a parameterized method to add a new feature to the **Vehicle** class: the ability to compute the amount of fuel needed for a given distance. This new method is called **FuelNeeded( )**. This method takes the number of miles that you want to drive and returns the number of gallons of gas required. The **FuelNeeded( )** method is defined like this:

```
public double FuelNeeded(int miles) {
  return (double) miles / Mpg;
}
```

Notice that this method returns a value of type **double**. This is useful, since the amount of fuel needed for a given distance might not be an even number.

The entire **Vehicle** class that includes **FuelNeeded( )** is shown here:

```
/*
   Add a parameterized method that computes the
   fuel required for a given distance.
*/

using System;

class Vehicle {
  public int Passengers; // number of passengers
  public int FuelCap;    // fuel capacity in gallons
  public int Mpg;        // fuel consumption in miles per gallon

  // Return the range.
  public int Range() {
    return Mpg * FuelCap;
  }

  // Compute fuel needed for a given distance.
  public double FuelNeeded(int miles) {
    return (double) miles / Mpg;
  }
}

class CompFuel {
  static void Main() {
    Vehicle minivan = new Vehicle();
    Vehicle sportscar = new Vehicle();
    double gallons;
    int dist = 252;

      // Assign values to fields in minivan.
    minivan.Passengers = 7;
    minivan.FuelCap = 16;
    minivan.Mpg = 21;

    // Assign values to fields in sportscar.
    sportscar.Passengers = 2;
    sportscar.FuelCap = 14;
    sportscar.Mpg = 12;

    gallons = minivan.FuelNeeded(dist);

    Console.WriteLine("To go " + dist + " miles minivan needs " +
                      gallons + " gallons of fuel.");

    gallons = sportscar.FuelNeeded(dist);
```

Use a parameterized method to compute the fuel needed to drive the specified number of miles.

```
    Console.WriteLine("To go " + dist + " miles sportscar needs " +
                        gallons + " gallons of fuel.");
  }
}
```

The output from the program is shown here:

```
To go 252 miles minivan needs 12.0 gallons of fuel.
To go 252 miles sportscar needs 21.0 gallons of fuel.
```

Try This   Create a Help Class

If one were to try to summarize the essence of the class in a single sentence, it might be this: A class encapsulates functionality. Of course, sometimes the trick is knowing where one "functionality" ends and another begins. As a general rule, you will want your classes to be the building blocks of your larger application. To do this, each class must represent a single functional unit that performs clearly delineated actions. Thus, you will want your classes to be as small as possible—but no smaller! That is, classes that contain extraneous functionality confuse and destructure code, but classes that contain too little functionality are fragmented. What is the balance? It is at this point that the *science* of programming becomes the *art* of programming. Fortunately, most programmers find that this balancing act becomes easier with experience.

To begin gaining that experience, we will convert the help system developed in the Try This sections in Chapter 3 into a help class. Let's examine why this is a good idea. First, the help system defines one logical unit. It simply displays the syntax for C#'s control statements. Thus, its functionality is compact and well defined. Second, putting help in a class is an aesthetically pleasing approach. Whenever you want to offer the help system to a user, simply instantiate a help-system object. Finally, because help is encapsulated, it can be upgraded or changed without causing unwanted side effects in the programs that use it.

Step by Step

1. Create a new file called **HelpClassDemo.cs**. To save you some typing, you might want to copy the file from the final Try This section in Chapter 3, **Help3.cs**, into **HelpClassDemo.cs**.

2. To convert the help system into a class, you must first determine precisely what constitutes the help system. For example, in **Help3.cs**, there is code to display a menu, input the user's choice, check for a valid response, and display information about the item selected. The program also loops until a *q* is pressed. If you think about it, it is clear that the menu, the check for a valid response, and the display of the information are integral to the help system. How user input is obtained and whether repeated requests should be processed are not integral. Thus, you will create a class that displays the help information and the help menu and that checks for a valid selection. This functionality can be organized into methods, called **HelpOn( )**, **ShowMenu( )**, and **IsValid( )**.

(continued)

3. Create the **HelpOn( )** method, as shown here:

```
public void HelpOn(char what) {
  switch(what) {
    case '1':
      Console.WriteLine("The if:\n");
      Console.WriteLine("if(condition) statement;");
      Console.WriteLine("else statement;");
      break;
    case '2':
      Console.WriteLine("The switch:\n");
      Console.WriteLine("switch(expression) {");
      Console.WriteLine("  case constant:");
      Console.WriteLine("    statement sequence");
      Console.WriteLine("    break;");
      Console.WriteLine("  // ...");
      Console.WriteLine("}");
      break;
    case '3':
      Console.WriteLine("The for:\n");
      Console.Write("for(init; condition; iteration)");
      Console.WriteLine(" statement;");
      break;
    case '4':
      Console.WriteLine("The while:\n");
      Console.WriteLine("while(condition) statement;");
      break;
    case '5':
      Console.WriteLine("The do-while:\n");
      Console.WriteLine("do {");
      Console.WriteLine("  statement;");
      Console.WriteLine("} while (condition);");
      break;
    case '6':
      Console.WriteLine("The break:\n");
      Console.WriteLine("break; or break label;");
      break;
    case '7':
      Console.WriteLine("The continue:\n");
      Console.WriteLine("continue; or continue label;");
      break;
    case '8':
      Console.WriteLine("The goto:\n");
      Console.WriteLine("goto label;");
      break;
  }
  Console.WriteLine();
}
```

4. Create the **ShowMenu( )** method:

```
public void ShowMenu() {
  Console.WriteLine("Help on:");
  Console.WriteLine("  1. if");
  Console.WriteLine("  2. switch");
  Console.WriteLine("  3. for");
  Console.WriteLine("  4. while");
  Console.WriteLine("  5. do-while");
  Console.WriteLine("  6. break");
  Console.WriteLine("  7. continue");
  Console.WriteLine("  8. goto\n");
  Console.Write("Choose one (q to quit): ");
}
```

5. Create the **IsValid( )** method, shown here:

```
public bool IsValid(char ch) {
  if(ch < '1' | ch > '8' & ch != 'q') return false;
  else return true;
}
```

6. Assemble the foregoing methods into the **Help** class, shown here:

```
class Help {
  public void HelpOn(char what) {
    switch(what) {
      case '1':
        Console.WriteLine("The if:\n");
        Console.WriteLine("if(condition) statement;");
        Console.WriteLine("else statement;");
        break;
      case '2':
        Console.WriteLine("The switch:\n");
        Console.WriteLine("switch(expression) {");
        Console.WriteLine("  case constant:");
        Console.WriteLine("    statement sequence");
        Console.WriteLine("    break;");
        Console.WriteLine("  // ...");
        Console.WriteLine("}");
        break;
      case '3':
        Console.WriteLine("The for:\n");
        Console.Write("for(init; condition; iteration)");
        Console.WriteLine(" statement;");
        break;
      case '4':
        Console.WriteLine("The while:\n");
        Console.WriteLine("while(condition) statement;");
        break;
```

(continued)

```
        case '5':
          Console.WriteLine("The do-while:\n");
          Console.WriteLine("do {");
          Console.WriteLine("  statement;");
          Console.WriteLine("} while (condition);");
          break;
        case '6':
          Console.WriteLine("The break:\n");
          Console.WriteLine("break; or break label;");
          break;
        case '7':
          Console.WriteLine("The continue:\n");
          Console.WriteLine("continue; or continue label;");
          break;
        case '8':
          Console.WriteLine("The goto:\n");
          Console.WriteLine("goto label;");
          break;
      }
      Console.WriteLine();
    }

    public void ShowMenu() {
      Console.WriteLine("Help on:");
      Console.WriteLine("  1. if");
      Console.WriteLine("  2. switch");
      Console.WriteLine("  3. for");
      Console.WriteLine("  4. while");
      Console.WriteLine("  5. do-while");
      Console.WriteLine("  6. break");
      Console.WriteLine("  7. continue");
      Console.WriteLine("  8. goto\n");
      Console.Write("Choose one (q to quit): ");
    }

    public bool IsValid(char ch) {
      if(ch < '1' | ch > '8' & ch != 'q') return false;
      else return true;
    }

}
```

7. Finally, create a class called **HelpClassDemo.cs** that uses the new **Help** class. Have **Main( )** display help information until the user enters *q*. The entire listing for **HelpClassDemo.cs** is shown here:

```
// The Help system from Chapter 3 converted into a Help class.

using System;
```

```
class Help {
  public void HelpOn(char what) {
    switch(what) {
      case '1':
        Console.WriteLine("The if:\n");
        Console.WriteLine("if(condition) statement;");
        Console.WriteLine("else statement;");
        break;
      case '2':
        Console.WriteLine("The switch:\n");
        Console.WriteLine("switch(expression) {");
        Console.WriteLine("  case constant:");
        Console.WriteLine("    statement sequence");
        Console.WriteLine("    break;");
        Console.WriteLine("  // ...");
        Console.WriteLine("}");
        break;
      case '3':
        Console.WriteLine("The for:\n");
        Console.Write("for(init; condition; iteration)");
        Console.WriteLine(" statement;");
        break;
      case '4':
        Console.WriteLine("The while:\n");
        Console.WriteLine("while(condition) statement;");
        break;
      case '5':
        Console.WriteLine("The do-while:\n");
        Console.WriteLine("do {");
        Console.WriteLine("  statement;");
        Console.WriteLine("} while (condition);");
        break;
      case '6':
        Console.WriteLine("The break:\n");
        Console.WriteLine("break; or break label;");
        break;
      case '7':
        Console.WriteLine("The continue:\n");
        Console.WriteLine("continue; or continue label;");
        break;
      case '8':
        Console.WriteLine("The goto:\n");
        Console.WriteLine("goto label;");
        break;
    }
    Console.WriteLine();
  }
```

(continued)

```csharp
    // Display the help menu.
    public void ShowMenu() {
      Console.WriteLine("Help on:");
      Console.WriteLine("  1. if");
      Console.WriteLine("  2. switch");
      Console.WriteLine("  3. for");
      Console.WriteLine("  4. while");
      Console.WriteLine("  5. do-while");
      Console.WriteLine("  6. break");
      Console.WriteLine("  7. continue");
      Console.WriteLine("  8. goto\n");
      Console.Write("Choose one (q to quit): ");
    }

    // Test for a valid menu selection.
    public bool IsValid(char ch) {
      if(ch < '1' | ch > '8' & ch != 'q') return false;
      else return true;
    }

}

class HelpClassDemo {
  static void Main() {
    char choice;
    Help hlpobj = new Help();

    for(;;) {
      do {
        hlpobj.ShowMenu();
        do {
          choice = (char) Console.Read();
        } while(choice == '\n' | choice == '\r');

      } while( !hlpobj.IsValid(choice) );

      if(choice == 'q') break;

      Console.WriteLine("\n");

      hlpobj.HelpOn(choice);
    }
  }
}
```

When you try the program, you will find that it is functionally the same as the final version in Chapter 3. The advantage to this approach is that you now have a help system component that can be reused whenever it is needed.

Constructors

In the preceding examples, the instance variables of each **Vehicle** object had to be set manually using a sequence of statements, such as:

```
minivan.Passengers = 7;
minivan.FuelCap = 16;
minivan.Mpg = 21;
```

An approach like this would never be used in professionally written C# code. Aside from being error-prone (you might forget to set one of the fields), there is simply a better way to accomplish this task: the constructor.

A *constructor* initializes an object when it is created. It has the same name as its class and is syntactically similar to a method. However, constructors have no explicit return type. The general form of a constructor is shown here:

access class-name(param-list) {
  // constructor code
}

Typically, you will use a constructor to give initial values to the instance variables defined by the class, or to perform any other startup procedures required to create a fully formed object. Often, *access* is **public** because a constructor is usually called from outside its class. The *parameter-list* can be empty, or it can specify one or more parameters.

All classes have constructors, whether you define one or not, because C# automatically provides a default constructor that causes all member variables to be initialized to their default values. For most value types, the default value is zero. For **bool**, the default is **false**. For reference types, the default is null. However, once you define your own constructor, the default constructor is no longer used.

Here is a simple example that uses a constructor:

```
// A simple constructor.

using System;

class MyClass {
  public int x;

  public MyClass() {
    x = 10;
  }
}

class ConsDemo {
  static void Main() {
```

The constructor for **MyClass**.

```
    MyClass t1 = new MyClass();
    MyClass t2 = new MyClass();

    Console.WriteLine(t1.x + " " + t2.x);
  }
}
```

In this example, the constructor for **MyClass** is

```
public MyClass() {
  x = 10;
}
```

Notice that the constructor is specified as **public** because the constructor will be called from code defined outside of its class. As mentioned, most constructors are declared **public** for this reason. This constructor assigns the instance variable **x** of **MyClass** the value 10. The constructor is called by **new** when an object is created. For example, in the line

```
MyClass t1 = new MyClass();
```

the constructor **MyClass( )** is called on the **t1** object, giving **t1.x** the value 10. The same is true for **t2**. After construction, **t2.x** has the value 10. Thus, the output from the program is

```
10 10
```

Parameterized Constructors

In the preceding example, a parameterless constructor was used. While this is fine for some situations, most often, you will need a constructor that accepts one or more parameters. Parameters are added to a constructor in the same way that they are added to a method: Just declare them inside the parentheses after the constructor's name. For example, here, **MyClass** is given a parameterized constructor:

```
// A parameterized constructor.

using System;

class MyClass {
  public int x;

  public MyClass(int i) {
    x = i;                          ◄─────────── This constructor has a parameter.
  }
}

class ParmConsDemo {
  static void Main() {
    MyClass t1 = new MyClass(10);
```

```
    MyClass t2 = new MyClass(88);

    Console.WriteLine(t1.x + " " + t2.x);
  }
}
```

The output from this program is shown here:

```
10 88
```

In this version of the program, the **MyClass( )** constructor defines one parameter called **i**, which is used to initialize the instance variable, **x**. Thus, when this line executes,

```
MyClass t1 = new MyClass(10);
```

the value 10 is passed to **i**, which is then assigned to **x**.

Add a Constructor to the Vehicle Class

We can improve the **Vehicle** class by adding a constructor that automatically initializes the **Passengers**, **FuelCap**, and **Mpg** fields when an object is constructed. Pay special attention to how **Vehicle** objects are created.

```
// Add a constructor to Vehicle.

using System;

class Vehicle {
  public int Passengers; // number of passengers
  public int FuelCap;    // fuel capacity in gallons
  public int Mpg;        // fuel consumption in miles per gallon

  // This is a constructor for Vehicle.
  public Vehicle(int p, int f, int m) {
    Passengers = p;
    FuelCap = f;                                ◄——————— Constructor for Vehicle.
    Mpg = m;
  }

  // Return the range.
  public int Range() {
    return Mpg * FuelCap;
  }

  // Compute fuel needed for a given distance.
  public double FuelNeeded(int miles) {
    return (double) miles / Mpg;
  }
}
```

```
class VehConsDemo {
  static void Main() {

    // Construct complete vehicles.
    Vehicle minivan = new Vehicle(7, 16, 21);
    Vehicle sportscar = new Vehicle(2, 14, 12);
    double gallons;
    int dist = 252;

    gallons = minivan.FuelNeeded(dist);

    Console.WriteLine("To go " + dist + " miles minivan needs " +
                      gallons + " gallons of fuel.");

    gallons = sportscar.FuelNeeded(dist);

    Console.WriteLine("To go " + dist + " miles sportscar needs " +
                      gallons + " gallons of fuel.");

  }
}
```

Pass information to **Vehicle** through its constructor.

Both **minivan** and **sportscar** were initialized by the **Vehicle( )** constructor when they were created. Each object is initialized as specified in the parameters to its constructor. For example, in the following line:

```
Vehicle minivan = new Vehicle(7, 16, 21);
```

the values 7, 16, and 21 are passed to the **Vehicle( )** constructor when **new** creates the object. Thus, **minivan**'s copy of **Passengers**, **FuelCap**, and **Mpg** will contain the values 7, 16, and 21, respectively. Therefore, the output from this program is the same as that of the previous version.

The new Operator Revisited

Now that you know more about classes and their constructors, let's take a closer look at the **new** operator. It has this general form:

new *class-name(arg-list)*

Here, *class-name* is the name of the class that is being instantiated. The class name followed by parentheses specifies the constructor for the class, as described by the preceding section. If a class does not define its own constructor, **new** will use the default constructor supplied by C#.

Since memory is finite, it is possible that **new** will not be able to allocate memory for an object because insufficient memory exists. If this happens, a runtime exception will occur. (You will learn about exceptions in Chapter 9.) For the sample programs in this book, you won't need to worry about running out of memory, but you will need to consider this possibility in real-world programs that you write.

Ask the Expert

Q: Why don't I need to use new **for variables of the value types, such as** int **or** float?

A: In C#, a variable of a value type contains its own value. Memory to hold this value is automatically provided when the program is run. Thus, there is no need to explicitly allocate this memory using **new**. Conversely, a reference variable stores a reference to an object. The memory to hold this object is allocated dynamically during execution.

Not making the fundamental types, such as **int** or **char**, into reference types greatly improves the performance of your program. When using a reference type, there is a layer of indirection that adds overhead to each object access. This overhead is avoided by a value type.

As a point of interest, it is permitted to use **new** with the value types, as shown here:

```
int i = new int();
```

Doing so invokes the default constructor for type **int**, which initializes **i** to zero. In general, invoking **new** for a value type invokes the default constructor for that type. It does not, however, dynamically allocate memory. Frankly, most programmers do not use **new** with the value types.

Garbage Collection and Destructors

As you have seen, objects are dynamically allocated from a pool of free memory by using the **new** operator. Of course, memory is not infinite, and the free memory can be exhausted. Thus, it is possible for **new** to fail because there is insufficient free memory to create the desired object. For this reason, one of the key components of any dynamic allocation scheme is the recovery of free memory from unused objects, making that memory available for subsequent reallocation. In many programming languages, the release of previously allocated memory is handled manually. For example, in C++, you use the **delete** operator to free memory that was allocated. However, C# uses a different, more trouble-free approach: *garbage collection.*

C#'s garbage collection system reclaims objects automatically—occurring transparently, behind the scenes, without any programmer intervention. It works like this: When no references to an object exist, that object is assumed to be no longer needed, and the memory occupied by the object is released. This recycled memory can then be used for a subsequent allocation.

Garbage collection occurs only sporadically during the execution of your program. It will not occur simply because one or more objects exist that are no longer used. Thus, you can't know precisely when garbage collection will take place.

Destructors

It is possible to define a method that will be called just prior to an object's final destruction by the garbage collector. This method is called a *destructor,* and it can be used in some highly specialized situations to ensure that an object terminates cleanly. For example, you might use a destructor to ensure that a system resource owned by an object is released. It must be stated at the outset that destructors are a very advanced feature that are applicable to certain specialized situations. They are not normally needed. However, because they are part of C#, they are briefly described here for completeness.

Destructors have this general form:

~class-name( ) {
  // destruction code
}

Here, *class-name* is the name of the class. Thus, a destructor is declared like a constructor, except that it is preceded with a ~ (tilde). Notice it has no return type.

It is important to understand that the destructor is called just prior to garbage collection. It is not called when a variable containing a reference to an object goes out of scope, for example. (This differs from destructors in C++, which *are* called when an object goes out of scope.) This means that you cannot know precisely when a destructor will be executed. Furthermore, it is possible for your program to end before garbage collection occurs, so a destructor might not get called at all.

The this Keyword

Before concluding this chapter, it is necessary to introduce **this**. When a method is called, it is automatically passed a reference to the invoking object (that is, the object on which the method is called). This reference is called **this**. Therefore, **this** refers to the object on which the method is acting. To understand **this**, first consider a program that creates a class called **Pwr** that computes the result of a number raised to some integer power:

```
using System;

class Pwr {
  public double b;
  public int e;
  public double val;

  public Pwr(double num, int exp) {
    b = num;
    e = exp;

    val = 1;
    for( ; exp>0; exp--) val = val * b;
  }
```

```
  public double GetPwr() {
    return val;
  }
}

class DemoPwr {
  static void Main() {
    Pwr x = new Pwr(4.0, 2);
    Pwr y = new Pwr(2.5, 1);
    Pwr z = new Pwr(5.7, 0);

    Console.WriteLine(x.b + " raised to the " + x.e +
                      " power is " + x.GetPwr());
    Console.WriteLine(y.b + " raised to the " + y.e +
                      " power is " + y.GetPwr());
    Console.WriteLine(z.b + " raised to the " + z.e +
                      " power is " + z.GetPwr());
  }
}
```

As you know, within a method, the other members of a class can be accessed directly, without any object or class qualification. Thus, inside **GetPwr( )**, the statement

```
return val;
```

means that the copy of **val** associated with the invoking object will be returned. However, the same statement can also be written like this:

```
return this.val;
```

Here, **this** refers to the object on which **GetPwr( )** was called. Thus, **this.val** refers to that object's copy of **val**. For example, if **GetPwr( )** had been invoked on **x**, then **this** in the preceding statement would have been referring to **x**. Writing the statement without using **this** is really just shorthand.

It is also possible to use **this** inside a constructor. In this case, **this** refers to the object that is being constructed. For example, inside **Pwr( )**, the statements

```
b = num;
e = exp;
```

can be written like this:

```
this.b = num;
this.e = exp;
```

Of course, there is no benefit in doing so in this case.

Here is the entire **Pwr** class written using the **this** reference:

```
// Demonstrate this.
class Pwr {
  public double b;
  public int e;
  public double val;

  public Pwr(double num, int exp) {
    this.b = num;
    this.e = exp;

    this.val = 1;
    for( ; exp>0; exp--) this.val = this.val * this.b;
  }

  public double GetPwr() {
    return this.val;
  }
}
```

Actually, no C# programmer would use **this** to write **Pwr** as just shown because nothing is gained and the standard form is easier. However, **this** has some important uses. For example, C# permits the name of a parameter or a local variable to be the same as the name of an instance variable. When this happens, the local name *hides* the instance variable. You can gain access to the hidden instance variable by referring to it through **this**. For example, the following is a syntactically valid way to write the **Pwr( )** constructor:

```
public Pwr(double b, int e) {
  this.b = b;
  this.e = e;

  val = 1;
  for( ; e>0; e--) val = val * b;
}
```

Here **this.b** refers to the **b** instance variable, not the parameter.

In this version, the names of the parameters are the same as the names of the instance variables, thus hiding them. However, **this** is used to "uncover" the instance variables.

Chapter 4 Self Test

1. What is the difference between a class and an object?

2. How is a class defined?

3. What does each object have its own copy of?

4. Using two separate statements, show how to declare an object called **counter** of a class called **MyCounter**, and assign it a reference to an object.

5. Show how a method called **MyMeth( )** is declared if it has a return type of **double** and has two **int** parameters called **a** and **b**.

6. How must a method return if it returns a value?

7. What name does a constructor have?

8. What does **new** do?

9. What is garbage collection and how does it work? What is a destructor?

10. What is **this**?

Chapter 5

More Data Types
and Operators

Key Skills & Concepts

- One-dimensional arrays

- Multidimensional arrays

- Jagged arrays

- The **Length** property

- Implicitly typed arrays

- Strings

- The **foreach** loop

- The bitwise operators

- The **?** operator

This chapter returns to the subject of C#'s data types and operators. It discusses arrays, the **string** type, the bitwise operators, and the **?** conditional operator. Along the way, the **foreach** loop is introduced.

Arrays

An *array* is a collection of variables of the same type that are referred to by a common name. In C#, arrays can have one or more dimensions, although the one-dimensional array is the most common. Arrays are used for a variety of purposes because they offer a convenient means of grouping together related variables. For example, you might use an array to hold a record of the daily high temperature for a month, a list of users logged onto a network, or your collection of programming books.

The principal advantage of an array is that it organizes data in such a way that it can be easily manipulated. For example, if you have an array containing the incomes for a selected group of households, it is easy to compute the average income by cycling through the array. Also, arrays organize data in such a way that it can be easily sorted.

Although arrays in C# can be used just like arrays in many other programming languages, they have one special attribute: They are implemented as objects. This fact is one reason that a discussion of arrays was deferred until objects had been introduced. By implementing arrays as objects, several important advantages are gained, not the least of which is that unused arrays can be garbage-collected.

One-Dimensional Arrays

A one-dimensional array is a list of related variables. Such lists are common in programming. For example, you might use a one-dimensional array to store the account numbers of the active users on a network. Another array might be used to store the current batting averages for a baseball team.

Since arrays in C# are implemented as objects, two steps are needed to obtain one for use in your program. First, you must declare a variable that can refer to an array. Second, you must create an instance of the array by use of **new**. Therefore, to declare a one-dimensional array, you will typically use this general form:

type[ ] *array-name* = new *type*[*size*];

Here, *type* declares the *element type* of the array. The element type determines the data type of the elements that comprise the array. Notice the square brackets that follow *type*. They indicate that a reference to a one-dimensional array is being declared. The number of elements that the array will hold is determined by *size*.

Here is an example. The following creates an **int** array of ten elements and links it to an array reference variable named **sample**:

```
int[] sample = new int[10];
```

The **sample** variable holds a reference to the memory allocated by **new**. This memory is large enough to hold ten elements of type **int**.

As is the case when creating an instance of a class, it is possible to break the preceding declaration in two. For example:

```
int[] sample;
sample = new int[10];
```

In this case, when **sample** is first created, it refers to no physical object. It is only after the second statement executes that **sample** refers to an array.

An individual element within an array is accessed by use of an index. An *index* describes the position of an element within an array. In C#, all arrays have zero as the index of their first element. Because **sample** has ten elements, it has index values of 0 through 9. To index an array, specify the number of the element you want, surrounded by square brackets. Thus, the first element in **sample** is **sample[0]**, and the last element is **sample[9]**. For example, the following program loads **sample** with the numbers 0 through 9:

```
// Demonstrate a one-dimensional array.

using System;

class ArrayDemo {
  static void Main() {
    int[] sample = new int[10];
    int i;
```

```
    for(i = 0; i < 10; i++)
      sample[i] = i;
                                        ———— Array indexes begin at zero.
    for(i = 0; i < 10; i++)
      Console.WriteLine("This is sample[" + i + "]: " + sample[i]);
  }
}
```

The output from the program is shown here:

```
This is sample[0]: 0
This is sample[1]: 1
This is sample[2]: 2
This is sample[3]: 3
This is sample[4]: 4
This is sample[5]: 5
This is sample[6]: 6
This is sample[7]: 7
This is sample[8]: 8
This is sample[9]: 9
```

Conceptually, the **sample** array looks like this:

0	1	2	3	4	5	6	7	8	9
sample [0]	sample [1]	sample [2]	sample [3]	sample [4]	sample [5]	sample [6]	sample [7]	sample [8]	sample [9]

Arrays are common in programming because they let you deal easily with large numbers of related variables. For example, the following program finds the minimum and maximum values stored in the **nums** array by cycling through the array using a **for** loop:

```
// Find the minimum and maximum values in an array.

using System;

class MinMax {
  static void Main() {
    int[] nums = new int[10];
    int min, max;

    nums[0] = 99;
    nums[1] = -10;
    nums[2] = 100123;
    nums[3] = 18;
```

```
    nums[4]  =  -978;
    nums[5]  =  5623;
    nums[6]  =  463;
    nums[7]  =  -9;
    nums[8]  =  287;
    nums[9]  =  49;

    min = max = nums[0];

    // Find the minimum and maximum value in the array.
    for(int i=1; i < 10; i++) {
      if(nums[i] < min) min = nums[i];
      if(nums[i] > max) max = nums[i];
    }

    Console.WriteLine("min and max: " + min + " " + max);
  }
}
```

The output from the program is shown here:

```
min and max: -978 100123
```

Initialize an Array

In the preceding program, the **nums** array was given values by hand, using ten separate assignment statements. While perfectly correct, there is an easier way to do this. Arrays can be initialized when they are created. The general form for initializing a one-dimensional array is shown here:

type[ ] *array-name* = { *val1*, *val2*, *val3*, ... , *valN* };

Here, the initial values are specified by *val1* through *valN*. They are assigned in sequence, left to right, in index order. C# automatically allocates an array large enough to hold the initializers that you specify. There is no need to explicitly use the **new** operator. For example, here is a better way to write the **MinMax** program:

```
// Use array initializers.

using System;

class MinMax {
  static void Main() {
    int[] nums = { 99, -10, 100123, 18, -978,          Array initializers.
                   5623, 463, -9, 287, 49 };
    int min, max;
```

```
    min = max = nums[0];
    for(int i=1; i < 10; i++) {
      if(nums[i] < min) min = nums[i];
      if(nums[i] > max) max = nums[i];
    }
    Console.WriteLine("Min and max: " + min + " " + max);
  }
}
```

As a point of interest, although not needed, you can use **new** when initializing an array. For example, this is a proper, but redundant, way to initialize **nums** in the foregoing program:

```
int[] nums = new int[] { 99, -10, 100123, 18, -978,
                         5623, 463, -9, 287, 49 };
```

While redundant here, the **new** form of array initialization is useful when you are assigning a new array to an already existent array reference variable. For example:

```
int[] nums;
nums = new int[] { 99, -10, 100123, 18, -978,
                   5623, 463, -9, 287, 49 };
```

In this case, **nums** is declared in the first statement and initialized by the second.

Boundaries Are Enforced

Array boundaries are strictly enforced in C#; it is a runtime error to overrun or underrun the end of an array. If you want to confirm this for yourself, try the following program that purposely overruns an array:

```
// Demonstrate an array overrun.

using System;

class ArrayErr {
  static void Main() {
    int[] sample = new int[10];

    // Generate an array overrun.
    for(int i = 0; i < 100; i++)
      sample[i] = i;              ← ———— Overrun the end of sample.
  }
}
```

As soon as **i** reaches 10, an **IndexOutOfRangeException** is generated and the program is terminated.

Try This Sort an Array

Because a one-dimensional array organizes data into an indexable linear list, it is the perfect data structure for sorting. Furthermore, sorting algorithms make some of the best examples of array handling. Towards that end, this example develops a version of the rather infamous *bubble sort*. As you may know, there are a number of different sorting algorithms. There are the quicksort, the shaker sort, and the Shell sort, to name just three. However, one of the simplest and easiest-to-understand sorting algorithms is the bubble sort. It is also one of the worst sorts in terms of performance (although it can sometimes be used effectively for sorting very small arrays). The bubble sort does have one useful characteristic, however: It makes an interesting example of array handling!

Step by Step

1. Create a file called **Bubble.cs**.

2. The bubble sort gets its name from the way it performs the sorting operation. It uses the repeated comparison and, if necessary, exchange of adjacent elements in the array. In this process, small values move toward one end and large ones toward the other end. The process is conceptually similar to bubbles finding their own level in a tank of water. The bubble sort operates by making several passes through the array, exchanging out-of-place elements when necessary. The number of passes required to ensure that the array is sorted is equal to one less than the number of elements in the array.

   Here is the code that forms the core of the bubble sort. The array being sorted here is called **nums**.

   ```
   // This is the bubble sort.
   for(a=1; a < size; a++)
     for(b=size-1; b >= a; b--) {
       if(nums[b-1] > nums[b]) { // if out of order
         // Exchange out-of-order elements.
         t = nums[b-1];
         nums[b-1] = nums[b];
         nums[b] = t;
       }
     }
   ```

   Notice that the sort relies on two **for** loops. The inner loop checks adjacent elements in the array, looking for out-of-order elements. When an out-of-order element pair is found, the two elements are exchanged. With each pass, the smallest element of those remaining moves into its proper location. The outer loop causes this process to repeat until the entire array has been sorted.

3. Here is the entire **Bubble** program:

   ```
   // Demonstrate the bubble sort.

   using System;
   ```

   (continued)

```
class Bubble {
  static void Main() {
    int[] nums = { 99, -10, 100123, 18, -978,
                   5623, 463, -9, 287, 49 };
    int a, b, t;
    int size;

    // Set the number of elements to sort.
    size = 10;

    // Display the original array.
    Console.Write("Original array is:");
    for(int i=0; i < size; i++)
      Console.Write(" " + nums[i]);
    Console.WriteLine();

    // This is the bubble sort.
    for(a=1; a < size; a++)
      for(b=size-1; b >= a; b--) {
        if(nums[b-1] > nums[b]) {
          // Exchange out-of-order elements.
          t = nums[b-1];
          nums[b-1] = nums[b];
          nums[b] = t;
        }
      }

    // Display the sorted array.
    Console.Write("Sorted array is:");
    for(int i=0; i < size; i++)
      Console.Write(" " + nums[i]);
    Console.WriteLine();
  }
}
```

The output from the program is shown here:

```
Original array is: 99 -10 100123 18 -978 5623 463 -9 287 49
Sorted array is: -978 -10 -9 18 49 99 287 463 5623 100123
```

4. As it is shown, **Bubble** sorts an array of **int**s, but you can change the type of data being sorted by changing the type of the **nums** array and **t**. For example, to sort an array of **double**s, both **nums** and **t** must be of type **double**.

5. As mentioned, although the bubble sort provides an excellent example of array handling, it is not a good sort in most cases. The best general-purpose sorting algorithm is the quicksort. The quicksort, however, relies on features of C# that are described in Chapter 6. Therefore, the creation of a quicksort is deferred until then.

Multidimensional Arrays

Although the one-dimensional array is the most commonly used, multidimensional arrays are certainly not rare. A multidimensional array is an array that has two or more dimensions, and an individual element is accessed through the combination of two or more indices.

Two-Dimensional Arrays

The simplest form of the multidimensional array is the two-dimensional array. In a two-dimensional array, the location of an element is specified by two indices. Think of a two-dimensional array as a table of information: one index indicates the row, the other indicates the column.

To declare a two-dimensional integer array **table** of size 10, 20, you would write

```
int[,] table = new int[10, 20];
```

Pay careful attention to the declaration. Notice that the two dimensions are separated by a comma. In the first part of the declaration, the syntax

```
[,]
```

indicates that a two-dimensional array reference variable is being created. When memory is actually allocated for the array using **new**, this syntax is used:

```
int[10, 20]
```

This creates a 10×20 array, and again, the comma separates the dimensions.

To access an element in a two-dimensional array, you must specify both indices, separating the two with a comma. For example, to assign the value 10 to location 3, 5 of array **table**, you would use

```
table[3, 5] = 10;
```

Here is a complete example. It loads a two-dimensional array with the numbers 1 through 12 and then displays the contents of the array.

```
// Demonstrate a two-dimensional array.

using System;

class TwoD {
  static void Main() {
    int t, i;
    int[,] table = new int[3, 4];    ◄——— Declare a 3 by 4 two-dimensional array.

    for(t=0; t < 3; ++t) {
      for(i=0; i < 4; ++i) {
        table[t,i] = (t*4)+i+1;
        Console.Write(table[t,i] + " ");
      }
```

```
        Console.WriteLine();
    }
  }
}
```

In this example, **table[0, 0]** will have the value 1, **table[0, 1]** the value 2, **table[0, 2]** the value 3, and so on. The value of **table[2, 3]** will be 12. Conceptually, the array will look like that shown in Figure 5-1.

Arrays of Three or More Dimensions

C# allows arrays with more than two dimensions. Here is the general form of a multidimensional array declaration:

type[,...,] name = new *type[size1,size2,...,sizeN]*;

For example, the following declaration creates a 4×10×3 three-dimensional integer array:

```
int[,,] multidim = new int[4, 10, 3];
```

To assign element 2, 4, 1 of **multidim** the value 100, use this statement:

```
multidim[2, 4, 1] = 100;
```

Initialize Multidimensional Arrays

A multidimensional array can be initialized by enclosing each dimension's initializer list within its own set of curly braces. For example, the general form of array initialization for a two-dimensional array is shown here:

type[,] array_name = {
  { *val, val, val, ..., val* },
  { *val, val, val, ..., val* },

  .

  .

  .

  { *val, val, val, ..., val* }
};

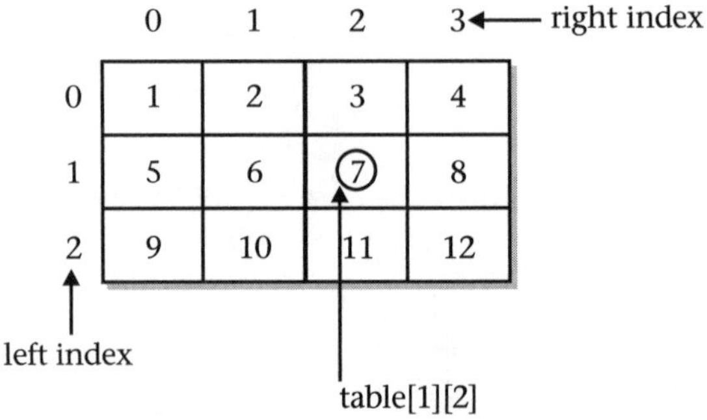

Figure 5-1   A conceptual view of the **table** array created by the **TwoD** program

Here, *val* indicates an initialization value. Each inner block designates a row. Within each row, the first value will be stored in the first position of the row, the second value in the second position, and so on. Notice that commas separate the initializer blocks and that a semicolon follows the closing curly brace.

For example, the following program initializes an array called **sqrs** with the numbers 1 through 5 and their squares:

```
// Initialize a two-dimensional array.

using System;

class Squares {
  static void Main() {
    int[,] sqrs = {
      { 1, 1 },
      { 2, 4 },
      { 3, 9 },          <───────── Notice how each row has its own set of initializers.
      { 4, 16 },
      { 5, 25 },
    };
    int i, j;

    for(i=0; i < 5; i++) {
      for(j=0; j < 2; j++)
        Console.Write(sqrs[i,j] + " ");
      Console.WriteLine();
    }
  }
}
```

Here is the output from the program:

```
1 1
2 4
3 9
4 16
5 25
```

Jagged Arrays

In the preceding examples, when you created a two-dimensional array, you were creating what C# calls a *rectangular array*. Thinking of two-dimensional arrays as tables, a rectangular array is a two-dimensional array in which the length of each row is the same for the entire array. However, C# also allows you to create a special type of two-dimensional array called a *jagged array*. A jagged array is an *array of arrays* in which the length of each array can differ. Thus, a jagged array can be used to create a table in which the row lengths are not the same.

Jagged arrays are declared by using sets of square brackets to indicate each dimension. For example, to declare a two-dimensional jagged array, you will use this general form:

type[ ] [ ] *array-name* = new *type*[*size*][ ];

Here, *size* indicates the number of rows in the array. The rows themselves have not been allocated. Instead, the rows are allocated individually. This allows for the length of each row to vary. For example, the following code allocates memory for the first dimension of **jagged** when it is declared. It then allocates the second dimensions manually.

```
int[][] jagged = new int[3][];
jagged[0] = new int[2];
jagged[1] = new int[3];
jagged[2] = new int[4];
```

After this sequence executes, jagged looks like this:

jagged [0][0]	jagged [0][1]		
jagged [1][0]	jagged [1][1]	jagged [1][2]	
jagged [2][0]	jagged [2][1]	jagged [2][2]	jagged [2][3]

It is easy to see how jagged arrays got their name!

Once a jagged array has been created, an element is accessed by specifying each index within its own set of brackets. For example, to assign the value 10 to element 2, 1 of **jagged**, you would use this statement:

```
jagged[2][1] = 10;
```

Note that this differs from the syntax that is used to access an element of a rectangular array.

Here is an example that uses a jagged two-dimensional array. Assume that you are writing a program that stores the number of passengers that ride an airport shuttle. If the shuttle runs ten times a day during the week and twice a day on Saturday and Sunday, you could use the **riders** array shown in the following program to store the information. Notice that the length of the second dimension for the first five dimensions is 10 and that the length of the second dimension for the last two dimensions is 2.

```
// Demonstrate jagged arrays.

using System;

class Jagged {
  static void Main() {
    int[][] riders = new int[7][];
```

```
riders[0] = new int[10];
riders[1] = new int[10];
riders[2] = new int[10];          Here, the second dimensions
riders[3] = new int[10];          are 10 elements long.
riders[4] = new int[10];

riders[5] = new int[2];
riders[6] = new int[2];           But here, they are 2 elements long.

int i, j;

// Fabricate some data.
for(i=0; i < 5; i++)
  for(j=0; j < 10; j++)
    riders[i][j] = i + j + 10;
for(i=5; i < 7; i++)
  for(j=0; j < 2; j++)
    riders[i][j] = i + j + 10;

Console.WriteLine("Riders per trip during the week:");
for(i=0; i < 5; i++) {
  for(j=0; j < 10; j++)
    Console.Write(riders[i][j] + " ");
  Console.WriteLine();
}
Console.WriteLine();

Console.WriteLine("Riders per trip on the weekend:");
for(i=5; i < 7; i++) {
  for(j=0; j < 2; j++)
    Console.Write(riders[i][j] + " ");
  Console.WriteLine();
  }
 }
}
```

Jagged arrays will not be used by all applications, but they can be very effective in some situations. For example, if you need a very large two-dimensional array that is sparsely populated (that is, one in which not all of the elements will be used), then a jagged array might be a perfect solution.

Assign Array References

As with other objects, when you assign one array reference variable to another, you are simply making both variables refer to the same array. You are not causing a copy of the array to be made, nor are you causing the contents of one array to be copied to the other. For example, consider this program:

```
// Assign array reference variables.

using System;

class AssignARef {
  static void Main() {
    int i;

    int[] nums1 = new int[10];
    int[] nums2 = new int[10];

    // Give nums1 and nums2 some values.
    for(i=0; i < 10; i++) nums1[i] = i;
    for(i=0; i < 10; i++) nums2[i] = -i;

    Console.Write("Here is nums1: ");
    for(i=0; i < 10; i++)
      Console.Write(nums1[i] + " ");
    Console.WriteLine();

    Console.Write("Here is nums2: ");
    for(i=0; i < 10; i++)
      Console.Write(nums2[i] + " ");
    Console.WriteLine();

    // Now nums2 refers to nums1.
    nums2 = nums1;                      ←———————— Assign one array reference to another.

    Console.Write("Here is nums2 after assignment: ");
    for(i=0; i < 10; i++)
      Console.Write(nums2[i] + " ");
    Console.WriteLine();

    // Operate on nums1 array through nums2.
    nums2[3] = 99;

    Console.Write("Here is nums1 after change through nums2: ");
    for(i=0; i < 10; i++)
      Console.Write(nums1[i] + " ");
    Console.WriteLine();
  }
}
```

The output from the program is shown here:

```
Here is nums1: 0 1 2 3 4 5 6 7 8 9
Here is nums2: 0 -1 -2 -3 -4 -5 -6 -7 -8 -9
Here is nums2 after assignment: 0 1 2 3 4 5 6 7 8 9
Here is nums1 after change through nums2: 0 1 2 99 4 5 6 7 8 9
```

As the output shows, after the assignment of **nums1** to **nums2**, both array reference variables refer to the same object.

Use the Length Property with Arrays

A number of benefits result because C# implements arrays as objects. One comes from the fact that each array has associated with it a **Length** property that contains the number of elements that an array can hold. Thus, each array provides a means by which its length can be determined. Here is a program that demonstrates the **Length** property:

```
// Use the Length array property.

using System;

class LengthDemo {
  static void Main() {
    int[] list = new int[10];
    int[,] twoD = new int[3, 4];
    int[] nums = { 1, 2, 3 };

    // A variable-length table.
    int[][] table = new int[3][];

    // Add second dimensions.
    table[0] = new int[] {1, 2, 3};
    table[1] = new int[] {4, 5};
    table[2] = new int[] {6, 7, 8, 9};

    Console.WriteLine("length of list is " + list.Length);
    Console.WriteLine("length of twoD is " + twoD.Length);
    Console.WriteLine("length of nums is " + nums.Length);
    Console.WriteLine("length of table is " + table.Length);
    Console.WriteLine("length of table[0] is " + table[0].Length);
    Console.WriteLine("length of table[1] is " + table[1].Length);
    Console.WriteLine("length of table[2] is " + table[2].Length);
    Console.WriteLine();

    // Use Length to initialize list.
    for(int i=0; i < list.Length; i++)
      list[i] = i * i;
```

Show the length of the arrays.

Use **Length** to control a **for** loop.

```
    Console.Write("Here is list: ");
    // now use Length to display list
    for(int i=0; i < list.Length; i++)
      Console.Write(list[i] + " ");
    Console.WriteLine();
  }
}
```

This program displays the following output:

```
length of list is 10
length of twoD is 12
length of nums is 3
length of table is 3
length of table[0] is 3
length of table[1] is 2
length of table[2] is 4

Here is list: 0 1 4 9 16 25 36 49 64 81
```

There are several points of interest in this program. First, the length of **list**, which is a one-dimensional array, is equal to its declared length of 10. Second, the length of **twoD**, a 3 by 4 two-dimensional array, is 12, which is the total number of elements that it contains. In general, the length of a multidimensional array is equal to all of the elements that it can hold. However, this situation is different for jagged arrays.

As you know, a jagged array is an array of arrays. Therefore, in the program, **table** is a jagged array that has two dimensions. Pay special attention to the way **Length** is used with it. First, the expression

```
table.Length
```

obtains the number of *arrays* stored in **table**, which, in this case, is 3. To obtain the length of any individual array in **table**, use an expression such as this:

```
table[0].Length
```

which, in this case, obtains the length of the first array, which is 3.

One other thing to notice in **LengthDemo** is the way that **list.Length** is used by the **for** loops to govern the number of iterations that take place. Since each array carries with it its own length, you can use this information rather than manually keeping track of an array's size. Keep in mind that the value of **Length** has nothing to do with the number of elements that you are actually using. It contains the number of elements that the array is capable of holding.

The inclusion of the **Length** property simplifies many algorithms by making certain types of array operations easier—and safer—to perform. For example, the following program uses **Length** to copy one array to another while preventing an array overrun and its attendant runtime exception:

```
// Use Length property to help copy an array.

using System;

class ACopy {
  static void Main() {
    int i;
    int[] nums1 = new int[10];
    int[] nums2 = new int[10];

    for(i=0; i < nums1.Length; i++) nums1[i] = i;

    // Copy nums1 to nums2.
    if(nums2.Length >= nums1.Length)
      for(i = 0; i < nums2.Length; i++)
        nums2[i] = nums1[i];

    for(i=0; i < nums2.Length; i++)
      Console.Write(nums2[i] + " ");
  }
}
```

Confirm that the target array is large enough to hold all the elements from the source array.

Here, **Length** helps perform two important functions. First, it is used to confirm that the target array is large enough to hold the contents of the source array. Second, it provides the termination condition of the **for** loop that performs the copy. Of course, in this simple example, the size of the arrays is easily known, but this same approach can be applied to a wide range of more challenging situations.

Create an Implicitly Typed Array

As explained in Chapter 2, C# 3.0 adds the ability to declare implicitly typed variables by the use of the **var** keyword. These are variables whose type is determined by the compiler, based on the type of the initializing expression. Thus, all implicitly typed variables must be initialized. Using the same mechanism, it is also possible to create an implicitly typed array. As a general rule, implicitly typed arrays are for use in certain types of queries involving LINQ, which is described later in this book. In most other cases, you will use the "normal" array declaration approach. Implicitly typed arrays are introduced here for completeness.

An implicitly typed array is declared using the keyword **var**, but you *do not* follow **var** with [ ]. Furthermore, the array must be initialized. It is the type of initializer that determines the element type of the array. All of the initializers must be of the same or a compatible type. Here is an example of an implicitly typed array:

```
var vals = new[] { 1, 2, 3, 4, 5 };
```

This creates an array of **int** that is five elements long. A reference to that array is assigned to **vals**. Thus, the type of **vals** is "array of **int**" and it has five elements. Again, notice that **var** is not followed by [ ]. Also, even though the array is being initialized, you must include **new[ ]**. It's not optional in this context.

Here is another example. It creates a two-dimensional array of **double**.

```
var vals = new[,] { {1.1, 2.2}, {3.3, 4.4},{ 5.5, 6.6} };
```

In this case, **vals** has the dimensions 2 by 3.

As mentioned, implicitly typed arrays are most applicable to LINQ-based queries. They are not meant for general use. In most cases, you should use explicitly typed arrays.

Try This Create a Simple Queue Class

As you may know, a *data structure* is a means of organizing data. The simplest data structure is the array, which is a linear list that supports random access to its elements. Arrays are often used as the underpinning for more sophisticated data structures, such as stacks and queues. A *stack* is a list in which elements can be accessed in first-in, last-out (FILO) order only. A *queue* is a list in which elements can be accessed in first-in, first-out (FIFO) order only. Thus, a stack is like a stack of plates on a table; the first down is the last to be used. A queue is like a line at a bank; the first in line is the first served.

What makes data structures such as stacks and queues interesting is that they combine storage for information with the methods that access that information. Thus, stacks and queues are *data engines* in which storage and retrieval are provided by the data structure itself and not manually by your program. Such a combination is, obviously, an excellent choice for a class, and in this project, you will create a simple queue class.

In general, queues support two basic operations: *put* and *get*. Each *put* operation places a new element on the end of the queue. Each *get* operation retrieves the next element from the front of the queue. Queue operations are consumptive. Once an element has been retrieved, it cannot be retrieved again. The queue can also become full if there is no space available to store an item, and it can become empty if all of the elements have been removed.

There are many different ways to implement a queue. For the sake of brevity, the one we will use is probably the simplest. It creates a single-use, fixed-size queue in which empty locations *are not* reused. Thus, the queue eventually becomes exhausted and must be discarded. While such queues are quite limited, they are occasionally very useful. For example, such a queue might hold a list of data produced by one process and consumed by another. In this situation, neither the producer nor the consumer would want to reuse a queue. When more data is generated, a new queue is created. The previous queue is simply discarded and eventually garbage-collected.

Of course, much more sophisticated queues are possible. Later in this book, you will see another way to implement a queue, called a *circular queue,* that reuses empty locations in the underlying array when elements are removed. Thus, a circular queue can continue to have elements put in as long as elements are also being taken out. You will also see how to create a dynamic queue, which will automatically expand to hold more elements. But for now, a simple queue will do.

Step by Step

1. Create a file called **QDemo.cs**.

2. Although there are other ways to support a queue, the method we will use is based upon an array. That is, an array will provide the storage for the items put into the queue. This array will be accessed through two indices. The *put* index determines where the next element of data will be stored. The *get* index indicates at what location the next element of data will be obtained. Keep in mind that the *get* operation is consumptive, and it is not possible to retrieve the same element twice. Although the queue that we will be creating stores characters, the same logic can be used to store any type of object. Begin creating the **SimpleQueue** class with these lines:

```
class SimpleQueue {
  public char[] q; // this array holds the queue
  public int putloc, getloc; // the put and get indices
```

3. The constructor for the **SimpleQueue** class creates a queue of a given size. Here is the **SimpleQueue** constructor:

```
public SimpleQueue(int size) {
  q = new char[size+1]; // allocate memory for queue
  putloc = getloc = 0;
}
```

Notice that the queue is created one size larger than the size specified in **size**. Because of the way the queue algorithm will be implemented, one array location will be unused, so the array must be created one size larger than the requested queue size. The **putloc** and **getloc** indices are initially set to zero.

4. The **Put( )** method, which stores elements, is shown next:

```
// Put a character into the queue.
public void Put(char ch) {
  if(putloc==q.Length-1) {
    Console.WriteLine(" -- Queue is full.");
    return;
  }

  putloc++;
  q[putloc] = ch;
}
```

The method begins by checking for a queue-full condition. If **putloc** is equal to the last location in the **q** array, there is no more room in which to store elements. Otherwise, **putloc** is incremented and the new element is stored at that location. Thus, **putloc** is always the index of the last element stored.

(continued)

5. To retrieve elements, use the **Get( )** method, shown next:

```
// Get a character from the queue.
public char Get() {
  if(getloc == putloc) {
    Console.WriteLine(" -- Queue is empty.");
    return (char) 0;
  }

  getloc++;
  return q[getloc];
}
```

Notice first the check for queue-empty. If **getloc** and **putloc** both index the same element, the queue is assumed to be empty. This is why **getloc** and **putloc** were both initialized to zero by the **SimpleQueue** constructor. Next, **getloc** is incremented and the next element is returned. Thus, **getloc** always indicates the location of the last element retrieved.

6. Here is the entire **QDemo.cs** program:

```
// A simple queue class for characters.

using System;

class SimpleQueue {
  public char[] q; // this array holds the queue
  public int putloc, getloc; // the put and get indices

  public SimpleQueue(int size) {
    q = new char[size+1]; // allocate memory for queue
    putloc = getloc = 0;
  }

  // Put a character into the queue.
  public void Put(char ch) {
    if(putloc==q.Length-1) {
      Console.WriteLine(" -- Queue is full.");
      return;
    }

    putloc++;
    q[putloc] = ch;
  }

  // Get a character from the queue.
  public char Get() {
    if(getloc == putloc) {
      Console.WriteLine(" -- Queue is empty.");
      return (char) 0;
    }
```

```
      getloc++;
      return q[getloc];
    }
}

// Demonstrate the SimpleQueue class.
class QDemo {
  static void Main() {
    SimpleQueue bigQ = new SimpleQueue(100);
    SimpleQueue smallQ = new SimpleQueue(4);
    char ch;
    int i;

    Console.WriteLine("Using bigQ to store the alphabet.");
    // put some numbers into bigQ
    for(i=0; i < 26; i++)
      bigQ.Put((char) ('A' + i));

    // Retrieve and display elements from bigQ.
    Console.Write("Contents of bigQ: ");
    for(i=0; i < 26; i++) {
      ch = bigQ.Get();
      if(ch != (char) 0) Console.Write(ch);
    }

    Console.WriteLine("\n");

    Console.WriteLine("Using smallQ to generate errors.");

    // Now, use smallQ to generate some errors.
    for(i=0; i < 5; i++) {
      Console.Write("Attempting to store " +
                        (char) ('Z' - i));

      smallQ.Put((char) ('Z' - i));

      Console.WriteLine();
    }
    Console.WriteLine();

    // More errors on smallQ.
    Console.Write("Contents of smallQ: ");
    for(i=0; i < 5; i++) {
      ch = smallQ.Get();

      if(ch != (char) 0) Console.Write(ch);
    }
  }
}
```

(continued)

7. The output produced by the program is shown here:

```
Using bigQ to store the alphabet.
Contents of bigQ: ABCDEFGHIJKLMNOPQRSTUVWXYZ

Using smallQ to generate errors.
Attempting to store Z
Attempting to store Y
Attempting to store X
Attempting to store W
Attempting to store V -- Queue is full.

Contents of smallQ: ZYXW -- Queue is empty.
```

8. On your own, try modifying **SimpleQueue** so that it stores other types of objects. For example, have it store **int**s or **double**s.

The foreach Loop

In Chapter 3, it was mentioned that C# defines a loop called **foreach**, but a discussion of that statement was deferred until you knew more about C#. The time for that discussion has come.

The **foreach** loop is used to cycle through the elements of a *collection*. A collection is a group of objects. C# defines several types of collections, of which one is an array. The general form of **foreach** is shown here:

foreach(*type loopvar* in *collection*) *statement*;

Here, *type loopvar* specifies the type and name of an *iteration variable*. The iteration variable receives the value of the next element in the collection each time the **foreach** loop iterates. The collection being cycled through is specified by *collection,* which, for the rest of this discussion, is an array. Thus, *type* must be the same as (or compatible with) the element type of the array. Beginning with C# 3.0, *type* can also be **var**, in which case the compiler determines the type based on the element type of the array. This can be useful when working with certain queries, as described later in this book. Normally, you will explicitly specify the type.

Here is how the **foreach** works. When the loop begins, the first element in the array is obtained and assigned to *loopvar.* Each subsequent iteration obtains the next element from the array and stores it in *loopvar.* The loop ends when there are no more elements to obtain. Thus, the **foreach** cycles through the array one element at a time, from start to finish.

One important point to remember about **foreach** is that the iteration variable *loopvar* is read-only. This means that you can't change the contents of an array by assigning the iteration variable a new value.

Here is a simple example that uses **foreach**. It creates an array of integers and gives it some initial values. It then uses a **foreach** loop to display those values, computing the summation in the process.

```
// Use foreach

using System;

class ForeachDemo {
  static void Main() {
    int sum = 0;
    int[] nums = new int[10];

    // Give nums some values.
    for(int i = 0; i < 10; i++)
      nums[i] = i;

    // Use foreach to display and sum the values.
    foreach(int x in nums) {
      Console.WriteLine("Value is: " + x);
      sum += x;
    }
    Console.WriteLine("Summation: " + sum);
  }
}
```

Cycle through **nums** using a **foreach** loop.

The output from the program is shown here:

```
Value is: 0
Value is: 1
Value is: 2
Value is: 3
Value is: 4
Value is: 5
Value is: 6
Value is: 7
Value is: 8
Value is: 9
Summation: 45
```

As this output shows, the **foreach** cycles through an array in sequence from the lowest index to the highest.

The **foreach** also works on multidimensional arrays. It returns those elements in row order, from first to last.

```
// Use foreach on a two-dimensional array.

using System;

class ForeachDemo2 {
  static void Main() {
    int sum = 0;
    int[,] nums = new int[3,5];
```

```
    // Give nums some values.
    for(int i = 0; i < 3; i++)
      for(int j=0; j < 5; j++)
        nums[i,j] = (i+1)*(j+1);

    // Use foreach to display and sum the values.
    foreach(int x in nums) {
      Console.WriteLine("Value is: " + x);
      sum += x;
    }
    Console.WriteLine("Summation: " + sum);
  }
}
```

The output from this program is shown here:

```
Value is: 1
Value is: 2
Value is: 3
Value is: 4
Value is: 5
Value is: 2
Value is: 4
Value is: 6
Value is: 8
Value is: 10
Value is: 3
Value is: 6
Value is: 9
Value is: 12
Value is: 15
Summation: 90
```

Since the **foreach** can only cycle through an array from start to finish, you might think that its use is limited. However, this is not true. A large number of algorithms require exactly this mechanism. For example, here is another way to write the **MinMax** class shown earlier in this chapter that obtains the minimum and maximum from a set of values:

```
/* Find the minimum and maximum values in an array
   by using a foreach loop. */

using System;

class MinMax {
  static void Main() {
    int[] nums = { 99, -10, 100123, 18, -978,
                   5623, 463, -9, 287, 49 };
    int min, max;
```

```
    min = max = nums[0];
    foreach(int val in nums) {
      if(val < min) min = val;
      if(val > max) max = val;
    }
    Console.WriteLine("Min and max: " + min + " " + max);
  }
}
```

The **foreach** is an excellent choice in this application because the finding of a minimum or maximum value requires examining each element. Other types of **foreach** applications include such things as computing an average, searching a list, and copying an array.

Strings

From a day-to-day programming standpoint, one of the most important of C#'s data types is **string**. **string** defines and supports character strings. In many other programming languages, a string is an array of characters. This is not the case with C#. In C#, strings are objects. Thus, **string** is a reference type.

Actually, you have been using the **string** class since Chapter 1, but you did not know it. When you create a string literal, you are actually creating a **string** object. For example, in the statement

```
Console.WriteLine("In C#, strings are objects.");
```

the string "In C#, strings are objects." is automatically made into a **string** object by C#. Thus, the use of the **string** class has been "below the surface" in the preceding programs. In this section, you will learn to handle them explicitly. Be aware, however, that the **string** class is quite large, and we will only scratch its surface here. It is a class that you will want to explore more fully on your own.

Construct a String

The easiest way to construct a **string** is to use a string literal. For example, here **str** is a **string** reference variable that is assigned a reference to a string literal:

```
string str = "C# strings are powerful.";
```

In this case, **str** is initialized to the character sequence "C# strings are powerful."

You can also create a **string** from a **char** array. For example:

```
char[] chrs = {'t', 'e', 's', 't'};
string str = new string(chrs);
```

Once you have created a **string** object, you can use it nearly anywhere that a string literal is allowed. For example, you can use a **string** object as an argument to **WriteLine( )**, as shown in this example:

```
// Introduce string.

using System;

class StringDemo {
  static void Main() {

    char[] charray = {'A', ' ', 's', 't', 'r', 'i', 'n', 'g', '.' };
    string str1 = new string(charray);
    string str2 = "Another string.";

    Console.WriteLine(str1);
    Console.WriteLine(str2);
  }
}
```

Construct **string** objects from a **char** array and from a string literal.

Use **string** objects in a coll to **WriteLine( )**.

The output from the program is shown here:

```
A string.
Another string.
```

Operating on Strings

The **string** class contains several methods that operate on strings. Here are a few:

static string Copy(string *str*)	Returns a copy of *str*.
int CompareTo(string *str*)	Returns less than zero if the invoking string is less than *str*, greater than zero if the invoking string is greater than *str*, and zero if the strings are equal.
int IndexOf(string *str*)	Searches the invoking string for the substring specified by *str*. Returns the index of the first match, or −1, on failure.
int LastIndexOf(string *str*)	Searches the invoking string for the substring specified by *str*. Returns the index of the last match, or −1, on failure.

The **string** type also includes the **Length** property, which contains the length of the string.

To obtain the value of an individual character of a string, you simply use an index. For example:

```
string str = "test";
Console.WriteLine(str[0]);
```

This displays "t". Like arrays, string indices begin at zero. One important point, however, is that you cannot assign a new value to a character within a string using an index. An index can only be used to obtain a character.

To test two strings for equality, you can use the = = operator. Normally, when the = = operator is applied to object references, it determines if both references refer to the same object. This differs for objects of type **string**. When the = = is applied to two **string** references, the contents of the strings themselves are compared for equality. The same is true for the **!=** operator: When comparing **string** objects, the contents of the strings are compared. For other types of string comparisons, you will need to use the **CompareTo( )** method.

Here is a program that demonstrates several string operations:

```
// Some string operations.

using System;

class StrOps {
  static void Main() {
    string str1 =
      "When it comes to .NET programming, C# is #1.";
    string str2 = string.Copy(str1);
    string str3 = "C# strings are powerful.";
    int result, idx;

    Console.WriteLine("Length of str1: " +
                      str1.Length);

    // Display str1, one char at a time.
    for(int i=0; i < str1.Length; i++)
      Console.Write(str1[i]);
    Console.WriteLine();

    if(str1 == str2)
      Console.WriteLine("str1 == str2");
    else
      Console.WriteLine("str1 != str2");

    if(str1 == str3)
      Console.WriteLine("str1 == str3");
    else
      Console.WriteLine("str1 != str3");

    result = str1.CompareTo(str3);
    if(result == 0)
      Console.WriteLine("str1 and str3 are equal");
    else if(result < 0)
      Console.WriteLine("str1 is less than str3");
    else
      Console.WriteLine("str1 is greater than str3");

    // Assign a new string to str2.
    str2 = "One Two Three One";
```

```
    idx = str2.IndexOf("One");
    Console.WriteLine("Index of first occurrence of One: " + idx);
    idx = str2.LastIndexOf("One");
    Console.WriteLine("Index of last occurrence of One: " + idx);

  }
}
```

This program generates the following output:

```
Length of str1: 44
When it comes to .NET programming, C# is #1.
str1 == str2
str1 != str3
str1 is greater than str3
Index of first occurrence of One: 0
Index of last occurrence of One: 14
```

You can *concatenate* (join together) two strings using the **+** operator. For example, this statement:

```
string str1 = "One";
string str2 = "Two";
string str3 = "Three";
string str4 = str1 + str2 + str3;
```

initializes **str4** with the string "OneTwoThree."

Arrays of Strings

Like any other data type, strings can be assembled into arrays. For example:

```
// Demonstrate string arrays.

using System;

class StringArrays {
  static void Main() {
    string[] str = { "This", "is", "a", "test." };   ◄——— An array of strings.

    Console.WriteLine("Original array: ");
    for(int i=0; i < str.Length; i++)
      Console.Write(str[i] + " ");
    Console.WriteLine("\n");

    // Change a string.
    str[1] = "was";
    str[3] = "test, too!";
```

```
      Console.WriteLine("Modified array: ");
      for(int i=0; i < str.Length; i++)
        Console.Write(str[i] + " ");
  }
}
```

Here is the output from this program:

```
Original array:
This is a test.

Modified array:
This was a test, too!
```

Strings Are Immutable

Here is something that might surprise you: The contents of a **string** object are immutable. That is, once created, the character sequence comprising that string cannot be altered. This restriction allows strings to be implemented more efficiently. Even though this probably sounds like a serious drawback, it isn't. When you need a string that is a variation on one that already exists, simply create a new string that contains the desired changes. Since unused string objects are automatically garbage-collected, you don't even need to worry about what happens to the discarded strings.

It must be made clear, however, that **string** reference variables may, of course, change which object they refer to. It is just that the contents of a specific **string** object cannot be changed after it is created.

To fully understand why immutable strings are not a hindrance, we will use another of **string**'s methods: **Substring( )**. The **Substring( )** method returns a new string that contains a specified portion of the invoking string. Because a new **string** object is manufactured that contains the substring, the original string is unaltered and the rule of immutability is still intact. The form of **Substring( )** that we will be using is shown here:

string Substring(int *startIndex*, int *len*)

Here, *startIndex* specifies the beginning index, and *len* specifies the length of the substring.

Here is a program that demonstrates **Substring( )** and the principle of immutable strings:

```
// Use Substring().

using System;

class SubStr {
  static void Main() {
    string orgstr = "C# makes strings easy.";

    // Construct a substring.
    string substr = orgstr.Substring(5, 12);
```

This creates a new string that contains the desired substring.

Ask the Expert

Q: You say that once created, string objects are immutable. I understand that, from a practical point of view, this is not a serious restriction, but what if I want to create a string that *can* be changed?

A: You're in luck. C# offers a class called **StringBuilder** that is in the **System.Text** namespace. It creates string objects that can be changed. However, for most purposes, you will want to use **string**, not **StringBuilder**.

```
    Console.WriteLine("orgstr: " + orgstr);
    Console.WriteLine("substr: " + substr);
  }
}
```

Here is the output from the program:

```
orgstr: C# makes strings easy.
substr: kes strings
```

As you can see, the original string **orgstr** is unchanged and **substr** contains the substring.

The Bitwise Operators

In Chapter 2, you learned about C#'s arithmetic, relational, and logical operators. While these are the most commonly used, C# provides additional operators that expand the set of problems to which C# can be applied: the bitwise operators. The bitwise operators act directly upon the bits of their operands. They are defined only for integer operands. They cannot be used on **bool**, **float**, **double**, or **class** types.

They are called the *bitwise* operators because they are used to test, set, or shift the bits that comprise an integer value. Bitwise operations are important to a wide variety of systems-level programming tasks, such as when status information from a device must be interrogated or constructed. Table 5-1 lists the bitwise operators.

Operator	Result
&	Bitwise AND
|	Bitwise OR
^	Bitwise exclusive OR (XOR)
>>	Shift right
<<	Shift left
~	One's complement (unary NOT)

Table 5-1 The Bitwise Operators

The Bitwise AND, OR, XOR, and NOT Operators

The bitwise operators AND, OR, XOR, and NOT are, respectively, **&**, |, ^, and ~. They perform the same operations as their Boolean logic equivalents described in Chapter 2. The difference is that the bitwise operators work on a bit-by-bit basis. The following table shows the outcome of each operation using 1's and 0's:

p	q	p & q	p | q	p ^ q	~p
0	0	0	0	0	1
1	0	0	1	1	0
0	1	0	1	1	1
1	1	1	1	0	0

In terms of its most common usage, you can think of the bitwise AND as a way to turn bits off. That is, any bit that is 0 in either operand will cause the corresponding bit in the outcome to be set to 0. For example:

```
   1 1 0 1 0 0 1 1
&  1 0 1 0 1 0 1 0
   ---------------
   1 0 0 0 0 0 1 0
```

The following program demonstrates the **&** by turning any lowercase letter into uppercase by resetting the sixth bit to 0. As the ASCII character set (which is a subset of Unicode) is defined, the lowercase letters are the same as the uppercase ones, except that the lowercase ones are greater in value by exactly 32. Therefore, to transform a lowercase letter to uppercase, just turn off the sixth bit, as this program illustrates:

```
// Uppercase letters.

using System;

class UpCase {
  static void Main() {
    char ch;

    for(int i=0; i < 10; i++) {
      ch = (char) ('a' + i);
      Console.Write(ch);

      // This statement turns off the 6th bit.
      ch = (char) (ch & 65503); // ch is now uppercase
                        ↑
                        └──────── Use the AND operator.
      Console.Write(ch + " ");
    }
  }
}
```

The output from this program is shown here:

```
aA bB cC dD eE fF gG hH iI jJ
```

The value 65,503 used in the AND operation is the decimal representation of 1111 1111 1101 1111. Thus, the AND operation leaves all bits in **ch** unchanged, except for the sixth one, which is set to zero.

The AND operator is also useful when you want to determine whether a bit is on or off. For example, this statement determines if bit 4 in **status** is set:

```
if((status & 8) != 0) Console.WriteLine("bit 4 is on");
```

The reason 8 is used is that it translates into a binary value that has only the fourth bit set. Therefore, the **if** statement can succeed only when bit 4 of **status** is also on. An interesting use of this concept is to show the bits of a **byte** value in binary format:

```
// Display the bits within a byte.

using System;

class BitsInByte {
  static void Main() {
    byte val;

    val = 123;
    for(int t=128; t > 0; t = t/2) {
      if((val & t) != 0) Console.Write("1 ");      ⟵——— Display the bits within a byte.
      else Console.Write("0 ");
    }
  }
}
```

The output is shown here:

```
0 1 1 1 1 0 1 1
```

The **for** loop successively tests each bit in **val**, using the bitwise AND, to determine if it is on or off. If the bit is on, the digit **1** is displayed; otherwise, **0** is displayed.

The bitwise OR can be used to turn bits on. Any bit that is set to 1 in either operand will cause the corresponding bit in the variable to be set to 1. For example:

```
  1 1 0 1 0 0 1 1
| 1 0 1 0 1 0 1 0
  ---------------
  1 1 1 1 1 0 1 1
```

We can make use of the OR to change the uppercasing program into a lowercasing program, as shown here:

```
// Lowercase letters.

using System;

class LowCase {
  static void Main() {
    char ch;

    for(int i=0; i < 10; i++) {
      ch = (char) ('A' + i);
      Console.Write(ch);

      // This statement turns on the 6th bit.
      ch = (char) (ch | 32); // ch is now lowercase

      Console.Write(ch + " ");            Use the OR operator.
    }
  }
}
```

The output from this program is shown here:

```
Aa Bb Cc Dd Ee Ff Gg Hh Ii Jj
```

The program works by ORing each character with the value 32, which is 0000 0000 0010 0000 in binary. Thus, 32 is the value that produces a value in binary in which only the sixth bit is set. When this value is ORed with any other value, it produces a result in which the sixth bit is set and all other bits remain unchanged. As explained, for the ASCII characters, this means that each uppercase letter is transformed into its lowercase equivalent.

An exclusive OR, usually abbreviated XOR, will set a bit on if, and only if, the bits being compared are different, as illustrated here:

```
  0 1 1 1 1 1 1 1
^ 1 0 1 1 1 0 0 1
  ---------------
  1 1 0 0 0 1 1 0
```

The XOR operation has an interesting property that is useful in a variety of situations. When some value X is XORed with another value Y and then that result is XORed with Y again, X is produced. That is, given the sequence

R1 = X ^ Y;

R2 = R1 ^ Y;

R2 is the same value as X. Thus, the outcome of a sequence of two XORs using the same value produces the original value.

To see this feature of the XOR in action, we will create a simple cipher in which some integer is the key that is used to both encode and decode a message by XORing the characters in that message. To encode, the XOR operation is applied the first time, yielding the ciphertext. To decode, the XOR is applied a second time, yielding the plaintext. Of course, such a cipher has no practical value, being trivially easy to break. It does, however, provide an interesting way to demonstrate the effects of the XOR, as the following program shows:

```
// Demonstrate the XOR.

using System;

class Encode {
  static void Main() {
    string msg = "This is a test";
    string encmsg = "";
    string decmsg = "";
    int key = 88;

    Console.Write("Original message: ");
    Console.WriteLine(msg);

    // Encode the message.
    for(int i=0; i < msg.Length; i++)
      encmsg = encmsg + (char) (msg[i] ^ key);

    Console.Write("Encoded message: ");
    Console.WriteLine(encmsg);

    // Decode the message.
    for(int i=0; i < msg.Length; i++)
      decmsg = decmsg + (char) (encmsg[i] ^ key);

    Console.Write("Decoded message: ");
    Console.WriteLine(decmsg);
  }
}
```

This constructs the encoded string.

This constructs the decoded string.

Here is the output:

```
Original message: This is a test
Encoded message: 01+x1+x9x,=+,
Decoded message: This is a test
```

As you can see, the result of two XORs using the same key produces the decoded message. (Remember, this simple XOR cipher is not suitable for any real-world, practical use because it is inherently insecure.)

The unary 1's complement (NOT) operator reverses the state of all the bits of the operand. For example, if some integer called **A** has the bit pattern 1001 0110, then ~**A** produces a result with the bit pattern 0110 1001.

The following program demonstrates the NOT operator by displaying a number and its complement in binary:

```
// Demonstrate the bitwise NOT.

using System;

class NotDemo {
  static void Main() {
    sbyte b = -34;

    for(int t=128; t > 0; t = t/2) {
      if((b & t) != 0) Console.Write("1 ");
      else Console.Write("0 ");
    }
    Console.WriteLine();

    // Reverse all bits.
    b = (sbyte) ~b;                                  Use the NOT operator.

    for(int t=128; t > 0; t = t/2) {
      if((b & t) != 0) Console.Write("1 ");
      else Console.Write("0 ");
    }
  }
}
```

Here is the output:

```
1 1 0 1 1 1 1 0
0 0 1 0 0 0 0 1
```

The Shift Operators

In C#, it is possible to shift the bits that comprise a value to the left or to the right by a specified amount. C# defines the two bit-shift operators shown here:

<<	Left shift
>>	Right shift

The general forms for these operators are shown here:

value << num-bits

value >> num-bits

Here, *value* is the value being shifted by the number of bit positions specified by *num-bits*.

A left shift causes all bits within the specified value to be shifted left one position and a zero bit to be brought in on the right. A right shift causes all bits to be shifted right one position. In the case of a right shift on an unsigned value, a zero is brought in on the left. In the case of a right shift on a signed value, the sign bit is preserved. Recall that negative numbers are represented by setting the high-order bit of an integer to 1. Thus, if the value being shifted is negative, each right-shift brings in a 1 on the left. If the value is positive, each right shift brings in a 0 on the left.

For both left and right shifts, the bits shifted out are lost. Thus, a shift is not a rotate, and there is no way to retrieve a bit that has been shifted out.

Here is a program that graphically illustrates the effect of a left and right shift. An integer is given an initial value of 1, which means that its low-order bit is set. Then, a series of eight shifts is performed on the integer. After each shift, the lower eight bits of the value are shown. The process is then repeated, except that a 1 is put in the eighth bit position and right shifts are performed.

```csharp
// Demonstrate the shift << and >> operators.

using System;

class ShiftDemo {
  static void Main() {
    int val = 1;

    for(int i = 0; i < 8; i++) {
      for(int t=128; t > 0; t = t/2) {
        if((val & t) != 0) Console.Write("1 ");
        else Console.Write("0 ");
      }
      Console.WriteLine();
      val = val << 1; // left shift          Left shift val.
    }
    Console.WriteLine();

    val = 128;
    for(int i = 0; i < 8; i++) {
      for(int t=128; t > 0; t = t/2) {
        if((val & t) != 0) Console.Write("1 ");
        else Console.Write("0 ");
      }
      Console.WriteLine();
      val = val >> 1; // right shift          Right shift val.
    }
  }
}
```

Ask the Expert

Q: Since binary is based on powers of 2, can the shift operators be used as a shortcut for multiplying or dividing an integer by 2?

A: Yes. The bitwise shift operators can be used to perform a multiplication or division by 2. A shift left doubles a value. A shift right halves it. Of course, this only works as long as you are not shifting bits off one end or the other.

The output from the program is shown here:

```
0 0 0 0 0 0 0 1
0 0 0 0 0 0 1 0
0 0 0 0 0 1 0 0
0 0 0 0 1 0 0 0
0 0 0 1 0 0 0 0
0 0 1 0 0 0 0 0
0 1 0 0 0 0 0 0
1 0 0 0 0 0 0 0

1 0 0 0 0 0 0 0
0 1 0 0 0 0 0 0
0 0 1 0 0 0 0 0
0 0 0 1 0 0 0 0
0 0 0 0 1 0 0 0
0 0 0 0 0 1 0 0
0 0 0 0 0 0 1 0
0 0 0 0 0 0 0 1
```

Bitwise Compound Assignments

All of the binary bitwise operators can be used in compound assignments. For example, the following two statements both assign to **x** the outcome of an XOR of **x** with the value 127:

```
x = x ^ 127;
x ^= 127;
```

Try This   Create a ShowBits Class

Earlier in this chapter, you saw the **BitsInByte** class that displays the bits that make up a **byte**. One drawback to **BitsInByte** is that it works only with **byte** values. A more useful class would show the bit pattern for any type of integer value. Fortunately, such a class is easy to create, and the program developed here shows how. It creates a class called **ShowBits** that allows the bits

(continued)

in any type of unsigned integer value to be displayed. (You can also use **ShowBits** to display the bits in a signed integer value, but you will need to cast it to its unsigned equivalent.) Being able to see the bits in a value can be quite useful in a variety of situations. For example, if you are receiving raw data from a device that is being transmitted via the Internet, being able to watch the data in its binary form could be helpful if the device malfunctions.

Step by Step

1. Create a file called **ShowBitsDemo.cs**.

2. Begin the **ShowBits** class, as shown here:

```
class ShowBits {
  public int numbits;

  public ShowBits(int n) {
    numbits = n;
  }
```

ShowBits creates objects that display a specified number of bits. For example, to create an object that will display the low-order eight bits of some value, use

```
ShowBits b = new ShowBits(8);
```

The number of bits to display is stored in **numbits**.

3. To actually display the bit pattern, **ShowBits** provides the method **Show( )**, which is shown here:

```
public void Show(ulong val) {
  ulong mask = 1;

  // Left shift a 1 into the proper position.
  mask <<= numbits-1;

  int spacer = 0;
  for(; mask != 0; mask >>= 1) {
    if((val & mask) != 0) Console.Write("1");
    else Console.Write("0");
    spacer++;
    if((spacer % 8) == 0) {
      Console.Write(" ");
      spacer = 0;
    }
  }
  Console.WriteLine();
}
```

Notice that **Show( )** specifies one **ulong** parameter. This does not mean that you must pass **Show( )** a **ulong** value, however. Because of C#'s implicit conversions, any unsigned integer type can be passed to **Show( )**. (To display a signed integer value, just cast it to its corresponding unsigned type.) The number of bits displayed is determined by the value stored in **numbits**. After each group of eight bits, **Show( )** outputs a space. This makes it easier to read the binary values of long bit patterns.

4. The following program called **ShowBitsDemo** demonstrates the **ShowBits** class:

```
// A class that displays the binary representation of a value.

using System;

class ShowBits {
  public int numbits;

  public ShowBits(int n) {
    numbits = n;
  }

  public void Show(ulong val) {
    ulong mask = 1;

    // Left shift a 1 into the proper position.
    mask <<= numbits-1;

    int spacer = 0;
    for(; mask != 0; mask >>= 1) {
      if((val & mask) != 0) Console.Write("1");
      else Console.Write("0");
      spacer++;
      if((spacer % 8) == 0) {
        Console.Write(" ");
        spacer = 0;
      }
    }
    Console.WriteLine();
  }
}

// Demonstrate ShowBits.
class ShowBitsDemo {
  static void Main() {
    ShowBits b = new ShowBits(8);
    ShowBits i = new ShowBits(32);
    ShowBits li = new ShowBits(64);

    Console.WriteLine("123 in binary: ");
    b.Show(123);
```

(continued)

```
Console.WriteLine("\n87987 in binary: ");
i.Show(87987);

Console.WriteLine("\n237658768 in binary: ");
li.Show(237658768);

// You can also show low-order bits of any integer.
Console.WriteLine("\nLow order 8 bits of 87987 in binary: ");
b.Show(87987);
    }
}
```

5. The output from **ShowBitsDemo** is shown here:

```
123 in binary:
01111011

87987 in binary:
00000000 00000001 01010111 10110011

237658768 in binary:
00000000 00000000 00000000 00000000 00001110 00101010 01100010
10010000

Low order 8 bits of 87987 in binary:
10110011
```

The ? Operator

One of C#'s most fascinating operators is the **?**, which is C#'s conditional operator. The **?** operator is often used to replace **if-else** statements of this general form:

if (*condition*)
  variable = *expression1*;
else
  variable = *expression2*;

Here, the value assigned to *variable* depends upon the outcome of the *condition* controlling the **if**.

The **?** is called a *ternary operator* because it requires three operands. It takes the general form

Exp1 ? *Exp2* : *Exp3*;

where *Exp1* is a **bool** expression, and *Exp2* and *Exp3* are expressions. The type of *Exp2* and *Exp3* must be the same (or compatible). Notice the use and placement of the colon.

The value of a **?** expression is determined like this: *Exp1* is evaluated. If it is true, then *Exp2* is evaluated and becomes the value of the entire **?** expression. If *Exp1* is false, then *Exp3* is evaluated and its value becomes the value of the expression. Consider this example, which assigns **absval** the absolute value of **val**:

```
absval = val < 0 ? -val : val; // get absolute value of val
```

Here, **absval** will be assigned the value of **val** if **val** is zero or greater. If **val** is negative, then **absval** will be assigned the negative of that value (which yields a positive value). The same code written using the **if-else** structure would look like this:

```
if (val < 0) absval  = -val;
else absval = val;
```

Here is another example of the **?** operator. This program divides two numbers, but will not allow a division by zero:

```
// Prevent a division by zero using the ?.

using System;

class NoZeroDiv {
  static void Main() {
    int result;

    for(int i = -5; i < 6; i++) {
      result = i != 0 ? 100 / i : 0;          This prevents a divide-by-zero.
      if(i != 0)
        Console.WriteLine("100 / " + i + " is " + result);
    }
  }
}
```

The output from the program is shown here:

```
100 / -5 is -20
100 / -4 is -25
100 / -3 is -33
100 / -2 is -50
100 / -1 is -100
100 / 1 is 100
100 / 2 is 50
100 / 3 is 33
100 / 4 is 25
100 / 5 is 20
```

Pay special attention to this line from the program:

```
result = i != 0 ? 100 / i : 0;
```

Here, **result** is assigned the outcome of the division of 100 by **i**. However, this division takes place only if **i** is not zero. When **i** is zero, a placeholder value of zero is assigned to **result**.

You don't actually have to assign the value produced by the **?** to some variable. For example, you could use the value as an argument in a call to a method. Or, if the expressions are all of type **bool**, the **?** can be used as the conditional expression in a loop or **if** statement. For example, here is the preceding program rewritten a bit more compactly. It produces the same output as before.

```
// Prevent a division by zero using the ?.

using System;

class NoZeroDiv2 {
  static void Main() {

    for(int i = -5; i < 6; i++)
      if(i != 0 ? true : false)
        Console.WriteLine("100 / " + i +
                          " is " + 100 / i);

  }
}
```

Here, the **?** operator is moved into the **if** statement.

Notice the **if** statement. If **i** is zero, then the outcome of the **if** is false, the division by zero is prevented, and no result is displayed. Otherwise, the division takes place.

Chapter 5 Self Test

1. Show how to declare a one-dimensional array of 12 **double**s.

2. Show how to declare a 4 by 5, two-dimensional array of **int**s.

3. Show how to declare a jagged two-dimensional **int** array in which the first dimension is 5.

4. Show how to initialize a one-dimensional **int** array with the values 1 through 5.

5. Explain **foreach**. Show its general form.

6. Write a program that uses an array to find the average of ten **double** values. Use any ten values you like.

7. Change the bubble sort in the first Try This section so that it sorts an array of strings. Demonstrate that it works.

8. What is the difference between the **string** methods **IndexOf( )** and **LastIndexOf( )**?

9. Expanding on the **Encode** cipher class, modify it so that it uses an eight-character string as the key.

10. Can the bitwise operators be applied to the **double** type?

11. Show how this sequence can be rewritten using the **?** operator:

```
if (x < 0)  y = 10;
else y = 20;
```

12. In the following fragment, is the **&** a bitwise or logical operator? Why?

```
bool a, b;
// ...
if (a & b)  ...
```

Chapter 6

A Closer Look at Methods and Classes

Key Skills & Concepts

- Control access to members

- Pass objects to a method

- Return objects from a method

- Use **ref** and **out** parameters

- Overload methods

- Overload constructors

- Return values from **Main( )**

- Pass arguments to **Main( )**

- Recursion

- The **static** modifier

This chapter continues our examination of classes and methods. It begins by explaining how to control access to the members of a class. It then discusses the passing and returning of objects, method overloading, the various forms of **Main( )**, recursion, and the use of the keyword **static**.

Controlling Access to Class Members

In its support for encapsulation, the class provides two major benefits. First, it links data with the code that manipulates it. You have been taking advantage of this aspect of the class since Chapter 4. Second, it provides the means by which access to members can be controlled. This feature is examined here.

Although C#'s approach is a bit more sophisticated, in essence, there are two basic types of class members: public and private. A *public* member can be freely accessed by code defined outside of its class. This is the type of class member that we have been using up to this point. A *private* member can be accessed only by other methods defined by its class. It is through the use of private members that access is controlled.

Restricting access to a class' members is a fundamental part of object-oriented programming because it helps prevent the misuse of an object. By allowing access to private data only through a well-defined set of methods, you can prevent improper values from being assigned to that data—by performing a range-check, for example. It is not possible for code outside the class to set the value of a private member directly. You can also control precisely how and when the data within an object is used. Thus, when correctly implemented, a class creates a "black box" that can be used, but the inner workings of it are not open to tampering.

C#'s Access Specifiers

Member access control is achieved through the use of four *access specifiers:* **public**, **private**, **protected**, and **internal**. In this chapter we will be concerned with **public** and **private**. The **protected** modifier applies only when inheritance is involved, and is described in Chapter 7. The **internal** modifier applies mostly to the use of an *assembly,* which in the case of C# means a program, project, or component. The **internal** modifier is briefly described in Chapter 15.

When a member of a class is modified by the **public** specifier, that member can be accessed by any other code in your program. This includes methods defined inside other classes.

When a member of a class is specified as **private**, that member can be accessed only by other members of its class. Thus, methods in other classes are not able to access a **private** member of another class. As explained in Chapter 4, if no access specifier is used, a class member is private to its class by default. Thus, the **private** specifier is optional when creating private class members.

An access specifier precedes the rest of a member's type specification. That is, it must begin a member's declaration statement. Here are some examples:

```
public string ErrorMsg;
private double bal;
private bool isError(byte status) { // ...
```

To understand the difference between **public** and **private**, consider the following program:

```
// Public vs private access.

using System;                        These are private to MyClass.

class MyClass {                                    |
  private int alpha; // private access explicitly specified
  int beta;          // private access by default
  public int gamma;  // public access

  /* Methods to access alpha and beta. It is OK for a member
     of a class to access a private member of the same class. */

  public void SetAlpha(int a) {
    alpha = a;
  }

  public int GetAlpha() {
    return alpha;
  }

  public void SetBeta(int a) {
    beta = a;
  }
```

```
  public int GetBeta() {
    return beta;
  }
}

class AccessDemo {
  static void Main() {
    MyClass ob = new MyClass();

    // Access to alpha and beta is allowed only through methods.
    ob.SetAlpha(-99);
    ob.SetBeta(19);
    Console.WriteLine("ob.alpha is " + ob.GetAlpha());
    Console.WriteLine("ob.beta is " + ob.GetBeta());

    // You cannot access alpha or beta like this:
//  ob.alpha = 10; // Wrong! alpha is private!        Wrong! alpha and beta
//  ob.beta = 9;   // Wrong! beta is private!          are private.

    // It is OK to directly access gamma because it is public.
    ob.gamma = 99;          OK because gamma is public.
  }
}
```

As you can see, inside the **MyClass** class, **alpha** is explicitly specified as **private**, **beta** is private by default, and **gamma** is specified as **public**. Because **alpha** and **beta** are private, they cannot be accessed by code outside of their class. Therefore, inside the **AccessDemo** class, neither can be used directly. Each must be accessed through public methods, such as **SetAlpha( )** and **GetAlpha( )**. For example, if you were to remove the comment symbol from the beginning of the following line:

```
//  ob.alpha = 10; // Wrong! alpha is private!
```

you would not be able to compile this program because of the access violation. Although access to **alpha** by code outside of **MyClass** is not allowed, methods defined within **MyClass** can freely access it, as the **SetAlpha( )** and **GetAlpha( )** methods show. The same is true for **beta**.

The key point is this: A private member can be used freely by other members of its class, but it cannot be accessed by code outside its class.

To see how access control can be applied to a more practical example, consider the following program that implements a "fail-soft" **int** array in which boundary errors are prevented, thus avoiding a runtime exception. This is accomplished by encapsulating the array as a private member of a class, allowing access to the array only through member methods. With this approach, any attempt to access the array beyond its boundaries can be prevented, with such an attempt failing gracefully (thus resulting in a "soft" landing rather than a "crash"). The fail-soft array is implemented by the **FailSoftArray** class, shown here:

```
/* This class implements a "fail-soft" array that prevents
   runtime errors. */
```

```
using System;

class FailSoftArray {
  private int[] a;      // reference to array
  private int errval; // value to return if Get() fails

  public int Length; // Length is public
```

Notice that these are private.

```
  /* Construct array given its size and the value to
     return if Get() fails. */
  public FailSoftArray(int size, int errv) {
    a = new int[size];
    errval = errv;
    Length = size;
  }

  // Return value at given index.
  public int Get(int index) {
    if(ok(index)) return a[index];
    return errval;
  }

  // Put a value at an index. Return false on failure.
  public bool Put(int index, int val) {
    if(ok(index)) {
      a[index] = val;
      return true;
    }
    return false;
  }

  // Return true if index is within bounds.
  private bool ok(int index) {
    if(index >= 0 & index < Length) return true;
    return false;
  }
}

// Demonstrate the fail-soft array.
class FSDemo {
  static void Main() {
    FailSoftArray fs = new FailSoftArray(5, -1);
    int x;

    // Show quiet failures.
    Console.WriteLine("Fail quietly.");
    for(int i=0; i < (fs.Length * 2); i++)
      fs.Put(i, i*10);
```

Trap an out-of-bounds index.

A private method.

```
        for(int i=0; i < (fs.Length * 2); i++) {
          x = fs.Get(i);
          if(x != -1) Console.Write(x + " ");
        }
        Console.WriteLine("");

        // Now, handle failures.
        Console.WriteLine("\nFail with error reports.");
        for(int i=0; i < (fs.Length * 2); i++)
          if(!fs.Put(i, i*10))
            Console.WriteLine("Index " + i + " out-of-bounds");

        for(int i=0; i < (fs.Length * 2); i++) {
          x = fs.Get(i);
          if(x != -1) Console.Write(x + " ");
          else
            Console.WriteLine("Index " + i + " out-of-bounds");
        }
      }
    }
}
```

The output from the program is shown here:

```
Fail quietly.
0 10 20 30 40

Fail with error reports.
Index 5 out-of-bounds
Index 6 out-of-bounds
Index 7 out-of-bounds
Index 8 out-of-bounds
Index 9 out-of-bounds
0 10 20 30 40 Index 5 out-of-bounds
Index 6 out-of-bounds
Index 7 out-of-bounds
Index 8 out-of-bounds
Index 9 out-of-bounds
```

Let's look closely at this example. Inside **FailSoftArray** are defined three private members. The first is **a**, which stores a reference to the array that will actually hold information. The second is **errval**, which is the value that will be returned when a call to **Get( )** fails. The third is the private method **ok( )**, which determines if an index is within bounds. Thus, these three members can be used only by other members of the **FailSoftArray** class. Specifically, **a** and **errval** can be used only by other methods in the class, and **ok( )** can be called only by other members of **FailSoftArray**. The rest of the class members are **public** and can be called by any other code in a program that uses **FailSoftArray**.

When a **FailSoftArray** object is constructed, you must specify the size of the array and the value that you want to return if a call to **Get( )** fails. The error value must be a value that

Ask the Expert

Q: While it is true that the "fail-soft" array example prevents an array overrun, it does so at the expense of the normal array-indexing syntax. Is there a better way to create a "fail-soft" array?

A: Yes. As you will see in Chapter 7, C# includes a special type of class member called an *indexer*, which allows you to index a class object like an array. There is also a better way to handle the **Length** field by making it into a *property*. This is also described in Chapter 7.

would otherwise not be stored in the array. Once constructed, the actual array referred to by **a** and the error value stored in **errval** cannot be accessed by users of the **FailSoftArray** object. Thus, they are not open to misuse. For example, the user cannot try to index **a** directly, possibly exceeding its bounds. Access is available only through the **Get( )** and **Put( )** methods.

The **ok( )** method is **private** mostly for the sake of illustration. It would be harmless to make it **public** because it does not modify the object. However, since it is used internally by the **FailSoftArray** class, it can be **private**.

Notice that the **Length** instance variable is **public**. This is in keeping with the way that C# implements arrays. To obtain the length of a **FailSoftArray**, simply use its **Length** member.

To use a **FailSoftArray** array, call **Put( )** to store a value at the specified index. Call **Get( )** to retrieve a value from a specified index. If the index is out of bounds, **Put( )** returns **false** and **Get( )** returns **errval**.

Since class members are private by default, there is no reason to explicitly declare them using **private**. Therefore, from this point forward, this book will not redundantly declare class members as **private**. Just remember that if a class member is not preceded by an access modifier, its access is private.

Try This   Improve the SimpleQueue Class

You can use private access to make a rather important improvement to the **SimpleQueue** class developed in Chapter 5. In that version, all members of the **SimpleQueue** class were public. This means that it would be possible for a program that uses a **SimpleQueue** to directly access the underlying array, possibly accessing its elements out of turn. Since the entire point of a queue is to provide a first-in, first-out list, allowing out-of-order access is not desirable. It would also be possible for a malicious programmer to alter the values stored in the **putloc** and **getloc** indices, thus corrupting the queue. Fortunately, these types of problems are easy to prevent by making parts of **SimpleQueue** private.

(continued)

Step by Step

1. Copy the original **SimpleQueue** to a new file called **SimpleQueue.cs**.

2. In the **SimpleQueue** class, remove the **public** specifier to the **q** array and the indices **putloc** and **getloc**, as shown here:

```
// An improved queue class for characters.
class SimpleQueue {

  // These are now private.
  char[] q; // this array holds the queue
  int putloc, getloc; // the put and get indices

  public SimpleQueue(int size) {
    q = new char[size+1]; // allocate memory for queue
    putloc = getloc = 0;
  }

  // Put a character into the queue.
  public void Put(char ch) {
    if(putloc==q.Length-1) {
      Console.WriteLine(" -- Queue is full.");
      return;
    }

    putloc++;
    q[putloc] = ch;
  }

  // Get a character from the queue.
  public char Get() {
    if(getloc == putloc) {
      Console.WriteLine(" -- Queue is empty.");
      return (char) 0;
    }

    getloc++;
    return q[getloc];
  }
}
```

3. Changing **q**, **putloc**, and **getloc** from public access to private access has no effect on a program that properly uses **SimpleQueue**. For example, it still works fine with the **QDemo** class from Chapter 5. However, it prevents the improper use of a **SimpleQueue**. For example, the last two statements are illegal:

```
SimpleQueue test = new SimpleQueue(10);
```

```
test.q[0] = 'X'; // wrong!
test.putloc = -100; // won't work!
```

4. Now that **q**, **putloc**, and **getloc** are private, the **SimpleQueue** class strictly enforces the
first-in, first-out attribute of a queue.

Pass an Object Reference to a Method

Up to this point, the examples in this book have been using value types, such as **int** or **double**,
as parameters to methods. However, it is both correct and common to pass an object reference
to methods. For example, consider the following simple program that stores the dimensions of
a three-dimensional block:

```
// Object references can be passed to methods.

using System;

class Block {
  int a, b, c;
  int volume;

  public Block(int i, int j, int k) {
    a = i;
    b = j;
    c = k;
    volume = a * b * c;
  }

  // Return true if ob defines same block.
  public bool SameBlock(Block ob) {
    if((ob.a == a) & (ob.b == b) & (ob.c == c)) return true;
    else return false;
  }

  // Return true if ob has same volume.
  public bool SameVolume(Block ob) {
    if(ob.volume == volume) return true;
    else return false;
  }
}

class PassOb {
  static void Main() {
    Block ob1 = new Block(10, 2, 5);
    Block ob2 = new Block(10, 2, 5);
    Block ob3 = new Block(4, 5, 5);
```

Use class type for
the parameter.

```
        Console.WriteLine("ob1 same dimensions as ob2: " +
                          ob1.SameBlock(ob2));
        Console.WriteLine("ob1 same dimensions as ob3: " +
                          ob1.SameBlock(ob3));
        Console.WriteLine("ob1 same volume as ob3: " +
                          ob1.SameVolume(ob3));
    }
}
```

Pass an object reference.

This program generates the following output:

```
ob1 same dimensions as ob2: True
ob1 same dimensions as ob3: False
ob1 same volume as ob3: True
```

The **SameBlock( )** and **SameVolume( )** methods compare the invoking object with the object passed as an argument. For **SameBlock( )**, the dimensions of the objects are compared, and **true** is returned only if the two blocks are identical. For **SameVolume( )**, the two blocks are compared only to determine if they have the same volume. In both cases, notice that the parameter **ob** specifies **Block** as its type. As this example shows, syntactically, reference types are passed to methods in the same way as are the value types.

How Arguments Are Passed

As the preceding example demonstrated, passing an object reference to a method is a straightforward task. However, there are some nuances that the example did not show. In certain cases, the effects of passing an object reference will be different from those experienced when passing a value type. To see why, you need to understand the two ways in which an argument can be passed to a subroutine.

The first way is *call-by-value*. This method copies the *value* of an argument into the formal parameter of the subroutine. Therefore, changes made to the parameter of the subroutine have no effect on the argument. The second way an argument can be passed is *call-by-reference*. In this method, a *reference* to an argument (not the value of the argument) is passed to the parameter. Inside the subroutine, this reference is used to access the actual argument specified in the call. This means that changes made to the parameter will affect the argument used to call the subroutine.

By default, C# uses call-by-value, which means that a copy of the argument is made and given to the receiving parameter. Thus, when you pass a value type, such as **int** or **double**, what occurs to the parameter that receives the argument has no effect outside the method. For example, consider the following program:

```
// Simple types are passed by value.

using System;

class Test {
  // This method causes no change to the arguments used in the call.
  public void NoChange(int i, int j) {
```

```
    i = i + j;          ◄──── This does not change the arguments outside of NoChange( ).
    j = -j;
  }
}

class CallByValue {
  static void Main() {
    Test ob = new Test();

    int a = 15, b = 20;

    Console.WriteLine("a and b before call: " +
                      a + " " + b);

    ob.NoChange(a, b);

    Console.WriteLine("a and b after call: " +
                      a + " " + b);
  }
}
```

The output from this program is shown here:

```
a and b before call: 15 20
a and b after call: 15 20
```

As you can see, the operations that occur inside **NoChange( )** have no effect on the values of **a** and **b** used in the call.

When you pass an object reference to a method, the situation is a bit more complicated. Technically, the object reference itself is passed by value. Thus, a copy of the reference is made and changes to the parameter will not affect the argument. (For example, making the parameter refer to a new object will not change the object to which the argument refers.) However—and this is a big however—changes *made to the object* being referred to by the parameter *will* affect the object referred to by the argument because they are one and the same. Let's see why.

Recall that when you create a variable of a class type, you are creating a reference to an object, not the object itself. The object is allocated via **new**, and a reference to it is assigned to the reference variable. When you use a reference variable as an argument to a method, the parameter receives a reference to the same object as that referred to by the argument. Thus, the argument and parameter will both refer to the same object. This means that objects are passed to methods by use of what is effectively call-by-reference. Changes to the object inside the method *do* affect the object used as an argument. For example, consider the following program:

```
// Objects are implicitly passed by reference.

using System;

class Test {
  public int a, b;
```

```
   public Test(int i, int j) {
     a = i;
     b = j;
   }

   /* Pass an object. Now, ob.a and ob.b in object
      used in the call will be changed. */
   public void Change(Test ob) {
     ob.a = ob.a + ob.b;          ◄──── This will change the argument.
     ob.b = -ob.b;
   }
}

class CallByRef {
  static void Main() {
    Test ob = new Test(15, 20);

    Console.WriteLine("ob.a and ob.b before call: " +
                      ob.a + " " + ob.b);

    ob.Change(ob);

    Console.WriteLine("ob.a and ob.b after call: " +
                      ob.a + " " + ob.b);
  }
}
```

This program generates the following output:

```
ob.a and ob.b before call: 15 20
ob.a and ob.b after call: 35 -20
```

As you can see, in this case, the actions inside **Change( )** have affected the object used as an argument.

To review: When an object reference is passed to a method, the reference itself is passed by use of call-by-value. Thus, a copy of that reference is made. However, since the value being passed refers to an object, the copy of that value will still refer to the same object as its corresponding argument.

Using ref and out Parameters

As just explained, by default, value types, such as **int** or **char**, are passed by value to a method. This means that changes to the parameter that receives a value type will not affect the actual argument used in the call. You can, however, alter this behavior. Through the use of the **ref** and **out** keywords, it is possible to pass any of the value types by reference. Doing so allows a method to alter the argument used in the call.

Before going into the mechanics of using **ref** and **out**, it is useful to understand why you might want to pass a value type by reference. In general, there are two reasons: to allow a method to alter the contents of its arguments or to allow a method to return more than one value. Let's look at each reason in detail.

Often, you will want a method to be able to operate on the actual arguments that are passed to it. The quintessential example of this is a "swap" method that exchanges the values of its two arguments. Since value types are passed by value, it is not possible to write such a method that swaps the value of two **int**s, for example, using C#'s default call-by-value parameter-passing mechanism. The **ref** modifier solves this problem.

As you know, a **return** statement enables a method to return a value to its caller. However, a method can return *only one* value each time it is called. What if you need to return two or more pieces of information? For example, what if you want to create a method that computes the area of a rectangle and also determines if that rectangle is a square? To do this requires that two pieces of information be returned: the area and a value indicating square-ness. This method cannot be written using only a single return value. The **out** modifier solves this problem.

Using ref

The **ref** parameter modifier causes C# to create a call-by-reference rather than a call-by-value. The **ref** modifier is used when the method is declared and when it is called. Let's begin with a simple example. The following program creates a method called **Sqr( )** that returns in place the square of its integer argument. Notice the use and placement of **ref**.

```
// Use ref to pass a value type by reference.

using System;

class RefTest {
  // This method changes its arguments.
  public void Sqr(ref int i) {      ◄——— Here, ref precedes the parameter declaration.
    i = i * i;
  }
}

class RefDemo {
  static void Main() {
    RefTest ob = new RefTest();

    int a = 10;

    Console.WriteLine("a before call: " + a);

    ob.Sqr(ref a);    ◄——— Here, ref precedes the argument.

    Console.WriteLine("a after call: " + a);
  }
}
```

Notice that **ref** precedes the entire parameter declaration in the method and that it precedes the name of the argument when the method is called. The output from this program, shown here, confirms that the value of the argument, **a**, was indeed modified by **Sqr( )**:

```
a before call: 10
a after call: 100
```

Using **ref**, it is now possible to write a method that exchanges the values of its two value-type arguments. For example, here is a program that contains a method called **Swap( )** that exchanges the values of the two integer arguments with which it is called:

```
// Swap two values.

using System;

class SwapDemo {
  // This method exchanges its arguments.
  public void Swap(ref int a, ref int b) {
    int t;

    t = a;
    a = b;
    b = t;
  }
}

class SwapIt {
  static void Main() {
    SwapDemo ob = new SwapDemo();

    int x = 10, y = 20;

    Console.WriteLine("x and y before call: " + x + " " + y);

    ob.Swap(ref x, ref y);

    Console.WriteLine("x and y after call: " + x + " " + y);
  }
}
```

The output from this program is shown here:

```
x and y before call: 10 20
x and y after call: 20 10
```

Here is one important point to understand about **ref**: An argument passed by **ref** must be assigned a value prior to the call. The reason for this is that the method that receives such an argument assumes that the parameter refers to a valid value. Thus, using **ref**, you cannot use a method to give an argument an initial value.

Using out

Sometimes you will want to use a reference parameter to receive a value from a method but not pass in a value. For example, you might have a method that performs some function, such as opening a network socket, that returns a success/fail code in a reference parameter. In this case, there is no information to pass into the method, but there is information to pass back out. The problem with this scenario is that a **ref** parameter must be initialized to a value prior to the call. Thus, to use a **ref** parameter would require giving the argument a dummy value just to satisfy this constraint. Fortunately, C# provides a better alternative: the **out** parameter.

An **out** parameter is similar to a **ref** parameter with this one exception: It can only be used to pass a value out of a method. It is not necessary (or useful) to give the variable used as an **out** parameter an initial value prior to calling the method. The method will give the variable a value. Furthermore, inside the method, an **out** parameter is always considered *unassigned;* that is, it is assumed to have no initial value. Instead, the method *must* assign the parameter a value prior to the method's termination. Thus, after the call to the method, the variable referred to by an **out** parameter will contain a value.

Here is an example that uses an **out** parameter. The method **RectInfo( )** returns the area of a rectangle given the lengths of its sides. In the parameter **isSquare**, it returns **true** if the rectangle is a square and **false** otherwise. Thus, **RectInfo( )** returns two pieces of information to the caller.

```
// Use an out parameter.

using System;

class Rectangle {
  int side1;
  int side2;

  public Rectangle(int i, int j) {
    side1 = i;
    side2 = j;
  }

  // Return area and determine if square.
  public int RectInfo(out bool isSquare) {
    if(side1==side2) isSquare = true;
    else isSquare = false;

    return side1 * side2;
  }
}

class OutDemo {
  static void Main() {
    Rectangle rect = new Rectangle(10, 23);
```

Pass information out of the method via an **out** parameter.

```
        int area;
        bool isSqr;

        area = rect.RectInfo(out isSqr);

        if(isSqr) Console.WriteLine("rect is a square.");
        else Console.WriteLine("rect is not a square.");

        Console.WriteLine("Its area is " + area + ".");
    }
}
```

Notice that **isSqr** is not assigned a value prior to the call to **RectInfo( )**. This would not be allowed if the parameter to **RectInfo( )** had been a **ref** rather than an **out** parameter. After the method returns, **isSqr** contains either **true** or **false**, depending upon whether the rectangle is square or not. The area is returned via the **return** statement. The output from this program is shown here:

```
rect is not a square.
Its area is 230.
```

Ask the Expert

Q: Can ref and out be used on reference-type parameters, such as when passing a reference to an object?

A: Yes. When **ref** or **out** modifies a reference-type parameter, it causes the reference itself to be passed by reference. This allows a method to change what the reference is referring to. Consider the following program:

```
// Use ref on an object parameter.
using System;

class Test {
  public int a;

  public Test(int i) {
    a = i;
  }
  // This will not change the argument.
  public void NoChange(Test o) {
    Test newob = new Test(0);
    o = newob; // this has no effect outside of NoChange()
  }
```

```
    // This will change what the argument refers to.
    public void Change(ref Test o) {
      Test newob = new Test(0);
      o = newob; // this affects the calling argument.
    }
  }

class CallObjByRef {
  static void Main() {
    Test ob = new Test(100);

    Console.WriteLine("ob.a before call: " + ob.a);

    ob.NoChange(ob);
    Console.WriteLine("ob.a after call to NoChange(): " + ob.a);

    ob.Change(ref ob);
    Console.WriteLine("ob.a after call to Change(): " + ob.a);
  }
}
```

The output from this program is shown here:

```
ob.a before call: 100
ob.a after call to NoChange(): 100
ob.a after call to Change(): 0
```

As you can see, when **o** is assigned a reference to a new object inside **NoChange( )**, there is no effect on the argument **ob** inside **Main( )**. However, inside **Change( )**, which uses a **ref** parameter, assigning a new object to **o** does change the object referred to by **ob** inside **Main( )**.

Using a Variable Number of Arguments

When you create a method, you usually know in advance the number of arguments that you will be passing to it, but this is not always the case. Sometimes you will want to create a method that can be passed an arbitrary number of arguments. For example, consider a method that finds the smallest of a set of values. Such a method might be passed as few as two values, or three, or four, and so on. In all cases, you want that method to return the smallest value. Such a method cannot be created using normal parameters. Instead, you must use a special type of parameter that stands for an arbitrary number of parameters. This is done by creating a **params** parameter.

The **params** modifier is used to declare an array parameter that will be able to receive zero or more arguments. The number of elements in the array will be equal to the number of arguments passed to the method. Your program then accesses the array to obtain the arguments.

Here is an example that uses **params** to create a method called **MinVal( )**, which returns the minimum value from a set of values:

```csharp
// Demonstrate params.

using System;

class Min {
  public int MinVal(params int [] nums) {      Create a variable-length parameter
    int m;                                      by using params.

    if(nums.Length == 0) {
      Console.WriteLine("Error: no arguments.");
      return 0;
    }

    m = nums[0];
    for(int i=1; i < nums.Length; i++)
      if(nums[i] < m) m = nums[i];

    return m;
  }
}

class ParamsDemo {
  static void Main() {
    Min ob = new Min();
    int min;
    int a = 10, b = 20;

    // Call with two values.
    min = ob.MinVal(a, b);
    Console.WriteLine("Minimum is " + min);

    // Call with 3 values.
    min = ob.MinVal(a, b, -1);
    Console.WriteLine("Minimum is " + min);

    // Call with 5 values.
    min = ob.MinVal(18, 23, 3, 14, 25);
    Console.WriteLine("Minimum is " + min);

    // Can call with an int array, too.
    int[] args = { 45, 67, 34, 9, 112, 8 };
    min = ob.MinVal(args);
    Console.WriteLine("Minimum is " + min);
  }
}
```

The output from the program is shown here:

```
Minimum is 10
Minimum is -1
Minimum is 3
Minimum is 8
```

Each time **MinVal( )** is called, the arguments are passed to it via the **nums** array. The length of the array equals the number of elements. Thus, you can use **MinVal( )** to find the minimum of any number of values.

Although you can pass a **params** parameter any number of arguments, they all must be of a type compatible with the array type specified by the parameter. For example, calling **MinVal( )** like this:

```
min = ob.MinVal(1, 2.2);
```

is illegal because there is no implicit conversion from **double** (2.2) to **int**, which is the type of **nums** in **MinVal( )**.

When using **params**, you need to be careful about boundary conditions because a **params** parameter can accept any number of arguments—*even zero!* For example, it is syntactically valid to call **MinVal( )** as shown here:

```
min = ob.MinVal(); // no arguments
min  = ob.MinVal(3); // 1 argument
```

This is why there is a check in **MinVal( )** to confirm that at least one element is in the **nums** array before there is an attempt to access that element. If the check was not there, a runtime exception would result if **MinVal( )** were called with no arguments. (Later in this book, when exceptions are discussed, you will see a better way to handle these types of errors.) Furthermore, the code in **MinVal( )** was written in such a way as to permit calling **MinVal( )** with one argument. In that situation, the lone argument is returned.

A method can have normal parameters and a variable-length parameter. For example, in the following program, the method **ShowArgs( )** takes one **string** parameter and then a **params** integer array:

```
// Use regular parameter with a params parameter.

using System;

class MyClass {
  public void ShowArgs(string msg, params int[] nums) {
    Console.Write(msg + ": ");

    foreach(int i in nums)
      Console.Write(i + " ");

    Console.WriteLine();
```

This method has one normal parameter and one **params** parameter.

```
    }
  }

class ParamsDemo2 {
  static void Main() {
    MyClass ob = new MyClass();

    ob.ShowArgs("Here are some integers",
                1, 2, 3, 4, 5);

    ob.ShowArgs("Here are two more",
                17, 20);

  }
}
```

This program displays the following output:

```
Here are some integers: 1 2 3 4 5
Here are two more: 17 20
```

In cases where a method has regular parameters and a **params** parameter, the **params** parameter must be the last one in the parameter list. Furthermore, in all situations, there must be only one **params** parameters.

Returning Objects

A method can return any type of data, including class types. For example, the class **ErrorMsg** could be used to report errors. Its method, **GetErrorMsg( )**, returns a **string** object that contains a description of an error based upon the error code that it is passed.

```
// Return a string object.

using System;

class ErrorMsg {
  string[] msgs = {
    "Output Error",
    "Input Error",
    "Disk Full",
    "Index Out-Of-Bounds"
  };

  // Return the error message.
  public string GetErrorMsg(int i) {    ◄──── Return an object of type string.
    if(i >=0 & i < msgs.Length)
      return msgs[i];
    else
```

```
      return "Invalid Error Code";
    }
  }

class ErrMsg {
  static void Main() {
    ErrorMsg err = new ErrorMsg();

    Console.WriteLine(err.GetErrorMsg(2));
    Console.WriteLine(err.GetErrorMsg(19));
  }
}
```

Its output is shown here:

```
Disk Full
Invalid Error Code
```

You can, of course, also return objects of classes that you create. For example, here is a reworked version of the preceding program that creates two error classes. One is called **Err**, and it encapsulates an error message along with a severity code. The second is called **ErrorInfo**. It defines a method called **GetErrorInfo( )** that returns an **Err** object.

```
// Return a programmer-defined object.

using System;

class Err {
  public string Msg; // error message
  public int Severity; // code indicating severity of error

  public Err(string m, int s) {
    Msg = m;
    Severity  = s;
  }
}

class ErrorInfo {
  string[] msgs = {
    "Output Error",
    "Input Error",
    "Disk Full",
    "Index Out-Of-Bounds"
  };
  int[] howbad = { 3, 3, 2, 4 };

  public Err GetErrorInfo(int i) {     ◄——— Return an object of type Err.
    if(i >=0 & i < msgs.Length)
```

```
          return new Err(msgs[i], howbad[i]);
      else
          return new Err("Invalid Error Code", 0);
    }
}

class ErrInfo {
  static void Main() {
    ErrorInfo err = new ErrorInfo();
    Err e;

    e = err.GetErrorInfo(2);
    Console.WriteLine(e.Msg + " severity: " + e.Severity);

    e = err.GetErrorInfo(19);
    Console.WriteLine(e.Msg + " severity: " + e.Severity);
  }
}
```

Here is the output:

```
Disk Full severity: 2
Invalid Error Code severity: 0
```

Each time **GetErrorInfo( )** is invoked, a new **Err** object is created and a reference to it is returned to the calling routine. This object is then used within **Main( )** to display the error message and severity code.

When an object is returned by a method, it remains in existence until there are no more references to it. At that point, it is subject to garbage collection. Thus, an object won't be destroyed just because the method that created it terminates.

Method Overloading

In this section, you will learn about one of C#'s most exciting features: method overloading. In C#, two or more methods within the same class can share the same name, as long as their parameter declarations are different. When this is the case, the methods are said to be *overloaded,* and the process is referred to as *method overloading.* Method overloading is one of the ways that C# implements polymorphism.

In general, to overload a method, simply declare different versions of it. The compiler takes care of the rest. You must observe one important restriction: The type and/or number of the parameters of each overloaded method must differ. It is not sufficient for two methods to differ only in their return types. They must differ in the types or number of their parameters. (Return types do not provide sufficient information in all cases for C# to decide which method to use.) Of course, overloaded methods *may* differ in their return types, too. When an overloaded method is called, the version of the method whose parameters match the arguments is executed.

Here is a simple example that illustrates method overloading:

```
// Demonstrate method overloading.

using System;

class Overload {
  public void OvlDemo() {        ◄──── First version.
    Console.WriteLine("No parameters");
  }

  // Overload OvlDemo for one integer parameter.
  public void OvlDemo(int a) {    ◄──── Second version.
    Console.WriteLine("One parameter: " + a);
  }

  // Overload OvlDemo for two integer parameters.
  public int OvlDemo(int a, int b) {    ◄──── Third version.
    Console.WriteLine("Two parameters: " + a + " " + b);
    return a + b;
  }

  // Overload OvlDemo for two double parameters.
  public double OvlDemo(double a, double b) {    ◄──── Fourth version.
    Console.WriteLine("Two double parameters: " +
                       a + " "+ b);
    return a + b;
  }
}

class OverloadDemo {
  static void Main() {
    Overload ob = new Overload();
    int resI;
    double resD;

    // Call all versions of OvlDemo().
    ob.OvlDemo();
    Console.WriteLine();

    ob.OvlDemo(2);
    Console.WriteLine();

    resI = ob.OvlDemo(4, 6);
    Console.WriteLine("Result of ob.OvlDemo(4, 6): " +
                       resI);
    Console.WriteLine();

    resD = ob.OvlDemo(1.1, 2.32);
```

```
        Console.WriteLine("Result of ob.OvlDemo(1.1, 2.2): " +
                           resD);
    }
}
```

This program generates the following output:

```
No parameters

One parameter: 2

Two parameters: 4 6
Result of ob.OvlDemo(4, 6): 10

Two double parameters: 1.1 2.2
Result of ob.OvlDemo(1.1, 2.2): 3.42
```

As you can see, **OvlDemo( )** is overloaded four times. The first version takes no parameters, the second takes one integer parameter, the third takes two integer parameters, and the fourth takes two **double** parameters. Notice that the first two versions of **OvlDemo( )** return **void** and the second two return a value. This is perfectly valid, but as explained, overloading is not affected one way or the other by the return type of a method. Thus, attempting to use these two versions of **OvlDemo( )** will cause an error.

```
// One OvlDemo(int) is OK.
public void OvlDemo(int a) {
  Console.WriteLine("One parameter: " + a);
}
```

Return types cannot be used to differentiate overloaded methods.

```
/* Error! Two OvlDemo(int)s are not OK even though
   return types differ. */
public int OvlDemo(int a) {
  Console.WriteLine("One parameter: " + a);
  return a * a;
}
```

As the comments suggest, the difference in their return types is an insufficient difference for the purposes of overloading.

As you will recall from Chapter 2, C# provides certain implicit type conversions. These conversions also apply to parameters of overloaded methods. For example, consider the following:

```
// Implicit type conversions can affect overloaded method resolution.

using System;

class Overload2 {
  public void MyMeth(int x) {
    Console.WriteLine("Inside MyMeth(int): " + x);
  }
```

```
    public void MyMeth(double x) {
      Console.WriteLine("Inside MyMeth(double): " + x);
    }
}

class TypeConv {
  static void Main() {
    Overload2 ob = new Overload2();

    int i = 10;
    double d = 10.1;

    byte b = 99;
    short s = 10;
    float f = 11.5F;


    ob.MyMeth(i); // calls ob.MyMeth(int)
    ob.MyMeth(d); // calls ob.MyMeth(double)

    ob.MyMeth(b); // calls ob.MyMeth(int) -- type conversion
    ob.MyMeth(s); // calls ob.MyMeth(int) -- type conversion
    ob.MyMeth(f); // calls ob.MyMeth(double) -- type conversion
  }
}
```

The output from the program is shown here:

```
Inside MyMeth(int): 10
Inside MyMeth(double): 10.1
Inside MyMeth(int): 99
Inside MyMeth(int): 10
Inside MyMeth(double): 11.5
```

In this example, only two versions of **MyMeth( )** are defined: one that has an **int** parameter and one that has a **double** parameter. However, it is possible to pass **MyMeth( )** a **byte**, **short**, or **float** value. In the case of **byte** and **short**, C# automatically converts them to **int**. Thus, **MyMeth(int)** is invoked. In the case of **float**, the value is converted to **double** and **MyMeth(double)** is called.

It is important to understand, however, that the implicit conversions apply only if there is no direct match between the types of a parameter and an argument. For example, here is the preceding program with the addition of a version of **MyMeth( )** that specifies a **byte** parameter:

```
// Add MyMeth(byte).

using System;

class Overload2 {
  public void MyMeth(byte x) {
```

```
      Console.WriteLine("Inside MyMeth(byte): " + x);
  }

  public void MyMeth(int x) {
    Console.WriteLine("Inside MyMeth(int): " + x);
  }

  public void MyMeth(double x) {
    Console.WriteLine("Inside MyMeth(double): " + x);
  }
}

class TypeConv {
  static void Main() {
    Overload2 ob = new Overload2();

    int i = 10;
    double d = 10.1;

    byte b = 99;
    short s = 10;
    float f = 11.5F;

    ob.MyMeth(i); // calls ob.MyMeth(int)
    ob.MyMeth(d); // calls ob.MyMeth(double)

    ob.MyMeth(b); // calls ob.MyMeth(byte) -- now, no type conversion

    ob.MyMeth(s); // calls ob.MyMeth(int) -- type conversion
    ob.MyMeth(f); // calls ob.MyMeth(double) -- type conversion
  }
}
```

Now when the program is run, the following output is produced:

```
Inside MyMeth(int): 10
Inside MyMeth(double): 10.1
Inside MyMeth(byte): 99
Inside MyMeth(int): 10
Inside MyMeth(double): 11.5
```

In this version, since there is a version of **MyMeth( )** that takes a **byte** argument, when **MyMeth( )** is called with a **byte** argument, **MyMeth(byte)** is invoked and the automatic conversion to **int** does not occur.

Both **ref** and **out** participate in overload resolution. For example, the following define two distinct and separate methods:

```
public void MyMeth(int x) {
  Console.WriteLine("Inside MyMeth(int): " + x);
}
```

```
public void MyMeth(ref int x) {
  Console.WriteLine("Inside MyMeth(ref int): " + x);
}
```

Thus,

```
ob.MyMeth(i)
```

invokes **MyMeth(int x)**, but

```
ob.MyMeth(ref i)
```

invokes **MyMeth(ref int x)**.

One important point: Although **ref** and **out** participate in overload resolution, the difference between the two alone is not sufficient. Thus, these two versions of **MyMeth( )** are invalid:

```
// This won't compile.
public void MyMeth(out int x) { // ...
public void MyMeth(ref int x) { // ...
```

In this case, the compiler cannot differentiate between the versions of **MyMeth( )** simply because one uses **ref** and one uses **out**.

Method overloading supports polymorphism because it is one way that C# implements the "one interface, multiple methods" paradigm. To understand how, consider the following. In languages that do not support method overloading, each method must be given a unique name. However, frequently, you will want to implement essentially the same method for different types of data. Consider the absolute value function. In languages that do not support overloading, there are usually three or more versions of this function, each with a slightly different name. For instance, in C, the function **abs( )** returns the absolute value of an integer, **labs( )** returns the absolute value of a long integer, and **fabs( )** returns the absolute value of a floating-point value.

Since C does not support overloading, each of the absolute value functions needs its own name, even though all three functions do essentially the same thing. This makes the situation more complex conceptually than it actually is. Although the underlying concept of each function is the same, you still have three names to remember. This situation does not occur in C#, because each absolute value method can use the same name. Indeed, C#'s standard class library includes an absolute value method, called **Abs( )**. This method is overloaded by C#'s **System.Math** class to handle the numeric types. C# determines which version of **Abs( )** to call based upon the type of argument.

The value of overloading is that it allows related methods to be accessed through a common name. Thus, the name **Abs** represents the *general action* that is being performed. It is left to the compiler to choose the right *specific* version for a particular circumstance. You, the programmer, need only remember the general operation. Through the application of polymorphism, several names have been reduced to one. Although this example is fairly simple, if you expand the concept, you can see how overloading can help manage greater complexity.

Ask the Expert

Q: I've heard the term *signature* used by C# programmers. What is it?

A: As it applies to C#, a signature is the name of a method plus its parameter list. Thus, for the purposes of overloading, no two methods within the same class can have the same signature. Notice that a signature does not include the return type, since it is not used by C# for overload resolution.

When you overload a method, each version of that method can perform any activity you desire. There is no rule stating that overloaded methods must relate to one another. However, from a stylistic point of view, method overloading implies a relationship. Thus, while you can use the same name to overload unrelated methods, you should not. For example, you could use the name **sqr** to create methods that return the *square* of an integer and the *square root* of a floating-point value. But these two operations are fundamentally different. Applying method overloading in this manner defeats its original purpose. In practice, you should only overload closely related operations.

Overloading Constructors

Like methods, constructors can also be overloaded. Doing so allows you to construct objects in a variety of ways. For example, consider the following program:

```
// Demonstrate an overloaded constructor.

using System;

class MyClass {
  public int x;

  public MyClass() {
    Console.WriteLine("Inside MyClass().");
    x = 0;
  }

  public MyClass(int i) {
    Console.WriteLine("Inside MyClass(int).");
    x = i;
  }

  public MyClass(double d) {
    Console.WriteLine("Inside MyClass(double).");
    x = (int) d;
  }
```

Construct an object in a variety of ways.

```
 public MyClass(int i, int j) {
     Console.WriteLine("Inside MyClass(int, int).");
     x = i * j;
   }
}

class OverloadConsDemo {
  static void Main() {
    MyClass t1 = new MyClass();
    MyClass t2 = new MyClass(88);
    MyClass t3 = new MyClass(17.23);
    MyClass t4 = new MyClass(2, 4);

    Console.WriteLine("t1.x: " + t1.x);
    Console.WriteLine("t2.x: " + t2.x);
    Console.WriteLine("t3.x: " + t3.x);
    Console.WriteLine("t4.x: " + t4.x);
  }
}
```

Construct an object in a variety of ways.

The output from the program is shown here:

```
Inside MyClass().
Inside MyClass(int).
Inside MyClass(double).
Inside MyClass(int, int).
t1.x: 0
t2.x: 88
t3.x: 17
t4.x: 8
```

MyClass( ) is overloaded four ways, each constructing an object differently. The proper constructor is called based upon the arguments specified when **new** is executed. By overloading a class' constructor, you give the user of your class flexibility in the way objects are constructed.

One of the most common reasons that constructors are overloaded is to allow one object to initialize another. For example, consider this program that uses the **Summation** class to compute the summation of an integer value:

```
// Initialize one object with another.

using System;

class Summation {
  public int Sum;

  // Construct from an int.
  public Summation(int num) {
    Sum = 0;
```

```
    for(int i=1; i <= num; i++)
      Sum += i;
  }

  // Construct from another object.
  public Summation(Summation ob) {      ◄──────── Construct one object from another.
    Sum = ob.Sum;
  }
}

class SumDemo {
  static void Main() {
    Summation s1 = new Summation(5);
    Summation s2 = new Summation(s1);

    Console.WriteLine("s1.Sum: " + s1.Sum);
    Console.WriteLine("s2.Sum: " + s2.Sum);
  }
}
```

The output is shown here:

```
s1.Sum: 15
s2.Sum: 15
```

Often, as this example shows, an advantage of providing a constructor that uses one object to initialize another is efficiency. In this case, when **s2** is constructed, it is not necessary to recompute the summation. Of course, even in cases when efficiency is not an issue, it is often useful to provide a constructor that makes a copy of an object.

Invoking an Overloaded Constructor Through this

When working with overloaded constructors, it is sometimes useful for one constructor to invoke another. In C#, this is accomplished by using another form of the **this** keyword. The general form is shown here:

constructor-name(*parameter-list1*) : this(*parameter-list2*) {
  // ... body of constructor, which may be empty
}

When the constructor is executed, the overloaded constructor that matches the parameter list specified by *parameter-list2* is first executed. Then, if there are any statements inside the original constructor, they are executed. Here is an example:

```
// Demonstrate invoking a constructor through this.

using System;

class XYCoord {
  public int x, y;
```

```
  public XYCoord() : this(0, 0) {
    Console.WriteLine("Inside XYCoord()");
  }

  public XYCoord(XYCoord obj) : this(obj.x, obj.y) {
    Console.WriteLine("Inside XYCoord(XYCoord obj)");
  }

  public XYCoord(int i, int j) {
    Console.WriteLine("Inside XYCoord(XYCoord(int, int)");
    x = i;
    y = j;
  }
}

class OverloadConsDemo {
  static void Main() {
    XYCoord t1 = new XYCoord();
    XYCoord t2 = new XYCoord(8, 9);
    XYCoord t3 = new XYCoord(t2);

    Console.WriteLine("t1.x, t1.y: " + t1.x + ", " + t1.y);
    Console.WriteLine("t2.x, t2.y: " + t2.x + ", " + t2.y);
    Console.WriteLine("t3.x, t3.y: " + t3.x + ", " + t3.y);
  }
}
```

Use **this** to invoke an overloaded constructor.

The output from the program is shown here:

```
Inside XYCoord(XYCoord(int, int)
Inside XYCoord()
Inside XYCoord(XYCoord(int, int)
Inside XYCoord(XYCoord(int, int)
Inside XYCoord(XYCoord obj)
t1.x, t1.y: 0, 0
t2.x, t2.y: 8, 9
t3.x, t3.y: 8, 9
```

Here is how the program works. In the **XYCoord** class, the only constructor that actually initializes the **x** and **y** fields is **XYCoord(int, int)**. The other two constructors simply invoke **XYCoord(int, int)** through **this**. For example, when object **t1** is created, its constructor, **XYCoord( )**, is called. This causes **this(0, 0)** to be executed, which, in this case, translates into a call to **XYCoord(0, 0)**.

One reason why invoking overloaded constructors through **this** can be useful is that it can prevent the unnecessary duplication of code. In the foregoing example, there is no reason for all three constructors to duplicate the same initialization sequence, which the use of **this** avoids. Another advantage is that you can create constructors with implied "default arguments," which are used when these arguments are not explicitly specified. For example, you could create another **XYCoord** constructor, as shown here:

```
public XYCoord(int x) : this(x, x) { }
```

This constructor automatically defaults the **y** coordinate to the same value as the **x** coordinate. Of course, it is wise to use such "default arguments" carefully because their misuse could easily confuse users of your classes.

Try This Overload the SimpleQueue Constructor

In this project you will enhance the **SimpleQueue** class developed in the previous Try This section by giving it two additional constructors. The first will construct a new queue from another queue. The second will construct a queue, giving it initial values. As you will see, adding these constructors enhances the usability of **SimpleQueue** substantially.

Step by Step

1. Create a file called **QDemo2.cs**, and copy the updated **SimpleQueue** class from the previous Try This section into it.

2. Add the following constructor, which constructs a queue from a queue:

```
// Construct a SimpleQueue from a SimpleQueue.
public SimpleQueue(SimpleQueue ob) {
  putloc = ob.putloc;
  getloc = ob.getloc;
  q = new char[ob.q.Length];

  // Copy elements
  for(int i=getloc+1; i <= putloc; i++)
    q[i] = ob.q[i];
}
```

Look closely at this constructor. It initializes **putloc** and **getloc** to the values contained in the **ob** parameter. It then allocates a new array to hold the queue and copies the elements from **ob** into that array. Once constructed, the new queue will be an identical copy of the original, but both will be completely separate objects.

3. Add the constructor that initializes the queue from a character array, as shown here:

```
// Construct a SimpleQueue with initial values.
public SimpleQueue(char[] a) {
  putloc = 0;
  getloc = 0;
  q = new char[a.Length+1];

  for(int i = 0; i < a.Length; i++) Put(a[i]);
}
```

This constructor creates a queue large enough to hold the characters in **a** and then stores those characters in the queue. Because of the way the queue algorithm works, the length of the queue must be 1 greater than the array.

4. Here is the complete updated **SimpleQueue** class, along with the **QDemo2** class, which demonstrates it:

```
// A queue class for characters.

using System;

class SimpleQueue {

  // These are now private.
  char[] q; // this array holds the queue
  int putloc, getloc; // the put and get indices

  // Construct an empty SimpleQueue given its size.
  public SimpleQueue(int size) {
    q = new char[size+1]; // allocate memory for queue
    putloc = getloc = 0;
  }

  // Construct a SimpleQueue from a SimpleQueue.
  public SimpleQueue(SimpleQueue ob) {
    putloc = ob.putloc;
    getloc = ob.getloc;
    q = new char[ob.q.Length];

    // Copy elements.
    for(int i=getloc+1; i <= putloc; i++)
      q[i] = ob.q[i];
  }

  // Construct a SimpleQueue with initial values.
  public SimpleQueue(char[] a) {
    putloc = 0;
    getloc = 0;
    q = new char[a.Length+1];

    for(int i = 0; i < a.Length; i++) Put(a[i]);
  }

  // Put a character into the queue.
  public void Put(char ch) {
    if(putloc==q.Length-1) {
      Console.WriteLine(" -- Queue is full.");
      return;
```

(continued)

```csharp
    }

    putloc++;
    q[putloc] = ch;
  }

  // Get a character from the queue.
  public char Get() {
    if(getloc == putloc) {
      Console.WriteLine(" -- Queue is empty.");
      return (char) 0;
    }

    getloc++;
    return q[getloc];
  }
}

// Demonstrate the SimpleQueue class.
class QDemo2 {
  static void Main() {
    // Construct 10-element empty queue.
    SimpleQueue q1 = new SimpleQueue(10);

    char[] name = {'T', 'o', 'm'};

    // Construct queue from array.
    SimpleQueue q2 = new SimpleQueue(name);

    char ch;
    int i;

    // Put some characters into q1.
    for(i=0; i < 10; i++)
      q1.Put((char) ('A' + i));

    // Construct queue from another queue.
    SimpleQueue q3 = new SimpleQueue(q1);

    // Show the queues.
    Console.Write("Contents of q1: ");
    for(i=0; i < 10; i++) {
      ch = q1.Get();
      Console.Write(ch);
    }

    Console.WriteLine("\n");
```

```
        Console.Write("Contents of q2: ");
        for(i=0; i < 3; i++) {
          ch = q2.Get();
          Console.Write(ch);
        }

        Console.WriteLine("\n");

        Console.Write("Contents of q3: ");
        for(i=0; i < 10; i++) {
          ch = q3.Get();
          Console.Write(ch);
        }
      }
    }
  }
```

5. The output from the program is shown here:

```
Contents of q1: ABCDEFGHIJ

Contents of q2: Tom

Contents of q3: ABCDEFGHIJ
```

The Main( ) Method

Up to this point, you have been using one form of **Main( )**. However, there are several overloaded forms of **Main( )**. Some can be used to return a value, and some can receive arguments. Each is examined here.

Returning Values from Main( )

When a program ends, you can return a value to the calling process (often the operating system) by returning a value from **Main( )**. To do so, you can use this form of **Main( )**:

static int Main( )

Notice that instead of being declared **void**, this version of **Main( )** has a return type of **int**.

Usually, the return value from **Main( )** indicates whether the program ended normally or due to some abnormal condition. By convention, a return value of 0 usually indicates normal termination. All other values indicate that some type of error occurred.

Passing Arguments to Main( )

Many programs accept what are called *command-line* arguments. A command-line argument is the information that directly follows the program's name on the command line when it is executed. For C# programs, these arguments are then passed to the **Main( )** method. To receive the arguments, you must use one of these forms of **Main( )**:

static void Main(string[ ] *args*)

static int Main(string[ ] *args*)

The first form returns **void**; the second can be used to return an integer value, as described in the preceding section. For both, the command-line arguments are stored as strings in the **string** array passed to **Main( )**. The length of the *args* array will be equal to the number of command-line arguments.

For example, the following program displays all of the command-line arguments that it is called with:

```
// Display all command-line information.

using System;

class CLDemo {
  static void Main(string[] args) {
    Console.WriteLine("There are " + args.Length +
                      " command-line arguments.");

    Console.WriteLine("They are: ");
    for(int i=0; i < args.Length; i++)
      Console.WriteLine(args[i]);
  }
}
```

If **CLDemo** is executed like this:

```
CLDemo one two three
```

you will see the following output:

```
There are 3 command-line arguments.
They are:
one
two
three
```

To sample the way that command-line arguments can be used, consider the next program. It takes one command-line argument that specifies a person's name. It then searches through a two-dimensional array of strings for that name. If it finds a match, it displays that person's telephone number.

```
// A simple automated telephone directory.

using System;

class Phone {
  public static int Main(string[] args) {
    string[,] numbers = {
        { "Tom", "555-3322" },
        { "Mary", "555-8976" },
        { "Jon", "555-1037" },
        { "Rachel", "555-1400" },
    };
    int i;

    if(args.Length != 1) {
      Console.WriteLine("Usage: Phone <name>");
      return 1; // indicate improper command-line arguments
    }
    else {
      for(i=0; i < numbers.Length/2; i++) {
        if(numbers[i, 0] == args[0]) {
          Console.WriteLine(numbers[i, 0] + ": " +
                              numbers[i, 1]);
          break;
        }
      }
      if(i == numbers.Length/2)
        Console.WriteLine("Name not found.");
    }
    return 0;
  }
}
```

Here is a sample run:

```
C>Phone Mary
Mary: 555-8976
```

There are two interesting things in this program. First, notice how the program confirms that a command-line argument is present by checking the length of **args**. If the number of arguments is incorrect, execution is terminated. This confirmation is very important and can be generalized. When a program relies on there being one or more command-line arguments, it must always confirm that the proper arguments have been supplied. Failure to do this will often lead to a program crash!

Second, notice how the program returns a termination code. If the required command line is not present, then 1 is returned, indicating abnormal termination. Otherwise, 0 is returned when the program ends.

Recursion

In C#, a method can call itself. This process is called *recursion,* and a method that calls itself is said to be *recursive.* In general, recursion is the process of defining something in terms of itself and is somewhat similar to a circular definition. The key component of a recursive method is that it contains a statement that executes a call to itself. Recursion is a powerful control mechanism.

The classic example of recursion is the computation of the factorial of a number. The factorial of a number *N* is the product of all the whole numbers between 1 and *N*. For example, 3 factorial is $1 \times 2 \times 3$, or 6. The following program shows a recursive way to compute the factorial of a number. For comparison purposes, a nonrecursive equivalent is also included.

```
// A simple example of recursion.

using System;

class Factorial {
  // This is a recursive method.
  public int FactR(int n) {
    if(n==1) return 1;
    else return FactR(n-1) * n;    ◄──── Execute a recursive call to FactR( ).
  }

  // This is an iterative equivalent.
  public int FactI(int n) {
    int t, result;

    result = 1;
    for(t=1; t <= n; t++) result *= t;
    return result;
  }
}

class Recursion {
  static void Main() {
    Factorial f = new Factorial();

    Console.WriteLine("Factorials using recursive method.");
    Console.WriteLine("Factorial of 3 is " + f.FactR(3));
    Console.WriteLine("Factorial of 4 is " + f.FactR(4));
    Console.WriteLine("Factorial of 5 is " + f.FactR(5));
    Console.WriteLine();

    Console.WriteLine("Factorials using iterative method.");
    Console.WriteLine("Factorial of 3 is " + f.FactI(3));
    Console.WriteLine("Factorial of 4 is " + f.FactI(4));
    Console.WriteLine("Factorial of 5 is " + f.FactI(5));
  }
}
```

The output from this program is shown here:

```
Factorials using recursive method.
Factorial of 3 is 6
Factorial of 4 is 24
Factorial of 5 is 120

Factorials using iterative method.
Factorial of 3 is 6
Factorial of 4 is 24
Factorial of 5 is 120
```

The operation of the nonrecursive method **FactI( )** should be clear. It uses a loop starting at 1 and progressively multiplies each number by the moving product.

The operation of the recursive **FactR( )** is a bit more complex. When **FactR( )** is called with an argument of 1, the method returns 1; otherwise, it returns the product of **FactR(n–1)*n**. To evaluate this expression, **FactR( )** is called with **n–1**. This process repeats until **n** equals 1 and the calls to the method begin returning. For example, when the factorial of 2 is calculated, the first call to **FactR( )** will cause a second call to be made with an argument of 1. This call will return 1, which is then multiplied by 2 (the original value of **n**). The answer is then 2. You might find it interesting to insert **WriteLine( )** statements into **FactR( )** that show at what level each call is and what the intermediate results are.

When a method calls itself, new local variables and parameters are allocated storage on the system stack, and the method code is executed with these new variables from the start. (A recursive call *does not* make a new copy of the method.) As each recursive call returns, the old local variables and parameters are removed from the stack, and execution resumes at the point of the call inside the method. Recursive methods could be said to "telescope" out and back.

Recursive versions of many routines may execute a bit more slowly than the iterative equivalent because of the added overhead of the additional method calls. Too many recursive calls to a method could cause a stack overrun. Because storage for parameters and local variables is on the stack and each new call creates a new copy of these variables, it is possible that the stack could be exhausted. If this occurs, the CLR will throw an exception. However, you probably will not have to worry about this unless a recursive routine runs wild.

The main advantage to recursion is that some types of algorithms can be implemented more clearly and simply recursively than they can be iteratively. For example, the quicksort sorting algorithm is quite difficult to implement in an iterative way. Also, some problems, especially AI-related ones, seem to lend themselves to recursive solutions.

When writing recursive methods, you must have a conditional statement somewhere, such as an **if**, to force the method to return without the recursive call being executed. If you don't do this, once you call the method, it will never return. This type of error is very common when working with recursion. Use **WriteLine( )** statements liberally so that you can watch what is going on and abort execution if you see that you have made a mistake.

Understanding static

There will be times when you want to define a class member that will be used independently of any object of that class. Normally, a class member must be accessed through an object of its class, but it is possible to create a member that can be used by itself, without reference to a specific instance. To create such a member, precede its declaration with the keyword **static**. When a member is declared **static**, it can be accessed before any objects of its class are created and without reference to any object. You can declare both methods and variables to be **static**. The most common example of a **static** member is **Main( )**, which is declared **static** because it must be called by the operating system when your program begins.

Outside the class, to use a **static** member, you must specify the name of its class, followed by the dot operator. No object needs to be created. In fact, a **static** member cannot be accessed through an object instance. It must be accessed through its class name. For example, assume a **static** variable called **count** that is a member of a class called **Timer**. To assign **count** the value 10, use this line:

```
Timer.count = 10;
```

This format is similar to that used to access normal instance variables through an object, except that the class name is used. A **static** method can be called in the same way—by use of the dot operator on the name of the class.

Variables declared as **static** are, essentially, global variables. When objects of its class are declared, no copy of a **static** variable is made. Instead, all instances of the class share the same **static** variable. A **static** variable is initialized before its class is used. If no explicit initializer is specified, it is initialized to zero for numeric types, null in the case of reference types, or **false** for variables of type **bool**. Thus, a **static** variable always has a value.

The difference between a **static** method and a normal method is that the **static** method can be called through its class name, without any instance of that class being created. You have seen an example of this already: the **Sqrt( )** method, which is a **static** method within C#'s **System.Math** class.

Here is an example that declares a **static** variable and a **static** method:

```csharp
// Use static.

using System;

class StaticDemo {

  // A static variable.
  public static int Val = 100;   ◄——— A static variable.

  // A static method.
  public static int ValDiv2() {   ◄——— A static method.
    return Val/2;
  }
}
```

```
class SDemo {
  static void Main() {

    Console.WriteLine("Initial value of StaticDemo.Val is "
                       + StaticDemo.Val);

    StaticDemo.Val = 8;
    Console.WriteLine("StaticDemo.Val is " + StaticDemo.Val);
    Console.WriteLine("StaticDemo.ValDiv2(): " +
                       StaticDemo.ValDiv2());
  }
}
```

The output is shown here:

```
Initial value of StaticDemo.Val is 100
StaticDemo.Val is 8
StaticDemo.ValDiv2(): 4
```

As the output shows, a **static** variable is initialized before any object of its class is created. There are several restrictions that apply to **static** methods:

- A **static** method does not have a **this** reference. This is because a **static** method does not execute relative to any object.

- A **static** method can directly call only other **static** methods of its class. It cannot directly call an instance method of its class. The reason is that instance methods operate on specific objects, but a **static** method is not called on an object. Thus, on what object would the **instance** method operate?

- A similar restriction applies to **static** data. A **static** method can directly access only other **static** data of its class. It cannot operate on an instance variable of its class because there is no object to operate on.

For example, in the following class, the **static** method **ValDivDenom( )** is illegal:

```
class StaticError {
  public int Denom = 3; // a normal instance variable
  public static int Val = 1024; // a static variable

  /* Error! Can't directly access a non-static variable
     from within a static method. */
  public static int ValDivDenom() {
    return Val/Denom; // won't compile!
  }
}
```

Here, **Denom** is a normal instance variable that cannot be accessed within a **static** method. However, the use of **Val** is okay, since it is a **static** variable.

The same problem occurs when trying to call a non-**static** method from within a **static** method of the same class. For example:

```
using System;

class AnotherStaticError {

  // A non-static method.
  public void NonStaticMeth() {
     Console.WriteLine("Inside NonStaticMeth().");
  }

  /* Error! Can't directly call a non-static method
     from within a static method. */
  public static void StaticMeth() {
    NonStaticMeth(); // won't compile
  }
}
```

In this case, the attempt to call a non-**static** (that is, instance method) from a **static** method causes a compile-time error.

It is important to understand that although a **static** method cannot directly call instance methods or access instance variables of its class, it *can* call an instance method or access an instance variable if it does so through an object of its class. It just cannot use an instance variable or method directly, without an object qualification. For example, this fragment is perfectly valid:

```
class MyClass {
  // A non-static method.
  public void NonStaticMeth() {
     Console.WriteLine("Inside NonStaticMeth().");
  }

  /* Can call a non-static method through an
     object reference from within a static method. */
  public static void StaticMeth(MyClass ob) {
    ob.NonStaticMeth(); // this is OK
  }
}
```

Static Constructors and Classes

There are two other uses of **static** that are typically applied in situations more advanced than those described in this chapter. However, for the sake of completeness, they are briefly described here.

In addition to variables and methods, it is possible to specify a constructor as **static**. For example,

```
class Sample {
  // ...
  static Sample() { ...
```

Here, **Sample( )** is declared **static** and is, therefore, a **static** constructor for the **Sample** class. A **static** constructor is called automatically when the class is first loaded, before any objects are created and before any instance constructors are called. Thus, the primary use for a **static** constructor is to initialize features that apply to the class as a whole, rather than to an instance of the class. A **static** constructor cannot have access modifiers and cannot be called directly by your program. Furthermore, it has the same restrictions as **static** methods, described earlier.

Beginning with C# 2.0, you can also specify a class as **static**. For example,

```
static class Test { // ...
```

A **static** class has two important features. First, no object of a **static** class can be created. Second, a **static** class must contain only **static** members. A primary use of a **static** class is found when working with extension methods, which is an advanced feature added by C# 3.0.

Try This   The Quicksort

In Chapter 5 you were shown a simple sorting method called the bubble sort. It was mentioned that substantially better sorts exist. Here you will develop a version of one of the best: the quicksort. The quicksort, invented and named by C.A.R. Hoare, is the best general-purpose sorting algorithm currently available. The reason it could not be shown in Chapter 5 is that the best implementations of the quicksort rely on recursion. Thus, it makes an excellent example to show the power of recursion in action. The version we will develop sorts a character array, but the logic can be adapted to sort any type of object you like.

The quicksort is built on the idea of *partitions*. The general procedure is to select a value, called the *comparand,* and then to partition the array into two sections. All elements greater than or equal to the partition value are put on one side, and those less than the value are put on the other. This process is then repeated for each remaining section until the array is sorted. For example, given the array **fedacb** and using the value **d** as the comparand, the first pass of the quicksort would rearrange the array as follows:

| Initial | f e d a c b |
| Pass 1 | b c a d e f |

This process is then repeated for each section—that is, **bca** and **def**. As you can see, the process is essentially recursive in nature and, indeed, the cleanest implementation of quicksort is as a recursive method.

(continued)

You can select the comparand value in two ways. You can either choose it at random, or you can select it by averaging a small set of values taken from the array. For optimal sorting, you should select a value that is precisely in the middle of the range of values. However, this is not easy to do for most sets of data. In the worst case, the value chosen is at one extremity. Even in this case, however, quicksort still performs correctly. The version of quicksort that we will develop selects the middle element of the array as the comparand.

One other point before we begin. Although developing your own sorting methods is both instructive and enjoyable, you won't often need to. The reason is that C# provides library methods that sort arrays and other collections of objects. For example, the method **System.Array.Sort( )** can sort an array. As you might expect, it, too, is implemented as a quicksort!

Step by Step

1. Create a file called **QSDemo.cs**.

2. Create the **Quicksort** class shown here:

```
// A simple version of the Quicksort.

using System;

class Quicksort {

  // Set up a call to the actual quicksort method.
  public static void QSort(char[] items) {
    if(items.Length == 0) return;
    qs(items, 0, items.Length-1);
  }

  // A recursive version of quicksort for characters.
  private static void qs(char[] items, int left, int right)
  {
    int i, j;
    char x, y;

    i = left; j = right;
    x = items[(left+right)/2];

    do {
      while((items[i] < x) && (i < right)) i++;
      while((x < items[j]) && (j > left)) j--;

      if(i <= j) {
        y = items[i];
        items[i] = items[j];
        items[j] = y;
        i++; j--;
      }
    } while(i <= j);
```

```
      if(left < j) qs(items, left, j);
      if(i < right) qs(items, i, right);
  }
}
```

To keep the interface to the quicksort simple, the **Quicksort** class provides the **QSort( )** method, which sets up a call to the actual quicksort method, **qs( )**. This enables the quicksort to be called with just the name of the array to be sorted, without having to provide an initial partition. Since **qs( )** is only used internally, it is specified as **private**.

3. To use the **Quicksort**, simply call **Quicksort.QSort( )**. Since **QSort( )** is specified as **static**, it must be called through its class rather than on an object. Thus, there is no need to create a **Quicksort** object. After the call returns, the array will be sorted. Remember, this version works only for character arrays, but you can adapt the logic to sort any type of arrays you want.

4. Here is a program that demonstrates **Quicksort**:

```
// A simple version of the quicksort.

using System;

class Quicksort {

  // Set up a call to the actual quicksort method.
  public static void QSort(char[] items) {
    if(items.Length == 0) return;
    qs(items, 0, items.Length-1);
  }

  // A recursive version of quicksort for characters.
  private static void qs(char[] items, int left, int right)
  {
    int i, j;
    char x, y;

    i = left; j = right;
    x = items[(left+right)/2];

    do {
      while((items[i] < x) && (i < right)) i++;
      while((x < items[j]) && (j > left)) j--;

      if(i <= j) {
        y = items[i];
        items[i] = items[j];
        items[j] = y;
        i++; j--;
```

(continued)

```
        }
    } while(i <= j);

    if(left < j) qs(items, left, j);
    if(i < right) qs(items, i, right);
    }
  }

class QSDemo {
  static void Main() {
    char[] a = { 'd', 'x', 'a', 'r', 'p', 'j', 'i' };
    int i;

    Console.Write("Original array: ");
    for(i=0; i < a.Length; i++) Console.Write(a[i]);

    Console.WriteLine();

    // Now, sort the array.
    Quicksort.QSort(a);

    Console.Write("Sorted array: ");
    for(i=0; i < a.Length; i++) Console.Write(a[i]);
  }
}
```

Chapter 6 Self Test

1. Given this fragment:

```
class X {
  int count;
```

is the following fragment correct?

```
class Y {
  static void Main() {
    X ob = new X();

    ob.count = 10;
```

2. An access specifier must _____ a member's declaration.

3. The complement of a queue is a stack. It uses first-in, last-out accessing and is often likened to a stack of plates. The first plate put on the table is the last plate used. Create a stack class called **Stack** that can hold characters. Call the methods that access the stack **Push( )**

and **Pop( )**. Allow the user to specify the size of the stack when it is created. Keep all other members of the **Stack** class private. Hint: You can use the **SimpleQueue** class as a model; just change the way that the data is accessed.

4. Given this class:

```
class Test {
  int a;
  Test(int i) { a = i; }
}
```

write a method called **Swap( )** that exchanges the contents of the objects referred to by two **Test** object references.

5. Is the following fragment correct?

```
class X {
  int meth(int a, int b) { ... }
  string meth(int a, int b) { ... }
```

6. Write a recursive method that displays the contents of a string backwards.

7. If all objects of a class need to share the same variable, how must you declare that variable?

8. What do **ref** and **out** do? How do they differ?

9. Show the four forms of **Main( )**.

10. Given this fragment, which of the following calls are legal?

```
void meth(int i, int j, params int [] args) { // ...
```

   A. meth(10, 12, 19);

   B. meth(10, 12, 19, 100);

   C. meth(10, 12, 19, 100, 200);

   D. meth(10, 12);

Chapter 7

Operator Overloading, Indexers, and Properties

Key Skills & Concepts

- Operator overloading fundamentals
- Overload binary operators
- Overload unary operators
- Overload relational operators
- Indexers
- Properties

This chapter examines three special types of class members: overloaded operators, indexers, and properties. Each of these expands the power of a class by improving its usability, its integration into C#'s type system, and its resiliency. Using these members, it is possible to create class types that look and feel like the built-in types. This *type extensibility* is an important part of the power of an object-oriented language such as C#.

Operator Overloading

C# allows you to define the meaning of an operator relative to a class that you create. This process is called *operator overloading.* By overloading an operator, you expand its usage to your class. The effects of the operator are completely under your control and may differ from class to class. For example, a class that defines a linked list might use the + operator to add an object to the list. A class that implements a stack might use the + to push an object onto the stack. Another class might use the + operator in an entirely different way.

When an operator is overloaded, none of its original meaning is lost. It is simply that a new operation, relative to a specific class, is added. Therefore, overloading the + to handle a linked list, for example, does not cause its meaning relative to integers (that is, addition) to be changed.

A principal advantage of operator overloading is that it allows you to seamlessly integrate a new class type into your programming environment. Once operators are defined for a class, you can operate on objects of that class using the normal C# expression syntax. You can even use an object in expressions involving other types of data.

Operator overloading is closely related to method overloading. To overload an operator, use the **operator** keyword to define an *operator method,* which defines the action of the operator.

The General Forms of an Operator Method

There are two forms of **operator** methods: one for unary operators and one for binary operators. The general form for each is shown here:

```
// General form for overloading a unary operator.
public static ret-type operator op(param-type operand)
{
  // operations
}
```

```
// General form for overloading a binary operator.
public static ret-type operator op(param-type1 operand1, param-type2 operand2)
{
  // operations
}
```

Here, the operator that you are overloading, such as **+** or **/,** is substituted for the *op*. The *ret-type* is the type of value returned by the specified operation. Although it can be of any type you choose, the return value is often of the same type as the class for which the operator is being overloaded. This correlation facilitates the use of the overloaded operator in expressions. For unary operators, the operand is passed in *operand.* For binary operators, the operands are passed in *operand1* and *operand2*.

For unary operators, the operand must be of the same type as the class for which the operator is being defined. For binary operators, at least one of the operands must be of the same type as the class. Thus, you cannot overload any C# operators for objects that you have not created. For example, you can't redefine **+** for **int** or **string**.

One other point: Operator parameters must not use the **ref** or **out** modifier.

Overloading Binary Operators

To see how operator overloading works, let's start with an example that overloads two binary operators: the **+** and the **−**. The following program creates a class called **ThreeD**, which maintains the coordinates of an object in three-dimensional space. The overloaded **+** adds the individual coordinates of one **ThreeD** object to another. The overloaded **−** subtracts the coordinates of one object from the other.

```
// An example of operator overloading.

using System;

// A three-dimensional coordinate class.
class ThreeD {
  int x, y, z; // 3-D coordinates

  public ThreeD() { x = y = z = 0; }
  public ThreeD(int i, int j, int k) { x = i; y = j; z = k; }
```

```
   // Overload binary +.
   public static ThreeD operator +(ThreeD op1, ThreeD op2)
   {
      ThreeD result = new ThreeD();          Overload + for ThreeD objects.

      /* This adds together the coordinates of the two points
         and returns the result. */
      result.x = op1.x + op2.x; // These are integer additions
      result.y = op1.y + op2.y; // and the + retains its original
      result.z = op1.z + op2.z; // meaning relative to them.

      return result;
   }

   // Overload binary -.
   public static ThreeD operator -(ThreeD op1, ThreeD op2)
   {
      ThreeD result = new ThreeD();          Overload - for ThreeD objects.

      /* Notice the order of the operands. op1 is the left
         operand and op2 is the right. */
      result.x = op1.x - op2.x; // these are integer subtractions
      result.y = op1.y - op2.y;
      result.z = op1.z - op2.z;

      return result;
   }

   // Show X, Y, Z coordinates.
   public void Show()
   {
      Console.WriteLine(x + ", " + y + ", " + z);
   }
}

class ThreeDDemo {
   static void Main() {
      ThreeD a = new ThreeD(1, 2, 3);
      ThreeD b = new ThreeD(10, 10, 10);
      ThreeD c = new ThreeD();

      Console.Write("Here is a: ");
      a.Show();
      Console.WriteLine();
      Console.Write("Here is b: ");
      b.Show();
      Console.WriteLine();
```

```
    c = a + b; // add a and b together
    Console.Write("Result of a + b: ");
    c.Show();
    Console.WriteLine();

    c = a + b + c; // add a, b and c together
    Console.Write("Result of a + b + c: ");
    c.Show();
    Console.WriteLine();

    c = c - a; // subtract a
    Console.Write("Result of c - a: ");
    c.Show();
    Console.WriteLine();

    c = c - b; // subtract b
    Console.Write("Result of c - b: ");
    c.Show();
    Console.WriteLine();
  }
}
```

Use **ThreeD** objects and the + and – in expressions.

This program produces the following output:

```
Here is a: 1, 2, 3

Here is b: 10, 10, 10

Result of a + b: 11, 12, 13

Result of a + b + c: 22, 24, 26

Result of c - a: 21, 22, 23

Result of c - b: 11, 12, 13
```

Let's examine the preceding program carefully, beginning with the overloaded operator +. When two objects of type **ThreeD** are operated on by the + operator, the magnitudes of their respective coordinates are added together, as shown in **operator+( )**. Notice, however, that this method does not modify the value of either operand. Instead, a new object of type **ThreeD**, which contains the result of the operation, is returned by the method. To understand why the + operation does not change the contents of either object, think about the standard arithmetic + operation as applied like this: 10 + 12. The outcome of this operation is 22, but neither 10 nor 12 is changed by it. Although there is no rule that prevents an overloaded operator from altering the value of one of its operands, it is best for the actions of an overloaded operator to be consistent with its usual meaning.

Notice that **operator+( )** returns an object of type **ThreeD**. Although the method could have returned any valid C# type, the fact that it returns a **ThreeD** object allows the + operator to be used in compound expressions, such as **a+b+c**. Here, **a+b** generates a result that is of type **ThreeD**. This value can then be added to **c**. Had any other type of value been generated by **a+b**, such an expression would not work.

Here is another important point: When the coordinates are added together inside **operator+( )**, the addition of the individual coordinates results in an integer addition. This is because the individual coordinates, **x**, **y**, and **z**, are integer quantities. The fact that the + operator is overloaded for objects of type **ThreeD** has no effect on the + as it is applied to integer values.

Now, look at **operator–( )**. The – operator works just like the + operator, except that the order of the parameters is important. Recall that addition is commutative, but subtraction is not. (That is, A – B is not the same as B – A!) For all binary operators, the first parameter to an operator method will contain the left operand. The second parameter will contain the operand on the right. When implementing overloaded versions of the non-commutative operators, you must remember which operand is on the left and which is on the right.

Overloading Unary Operators

The unary operators are overloaded just like the binary operators. The main difference, of course, is that there is only one operand. For example, here is a method that overloads the unary minus for the **ThreeD** class:

```
// Overload unary -.
public static ThreeD operator -(ThreeD op)
{
  ThreeD result = new ThreeD();

  result.x = -op.x;
  result.y = -op.y;
  result.z = -op.z;

  return result;
}
```

Here, a new object is created that contains the negated fields of the operand. This object is then returned. Notice that the operand is unchanged. Again, this is in keeping with the usual meaning of the unary minus. For example, in an expression such as

```
a = -b
```

a receives the negation of **b**, but **b** is not changed.

In C#, overloading ++ and – – is quite easy; simply return the incremented or decremented value, but don't change the invoking object. C# will automatically handle that for you, taking into account the difference between the prefix and postfix forms. For example, here is an **operator++( )** method for the **ThreeD** class:

```
// Overload unary ++.
public static ThreeD operator ++(ThreeD op)
{
  ThreeD result = new ThreeD();
```

```
   // Return the incremented result.
   result.x = op.x + 1;
   result.y = op.y + 1;
   result.z = op.z + 1;

   return result;
}
```

Here is an expanded version of the previous example program that demonstrates the unary – and the ++ operator:

```
// More operator overloading.

using System;

// A three-dimensional coordinate class.
class ThreeD {
  int x, y, z; // 3-D coordinates

  public ThreeD() { x = y = z = 0; }
  public ThreeD(int i, int j, int k) { x = i; y = j; z = k; }

  // Overload binary +.
  public static ThreeD operator +(ThreeD op1, ThreeD op2)
  {
    ThreeD result = new ThreeD();

    /* This adds together the coordinates of the two points
       and returns the result. */
    result.x = op1.x + op2.x; // These are integer additions
    result.y = op1.y + op2.y; // and the + retains its original
    result.z = op1.z + op2.z; // meaning relative to them.

    return result;
  }

  // Overload binary -.
  public static ThreeD operator -(ThreeD op1, ThreeD op2)
  {
    ThreeD result = new ThreeD();

    /* Notice the order of the operands. op1 is the left
       operand and op2 is the right. */
    result.x = op1.x - op2.x; // these are integer subtractions
    result.y = op1.y - op2.y;
    result.z = op1.z - op2.z;

    return result;
  }
```

```
// Overload unary -.
public static ThreeD operator -(ThreeD op)      ◄──── Implement unary minus for ThreeD.
{
  ThreeD result = new ThreeD();

  result.x = -op.x;
  result.y = -op.y;
  result.z = -op.z;

  return result;
}

// Overload unary ++.
public static ThreeD operator ++(ThreeD op)      ◄──── Implement ++ for ThreeD.
{
  ThreeD result = new ThreeD();

  // Return the incremented result.
  result.x = op.x + 1;
  result.y = op.y + 1;
  result.z = op.z + 1;

  return result;
}

// Show X, Y, Z coordinates.
public void Show()
{
  Console.WriteLine(x + ", " + y + ", " + z);
}
}

class ThreeDDemo {
  static void Main() {
    ThreeD a = new ThreeD(1, 2, 3);
    ThreeD b = new ThreeD(10, 10, 10);
    ThreeD c = new ThreeD();

    Console.Write("Here is a: ");
    a.Show();
    Console.WriteLine();
    Console.Write("Here is b: ");
    b.Show();
    Console.WriteLine();

    c = a + b; // add a and b together
    Console.Write("Result of a + b: ");
    c.Show();
    Console.WriteLine();
```

```
c = a + b + c; // add a, b and c together
Console.Write("Result of a + b + c: ");
c.Show();
Console.WriteLine();

c = c - a; // subtract a
Console.Write("Result of c - a: ");
c.Show();
Console.WriteLine();

c = c - b; // subtract b
Console.Write("Result of c - b: ");
c.Show();
Console.WriteLine();

c = -a; // assign -a to c
Console.Write("Result of -a: ");
c.Show();
Console.WriteLine();

c = a++; // post-increment a
Console.WriteLine("Given c = a++");
Console.Write("c is ");
c.Show();
Console.Write("a is ");
a.Show();

// Reset a to 1, 2, 3
a = new ThreeD(1, 2, 3);
Console.Write("\nResetting a to ");
a.Show();

c = ++a; // pre-increment a
Console.WriteLine("\nGiven c = ++a");
Console.Write("c is ");
c.Show();
Console.Write("a is ");
a.Show();
  }
}
```

The output from the program is shown here:

```
Here is a: 1, 2, 3

Here is b: 10, 10, 10

Result of a + b: 11, 12, 13
```

```
Result of a + b + c: 22, 24, 26

Result of c - a: 21, 22, 23

Result of c - b: 11, 12, 13

Result of -a: -1, -2, -3

Given c = a++
c is 1, 2, 3
a is 2, 3, 4

Resetting a to 1, 2, 3

Given c = ++a
c is 2, 3, 4
a is 2, 3, 4
```

Adding Flexibility

For any given class and operator, an operator method can, itself, be overloaded. For example, once again, consider the **ThreeD** class. To this point, you have seen how to overload the **+** so that it adds the coordinates of one **ThreeD** object to another. However, this is not the only way in which we might want to define addition for **ThreeD**. For example, it might be useful to add an integer value to each coordinate of a **ThreeD** object. Such an operation could be used to translate axes. To perform such an operation, you will need to overload **+** a second time, as shown here:

```
// Overload binary + for ThreeD + int.
public static ThreeD operator +(ThreeD op1, int op2)
{
  ThreeD result = new ThreeD();

  result.x = op1.x + op2;
  result.y = op1.y + op2;
  result.z = op1.z + op2;

  return result;
}
```

Notice that the second parameter is of type **int**. Thus, the preceding method allows an integer value to be added to each field of a **ThreeD** object. This is permissible because, as explained earlier, when overloading a binary operator, one of the operands must be of the same type as the class for which the operator is being overloaded. However, the other operand can be of any other type.

Here is a version of **ThreeD** that has two overloaded **+** methods:

```
// Overload addition for ThreeD + ThreeD, and for ThreeD + int.

using System;

// A three-dimensional coordinate class.
class ThreeD {
  int x, y, z; // 3-D coordinates

  public ThreeD() { x = y = z = 0; }
  public ThreeD(int i, int j, int k) { x = i; y = j; z = k; }

  // Overload binary + for ThreeD + ThreeD.
  public static ThreeD operator +(ThreeD op1, ThreeD op2)
  {
    ThreeD result = new ThreeD();

    /* This adds together the coordinates of the two points
       and returns the result. */
    result.x = op1.x + op2.x;
    result.y = op1.y + op2.y;
    result.z = op1.z + op2.z;

    return result;
  }

  // Overload binary + for ThreeD + int.
  public static ThreeD operator +(ThreeD op1, int op2)
  {
    ThreeD result = new ThreeD();

    result.x = op1.x + op2;
    result.y = op1.y + op2;
    result.z = op1.z + op2;

    return result;
  }

  // Show X, Y, Z coordinates.
  public void Show()
  {
    Console.WriteLine(x + ", " + y + ", " + z);
  }
}
```

Define **ThreeD** + integer.

```
class ThreeDDemo {
  static void Main() {
    ThreeD a = new ThreeD(1, 2, 3);
    ThreeD b = new ThreeD(10, 10, 10);
    ThreeD c = new ThreeD();

    Console.Write("Here is a: ");
    a.Show();
    Console.WriteLine();
    Console.Write("Here is b: ");
    b.Show();
    Console.WriteLine();

    c = a + b; // ThreeD + ThreeD
    Console.Write("Result of a + b: ");
    c.Show();
    Console.WriteLine();

    c = b + 10; // ThreeD + int
    Console.Write("Result of b + 10: ");
    c.Show();
  }
}
```

The output from this program is shown here:

```
Here is a: 1, 2, 3

Here is b: 10, 10, 10

Result of a + b: 11, 12, 13

Result of b + 10: 20, 20, 20
```

As the output confirms, when the **+** is applied to two **ThreeD** objects, their coordinates are added together. When the **+** is applied to a **ThreeD** object and an integer, the coordinates are increased by the integer value.

While the overloading of **+** just shown certainly adds a useful capability to the **ThreeD** class, it does not quite finish the job. Here is why. The **operator+(ThreeD, int)** method allows statements like this:

```
ob1 = ob2 + 10;
```

It does not, unfortunately, allow ones like this:

```
ob1 = 10 + ob2;
```

because the integer argument is the second argument, which is the right-hand operand. The trouble is that the preceding statement puts the integer argument on the left. To allow both forms of statements, you will need to overload the **+** yet another time. This version must have its first parameter as type **int** and its second parameter as type **ThreeD**. One version of the **operator+( )** method handles **ThreeD** + integer, and the other handles integer + **ThreeD**. Overloading the **+** (or any other binary operator) this way allows a built-in type to occur on either the left or right side of the operator. Here is a version of **ThreeD** that overloads the **+** operator as just described:

```
// Overload the + for ThreeD + ThreeD, ThreeD + int, and int + ThreeD.

using System;

// A three-dimensional coordinate class.
class ThreeD {
  int x, y, z; // 3-D coordinates

  public ThreeD() { x = y = z = 0; }
  public ThreeD(int i, int j, int k) { x = i; y = j; z = k; }

  // Overload binary + for ThreeD + ThreeD.
  public static ThreeD operator +(ThreeD op1, ThreeD op2)
  {
    ThreeD result = new ThreeD();
```

This handles **ThreeD** + **ThreeD**.

```
    /* This adds together the coordinates of the two points
       and returns the result. */
    result.x = op1.x + op2.x;
    result.y = op1.y + op2.y;
    result.z = op1.z + op2.z;

    return result;
  }
```

This handles **ThreeD** + integer.

```
  // Overload binary + for ThreeD + int.
  public static ThreeD operator +(ThreeD op1, int op2)
  {
    ThreeD result = new ThreeD();

    result.x = op1.x + op2;
    result.y = op1.y + op2;
    result.z = op1.z + op2;

    return result;
  }
```

This handles integer + **ThreeD**.

```
  // Overload binary + for int + ThreeD.
  public static ThreeD operator +(int op1, ThreeD op2)
  {
    ThreeD result = new ThreeD();
```

```
      result.x = op2.x + op1;
      result.y = op2.y + op1;
      result.z = op2.z + op1;

      return result;
    }

    // Show X, Y, Z coordinates.
    public void Show()
    {
      Console.WriteLine(x + ", " + y + ", " + z);
    }
  }

class ThreeDDemo {
  static void Main() {
    ThreeD a = new ThreeD(1, 2, 3);
    ThreeD b = new ThreeD(10, 10, 10);
    ThreeD c = new ThreeD();

    Console.Write("Here is a: ");
    a.Show();
    Console.WriteLine();
    Console.Write("Here is b: ");
    b.Show();
    Console.WriteLine();

    c = a + b; // ThreeD + ThreeD
    Console.Write("Result of a + b: ");
    c.Show();
    Console.WriteLine();

    c = b + 10; // ThreeD + int
    Console.Write("Result of b + 10: ");
    c.Show();
    Console.WriteLine();

    c = 15 + b; // int + ThreeD
    Console.Write("Result of 15 + b: ");
    c.Show();
  }
}
```

The output from this program is shown here:

```
Here is a: 1, 2, 3

Here is b: 10, 10, 10
```

```
Result of a + b: 11, 12, 13

Result of b + 10: 20, 20, 20

Result of 15 + b: 25, 25, 25
```

Overloading the Relational Operators

The relational operators, such as = = or <, can also be overloaded, and the process is straightforward. Usually, an overloaded relational operator returns a **true** or **false** value. This is in keeping with the normal usage of these operators and allows the overloaded relational operators to be used in conditional expressions. If you return a different type result, you are greatly restricting the operator's utility.

Here is a version of the **ThreeD** class that overloads the < and > operators. In this example, these operators compare **ThreeD** objects based on their distance from the origin. One object is greater than another if its distance from the origin is larger. One object is less than another if its distance from the origin is smaller than the other. Given two points, such an implementation could be used to determine which point lies on a larger sphere. If neither operator returns true, the two points lie on the same sphere. Of course, other ordering schemes are possible.

```
// Overload < and >.

using System;

// A three-dimensional coordinate class.
class ThreeD {
  int x, y, z; // 3-D coordinates

  public ThreeD() { x = y = z = 0; }
  public ThreeD(int i, int j, int k) { x = i; y = j; z = k; }
```

Returns true if **op1** is less than **op2**.

```
  // Overload <.
  public static bool operator <(ThreeD op1, ThreeD op2)
  {
    if(Math.Sqrt(op1.x * op1.x + op1.y * op1.y + op1.z * op1.z) <
       Math.Sqrt(op2.x * op2.x + op2.y * op2.y + op2.z * op2.z))
      return true;
    else
      return false;
  }
```

Returns true if **op1** is greater than **op2**.

```
  // Overload >.
  public static bool operator >(ThreeD op1, ThreeD op2)
  {
    if(Math.Sqrt(op1.x * op1.x + op1.y * op1.y + op1.z * op1.z) >
       Math.Sqrt(op2.x * op2.x + op2.y * op2.y + op2.z * op2.z))
      return true;
```

```
      else
        return false;
    }

    // Show X, Y, Z coordinates.
    public void Show()
    {
      Console.WriteLine(x + ", " + y + ", " + z);
    }
}

class ThreeDDemo {
  static void Main() {
    ThreeD a = new ThreeD(5, 6, 7);
    ThreeD b = new ThreeD(10, 10, 10);
    ThreeD c = new ThreeD(1, 2, 3);
    ThreeD d = new ThreeD(6, 7, 5);

    Console.Write("Here is a: ");
    a.Show();
    Console.Write("Here is b: ");
    b.Show();
    Console.Write("Here is c: ");
    c.Show();
    Console.Write("Here is d: ");
    d.Show();
    Console.WriteLine();

    if(a > c) Console.WriteLine("a > c is true");
    if(a < c) Console.WriteLine("a < c is true");
    if(a > b) Console.WriteLine("a > b is true");
    if(a < b) Console.WriteLine("a < b is true");

    if(a > d) Console.WriteLine("a > d is true");
    else if(a < d) Console.WriteLine("a < d is true");
    else Console.WriteLine("a and d are same distance from origin");
  }
}
```

The output from this program is shown here:

```
Here is a: 5, 6, 7
Here is b: 10, 10, 10
Here is c: 1, 2, 3
Here is d: 6, 7, 5

a > c is true
a < b is true
a and d are same distance from origin
```

There is an important restriction that applies to overloading the relational operators: You must overload them in pairs. For example, if you overload <, you must also overload >, and vice versa. The operator pairs are

= =	!=
<	>
<=	>=

Thus, if you overload <=, you must also overload >=, and if you overload = =, you must also overload !=.

NOTE

If you overload the = = and != operators, you will usually need to override **Object.Equals( )** and **Object.GetHashCode( )**. These methods and the technique of overriding are discussed in Chapter 8.

Operator Overloading Tips and Restrictions

The action of an overloaded operator as applied to the class for which it is defined need not bear any relationship to that operator's default usage as applied to C#'s built-in types. However, for the purposes of the structure and readability of your code, an overloaded operator should reflect, when possible, the spirit of the operator's original use. For example, the + relative to **ThreeD** is conceptually similar to the + relative to integer types. For instance, there would be little benefit in defining the + operator relative to some class in such a way that it acts more the way you would expect the / operator to perform. The central concept is that while you can give an overloaded operator any meaning you like, for clarity, it is best when its new meaning is related to its original meaning.

There are some restrictions to overloading operators. You cannot alter the precedence of any operator. You cannot alter the number of operands required by the operator, although your operator method could choose to ignore an operand. There are several operators that you cannot overload. Perhaps most significantly, you cannot overload any assignment operator, including the compound assignments, such as +=. Here are the other operators that cannot be overloaded. (Some of these operators will be covered later in this book.)

&&	( )	.	?
??	[ ]	| |	=
=>	->	as	checked
default	is	new	sizeof
typeof	unchecked		

One last point: The keywords **true** and **false** can also be used as unary operators for the purposes of overloading. They are overloaded relative to a class to determine whether an object is "true" or "false." Once these are overloaded for a class, you can use objects of that class to control an **if** statement, for example.

Ask the Expert

Q: Since I can't overload operators such as +=, what happens if I try to use += with an object of a class for which I have defined +, for example? More generally, what happens when I use any compound assignment on an object for which I have defined the operational part of that assignment?

A: In general, if you have defined an operator, when that operator is used in a compound assignment, your overloaded operator method is invoked. Thus, += automatically uses your version of **operator+( )**. For example, assuming the **ThreeD** class, if you use a sequence like this:

```
ThreeD a = new ThreeD(1, 2, 3);
ThreeD b = new ThreeD(10, 10, 10);

b += a; // add a and b together
```

ThreeD's **operator+( )** is automatically invoked, and **b** will contain the coordinates 11, 12, 13.

Indexers

As you know, array indexing is performed using the [ ] operator. It is possible to overload the [ ] operator for classes that you create, but you don't use an **operator** method. Instead, you create an *indexer*. An indexer allows an object to be indexed like an array. The main use of indexers is to support the creation of specialized arrays that are subject to one or more constraints. However, you can use an indexer for any purpose for which an array-like syntax is beneficial. Indexers can have one or more dimensions.

We will begin with one-dimensional indexers. One-dimensional indexers have this general form:

```
element-type this[int index] {
    // The get accessor.
    get {
        // return the value specified by index
    }
}

    // The set accessor.
    set {
        // set the value specified by index
    }
}
```

Here, *element-type* is the element type of the indexer. Thus, each element accessed by the indexer will be of type *element-type*. It corresponds to the element type of an array. The parameter *index* receives the index of the element being accessed. Technically, this parameter does not have to be of type **int**, but since indexers are typically used to provide array indexing, an integral type is customary.

Inside the body of the indexer are defined two *accessors* called **get** and **set**. An accessor is similar to a method, except that it does not declare a return type or parameters. The accessors are automatically called when the indexer is used, and both accessors receive *index* as a parameter. If the indexer is being assigned, such as when it's on the left side of an assignment statement, then the **set** accessor is called and the element specified by *index* must be set. Otherwise, the **get** accessor is called and the value associated with *index* must be returned. The **set** method also receives a value called **value**, which contains the value being assigned to the specified index.

One of the benefits of an indexer is that you can control precisely how an array is accessed, heading off improper accesses. For example, here is a better way to implement the "fail-soft" array created in Chapter 6. It uses an indexer, thus allowing the array to be accessed using the normal array notation.

```
// Improve the fail-soft array by adding an indexer.

using System;

class FailSoftArray {
  int[] a;      // reference to array

  public int Length; // Length is public

  public bool ErrFlag; // indicates outcome of last operation

  // Construct array given its size.
  public FailSoftArray(int size) {
    a = new int[size];
    Length = size;
  }

  // This is the indexer for FailSoftArray.
  public int this[int index] {            An indexer for FailSoftArray.
    // This is the get accessor.
    get {
      if(ok(index)) {
        ErrFlag = false;
        return a[index];
      } else {
        ErrFlag = true;
        return 0;
      }
    }
```

```
      // This is the set accessor.
      set {
        if(ok(index)) {
          a[index] = value;
          ErrFlag = false;
        }
        else ErrFlag = true;
      }
    }

    // Return true if index is within bounds.
    private bool ok(int index) {
      if(index >= 0 & index < Length) return true;
      return false;
    }
  }

// Demonstrate the improved fail-soft array.
class ImprovedFSDemo {
  static void Main() {
    FailSoftArray fs = new FailSoftArray(5);
    int x;

    // Show quiet failures.
    Console.WriteLine("Fail quietly.");
    for(int i=0; i < (fs.Length * 2); i++)
      fs[i] = i*10;                                    Invoke the indexer's set accessor.

    for(int i=0; i < (fs.Length * 2); i++) {
      x = fs[i];                                       Invoke the indexer's get accessor.
      if(x != -1) Console.Write(x + " ");
    }
    Console.WriteLine();

    // Now, generate failures.
    Console.WriteLine("\nFail with error reports.");
    for(int i=0; i < (fs.Length * 2); i++) {
      fs[i] = i*10;
      if(fs.ErrFlag)
        Console.WriteLine("fs[" + i + "] out-of-bounds");
    }

    for(int i=0; i < (fs.Length * 2); i++) {
      x = fs[i];
      if(!fs.ErrFlag) Console.Write(x + " ");
      else
        Console.WriteLine("fs[" + i + "] out-of-bounds");
    }
  }
}
```

The output from the program is shown here:

```
Fail quietly.
0 10 20 30 40 0 0 0 0 0

Fail with error reports.
fs[5] out-of-bounds
fs[6] out-of-bounds
fs[7] out-of-bounds
fs[8] out-of-bounds
fs[9] out-of-bounds
0 10 20 30 40 fs[5] out-of-bounds
fs[6] out-of-bounds
fs[7] out-of-bounds
fs[8] out-of-bounds
fs[9] out-of-bounds
```

This output is similar to that produced by the previous version of the program shown in Chapter 6. In this version, the indexer prevents the array boundaries from being overrun. Let's look closely at each part of the indexer. It begins with this line:

```
public int this[int index] {
```

This declares an indexer that operates on **int** elements. The index is passed in **index**. The indexer is public, allowing it to be used by code outside of its class.

The **get** accessor is shown here:

```
get {
  if(ok(index)) {
    ErrFlag = false;
    return a[index];
  } else {
    ErrFlag = true;
    return 0;
  }
}
```

The **get** accessor prevents array boundary errors. If the specified index is within bounds, the element corresponding to the index is returned. If it is out of bounds, no operation takes place and no overrun occurs. In this version of **FailSoftArray**, a variable called **ErrFlag** contains the outcome of each operation. This field can be examined after each operation to assess the success or failure of the operation. (In Chapter 10, you will see a better way to handle errors by using C#'s exception subsystem, but for now, using an error flag is an acceptable approach.)

The **set** accessor is shown here. It, too, prevents a boundary error.

```
set {
  if(ok(index)) {
    a[index] = value;
```

```
      ErrFlag = false;
    }
  else ErrFlag = true;
}
```

In this case, if **index** is within bounds, the value passed in **value** is assigned to the corresponding element. Otherwise, **ErrFlag** is set to **true**. Recall that in an accessor method, **value** is an automatic parameter that contains the value being assigned. You do not need to (nor can you) declare it.

It is not necessary for an indexer to provide both **get** and **set**. You can create a read-only indexer by implementing only the **get** accessor. You can create a write-only indexer by implementing only **set**.

It is important to understand that there is no requirement that an indexer actually operate on an array. It simply must provide functionality that appears "array-like" to the user of the indexer. For example, the following program has an indexer that acts like a read-only array that contains the powers of 2 from 0 to 15. Notice, however, that no actual array exists. Instead, the indexer simply computes the proper value for a given index.

```
// Indexers don't have to operate on actual arrays.

using System;

class PwrOfTwo {

  /* Access a logical array that contains
     the powers of 2 from 0 to 15. */
  public int this[int index] {
    // Compute and return power of 2.
    get {
      if((index >= 0) && (index < 16)) return Pwr(index);
      else return -1;
    }

    // There is no set accessor.
  }

  int Pwr(int p) {
    int result = 1;

    for(int i=0; i<p; i++)
      result *= 2;

    return result;
  }
}

class UsePwrOfTwo {
  static void Main() {
    PwrOfTwo pwr = new PwrOfTwo();
```

Here, no underlying array is used.

```
    Console.Write("First 8 powers of 2: ");
    for(int i=0; i < 8; i++)
      Console.Write(pwr[i] + " ");
    Console.WriteLine();

    Console.Write("Here are some errors: ");
    Console.Write(pwr[-1] + " " + pwr[17]);
  }
}
```

The output from the program is shown here:

```
First 8 powers of 2: 1 2 4 8 16 32 64 128
Here are some errors: -1 -1
```

Notice that the indexer for **PwrOfTwo** includes a **get** accessor, but no **set** accessor. As explained, this means that the indexer is read-only. Thus, a **PwrOfTwo** object can be used on the right side of an assignment statement, but not on the left. For example, attempting to add this statement to the preceding program won't work:

```
pwr[0] = 11; // won't compile
```

This statement will cause a compilation error because there is no **set** accessor defined for the indexer.

Multidimensional Indexers

You can create indexers for multidimensional arrays, too. For example, here is a two-dimensional fail-soft array. Pay close attention to the way that the indexer is declared.

```
// A two-dimensional fail-soft array.

using System;

class FailSoftArray2D {
  int[,] a; // reference to 2D array
  int rows, cols; // dimensions
  public int Length; // Length is public

  public bool ErrFlag; // indicates outcome of last operation

  // Construct array given its dimensions.
  public FailSoftArray2D(int r, int c) {
    rows = r;
    cols = c;
    a = new int[rows, cols];
    Length = rows * cols;
  }
```

```
      // This is the indexer for FailSoftArray2D.
      public int this[int index1, int index2] {                    A two-dimensional indexer.
        // This is the get accessor.
        get {
          if(ok(index1, index2)) {
            ErrFlag = false;
            return a[index1, index2];
          } else {
            ErrFlag = true;
            return 0;
          }
        }

        // This is the set accessor.
        set {
          if(ok(index1, index2)) {
            a[index1, index2] = value;
            ErrFlag = false;
          }
          else ErrFlag = true;
        }
      }

      // Return true if indexes are within bounds.
      private bool ok(int index1, int index2) {
        if(index1 >= 0 & index1 < rows &
          index2 >= 0 & index2 < cols)
            return true;

        return false;
      }
    }

    // Demonstrate a 2D indexer.
    class TwoDIndexerDemo {
      static void Main() {
        FailSoftArray2D fs = new FailSoftArray2D(3, 5);
        int x;

        // Show quiet failures.
        Console.WriteLine("Fail quietly.");
        for(int i=0; i < 6; i++)
          fs[i, i] = i*10;

        for(int i=0; i < 6; i++) {
          x = fs[i,i];
          if(x != -1) Console.Write(x + " ");
        }
```

```
      Console.WriteLine();

      // Now, generate failures.
      Console.WriteLine("\nFail with error reports.");
      for(int i=0; i < 6; i++) {
        fs[i,i] = i*10;
        if(fs.ErrFlag)
          Console.WriteLine("fs[" + i + ", " + i + "] out-of-bounds");
      }

      for(int i=0; i < 6; i++) {
        x = fs[i,i];
        if(!fs.ErrFlag) Console.Write(x + " ");
        else
          Console.WriteLine("fs[" + i + ", " + i + "] out-of-bounds");
      }
    }
}
```

The output from this program is shown here:

```
Fail quietly.
0 10 20 0 0 0

Fail with error reports.
fs[3, 3] out-of-bounds
fs[4, 4] out-of-bounds
fs[5, 5] out-of-bounds
0 10 20 fs[3, 3] out-of-bounds
fs[4, 4] out-of-bounds
fs[5, 5] out-of-bounds
```

Indexer Restrictions

There are two important restrictions to using indexers. First, because an indexer does not define a storage location, a value produced by an indexer cannot be passed as a **ref** or **out** parameter to a method. Second, an indexer cannot be declared **static**.

Ask the Expert

Q: Can indexers be overloaded?

A: Yes. The version executed will be the one that has the closest type-match between its parameter(s) and the argument(s) used as an index.

Properties

Another type of class member is the *property*. As a general rule, a property combines a field with the methods that access it. As some examples earlier in this book have shown, often, you will want to create a field that is available to users of an object, but you want to maintain control over what operations are allowed on that field. For instance, you might want to limit the range of values that can be assigned to that field. While it is possible to accomplish this goal through the use of a private variable, along with methods to access its value, a property offers a better, more streamlined approach.

Properties are similar to indexers. A property consists of a name, along with **get** and **set** accessors. The accessors are used to get and set the value of a variable. The key benefit of a property is that its name can be used in expressions and assignments like a normal variable, but in actuality, the **get** and **set** accessors are automatically invoked. This is similar to the way that an indexer's **get** and **set** accessors are automatically used.

The general form of a property is shown here:

```
type name {
   get {
      // get accessor code
   }

   set {
      // set accessor code
   }
}
```

Here, *type* specifies the type of the property, such as **int**, and *name* is the name of the property. Once the property has been defined, any use of *name* results in a call to its appropriate accessor. The **set** accessor automatically receives a parameter called **value** that contains the value being assigned to the property.

Properties do not define storage locations. Instead, a property typically manages access to a field defined elsewhere. The property itself does not provide this field. Thus, a field must be specified independently of the property. (The exception is the *auto-implemented* property added by C# 3.0, which is described shortly.)

Here is a simple example that defines a property called **MyProp**, which is used to access the field **prop**. In this case, the property allows only positive values to be assigned.

```
// A simple property example.

using System;

class SimpProp {
   int prop; // field being managed by MyProp

   public SimpProp() { prop = 0; }
```

```
  /* This is the property that supports access to the private
     instance variable prop. It allows only positive values. */
  public int MyProp {        ◄─────── A property called MyProp
    get {                             that controls access to prop.
      return prop;
    }
    set {
      if(value >= 0) prop = value;
    }
  }
}

// Demonstrate a property.
class PropertyDemo {
  static void Main() {
    SimpProp ob = new SimpProp();

    Console.WriteLine("Original value of ob.MyProp: " + ob.MyProp);

    ob.MyProp = 100; // assign value
    Console.WriteLine("Value of ob.MyProp: " + ob.MyProp);   ◄─────┐
                                               Use MyProp just like a variable.
    // Can't assign negative value to prop.
    Console.WriteLine("Attempting to assign -10 to ob.MyProp");
    ob.MyProp = -10;
    Console.WriteLine("Value of ob.MyProp: " + ob.MyProp);
  }
}
```

Output from this program is shown here:

```
Original value of ob.MyProp: 0
Value of ob.MyProp: 100
Attempting to assign -10 to ob.MyProp
Value of ob.MyProp: 100
```

Let's examine this program carefully. The program defines one private field, called **prop**, and a property called **MyProp** that manages access to **prop**. As explained, a property by itself does not define a storage location. Instead, most properties simply manage access to a field. Furthermore, because **prop** is private, it can be accessed *only* through **MyProp**.

The property **MyProp** is specified as **public** so that it can be accessed by code outside of its class. This makes sense because it provides access to **prop**, which is private. The **get** accessor simply returns the value of **prop**. The **set** accessor sets the value of **prop** if and only if that value is positive. Thus, the **MyProp** property controls what values **prop** can have. This is the essence of why properties are important.

The type of property defined by **MyProp** is called a read-write property because it allows its underlying field to be read and written. It is possible, however, to create read-only and write-only properties. To create a read-only property, define only a **get** accessor. To define a write-only property, define only a **set** accessor.

You can use a property to further improve the fail-soft array class. As you know, all arrays have a **Length** property associated with them. Up to now, the **FailSoftArray** class simply used a public integer field called **Length** for this purpose. This is not good practice, though, because it allows **Length** to be set to some value other than the length of the fail-soft array. (For example, a malicious programmer could intentionally corrupt its value.) We can remedy this situation by transforming **Length** into a read-only property, as shown in this version of **FailSoftArray**:

```
// Add Length property to FailSoftArray.

using System;

class FailSoftArray {
  int[] a; // reference to array
  int len; // length of array

  public bool ErrFlag; // indicates outcome of last operation

  // Construct array given its size.
  public FailSoftArray(int size) {
    a = new int[size];
    len = size;
  }

  // Read-only Length property.
  public int Length {                    Length is now a property rather than a field.
    get {
      return len;
    }
  }

  // This is the indexer for FailSoftArray.
  public int this[int index] {
    // This is the get accessor.
    get {
      if(ok(index)) {
        ErrFlag = false;
        return a[index];
      } else {
        ErrFlag = true;
        return 0;
      }
    }
```

```
    // This is the set accessor.
    set {
      if(ok(index)) {
        a[index] = value;
        ErrFlag = false;
      }
      else ErrFlag = true;
    }
  }

  // Return true if index is within bounds.
  private bool ok(int index) {
    if(index >= 0 & index < Length) return true;
    return false;
  }
}

// Demonstrate the improved fail-soft array.
class ImprovedFSDemo {
  static void Main() {
    FailSoftArray fs = new FailSoftArray(5);
    int x;

    // Can read Length.
    for(int i=0; i < (fs.Length); i++)
      fs[i] = i*10;

    for(int i=0; i < (fs.Length); i++) {
      x = fs[i];
      if(x != -1) Console.Write(x + " ");
    }
    Console.WriteLine();

    // fs.Length = 10; // Error, illegal!

  }
}
```

Now, **Length** is a read-only property that can be read but not assigned. To prove this to yourself, try removing the comment symbol preceding this line in the program:

```
// fs.Length = 10; // Error, illegal!
```

When you try to compile, you will receive an error message stating that **Length** is read-only.

Auto-Implemented Properties

Beginning with C# 3.0, it is possible to implement very simple properties without having to explicitly define the variable managed by the property. Instead, you can let the compiler automatically supply the underlying variable. This is called an *auto-implemented property*. It has the following general form:

type name { get; set; }

Here, *type* specifies the type of the property and *name* specifies the name. Notice that **get** and **set** are immediately followed by a semicolon. The accessors for an auto-implemented property have no bodies. This syntax tells the compiler to automatically create a storage location (sometimes referred to as a *backing field*) that holds the value. This variable is not named and is not directly available to you. Instead, it can only be accessed through the property.

Here is how a property called **UserCount** is declared using an auto-implemented property:

```
public int UserCount { get; set; }
```

Notice that no variable is explicitly declared. As explained, the compiler automatically generates an anonymous field that holds the value. Otherwise, **UserCount** acts like and is used like any other property.

Unlike normal properties, an auto-implemented property cannot be read-only or write-only. Both the **get** and **set** must be specified in all cases. However, you can approximate the same effect by declaring either **get** or **set** as **private**, as explained shortly.

Although auto-implemented properties offer convenience, their use is limited to those cases in which you do not need control over the getting or setting of the backing field. Remember, you cannot access the backing field directly. This means that there is no way to constrain the value an auto-implemented property can have. Thus, auto-implemented properties simply let the name of the property act as a proxy for the field itself. However, sometimes, this is exactly what you want. Also, they can be very useful in cases in which properties are used to expose functionality to a third party, possibly through a design tool.

Property Restrictions

Properties have some important restrictions. First, because a property does not define a storage location, it cannot be passed as a **ref** or **out** parameter to a method. Second, you cannot overload a property. (You *can* have two different properties that both access the same underlying variable, but this would be unusual.) Finally, a property should not alter the state of the underlying variable when the **get** accessor is called. Although this rule is not enforced by the compiler, such an alteration is semantically wrong. A **get** operation should not create side effects.

Use an Access Modifier with an Accessor

By default, the **set** and **get** accessors have the same accessibility as the indexer or property of which they are a part. For example, if the property is declared **public**, then, by default, the **get** and **set** accessors are also public. It is possible, however, to give **set** or **get** its own access modifier, such as **private**. In all cases, the access modifier for an accessor must be more restrictive than the access specification of its property or indexer.

There are a number of reasons why you may want to restrict the accessibility of an accessor. For example, you might want to let anyone obtain the value of a property, but allow only members of its class to set the property. To do this, declare the **set** accessor as **private**. For example, here is a property called **Max** that has its **set** accessor specified as **private**:

```
class MyClass {
  int maximum;
  // ...
  public int Max {
    get {
      return maximum;
    }
    private set { // the set accessor is private
      if(value < 0) maximum = -value;
      else maximum   = value;
    }
  }
  // ...
}
```

Notice that the **set** accessor is declared private.

Now, only code inside **MyClass** can set the value of **Max**, but any code can obtain its value.

Perhaps the most important use of restricting an accessor's access is found when working with auto-implemented properties. As explained, it is not possible to create a read-only or write-only, auto-implemented property because both the **get** and **set** accessors must be specified when the auto-implemented property is declared. However, you can gain much the same effect by declaring either **get** or **set** as **private**. For example, this declares what is effectively a read-only, auto-implemented **Length** property for the **FailSoftArray** class shown earlier:

```
public int Length { get; private set; }
```

Because **set** is **private**, **Length** can be set only by code within its class. Outside its class, an attempt to change **Length** is illegal. Thus, outside its class, **Length** is effectively read-only.

To try the auto-implemented version of **Length** with **FailSoftArray**, first remove the **len** variable. Then, replace each use of **len** inside **FailSoftArray** with **Length**. Here is the updated version of **FailSoftArray**, along with a **Main( )** to demonstrate it:

```
// Demonstrate the auto-implemented Length property to FailSoftArray.

using System;

class FailSoftArray {
  int[] a; // reference to array

  public bool ErrFlag; // indicates outcome of last operation

  // An auto-implemented, read-only Length property.
  public int Length { get; private set; }
```

An auto-implemented property.

```
// Construct array given its size.
public FailSoftArray(int size) {
   a = new int[size];
   Length = size;  ←——    Assignment to Length OK
}                          inside FailSoftArray.


// This is the indexer for FailSoftArray.
public int this[int index] {
   // This is the get accessor.
   get {
     if(ok(index)) {
       ErrFlag = false;
       return a[index];
     } else {
       ErrFlag = true;
       return 0;
     }
   }

   // This is the set accessor.
   set {
     if(ok(index)) {
       a[index] = value;
       ErrFlag = false;
     }
     else ErrFlag = true;
   }
}

// Return true if index is within bounds.
private bool ok(int index) {
 if(index >= 0 & index < Length) return true;
 return false;
}
}

// Demonstrate the auto-implemented Length property.
class AutoImpPropertyFSDemo {
  static void Main() {
    FailSoftArray fs = new FailSoftArray(5);
    int x;

    // Can read Length.
    for(int i=0; i < (fs.Length); i++)
      fs[i] = i*10;

    for(int i=0; i < (fs.Length); i++) {
      x = fs[i];
```

```
    if(x != -1) Console.Write(x + " ");
  }
  Console.WriteLine();
```

```
  // fs.Length = 10; // Error! Length's set accessor is private.
  }
}
```
Assignment to **Length** outside **FailSoftArray** is illegal.

This version of **FailSoftArray** works in the same way as the previous version, but it does not contain an explicitly declared backing field.

Try This ## Create a Set Class

As mentioned at the start of this chapter, operator overloading, indexers, and properties help you create classes that can be fully integrated into C#'s programming environment. Consider this point: By defining the necessary operators, indexers, and properties, you enable a class type to be used in a program in just the same way as you would use a built-in type. You can act on objects of that class through operators and indexers, and use objects of that class in expressions. Adding properties enables the class to provide an interface consistent with C#'s built-in objects. To illustrate the creation and integration of a new class into the C# environment, we will create a class called **Set** that defines a set type.

Before we begin, it is important to understand precisely what we mean by a set. For the purposes of this example, a *set* is a collection of unique elements. That is, no two elements in any given set can be the same. The ordering of a set's members is irrelevant. Thus, the set

{ A, B, C }

is the same as the set

{ A, C, B }

A set can also be empty.

Sets support a number of operations. The ones that we will implement are:

- Add an element to a set

- Remove an element from a set

- Set union

- Set difference

Adding an element to a set and removing an element from a set are self-explanatory operations. The other two warrant some explanation.

The *union* of two sets is a set that contains all of the elements from both sets. (Of course, no duplicate elements are allowed.) We will use the **+** operator to perform a set union.

(continued)

The *difference* between two sets is a set that contains those elements in the first set that are not part of the second set. We will use the – operator to perform a set difference. For example, given two sets S1 and S2, this statement removes the elements of S2 from S1, putting the result in S3:

S3 = S1 – S2

If S1 and S2 are the same, then S3 will be the null set.

Of course, there are several other operations that can be performed on sets. Some are developed in the Self Test section. Others you might find fun to try adding on your own.

For the sake of simplicity, the **Set** class stores sets of characters, but the same basic principles could be used to create a **Set** class capable of storing other types of elements.

Step by Step

1. Create a new file called **SetDemo.cs**.

2. Begin creating **Set** with the following lines:

```
class Set {
  char[] members; // this array holds the set

  // An auto-implemented, read-only Length property.
  public int Length { get; private set; }
```

Each set is stored in a **char** array referred to by **members**. The number of members actually in the set is represented by the auto-implemented **Length** property. Notice that outside the **Set** class, it is effectively read-only.

3. Add the following **Set** constructors:

```
// Construct a null set.
public Set() {
  Length = 0;
}

// Construct an empty set of a given size.
public Set(int size) {
  members = new char[size]; // allocate memory for set
  Length = 0; // no members when constructed
}

// Construct a set from another set.
public Set(Set s) {
  members = new char[s.Length]; // allocate memory for set
  for(int i=0; i < s.Length; i++) members[i] = s[i];
  Length = s.Length; // number of members
}
```

Sets can be constructed three ways. First, a null set can be created. A null set contains no members, nor does it allocate an array for members. Thus, a null set is simply a placeholder. Second, an empty set can be created of a given size. Finally, a set can be constructed from another set. In this case, the two sets contain the same members, but refer to separate objects.

4. Add the read-only indexer, as shown here:

```
// Implement read-only indexer.
public char this[int idx] {
  get {
    if(idx >= 0 & idx < Length) return members[idx];
    else return (char)0;
  }
}
```

The indexer returns a member of a set given its index. A bounds check is performed to prevent an array overrun. If the index is invalid, the null character is returned.

5. Add the **find( )** method shown here. This method determines if the element passed in **ch** is a member of the set. It returns the index of the element if it is found and –1 if the element is not part of the set. Notice that this method is private.

```
/* See if an element is in the set.
   Return the index of the element or -1 if not found. */
int find(char ch) {
  int i;

  for(i=0; i < Length; i++)
    if(members[i] == ch) return i;

  return -1;
}
```

6. Begin adding the set operators, starting with set addition. To do this, overload **+** for objects of type **Set**, as shown here. This version adds an element to a set.

```
// Add a unique element to a set.
public static Set operator +(Set ob, char ch) {

  // If ch is already in the set, return a copy of the
  // original set.
  if(ob.find(ch) != -1) {

    // Return a copy of the original set.
    return new Set(ob);

  } else { // Return a new set that contains the new element.
```

(continued)

```
// Make the new set one element larger than the original.
Set newset = new Set(ob.Length+1);

// Copy elements into the new set.
for(int i=0; i < ob.Length; i++)
  newset.members[i] = ob.members[i];

// Set the Length property.
newset.Length = ob.Length+1;

// Add new element to new set.
newset.members[newset.Length-1] = ch;

return newset; // return the new set
  }
}
```

This method bears some close examination. First, the **find( )** method is called to determine if **ch** is already part of the set. If it returns anything other than –1, **ch** is already in the set, so a copy of the original set is returned. Otherwise, a new set called **newset** is created that will hold the contents of the original set referred to by **ob**, plus the new element, **ch**. Notice that it is created one element larger than **ob** to accommodate the new element. Next, the original elements are copied into **newset**, and the length of **newset** is set to one greater than the original set. Next, **ch** is added to the end of **newset**. Finally, **newset** is returned. In all cases, the original set is untouched by this operation and a new set is returned. Thus, the returned set is separate and distinct from the set passed as an operand.

7. Next, overload – so that it removes an element from the set, as shown here:

```
// Remove an element from the set.
public static Set operator -(Set ob, char ch) {
  Set newset = new Set();
  int i = ob.find(ch); // i will be -1 if element not found

  // Copy and compress the remaining elements.
  for(int j=0; j < ob.Length; j++)
    if(j != i) newset = newset + ob.members[j];

  return newset;
}
```

First, a new null set is created. Second, **find( )** is called to determine whether **ch** is a member of the original set. Recall that **find( )** returns –1 if **ch** is not a member. Next, the elements of the original set are added to the new set, except for the element whose index matches that returned by **find( )**. Thus, the resulting set contains all of the elements of the original set, except for **ch**. If **ch** was not part of the original set to begin with, then the two sets are equivalent.

8. Overload the + and – again, as shown here. These versions implement set union and set difference.

```
// Set union.
public static Set operator +(Set ob1, Set ob2) {
  Set newset = new Set(ob1); // copy the first set

  // Add unique elements from second set.
  for(int i=0; i < ob2.Length; i++)
      newset = newset + ob2[i];

  return newset; // return updated set
}

// Set difference.
public static Set operator -(Set ob1, Set ob2) {
  Set newset = new Set(ob1); // copy the first set

  // Subtract elements from second set
  for(int i=0; i < ob2.Length; i++)
      newset = newset - ob2[i];

  return newset; // return updated set
}
```

As you can see, these methods utilize the previously defined versions of the + and – operators to help perform their operations. In the case of set union, a new set is created that contains the elements of the first set. Then, the elements of the second set are added. Because the + operation only adds an element if it is not already part of the set, the resulting set is the union (without duplication) of the two sets. The set difference operator subtracts matching elements.

9. Here is the complete code for the **Set** class, along with the **SetDemo** class that demonstrates it:

```
// A set class for characters.

using System;

class Set {
  char[] members; // this array holds the set

  // An auto-implemented, read-only Length property.
  public int Length { get; private set; }

  // Construct a null set.
  public Set() {
    Length = 0;
  }
```

(continued)

```csharp
// Construct an empty set of a given size.
public Set(int size) {
  members = new char[size]; // allocate memory for set
  Length = 0; // no members when constructed
}

// Construct a set from another set.
public Set(Set s) {
  members = new char[s.Length]; // allocate memory for set
  for(int i=0; i < s.Length; i++) members[i] = s[i];
  Length = s.Length; // number of members
}

// Implement read-only indexer.
public char this[int idx]{
  get {
    if(idx >= 0 & idx < Length) return members[idx];
    else return (char)0;
  }
}

/* See if an element is in the set.
   Return the index of the element or -1 if not found. */
int find(char ch) {
  int i;

  for(i=0; i < Length; i++)
    if(members[i] == ch) return i;

  return -1;
}

// Add a unique element to a set.
public static Set operator +(Set ob, char ch) {

  // If ch is already in the set, return a copy of the
  // original set.
  if(ob.find(ch) != -1) {

    // Return a copy of the original set.
    return new Set(ob);

  } else { // Return a new set that contains the new element.

    // Make the new set one element larger than the original.
    Set newset = new Set(ob.Length+1);
```

```
      // Copy elements into the new set.
      for(int i=0; i < ob.Length; i++)
        newset.members[i] = ob.members[i];

      // Set the Length property.
      newset.Length = ob.Length+1;

      // Add new element to new set.
      newset.members[newset.Length-1] = ch;

      return newset; // return the new set
    }
  }

  // Remove an element from the set.
  public static Set operator -(Set ob, char ch) {
    Set newset = new Set();
    int i = ob.find(ch); // i will be -1 if element not found

    // Copy and compress the remaining elements.
    for(int j=0; j < ob.Length; j++)
      if(j != i) newset = newset + ob.members[j];

    return newset;
  }

  // Set union.
  public static Set operator +(Set ob1, Set ob2) {
    Set newset = new Set(ob1); // copy the first set

    // Add unique elements from second set.
    for(int i=0; i < ob2.Length; i++)
        newset = newset + ob2[i];

    return newset; // return updated set
  }

  // Set difference.
  public static Set operator -(Set ob1, Set ob2) {
    Set newset = new Set(ob1); // copy the first set

    // Subtract elements from second set
    for(int i=0; i < ob2.Length; i++)
        newset = newset - ob2[i];

    return newset; // return updated set
  }

}
```

(continued)

```
// Demonstrate the Set class.
class SetDemo {
  static void Main() {
    // Construct 10-element empty Set.
    Set s1 = new Set();
    Set s2 = new Set();
    Set s3 = new Set();

    s1 = s1 + 'A';
    s1 = s1 + 'B';
    s1 = s1 + 'C';

    Console.Write("s1 after adding A B C: ");
    for(int i=0; i<s1.Length; i++)
      Console.Write(s1[i] + " ");
    Console.WriteLine();

    s1 = s1 - 'B';
    Console.Write("s1 after s1 = s1 - 'B': ");
    for(int i=0; i<s1.Length; i++)
      Console.Write(s1[i] + " ");
    Console.WriteLine();

    s1 = s1 - 'A';
    Console.Write("s1 after s1 = s1 - 'A': ");
    for(int i=0; i<s1.Length; i++)
      Console.Write(s1[i] + " ");
    Console.WriteLine();

    s1 = s1 - 'C';
    Console.Write("s1 after a1 = s1 - 'C': ");
    for(int i=0; i<s1.Length; i++)
      Console.Write(s1[i] + " ");
    Console.WriteLine("\n");

    s1 = s1 + 'A';
    s1 = s1 + 'B';
    s1 = s1 + 'C';
    Console.Write("s1 after adding A B C: ");
    for(int i=0; i<s1.Length; i++)
      Console.Write(s1[i] + " ");
    Console.WriteLine();

    s2 = s2 + 'A';
    s2 = s2 + 'X';
    s2 = s2 + 'W';
```

```
    Console.Write("s2 after adding A X W: ");
    for(int i=0; i<s2.Length; i++)
      Console.Write(s2[i] + " ");
    Console.WriteLine();

    s3 = s1 + s2;
    Console.Write("s3 after s3 = s1 + s2: ");
    for(int i=0; i<s3.Length; i++)
      Console.Write(s3[i] + " ");
    Console.WriteLine();

    s3 = s3 - s1;
    Console.Write("s3 after s3 - s1: ");
    for(int i=0; i<s3.Length; i++)
      Console.Write(s3[i] + " ");
    Console.WriteLine("\n");

    s2 = s2 - s2; // clear s2
    s2 = s2 + 'C'; // add ABC in reverse order
    s2 = s2 + 'B';
    s2 = s2 + 'A';

    Console.Write("s1 is now: ");
    for(int i=0; i<s1.Length; i++)
      Console.Write(s1[i] + " ");
    Console.WriteLine();

    Console.Write("s2 is now: ");
    for(int i=0; i<s2.Length; i++)
      Console.Write(s2[i] + " ");
    Console.WriteLine();

    Console.Write("s3 is now: ");
    for(int i=0; i<s3.Length; i++)
      Console.Write(s3[i] + " ");
    Console.WriteLine();
  }
}
```

The output from this program is shown here:

```
s1 after adding A B C: A B C
s1 after s1 = s1 - 'B': A C
s1 after s1 = s1 - 'A': C
s1 after a1 = s1 - 'C':

s1 after adding A B C: A B C
s2 after adding A X W: A X W
```

(continued)

```
s3 after s3 = s1 + s2: A B C X W
s3 after s3 - s1: X W

s1 is now: A B C
s2 is now: C B A
s3 is now: X W
```

Chapter 7 Self Test

1. Show the general form used for overloading a unary operator. Of what type must the parameter to the operator method be?

2. To allow operations involving a class type and a built-in type, what must you do?

3. Can the **?** be overloaded? Can you change the precedence of an operator?

4. What is an indexer? Show its general form.

5. In an indexer, what functions must its **get** and **set** accessors perform?

6. What is a property? Show its general form.

7. Does a property define a storage location? If not, where does a property store its value?

8. Can a property be passed as a **ref** or **out** argument?

9. What is an auto-implemented property?

10. For the **Set** class developed in the Try This section, define **<** and **>** such that they determine if one set is a subset or a superset of another set. Have **<** return **true** if the left set is a subset of the set on the right and **false** otherwise. Have **>** return **true** if the left set is a superset of the set on the right and **false** otherwise.

11. For the **Set** class, define the **&** so that it yields the intersection of two sets.

12. On your own, try adding other **Set** operators. For example, try defining I so that it yields the *symmetric difference* between two sets. (The symmetric difference consists of those elements that the two sets do not have in common.)

Chapter 8

Inheritance

Key Skills & Concepts

- Inheritance fundamentals
- Protected access
- Call base class constructors
- Multilevel class hierarchies
- Base class references to derived class objects
- Virtual methods
- Abstract classes
- **sealed**
- The **object** class

Inheritance is one of the three foundational principles of object-oriented programming because it allows the creation of hierarchical classifications. Using inheritance, you can create a general class that defines traits common to a set of related items. This class can then be inherited by other, more specific classes, each adding those things that are unique to it.

In the language of C#, a class that is inherited is called a *base class*. The class that does the inheriting is called a *derived class*. Therefore, a derived class is a specialized version of a base class. It inherits all of the variables, methods, properties, and indexers defined by the base class and adds its own, unique elements.

Inheritance Basics

C# supports inheritance by allowing one class to incorporate another class into its declaration. This is done by specifying a base class when a derived class is declared. Let's begin with a short example that illustrates several of the key features of inheritance. The following program creates a base class called **TwoDShape** that stores the width and height of a two-dimensional object, and creates a derived class called **Triangle**. Pay close attention to the way that **Triangle** is declared.

```
// A simple class hierarchy.
using System;

// A class for two-dimensional objects.
class TwoDShape {
  public double Width;
  public double Height;
```

```
  public void ShowDim() {
    Console.WriteLine("Width and height are " +
                         Width + " and " + Height);
  }
}

// Triangle is derived from TwoDShape.
class Triangle : TwoDShape {          Triangle inherits TwoDShape. Notice the syntax.
  public string Style;

  public double Area() {                Triangle can refer to the members of TwoDShape
    return Width * Height / 2;          as if they were part of Triangle.
  }

  public void ShowStyle() {
    Console.WriteLine("Triangle is " + Style);
  }
}

class Shapes {
  static void Main() {
    Triangle t1 = new Triangle();
    Triangle t2 = new Triangle();

    t1.Width = 4.0;
    t1.Height = 4.0;                    All members of Triangle are available to Triangle
    t1.Style = "isosceles";            objects, even those inherited from TwoDShape.

    t2.Width = 8.0;
    t2.Height = 12.0;
    t2.Style = "right";

    Console.WriteLine("Info for t1: ");
    t1.ShowStyle();
    t1.ShowDim();
    Console.WriteLine("Area is " + t1.Area());

    Console.WriteLine();

    Console.WriteLine("Info for t2: ");
    t2.ShowStyle();
    t2.ShowDim();
    Console.WriteLine("Area is " + t2.Area());
  }
}
```

The output from this program is shown here:

```
Info for t1:
Triangle is isosceles
Width and height are 4 and 4
Area is 8

Info for t2:
Triangle is right
Width and height are 8 and 12
Area is 48
```

Here, **TwoDShape** defines the attributes of a "generic" two-dimensional shape, such as a square, rectangle, triangle, and so on. The **Triangle** class creates a specific type of **TwoDShape**, in this case, a triangle. The **Triangle** class includes all of **TwoDShape** and adds the field **Style**, the method **Area( )**, and the method **ShowStyle( )**. **Style** stores a description of the type of triangle, **Area( )** computes and returns the area of the triangle, and **ShowStyle( )** displays the triangle's style.

Notice the syntax that is used to inherit a base class. The base class name follows the name of the derived class, and they are separated by a colon. The syntax for inheriting a class is remarkably simple and easy to use.

Because **Triangle** includes all of the members of its base class, **TwoDShape**, it can access **Width** and **Height** inside **Area( )**. Also, inside **Main( )**, objects **t1** and **t2** can refer to **Width** and **Height** directly, as if they were part of **Triangle**. Figure 8-1 depicts conceptually how **TwoDShape** is incorporated into **Triangle**.

Even though **TwoDShape** is a base for **Triangle**, it is also a completely independent, stand-alone class. Being a base class for a derived class does not mean that the base class cannot be used by itself. For example, the following is perfectly valid:

```
TwoDShape shape = new TwoDShape();

shape.Width = 10;
shape.Height = 20;

shape.ShowDim();
```

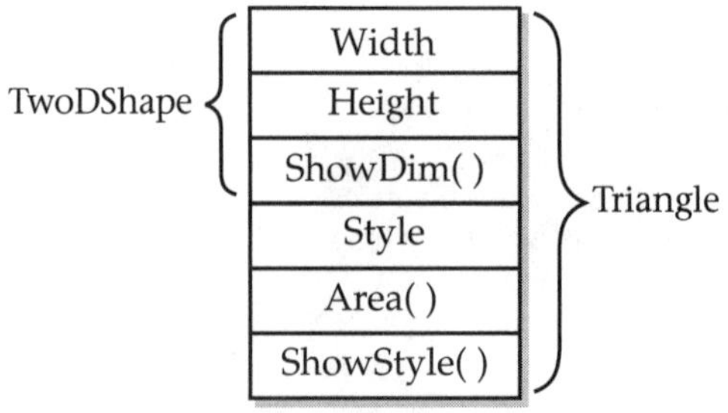

Figure 8-1 A conceptual depiction of the **Triangle** class

Of course, a **TwoDShape** object has no knowledge of or access to any class derived from **TwoDShape**.

The general form of a **class** declaration that inherits a base class is shown here:

```
class derived-class : base-class {
  // body of class
}
```

Notice that you can specify only one base class for any derived class that you create. C# does not support the inheritance of multiple base classes into a single derived class. (This differs from C++, in which you can inherit multiple base classes. Be aware of this when converting C++ code to C#.) You can, however, create a hierarchy of inheritance in which a derived class becomes a base class of another derived class. Of course, no class can be a base class of itself. In all cases, a derived class inherits all of the members of its base class. This includes instance variables, methods, properties, and indexers.

A major advantage of inheritance is that once you have created a base class that defines the attributes common to a set of objects, it can be used to create any number of more specific derived classes. Each derived class can precisely tailor its own classification. For example, here is another class derived from **TwoDShape** that encapsulates rectangles:

```
// A derived class of TwoDShape for rectangles.
class Rectangle : TwoDShape {
  // Return true if the rectangle is square.
  public bool IsSquare() {
    if(Width == Height) return true;
    return false;
  }

  public double Area() {
    return Width * Height;
  }
}
```

The **Rectangle** class includes **TwoDShape** and adds the methods **IsSquare( )**, which determines if the rectangle is square, and **Area( )**, which computes the area of a rectangle.

Member Access and Inheritance

As you learned in Chapter 6, members of a class are often declared as private to prevent their unauthorized use or tampering. Inheriting a class *does not* overrule the private access restriction. Thus, even though a derived class includes all of the members of its base class, it cannot access those members of the base class that are private. For example, if, as shown here, **Width** and **Height** are made private in **TwoDShape**, then **Triangle** will not be able to access them.

```
// Access to private members is not inherited.

// This example will not compile.
using System;
```

```
// A class for two-dimensional objects.
class TwoDShape {
  double Width;  // now private
  double Height; // now private

  public void ShowDim() {
    Console.WriteLine("Width and height are " +
                       Width + " and " + Height);
  }
}

// Triangle is derived from TwoDShape.
class Triangle : TwoDShape {
  public string Style;        Can't access private members of a base class.

  public double Area() {
    return Width * Height / 2; // Error! Can't access private member.
  }

  public void ShowStyle() {
    Console.WriteLine("Triangle is " + Style);
  }
}
```

The **Triangle** class will not compile because the reference to **Width** and **Height** inside the **Area( )** method causes an access violation. Since **Width** and **Height** are now private, they are accessible only by other members of their own class. Derived classes have no access to them.

Remember: A private class member will remain private to its class. It is not accessible by any code outside its class, including derived classes.

At first, you might think that it is a serious restriction that derived classes do not have access to the private members of base classes because it would prevent the use of private members in many situations. However, this is not true; C# provides various solutions. One is to use **protected** members, which is described in the next section. A second is to use public properties to provide access to private data.

As explained in the previous chapter, a property allows you to manage access to an instance variable. For example, you can enforce constraints on its values, or you can make the variable read-only. By making a property public but declaring its underlying variable private, a derived class can still use the property, but it cannot directly access the underlying private variable.

Here is a rewrite of the **TwoDShape** class that makes **Width** and **Height** into properties. In the process, it ensures that the values of **Width** and **Height** will be positive. This would allow you, for example, to specify the **Width** and **Height** using the coordinates of the shape in any quadrant of the Cartesian plane without having to first obtain their absolute values.

```
// Use properties to set and get private members.
using System;
```

```
// A class for two-dimensional objects.
class TwoDShape {
  double pri_width;
  double pri_height;

  // Properties for Width and Height.
  public double Width {
      get { return pri_width; }
      set { pri_width = value < 0 ? -value : value; }
  }

  public double Height {
      get { return pri_height; }
      set { pri_height = value < 0 ? -value : value; }
  }

  public void ShowDim() {
    Console.WriteLine("Width and height are " +
                      Width + " and " + Height);
  }
}

// A derived class of TwoDShape for triangles.
class Triangle : TwoDShape {
  public string Style;

  public double Area() {
    return Width * Height / 2;
  }

  public void ShowStyle() {
    Console.WriteLine("Triangle is " + Style);
  }
}

class Shapes2 {
  static void Main() {
    Triangle t1 = new Triangle();
    Triangle t2 = new Triangle();

    t1.Width = 4.0;
    t1.Height = 4.0;
    t1.Style = "isosceles";

    t2.Width = 8.0;
    t2.Height = 12.0;
    t2.Style = "right";
```

Here, **Width** and **Height** are properties.

Use of **Width** and **Height** now OK because access is through properties.

```
        Console.WriteLine("Info for t1: ");
        t1.ShowStyle();
        t1.ShowDim();
        Console.WriteLine("Area is " + t1.Area());

        Console.WriteLine();

        Console.WriteLine("Info for t2: ");
        t2.ShowStyle();
        t2.ShowDim();
        Console.WriteLine("Area is " + t2.Area());
    }
}
```

This program displays the same output as the previous version. The only difference is that now **Width** and **Height** are public properties that manage access to private instance variables.

Ask the Expert

Q: I have heard the terms "superclass" and "subclass" used in discussions of Java programming. Do these terms have meaning in C#?

A: What Java calls a superclass, C# calls a base class. What Java calls a subclass, C# calls a derived class. You will commonly hear both sets of terms applied to a class of either language, but this book will continue to use the standard C# terms. By the way, C++ also uses the base class, derived class terminology.

Using Protected Access

As explained in the preceding section, a private member of a base class is not accessible by a derived class. This would seem to imply that if you wanted a derived class to have access to some member in the base class, it would need to be public. Of course, making the member public also makes it available to all other code, which may not be desirable. Fortunately, this implication is wrong because C# allows you to create a *protected member*. A protected member is accessible within its class hierarchy, but private outside that hierarchy.

A protected member is created using the **protected** access modifier. When a member of a class is declared as **protected**, that member is, with one important exception, private. The exception occurs when a protected member is inherited. In this case, a protected member of the base class becomes a protected member of the derived class and is, therefore, accessible by the derived class. Therefore, by using **protected**, you can create class members that are private to their class but that can still be inherited and accessed by a derived class.

Here is a simple example that uses **protected**:

```
// Demonstrate protected.
using System;
```
            The fields **i** and **j** are declared protected.
```
class B {
  protected int i, j; // private to B, but accessible by D

  public void Set(int a, int b) {
    i = a;
    j = b;
  }

  public void Show() {
    Console.WriteLine(i + " " + j);
  }
}

class D : B {
  int k; // private

  // D can access B's i and j.
  public void SetK() {
    k = i * j;   ◄——————— D can access i and j because they are protected, not private.
  }

  public void Showk() {
    Console.WriteLine(k);
  }
}

class ProtectedDemo {
  static void Main() {
    D ob = new D();

    ob.Set(2, 3); // OK, known to D
    ob.Show();    // OK, known to D

    ob.SetK();  // OK, part of D
    ob.Showk(); // OK, part of D
  }
}
```

In this example, because **B** is inherited by **D** and because **i** and **j** are declared as **protected** in **B**, the **SetK( )** method can access them. If **i** and **j** had been declared as private by **B**, then **D** would not have access to them and the program would not compile.

Like **public** and **private**, **protected** status stays with a member no matter how many layers of inheritance are involved. Therefore, when a derived class is used as a base class for another derived class, any **protected** member of the initial base class that is inherited by the first derived class is also inherited as **protected** by a second derived class.

Although **protected** access is quite useful, it doesn't apply in all situations. For example, in the case of **TwoDShape** shown in the preceding section, we specifically want the **Width** and **Height** values to be publicly accessible. It's just that we want to manage the values that they are assigned. Therefore, declaring them **protected** is not an option. In this case, the use of properties supplies the proper solution, by controlling, rather than preventing, access. Remember, use **protected** when you want to create a member that is private throughout a class hierarchy, but is otherwise unrestricted. To manage access to a value, use a property.

Constructors and Inheritance

In a hierarchy, it is possible for both base classes and derived classes to have their own constructors. This raises an important question: What constructor is responsible for building an object of the derived class? The one in the base class, the one in the derived class, or both? The answer is this: The constructor for the base class constructs the base class portion of the object, and the constructor for the derived class constructs the derived class part. This makes sense, because the base class has no knowledge of or access to any element in a derived class. Thus, their construction must be separate. The preceding examples have relied upon the default constructors created automatically by C#, so this was not an issue. However, in practice, most classes will have constructors. Here, you will see how to handle this situation.

When only the derived class defines a constructor, the process is straightforward: Simply construct the derived class object. The base class portion of the object is constructed automatically using its default constructor. For example, here is a reworked version of **Triangle** that defines a constructor. It also makes **Style** private since it is now set by the constructor.

```
// Add a constructor to Triangle.
using System;

// A class for two-dimensional objects.
class TwoDShape {
  double pri_width;
  double pri_height;

  // Properties for Width and Height.
  public double Width {
    get { return pri_width; }
    set { pri_width = value < 0 ? -value : value; }
  }

  public double Height {
    get { return pri_height; }
    set { pri_height = value < 0 ? -value : value; }
  }
```

```
    public void ShowDim() {
      Console.WriteLine("Width and height are " +
                        Width + " and " + Height);
    }
}

// A derived class of TwoDShape for triangles.
class Triangle : TwoDShape {
  string Style;

  // Constructor
  public Triangle(string s, double w, double h) {    ◄─── Constructor for Triangle.
    Width = w;   // init the base class
    Height = h;  // init the base class   ◄─── Construct TwoDShape portion
                                               of a Triangle object.
    Style = s;   // init the derived class
  }

  public double Area() {
    return Width * Height / 2;
  }

  public void ShowStyle() {
    Console.WriteLine("Triangle is " + Style);
  }
}

class Shapes3 {
  static void Main() {
    Triangle t1 = new Triangle("isosceles", 4.0, 4.0);
    Triangle t2 = new Triangle("right", 8.0, 12.0);

    Console.WriteLine("Info for t1: ");
    t1.ShowStyle();
    t1.ShowDim();
    Console.WriteLine("Area is " + t1.Area());

    Console.WriteLine();

    Console.WriteLine("Info for t2: ");
    t2.ShowStyle();
    t2.ShowDim();
    Console.WriteLine("Area is " + t2.Area());
  }
}
```

Here, **Triangle**'s constructor initializes the members of **TwoDShape** that it inherits along with its own **Style** field. The output is the same as before.

When both the base class and the derived class define constructors, the process is a bit more complicated because both the base class and derived class constructors must be executed. In this case, you must use another of C#'s keywords: **base**, which has two uses. The first calls a base class constructor. The second is used to access a member of the base class that has been hidden by a member of a derived class. Here, we will look at its first use.

Calling Base Class Constructors

A derived class can call a constructor defined in its base class by using an expanded form of the derived class' constructor declaration and the **base** keyword. The general form of this expanded declaration is shown here:

derived-constructor(*parameter-list*) : base(*arg-list*) {
  // body of constructor
}

Here, *arg-list* specifies any arguments needed by the constructor in the base class. Notice the placement of the colon.

To see how **base** is used, consider the version **TwoDShape** in the following program. It defines a constructor that initializes the **Width** and **Height** properties. This constructor is then called by the **Triangle** constructor.

```
// Add constructors to TwoDShape.
using System;

// A class for two-dimensional objects.
class TwoDShape {
  double pri_width;
  double pri_height;

  // Constructor for TwoDShape.
  public TwoDShape(double w, double h) {    ◄——————— Constructor for TwoDShape.
    Width = w;
    Height = h;
  }

  // Properties for Width and Height.
  public double Width {
    get { return pri_width; }
    set { pri_width = value < 0 ? -value : value; }
  }

  public double Height {
    get { return pri_height; }
    set { pri_height = value < 0 ? -value : value; }
  }
```

```
  public void ShowDim() {
    Console.WriteLine("Width and height are " +
                      Width + " and " + Height);
  }
}

// A derived class of TwoDShape for triangles.
class Triangle : TwoDShape {
  string Style;

  // Call the base class constructor.
  public Triangle(string s, double w, double h) : base(w, h) {
    Style = s;
  }

  public double Area() {
    return Width * Height / 2;
  }

  public void ShowStyle() {
    Console.WriteLine("Triangle is " + Style);
  }
}

class Shapes4 {
  static void Main() {
    Triangle t1 = new Triangle("isosceles", 4.0, 4.0);
    Triangle t2 = new Triangle("right", 8.0, 12.0);

    Console.WriteLine("Info for t1: ");
    t1.ShowStyle();
    t1.ShowDim();
    Console.WriteLine("Area is " + t1.Area());

    Console.WriteLine();

    Console.WriteLine("Info for t2: ");
    t2.ShowStyle();
    t2.ShowDim();
    Console.WriteLine("Area is " + t2.Area());
  }
}
```

Use **base** to execute the **TwoDShape** constructor.

Here, **Triangle( )** calls **base** with the parameters **w** and **h**. This causes the **TwoDShape( )** constructor to be called, which initializes **Width** and **Height** using these values. **Triangle** no longer initializes these values itself. It need only initialize the value unique to it: **Style**. This leaves **TwoDShape** free to construct its subobject in any manner that it chooses. Furthermore, **TwoDShape** can add functionality about which existing derived classes have no knowledge, thus preventing existing code from breaking.

Any form of constructor defined by the base class can be called by **base**. The constructor executed will be the one that matches the arguments. For example, here are expanded versions of both **TwoDShape** and **Triangle** that include default constructors and constructors that take one argument.

```csharp
// Add more constructors to TwoDShape.
using System;

class TwoDShape {
  double pri_width;
  double pri_height;

  // Default constructor.
  public TwoDShape() {
    Width = Height = 0.0;
  }

  // Specify Width and Height.
  public TwoDShape(double w, double h) {
    Width = w;
    Height = h;
  }

  // Construct object with equal width and height.
  public TwoDShape(double x) {
    Width = Height = x;
  }

  // Properties for Width and Height.
  public double Width {
     get { return pri_width; }
     set { pri_width = value < 0 ? -value : value; }
  }

  public double Height {
     get { return pri_height; }
     set { pri_height = value < 0 ? -value : value; }
  }

  public void ShowDim() {
    Console.WriteLine("Width and height are " +
                       Width + " and " + Height);
  }
}

// A derived class of TwoDShape for triangles.
class Triangle : TwoDShape {
  string Style;
```

```
    /* A default constructor. This automatically invokes
       the default constructor of TwoDShape. */
    public Triangle() {
      Style = "null";
    }

    // Constructor that takes style, width, and height.
    public Triangle(string s, double w, double h) : base(w, h) {
      Style = s;
    }

    // Construct an isosceles triangle.
    public Triangle(double x) : base(x) {
      Style = "isosceles";
    }
```

Use **base** to call different forms of the **TwoDShape** constructor.

```
    public double Area() {
      return Width * Height / 2;
    }

    public void ShowStyle() {
      Console.WriteLine("Triangle is " + Style);
    }
  }

class Shapes5 {
  static void Main() {
    Triangle t1 = new Triangle();
    Triangle t2 = new Triangle("right", 8.0, 12.0);
    Triangle t3 = new Triangle(4.0);

    t1 = t2;

    Console.WriteLine("Info for t1: ");
    t1.ShowStyle();
    t1.ShowDim();
    Console.WriteLine("Area is " + t1.Area());

    Console.WriteLine();

    Console.WriteLine("Info for t2: ");
    t2.ShowStyle();
    t2.ShowDim();
    Console.WriteLine("Area is " + t2.Area());

    Console.WriteLine();

    Console.WriteLine("Info for t3: ");
    t3.ShowStyle();
```

```
        t3.ShowDim();
        Console.WriteLine("Area is " + t3.Area());

        Console.WriteLine();
    }
}
```

Here is the output from this version:

```
Info for t1:
Triangle is right
Width and height are 8 and 12
Area is 48

Info for t2:
Triangle is right
Width and height are 8 and 12
Area is 48

Info for t3:
Triangle is isosceles
Width and height are 4 and 4
Area is 8
```

Let's review the key concepts behind **base**. When a derived class specifies a **base** clause, it is calling the constructor of its immediate base class. Thus, **base** always refers to the base class immediately above the calling class. This is true even in a multileveled hierarchy. You pass arguments to the base constructor by specifying them as arguments to **base**. If no **base** clause is present, then the base class' default constructor is called automatically.

Inheritance and Name Hiding

It is possible for a derived class to define a member that has the same name as a member in its base class. When this happens, the member in the base class is hidden within the derived class. While this is not technically an error in C#, the compiler will issue a warning message. This warning alerts you to the fact that a name is being hidden. If your intent is to hide a base class member, then to prevent this warning, the derived class member must be preceded by the **new** keyword. Understand that this use of **new** is separate and distinct from its use when creating an object instance.

Here is an example of name hiding:

```
// An example of inheritance-related name hiding.
using System;

class A {
  public int i = 0;
}
```

```
// Create a derived class.
class B : A {
  new int i; // this i hides the i in A ◄─────── The i in A is hidden by the i
                                                 in B. Notice the use of new.
  public B(int b) {
    i = b; // i in B
  }

  public void Show() {
    Console.WriteLine("i in derived class: " + i);
  }
}

class NameHiding {
  static void Main() {
    B ob = new B(2);

    ob.Show();
  }
}
```

First, notice the use of **new**. In essence, it tells the compiler that you know a new variable called **i** is being created that hides the **i** in the base class **A**. If you leave **new** out, a warning is generated.

The output produced by this program is shown here:

```
i in derived class: 2
```

Since **B** defines its own instance variable called **i**, it hides the **i** in **A**. Therefore, when **Show( )** is invoked on an object of type **B**, the value of **i** as defined by **B** is displayed—not the one defined by **A**.

Using base to Access a Hidden Name

There is a second form of **base** that acts somewhat like **this**, except that it always refers to the base class of the derived class in which it is used. This usage has the following general form:

base.*member*

Here, *member* can be either a method or an instance variable. This form of **base** is most applicable to situations in which member names of a derived class hide members by the same name in the base class. Consider this version of the class hierarchy from the preceding example:

```
// Using base to overcome name hiding.
using System;

class A {
  public int i = 0;
}
```

```
// Create a derived class.
class B : A {
  new int i; // this i hides the i in A

  public B(int a, int b) {
    base.i = a; // this uncovers the i in A
    i = b; // i in B
  }

  public void Show() {
    // This displays the i in A.
    Console.WriteLine("i in base class: " + base.i);

    // This displays the i in B.
    Console.WriteLine("i in derived class: " + i);
  }
}

class UncoverName {
  static void Main() {
    B ob = new B(1, 2);

    ob.Show();
  }
}
```

← Here, **base.i** refers to the **i** in **A**.

This program displays the following:

```
i in base class: 1
i in derived class: 2
```

Although the instance variable **i** in **B** hides the **i** in **A**, **base** allows access to the **i** defined in the base class.

Hidden methods can also be called through the use of **base**. For example:

```
// Call a hidden method.
using System;

class A {
  public int i = 0;

  // Show() in A.
  public void Show() {
    Console.WriteLine("i in base class: " + i);
  }
}

// Create a derived class.
class B : A {
  new int i; // this i hides the i in A
```

```
   public B(int a, int b) {
     base.i = a; // this uncovers the i in A
     i = b; // i in B
   }

   // This hides Show() in A.
   new public void Show() {  ◄——— This Show( ) hides the one in A.
     base.Show(); // this calls Show() in A ◄——————— This calls the hidden Show( ).

     // This displays the i in B.
     Console.WriteLine("i in derived class: " + i);
   }
 }

class UncoverName {
  static void Main() {
    B ob = new B(1, 2);

    ob.Show();
  }
}
```

The output from the program is shown here:

```
i in base class: 1
i in derived class: 2
```

As you can see, **base.Show( )** calls the base class version of **Show( )**.

One other point: Notice that **new** is used in this program to tell the compiler that you know that a new method called **Show( )** is being created that hides the **Show( )** in **A**.

Try This Extend the Vehicle Class

To illustrate the power of inheritance, we will extend the **Vehicle** class first developed in Chapter 4. As you should recall, **Vehicle** encapsulates information about vehicles, including the number of passengers they can carry, their fuel capacity, and their fuel consumption rate. We can use the **Vehicle** class as a starting point from which more specialized classes are developed. For example, one type of vehicle is a truck. An important attribute of a truck is its cargo capacity. Thus, to create a **Truck** class, you can inherit **Vehicle**, adding an instance variable that stores the carrying capacity. In this project, you will create the **Truck** class. In the process, the instance variables in **Vehicle** will be made into auto-implemented properties in which the **set** accessors are specified as **protected**. This means that these values can be set by code in a derived class, but are not otherwise accessible.

(continued)

Step by Step

1. Create a file called **TruckDemo.cs**, and copy the last implementation of **Vehicle** from Chapter 4 into the file.

2. Convert the instance variables in **Vehicle** into auto-implemented properties. Specify the **set** accessors as **protected**, as shown here:

```
/* Auto-implemented properties for passengers,
   fuel capacity, and mileage. Notice that the
   set accessors are protected. */
public int Passengers { get; protected set; }

public int FuelCap { get; protected set; }

public int Mpg { get; protected set; }
```

As mentioned, making the **set** accessors **protected** means that they will be accessible by any classes derived from **Vehicle**, but will otherwise be private.

3. Create the **Truck** class as shown here:

```
// Use Vehicle to create a Truck specialization.
class Truck : Vehicle {

  // This is a constructor for Truck.
  public Truck(int p, int f, int m, int c) : base(p, f, m)
  {
    CargoCap = c;
  }

  // Auto-implemented property for cargo capacity in pounds.
  public int CargoCap { get; protected set; }
}
```

Here, **Truck** inherits **Vehicle** and adds the **CargoCap** property. Thus, **Truck** includes all of the general vehicle attributes defined by **Vehicle**. It need add only those items that are unique to its own class. Notice that **CargoCap** is also an auto-implemented property whose **set** accessor is specified as **protected**. This means that it will be accessible to any class that inherits **Truck**, but is otherwise private.

4. Here is an entire program that demonstrates the **Truck** class:

```
// Build a derived class of Vehicle for trucks.

using System;

class Vehicle {

  // This is a constructor for Vehicle.
  public Vehicle(int p, int f, int m) {
    Passengers = p;
```

```
      FuelCap = f;
      Mpg = m;
    }

    // Return the range.
    public int Range() {
      return Mpg * FuelCap;
    }

    // Compute fuel needed for a given distance.
    public double FuelNeeded(int miles) {
      return (double) miles / Mpg;
    }

    /* Auto-implemented properties for passengers,
       fuel capacity, and mileage. Notice that the
       set accessors are protected. */
    public int Passengers { get; protected set; }

    public int FuelCap { get; protected set; }

    public int Mpg { get; protected set; }
  }

// Use Vehicle to create a Truck specialization.
class Truck : Vehicle {

    // This is a constructor for Truck.
    public Truck(int p, int f, int m, int c) : base(p, f, m)
    {
      CargoCap = c;
    }

    // Auto-implemented property for cargo capacity in pounds.
    public int CargoCap { get; protected set; }
  }

class TruckDemo {
    static void Main() {

      // Construct some trucks.
      Truck semi = new Truck(2, 200, 7, 44000);
      Truck pickup = new Truck(3, 28, 15, 2000);

      double gallons;
      int dist = 252;

      gallons = semi.FuelNeeded(dist);
```

(continued)

```
Console.WriteLine("Semi can carry " + semi.CargoCap +
                  " pounds.");
Console.WriteLine("To go " + dist + " miles semi needs " +
                  gallons + " gallons of fuel.\n");

gallons = pickup.FuelNeeded(dist);

Console.WriteLine("Pickup can carry " + pickup.CargoCap +
                  " pounds.");
Console.WriteLine("To go " + dist + " miles pickup needs " +
                  gallons + " gallons of fuel.");
    }
}
```

5. The output from this program is shown here:

```
Semi can carry 44000 pounds.
To go 252 miles semi needs 36 gallons of fuel.

Pickup can carry 2000 pounds.
To go 252 miles pickup needs 16.8 gallons of fuel.
```

Many other types of classes can be derived from **Vehicle**. For example, the following skeleton creates an off-road class that stores the ground clearance of the vehicle:

```
// Create an off-road vehicle class.
class OffRoad : Vehicle {
  // Ground clearance in inches.
  public int GroundClearance { get; protected set; }
  // ...
}
```

The key point is that once you have created a base class that defines the general aspects of an object, that base class can be inherited to form specialized classes. Each derived class simply adds its own unique attributes. This is the essence of inheritance.

Creating a Multilevel Hierarchy

Up to this point, we have been using simple class hierarchies consisting of only a base class and a derived class. However, you can build hierarchies that contain as many layers of inheritance as you like. As mentioned, it is perfectly acceptable to use a derived class as a base class of another. For example, given three classes called **A**, **B**, and **C**, **C** can be derived from **B**, which can be derived from **A**. When this type of situation occurs, each derived class inherits all of the traits found in all of its base classes. In this case, **C** inherits all aspects of **B** and **A**.

To see how a multilevel hierarchy can be useful, consider the following program. In it, the derived class **Triangle** is used as a base class to create the derived class called **ColorTriangle**. **ColorTriangle** inherits all of the traits of **Triangle** and **TwoDShape**, and adds a field called **Color**, which holds the color of the triangle.

```
// A multilevel hierarchy.
using System;

class TwoDShape {
  double pri_width;
  double pri_height;

  // Default constructor.
  public TwoDShape() {
    Width = Height = 0.0;
  }

  // Constructor that takes width and height.
  public TwoDShape(double w, double h) {
    Width = w;
    Height = h;
  }

  // Specify width and height.
  public TwoDShape(double x) {
    Width = Height = x;
  }

  // Properties for Width and Height.
  public double Width {
     get { return pri_width; }
     set { pri_width = value < 0 ? -value : value; }
  }

  public double Height {
     get { return pri_height; }
     set { pri_height = value < 0 ? -value : value; }
  }

  public void ShowDim() {
    Console.WriteLine("Width and height are " +
                      Width + " and " + Height);
  }
}

// A derived class of TwoDShape for triangles.
class Triangle : TwoDShape {
  string Style;
```

```
  /* A default constructor. This invokes the default
     constructor of TwoDShape. */
  public Triangle() {
    Style = "null";
  }

  // Constructor that takes style, width, and height.
  public Triangle(string s, double w, double h) : base(w, h) {
    Style = s;
  }

  // Construct an isosceles triangle.
  public Triangle(double x) : base(x) {
    Style = "isosceles";
  }

  public double Area() {
    return Width * Height / 2;
  }

  public void ShowStyle() {
    Console.WriteLine("Triangle is " + Style);
  }
}

// Extend Triangle.
class ColorTriangle : Triangle {
  string Color;

  // Constructor for ColorTriangle.
  public ColorTriangle(string c, string s,
                       double w, double h) : base(s, w, h) {
    Color = c;
  }

  // Display the color.
  public void ShowColor() {
    Console.WriteLine("Color is " + Color);
  }
}

class Shapes6 {
  static void Main() {
    ColorTriangle t1 =
        new ColorTriangle("Blue", "right", 8.0, 12.0);
    ColorTriangle t2 =
        new ColorTriangle("Red", "isosceles", 2.0, 2.0);
```

ColorTriangle inherits **Triangle**, which is descended from **TwoDShape**. Therefore, it includes all members of both.

```
    Console.WriteLine("Info for t1: ");
    t1.ShowStyle();
    t1.ShowDim();
    t1.ShowColor();
    Console.WriteLine("Area is " + t1.Area());

    Console.WriteLine();

    Console.WriteLine("Info for t2: ");
    t2.ShowStyle();
    t2.ShowDim();
    t2.ShowColor();
    Console.WriteLine("Area is " + t2.Area());
  }
}
```

A **ColorTriangle** object can call methods defined by itself and its base classes.

The output of this program is shown here:

```
Info for t1:
Triangle is right
Width and height are 8 and 12
Color is Blue
Area is 48

Info for t2:
Triangle is isosceles
Width and height are 2 and 2
Color is Red
Area is 2
```

Because of inheritance, **ColorTriangle** can make use of the previously defined classes of **Triangle** and **TwoDShape**, adding only the extra information it needs for its own specific application. This is part of the value of inheritance—it allows the reuse of code.

This example illustrates one other important point: **base** always refers to the constructor in the closest base class. The **base** in **ColorTriangle** calls the constructor in **Triangle**. The **base** in **Triangle** calls the constructor in **TwoDShape**. In a class hierarchy, if a base class constructor requires parameters, then all derived classes must pass those parameters "up the line." This is true whether or not a derived class needs parameters of its own.

When Are Constructors Called?

In the foregoing discussion of inheritance and class hierarchies, an important question may have occurred to you: When a derived class object is created, whose constructor is executed first, the one in the derived class or the one defined by the base class? For example, given a derived class called **B** and a base class called **A**, is **A**'s constructor called before **B**'s, or vice versa? The answer is that in a class hierarchy, constructors are called in order of derivation, from base class to derived class. Furthermore, this order is the same whether or not **base** is used. If **base** is not used, then the default (parameterless) constructor of each base class will be executed. The following program illustrates this principle:

```
// Demonstrate when constructors are called.
using System;

// Create a base class.
class A {
  public A() {
    Console.WriteLine("Constructing A.");
  }
}

// Create a class derived from A.
class B : A {
  public B() {
    Console.WriteLine("Constructing B.");
  }
}

// Create a class derived from B.
class C : B {
  public C() {
    Console.WriteLine("Constructing C.");
  }
}

class OrderOfConstruction {
  static void Main() {

    C c = new C();
  }
}
```

The output from this program is shown here:

```
Constructing A
Constructing B
Constructing C
```

As you can see, the constructors are called in order of derivation.

It makes sense that constructors are executed in order of derivation. Because a base class has no knowledge of any derived class, any initialization it needs to perform is separate from and possibly prerequisite to any initialization performed by the derived class. Therefore, it must be executed first.

Base Class References and Derived Objects

As you know, C# is a strongly typed language. Aside from the standard conversions and automatic promotions that apply to its simple types, type compatibility is strictly enforced. Therefore, a reference variable for one class type cannot normally refer to an object of another class type. For example, consider the following program:

```
// This will not compile.
class X {
  int a;

  public X(int i) { a = i; }
}

class Y {
  int a;

  public Y(int i) { a = i; }
}

class IncompatibleRef {
  static void Main() {
    X x = new X(10);
    X x2;
    Y y = new Y(5);

    x2 = x; // OK, both of same type

    x2 = y; // Error, not of same type    ————— These references are not compatible.
  }
}
```

Here, even though class **X** and class **Y** are structurally the same, it is not possible to assign a reference of type **X** to a variable of type **Y**, because they have different types. In general, a reference variable can refer only to objects of its type.

There is, however, an important exception to C#'s strict type enforcement. A reference variable of a base class can be assigned a reference to an object of any class derived from that base class. This is legal because an instance of a derived type encapsulates an instance of the base type. Thus, a base class reference can refer to it. Here is an example:

```
// A base class reference can refer to a derived class object.
using System;

class X {
  public int a;

  public X(int i) {
    a = i;
  }
}
```

```
class Y : X {
  public int b;

  public Y(int i, int j) : base(j) {
    b = i;
  }
}

class BaseRef {
  static void Main() {
    X x = new X(10);
    X x2;
    Y y = new Y(5, 6);

    x2 = x; // OK, both of same type
    Console.WriteLine("x2.a: " + x2.a);

    x2 = y; // still OK because Y is derived from X
    Console.WriteLine("x2.a: " + x2.a);

    // X references know only about X members.
    x2.a = 19; // OK
//     x2.b = 27; // Error! X doesn't have b as a member.
  }
}
```

OK because **Y** is derived from **X**, thus **x2** can refer to **y**.

Here, **Y** is now derived from **X**; thus, it is permissible for **x2** to be assigned a reference to a **Y** object.

It is important to understand that it is the type of the reference variable—not the type of the object that it refers to—that determines what members can be accessed. That is, when a reference to a derived class object is assigned to a base class reference variable, you will have access only to those parts of the object defined by the base class. This is why **x2** can't access **b** even when it refers to a **Y** object. This makes sense, because the base class has no knowledge of what a derived class adds to it. This is why the last line of code in the program is commented out.

Although the preceding discussion may seem a bit esoteric, it has some important practical applications. One is described here. The other is discussed later in this chapter, when virtual methods are covered.

An important place where derived class references are assigned to base class variables is when constructors are called in a class hierarchy. As you know, it is common for a class to define a constructor that takes an object of its class as a parameter. This allows the class to construct a copy of an object. Classes derived from such a class can take advantage of this feature. For example, here are constructors for **TwoDShape** and **Triangle** that take an object of their class as a parameter.

```
class TwoDShape {
  // ...
  // Construct a copy of a TwoDShape object.
  public TwoDShape(TwoDShape ob) {
    Width = ob.Width;
    Height = ob.Height;
  }
  // ...

class Triangle : TwoDShape {
  // ...
  // Construct a copy of a Triangle object.
  public Triangle(Triangle ob) : base(ob) {
    Style = ob.Style;
  }
  // ...
```

Notice that the **Triangle** constructor receives an object of type **Triangle**, and it passes that object (through **base**) to the **TwoDShape** constructor. The key point is that **TwoDShape( )** is expecting a **TwoDShape** object. However, **Triangle( )** passes it a **Triangle** object. As explained, the reason this works is because a base class reference can refer to a derived class object. Thus, it is perfectly acceptable to pass **TwoDShape( )** a reference to an object of a class derived from **TwoDShape**. Because the **TwoDShape( )** constructor is initializing only those portions of the derived class object that are members of **TwoDShape**, it doesn't matter that the object might also contain other members added by derived classes.

Virtual Methods and Overriding

A *virtual method* is a method that is declared as **virtual** in a base class. The defining characteristic of a virtual method is that it can be redefined in one or more derived classes. Thus, each derived class can have its own version of a virtual method. Virtual methods are interesting because of what happens when one is called through a base class reference. In this situation, C# determines which version of the method to call based upon the *type* of the object *referred to* by the reference—and this determination is made *at runtime*. Thus, when different objects are referred to, different versions of the virtual method are executed. In other words, it is the type of the object being referred to (not the type of the reference) that determines which version of the virtual method will be executed. Therefore, if a base class contains a virtual method and classes are derived from that base class, then when different types of objects are referred to through a base class reference, different versions of the virtual method are executed.

You declare a method as virtual inside a base class by preceding its declaration with the keyword **virtual**. When a virtual method is redefined by a derived class, the **override** modifier is used. Thus, the process of redefining a virtual method inside a derived class is called *method overriding*. When overriding a method, the name, return type, and signature of the overriding method must be the same as the virtual method that is being overridden. Also, a virtual method cannot be specified as **static** or **abstract** (discussed later in this chapter).

Method overriding forms the basis for one of C#'s most powerful concepts: *dynamic method dispatch*. Dynamic method dispatch is the mechanism by which a call to an overridden method is resolved at runtime rather than at compile time. Dynamic method dispatch is important because this is how C# implements runtime polymorphism.

Here is an example that illustrates virtual methods and overriding:

```
// Demonstrate a virtual method.
using System;

class Base {
  // Create virtual method in the base class.
  public virtual void Who() {          ←——— Declare a virtual method.
    Console.WriteLine("Who() in Base");
  }
}

class Derived1 : Base {
  // Override Who() in a derived class.
  public override void Who() {  ←
    Console.WriteLine("Who() in Derived1");
  }
}                                                          Override the virtual
                                                           method.
class Derived2 : Base {
  // Override Who() again in another derived class.
  public override void Who() {  ←
    Console.WriteLine("Who() in Derived2");
  }
}

class OverrideDemo {
  static void Main() {
    Base baseOb = new Base();
    Derived1 dOb1 = new Derived1();
    Derived2 dOb2 = new Derived2();

    Base baseRef; // a base-class reference

    baseRef = baseOb;
    baseRef.Who();  ←

    baseRef = dOb1;                In each case, the version of **Who( )** to call is determined
    baseRef.Who();  ←             at runtime by the type of object being referred to.

    baseRef = dOb2;
    baseRef.Who();  ←
  }
}
```

The output from the program is shown here:

```
Who() in Base
Who() in Derived1
Who() in Derived2
```

This program creates a base class called **Base** and two derived classes of it, called **Derived1** and **Derived2**. **Base** declares a method called **Who( )**, and the derived classes override it. Inside the **Main( )** method, objects of type **Base**, **Derived1**, and **Derived2** are declared. Also, a reference of type **Base**, called **baseRef**, is declared. The program then assigns a reference to each type of object to **baseRef** and uses that reference to call **Who( )**. As the output shows, the version of **Who( )** that is executed is determined by the type of object being referred to at the time of the call, not by the class type of **baseRef**.

It is not necessary to override a virtual method. If a derived class does not provide its own version of a virtual method, then the one in the base class is used. For example:

```
/* When a virtual method is not overridden, the base
   class method is used. */
using System;

class Base {
  // Create virtual method in the base class.
  public virtual void Who() {
    Console.WriteLine("Who() in Base");
  }
}

class Derived1 : Base {
  // Override Who() in a derived class.
  public override void Who() {
    Console.WriteLine("Who() in Derived1");
  }
}

class Derived2 : Base {          ◄────────────── No override of Who( ) here.
  // This class does not override Who().
}

class NoOverrideDemo {
  static void Main() {
    Base baseOb = new Base();
    Derived1 dOb1 = new Derived1();
    Derived2 dOb2 = new Derived2();

    Base baseRef; // a base-class reference

    baseRef = baseOb;
    baseRef.Who();
```

```
        baseRef = dOb1;
        baseRef.Who();

        baseRef = dOb2;
        baseRef.Who(); // calls Base's Who()  ◄——————————— This calls Base's Who( ).
    }
}
```

The output from this program is shown here:

```
Who() in Base
Who() in Derived1
Who() in Base
```

Here, **Derived2** does not override **Who( )**. Thus, when **Who( )** is called on a **Derived2** object, the **Who( )** in **Base** is executed.

Ask the Expert

Q: Can properties be virtual?

A: Yes. Properties can be modified by the **virtual** keyword and overridden using **override**. The same is true for indexers.

Why Overridden Methods?

Overridden methods allow C# to support runtime polymorphism. Polymorphism is essential to object-oriented programming for one reason: It allows a general class to specify methods that will be common to all of its derivatives, while allowing derived classes to define the specific implementation of some or all of those methods. Overridden methods are another way that C# implements the "one interface, multiple methods" aspect of polymorphism.

Part of the key to successfully applying polymorphism is understanding that the base class and derived classes form a hierarchy that moves from lesser to greater specialization. Used correctly, the base class provides all elements that a derived class can use directly. It also defines those methods that the derived class must implement on its own. This allows the derived class the flexibility to define its own methods, yet still enforces a consistent interface. Thus, by combining inheritance with overridden methods, a base class can define the general form of the methods that will be used by all of its derived classes.

Applying Virtual Methods

To better understand the power of virtual methods, we will apply it to the **TwoDShape** class. In the preceding examples, each class derived from **TwoDShape** defines a method called **Area( )**. This suggests that it might be better to make **Area( )** a virtual method of the **TwoDShape** class, allowing each derived class to override it, and defining how the area is calculated for the type of shape that the class encapsulates. The following program does this. For convenience, it also adds an auto-implemented property called **Name** to **TwoDShape**. (This makes it easier to demonstrate the classes.)

```
// Use virtual methods and polymorphism.
using System;

class TwoDShape {
  double pri_width;
  double pri_height;

  // A default constructor.
  public TwoDShape() {
    Width = Height = 0.0;
    Name = "null";
  }

  // Specify all information.
  public TwoDShape(double w, double h, string n) {
    Width = w;
    Height = h;
    Name = n;
  }

  // Construct object with equal width and height.
  public TwoDShape(double x, string n) {
    Width = Height = x;
    Name = n;
  }

  // Construct a copy of a TwoDShape object.
  public TwoDShape(TwoDShape ob) {
    Width = ob.Width;
    Height = ob.Height;
    Name = ob.Name;
  }

  // Properties for Width, Height, and Name.
  public double Width {
    get { return pri_width; }
    set { pri_width = value < 0 ? -value : value; }
  }

  public double Height {
    get { return pri_height; }
    set { pri_height = value < 0 ? -value : value; }
  }

  public string Name { get; set; }
```

```
   public void ShowDim() {
     Console.WriteLine("Width and height are " +
                       Width + " and " + Height);
   }

   public virtual double Area() {                          Area( ) is now virtual.
     Console.WriteLine("Area() must be overridden");
     return 0.0;
   }
}

// A derived class of TwoDShape for triangles.
class Triangle : TwoDShape {
  string Style;

  // A default constructor.
  public Triangle() {
    Style = "null";
  }

  // Constructor that takes style, width, and height.
  public Triangle(string s, double w, double h) :
    base(w, h, "triangle") {
      Style = s;
  }

  // Construct an isosceles triangle.
  public Triangle(double x) : base(x, "triangle") {
    Style = "isosceles";
  }

  // Construct a copy of a Triangle object.
  public Triangle(Triangle ob) : base(ob) {
    Style = ob.Style;
  }

  // Override Area() for Triangle.
  public override double Area() {                    Override Area( ) for Triangle.
    return Width * Height / 2;
  }

  public void ShowStyle() {
    Console.WriteLine("Triangle is " + Style);
  }
}

// A derived class of TwoDShape for rectangles.
class Rectangle : TwoDShape {
```

```
// Constructor that takes width and height.
public Rectangle(double w, double h) :
  base(w, h, "rectangle"){ }

// Construct a square.
public Rectangle(double x) :
  base(x, "rectangle") { }

// Construct an object from an object.
public Rectangle(Rectangle ob) : base(ob) { }

// Return true if rectangle is square.
public bool IsSquare() {
  if(Width == Height) return true;
  return false;
}

// Override Area() for Rectangle.
public override double Area() {              ◄──────── Override Area( ) for Rectangle.
  return Width * Height;
}
}

class DynShapes {
  static void Main() {
    TwoDShape[] shapes = new TwoDShape[5];

    shapes[0] = new Triangle("right", 8.0, 12.0);
    shapes[1] = new Rectangle(10);
    shapes[2] = new Rectangle(10, 4);
    shapes[3] = new Triangle(7.0);
    shapes[4] = new TwoDShape(10, 20, "generic");

    for(int i=0; i < shapes.Length; i++) {
      Console.WriteLine("object is " + shapes[i].Name);
      Console.WriteLine("Area is " + shapes[i].Area());

      Console.WriteLine();                   ▲
    }                                        │  The proper version of Area( )
  }                                             is called for each shape.
}
```

The output from the program is shown here:

```
object is triangle
Area is 48

object is rectangle
```

```
Area is 100

object is rectangle
Area is 40

object is triangle
Area is 24.5

object is generic
Area() must be overridden
Area is 0
```

Let's examine this program closely. First, as explained, **Area( )** is declared as **virtual** in the **TwoDShape** class and is overridden by **Triangle** and **Rectangle**. Inside **TwoDShape**, **Area( )** is given a placeholder implementation that simply informs the user that this method must be overridden by a derived class. Each override of **Area( )** supplies an implementation that is suitable for the type of object encapsulated by the derived class. Thus, if you were to implement an ellipse class, for example, then **Area( )** would need to compute the area of an ellipse.

There is one other important feature in the preceding program. Notice in **Main( )** that **shapes** is declared as an array of **TwoDShape** objects. However, the elements of this array are assigned **Triangle**, **Rectangle**, and **TwoDShape** references. This is valid because a base class reference can refer to a derived class object. The program then cycles through the array, displaying information about each object. Although quite simple, this program illustrates the power of both inheritance and method overriding. The type of object stored in a base class reference variable is determined at runtime and acted on accordingly. If an object is derived from **TwoDShape**, then its area can be obtained by calling **Area( )**. The interface to this operation is the same, no matter what type of shape is being used.

Using Abstract Classes

Sometimes you will want to create a base class that defines only a generalized form that will be shared by all of its derived classes, leaving it to each derived class to fill in the details. Such a class determines the nature of the methods that the derived classes must implement, but does not, itself, provide an implementation of one or more of these methods. One way this situation can occur is when a base class is unable to create a meaningful implementation for a method. This is the case with the version of **TwoDShape** used in the preceding example. The definition of **Area( )** is simply a placeholder. It will not compute and display the area of any type of object.

As you will see as you create your own class libraries, it is not uncommon for a method to have no meaningful definition in the context of its base class. You can handle this situation two ways. One way, as shown in the previous example, is to simply have it report a warning message. While this approach can be useful in certain situations—such as debugging—it is not usually appropriate. You may have methods that *must* be overridden by the derived class in order for the derived class to have any meaning. Consider the class **Triangle**. It has no meaning if **Area( )** is not defined. In this case, you want some way to ensure that a derived class does, indeed, override all necessary methods. C#'s solution to this problem is the *abstract method*.

An abstract method is created by specifying the **abstract** type modifier. An abstract method contains no body and is, therefore, not implemented by the base class. Thus, a derived class must override it—it cannot simply use the version defined in the base class. As you can probably guess, an abstract method is automatically virtual, and there is no need to use the **virtual** modifier. In fact, it is an error to use **virtual** and **abstract** together.

To declare an abstract method, use this general form:

abstract *type name(parameter-list)*;

As you can see, no method body is present. The **abstract** modifier can be used only on instance methods. It cannot be applied to **static** methods.

A class that contains one or more abstract methods must also be declared as abstract by preceding its **class** declaration with the **abstract** specifier. Since an abstract class does not define a complete implementation, there can be no objects of an abstract class. Thus, attempting to create an object of an abstract class by using **new** will result in a compile-time error.

When a derived class inherits an abstract class, it must implement all of the abstract methods in the base class. If it doesn't, then the derived class must also be specified as **abstract**. Thus, the **abstract** attribute is inherited until such time as a complete implementation is achieved.

Using an abstract class, you can improve the **TwoDShape** class. Since there is no meaningful concept of area for an undefined two-dimensional figure, the following version of the preceding program declares **Area( )** as **abstract** inside **TwoDShape** and declares **TwoDShape** as **abstract**. This, of course, means that all classes derived from **TwoDShape** must override **Area( )**.

```
// Create an abstract class.
using System;

abstract class TwoDShape {          TwoDShape is now abstract.
  double pri_width;
  double pri_height;

  // A default constructor.
  public TwoDShape() {
    Width = Height = 0.0;
    Name = "null";
  }

  // Parameterized constructor.
  public TwoDShape(double w, double h, string n) {
    Width = w;
    Height = h;
    Name = n;
  }

  // Construct object with equal width and height.
  public TwoDShape(double x, string n) {
    Width = Height = x;
    Name = n;
  }
```

```csharp
// Construct an object from an object.
public TwoDShape(TwoDShape ob) {
  Width = ob.Width;
  Height = ob.Height;
  Name = ob.Name;
}

// Properties for Width, Height, and Name.
public double Width {
  get { return pri_width; }
  set { pri_width = value < 0 ? -value : value; }
}

public double Height {
  get { return pri_height; }
  set { pri_height = value < 0 ? -value : value; }
}

public string Name { get; set; }

public void ShowDim() {
  Console.WriteLine("Width and height are " +
                    Width + " and " + Height);
}

// Now, Area() is abstract.
public abstract double Area();
}
```

Area( ) is now abstract.

```csharp
// A derived class of TwoDShape for triangles.
class Triangle : TwoDShape {
  string Style;

  // A default constructor.
  public Triangle() {
    Style = "null";
  }

  // Constructor that takes style, width, and height.
  public Triangle(string s, double w, double h) :
    base(w, h, "triangle") {
      Style = s;
  }

  // Construct an isosceles triangle.
  public Triangle(double x) : base(x, "triangle") {
    Style = "isosceles";
  }
```

```
    // Construct an object from an object.
    public Triangle(Triangle ob) : base(ob) {
      Style = ob.Style;
    }

    // Override Area() for Triangle.
    public override double Area() {          ◄──────── Override Area( ) for Triangle.
      return Width * Height / 2;
    }

    public void ShowStyle() {
      Console.WriteLine("Triangle is " + Style);
    }
}

// A derived class of TwoDShape for rectangles.
class Rectangle : TwoDShape {
  // Constructor that takes width and height.
  public Rectangle(double w, double h) :
    base(w, h, "rectangle"){ }

  // Construct a square.
  public Rectangle(double x) :
    base(x, "rectangle") { }

  // Construct an object from an object.
  public Rectangle(Rectangle ob) : base(ob) { }

  // Return true if rectangle is square.
  public bool IsSquare() {
    if(Width == Height) return true;
    return false;
  }

  // Override Area() for Rectangle.
  public override double Area() {          ◄──────── Override Area( ) for Rectangle.
    return Width * Height;
  }
}

class AbsShape {
  static void Main() {
    TwoDShape[] shapes = new TwoDShape[4];

    shapes[0] = new Triangle("right", 8.0, 12.0);
    shapes[1] = new Rectangle(10);
    shapes[2] = new Rectangle(10, 4);
    shapes[3] = new Triangle(7.0);
```

```
      for(int i=0; i < shapes.Length; i++) {
        Console.WriteLine("object is " + shapes[i].Name);
        Console.WriteLine("Area is " + shapes[i].Area());

        Console.WriteLine();
      }
    }
  }
}
```

As the program illustrates, all derived classes *must* override **Area( )** (or also be declared **abstract**). To prove this to yourself, try creating a derived class that does not override **Area( )**. You will receive a compile-time error. Of course, it is still possible to create an object reference of type **TwoDShape**, which the program does. However, it is no longer possible to declare objects of type **TwoDShape**. Because of this, in **Main( )**, the **shapes** array has been shortened to 4 and a **TwoDShape** object is no longer created.

One last point: Notice that **TwoDShape** still includes the **ShowDim( )** method and that it is not modified by **abstract**. It is perfectly acceptable—indeed, quite common—for an abstract class to contain concrete methods that a derived class is free to use as-is. Only those methods declared as **abstract** must be overridden by derived classes.

Using sealed to Prevent Inheritance

As powerful and useful as inheritance is, sometimes you will want to prevent it. For example, you might have a class that encapsulates the initialization sequence of some specialized hardware device, such as a medical monitor. In this case, you don't want users of your class to be able to change the way the monitor is initialized, possibly setting the device incorrectly. Whatever the reason, in C#, it is easy to prevent a class from being inherited by using the keyword **sealed**.

To prevent a class from being inherited, precede its declaration with **sealed**. As you might expect, it is illegal to declare a class as both **abstract** and **sealed**, since an abstract class is incomplete by itself and relies upon its derived classes to provide complete implementations.

Here is an example of a **sealed** class:

```
sealed class A {  ←——————— This class can't be inherited.
  // ...
}

// The following class is illegal.
class B : A { // ERROR! Can't derive class A
  // ...
}
```

As the comments imply, it is illegal for **B** to inherit **A** since **A** is declared as **sealed**.

One other point: **sealed** can also be used on virtual methods to prevent further overrides. For example, assume a base class called **B** and a derived class called **D**. A method declared

virtual in **B** can be declared **sealed** by **D**. This would prevent any class that inherits **D** from overriding the method. This situation is illustrated by the following:

```
class B {
  public virtual void MyMethod() { /* ... */ }
}

class D : B {
  // This seals MyMethod() and prevents further overrides.
  sealed public override void MyMethod() { /* ... */ }
}

class X : D {
  // Error! MyMethod() is sealed!
  public override void MyMethod() { /* ... */ }
}
```

Now, this method can't be overridden.

Because **MyMethod( )** is sealed by **D**, it can't be overridden by **X**.

The object Class

C# defines one special class called **object** that is an implicit base class of all other classes and for all other types (including the value types). In other words, all C# types are derived from **object**. This means that a reference variable of type **object** can refer to an object of any other type. Also, since arrays are implemented as objects, a variable of type **object** can also refer to any array. Technically, the C# name **object** is just another name for **System.Object**, which is part of the .NET Framework class library.

The **object** class defines the following methods, which means that they are available in every object.

Method	Purpose
public virtual bool Equals(object *ob*)	Determines whether the invoking object is the same as the one referred to by *ob*.
public static bool Equals(object *ob1*, object *ob2*)	Determines whether *ob1* is the same as *ob2*.
protected virtual Finalize( )	Performs shutdown actions prior to garbage collection. In C#, **Finalize** is accessed through a destructor.
public virtual int GetHashCode( )	Returns the hash code associated with the invoking object.
public Type GetType( )	Obtains the type of an object at runtime.
protected object MemberwiseClone( )	Makes a "shallow copy" of the object. This is one in which the members are copied, but objects referred to by members are not.
public static bool ReferenceEquals(object *ob1*, object *ob2*)	Determines whether *ob1* and *ob2* refer to the same object.
public virtual string ToString( )	Returns a string that describes the object.

A few of these methods warrant some additional explanation. By default, the **Equals(object)** method determines if the invoking object refers to the same object as the one referred to by the argument. (That is, it determines if the two references are the same.) It returns **true** if the objects are the same and **false** otherwise. You can override this method in classes that you create. Doing so allows you to define what equality means relative to a class. For example, you could define **Equals(object)** so that it compares the contents of two objects for equality. The **Equals(object, object)** method invokes **Equals(object)** to compute its result.

The **GetHashCode( )** method returns a hash code associated with the invoking object. This hash code can be used with any algorithm that employs hashing as a means of accessing stored objects.

As mentioned in Chapter 7, if you overload the = = operator, then you will usually need to override **Equals(object)** and **GetHashCode( )**, because most of the time, you will want the = = operator and the **Equals(object)** method to function the same. When **Equals( )** is overridden, you should also override **GetHashCode( )** so that the two methods are compatible.

The **ToString( )** method returns a string that contains a description of the object on which it is called. Also, this method is automatically called when an object is output using **WriteLine( )**. Many classes override this method. Doing so allows them to tailor a description specifically for the types of objects that they create. For example:

```csharp
// Demonstrate ToString()
using System;

class MyClass {
  static int count = 0;
  int id;

  public MyClass() {
    id = count;
    count++;
  }

  public override string ToString() {          // Override ToString().
    return "MyClass object #" + id;
  }
}

class Test {
  static void Main() {
    MyClass ob1 = new MyClass();
    MyClass ob2 = new MyClass();
    MyClass ob3 = new MyClass();

    Console.WriteLine(ob1);
    Console.WriteLine(ob2);          // ToString() called automatically here.
    Console.WriteLine(ob3);

  }
}
```

The output from the program is shown here:

```
MyClass object #0
MyClass object #1
MyClass object #2
```

Boxing and Unboxing

As explained, all C# types, including the value types, are derived from **object**. Thus, a reference of type **object** can be used to refer to any other type, including value types. When an **object** reference refers to a value type, a process known as *boxing* occurs. Boxing causes the value of a value type to be stored in an object instance. Thus, a value type is "boxed" inside an object. This object can then be used like any other object. In all cases, boxing occurs automatically. You simply assign a value to an **object** reference. C# handles the rest.

Unboxing is the process of retrieving a value from an object. This action is performed using a cast from the **object** reference to the desired value type. Attempting to unbox an object into an incompatible type will result in a runtime error.

Here is a simple example that illustrates boxing and unboxing:

```
// A simple boxing/unboxing example.
using System;

class BoxingDemo {
  static void Main() {
    int x;
    object obj;

    x = 10;
    obj = x; // box x into an object          Here, the value of x is boxed.

    int y = (int)obj; // unbox obj into an int    Here, the value is unboxed.
    Console.WriteLine(y);
  }
}
```

This program displays the value 10. Notice that the value in **x** is boxed simply by assigning it to **obj**, which is an **object** reference. The integer value in **obj** is retrieved by casting **obj** to **int**.

Here is another, more interesting example of boxing. In this case, an **int** is passed as an argument to the **Sqr( )** method, which uses an **object** parameter.

```
// Boxing also occurs when passing values.
using System;

class BoxingDemo {
  static void Main() {
    int x;

    x = 10;
    Console.WriteLine("Here is x: " + x);
```

```
    // x is automatically boxed when passed to Sqr().
    x = BoxingDemo.Sqr(x);
    Console.WriteLine("Here is x squared: " + x);
  }

  static int Sqr(object o) {
    return (int)o * (int)o;
  }
}
```

The value in **x** is boxed when **Sqr( )** is called.

The output from the program is shown here:

```
Here is x: 10
Here is x squared: 100
```

Here, the value of x is automatically boxed when it is passed to **Sqr( )**.

Boxing and unboxing allow C#'s type system to be fully unified. All types derive from **object**. A reference to any type can be assigned to a variable of type **object**. Boxing/unboxing automatically handles the details for the value types. Furthermore, because all types are derived from **object**, they all have access to **object**'s methods. For example, consider the following rather surprising program:

```
// Boxing makes it possible to call methods on a value!
using System;

class MethOnValue {
  static void Main() {

    Console.WriteLine(186.ToString());

  }
}
```

Perfectly legal in C#!

This program displays 186. The reason is that the **ToString( )** method returns a string representation of the object on which it is called. In this case, the string representation of 186 is 186!

Chapter 8 Self Test

1. Does a base class have access to the members of a derived class? Does a derived class have access to the members of a base class?

2. Create a derived class of **TwoDShape** called **Circle**. Include an **Area( )** method that computes the area of the circle and a constructor that uses **base** to initialize the **TwoDShape** portion.

3. How do you prevent a derived class from having access to a member of a base class?

4. Describe the purpose of **base**.

5. Given the following hierarchy, in what order are the constructors for these classes called when a **Gamma** object is instantiated?

```
class Alpha { ...

class Beta : Alpha { ...

Class Gamma : Beta { ...
```

6. A base class reference can refer to a derived class object. Explain why this is important as it relates to method overriding.

7. What is an abstract class?

8. How do you prevent a class from being inherited?

9. Explain how inheritance, method overriding, and abstract classes are used to support polymorphism.

10. What class is a base class of every other class?

11. Explain boxing.

12. How can **protected** members be accessed?

Chapter 9

Interfaces, Structures, and Enumerations

Key Skills & Concepts

- Interface fundamentals
- Add properties and indexers to interfaces
- Inherit interfaces
- Explicit implementations
- Structures
- Enumerations

This chapter discusses one of C#'s most important features: the interface. An *interface* defines a set of methods that will be implemented by a class. An interface does not, itself, implement any method. It is a purely logical construct that describes a set of methods that a class will provide without dictating the specifics of the implementation.

Also discussed in this chapter are two more C# data types: *structures* and *enumerations*. Structures are similar to classes, except that they are handled as value types rather than as reference types. Enumerations are lists of named integer constants. Structures and enumerations contribute to the richness of the C# programming environment, providing elegant solutions to many programming problems.

Interfaces

In object-oriented programming, it is sometimes helpful to define what a class must do, but not how it will do it. You have already seen an example of this: the abstract method. An abstract method defines the signature for a method, but provides no implementation. A derived class must provide its own implementation of each abstract method defined by its base class. Thus, an abstract method specifies the *interface* to the method, but not the *implementation*. While abstract classes and methods are useful, it is possible to take this concept a step further. In C#, you can fully separate a class' interface from its implementation by using the keyword **interface**.

Interfaces are syntactically similar to abstract classes. However, in an interface, no method can include a body. That is, an interface provides no implementation whatsoever. It specifies what must be done, but not how. Once an interface is defined, any number of classes can implement it. Also, one class can implement any number of interfaces.

To implement an interface, a class must provide bodies (implementations) for the methods described by the interface. Each class is free to determine the details of its own implementation. Thus, two classes might implement the same interface in different ways, but each class still supports the same set of methods. Therefore, code that has knowledge of the interface can use objects of either class since the interface to those objects is the same. By providing the interface, C# allows you to fully utilize the "one interface, multiple methods" aspect of polymorphism.

Interfaces are declared by using the **interface** keyword. Here is a simplified form of an interface declaration:

```
interface name {
    ret-type method-name1(param-list);
    ret-type method-name2(param-list);
    // ...
    ret-type method-nameN(param-list);
}
```

The name of the interface is specified by *name*. Methods are declared using only their return type and signature. They are, essentially, abstract methods. As explained, in an interface, no method can have an implementation. Thus, each class that includes an interface must implement all of the methods declared by that interface. In an interface, methods are implicitly **public**, and no explicit access specifier is allowed.

Here is an example of **interface**. It specifies the interface to a class that generates a series of numbers.

```
public interface ISeries {
    int GetNext(); // return next number in series
    void Reset();  // restart
    void SetStart(int x); // set starting value
}
```

This interface is declared **public** so that it can be implemented by any class in any program.

In addition to method signatures, interfaces can declare the signatures for properties, indexers, and events. Events are described in Chapter 12, and we will be concerned with only methods, properties, and indexers here. Interfaces cannot have data members. They cannot define constructors, destructors, or operator methods. Also, no member can be declared as **static**.

Implementing Interfaces

Once an **interface** has been defined, one or more classes can implement that interface. To implement an interface, the name of the interface is specified after the class name in just the same way that a base class is specified. The general form of a class that implements an interface is shown here:

```
class class-name : interface-name {
    // class-body
}
```

The name of the interface being implemented is specified in *interface-name*.

When a class implements an interface, the class must implement the entire interface. It cannot pick and choose which parts to implement, for example.

Classes can implement more than one interface. To implement more than one interface, the interfaces are separated with a comma. A class can inherit a base class and implement one or more interfaces. In this case, the name of the base class must come first in the comma-separated list.

The methods that implement an interface must be declared **public**. The reason is that methods are implicitly public within an interface, so their implementations must also be public. Also, the type signature of the implementing method must match exactly the type signature specified in the **interface** definition.

Here is an example that implements the **ISeries** interface shown earlier. It creates a class called **ByTwos**, which generates a series of numbers, each two greater than the previous one.

```
// Implement ISeries.
class ByTwos : ISeries {          ◄────────── Implement the ISeries interface.
  int start;
  int val;

  public ByTwos() {
    start = 0;
    val = 0;
  }

  public int GetNext() {
    val += 2;
    return val;
  }

  public void Reset() {
    start = 0;
    val = 0;
  }

  public void SetStart(int x) {
    start = x;
    val = x;
  }
}
```

As you can see, **ByTwos** implements all three methods defined by **ISeries**. As explained, this is necessary, since a class cannot create a partial implementation of an interface.

Here is a class that demonstrates **ByTwos**:

```
// Demonstrate the ByTwos interface.
using System;

class ISeriesDemo {
  static void Main() {
    ByTwos ob = new ByTwos();
```

```
    for(int i=0; i < 5; i++)
      Console.WriteLine("Next value is " +
                          ob.GetNext());

    Console.WriteLine("\nResetting");
    ob.Reset();
    for(int i=0; i < 5; i++)
      Console.WriteLine("Next value is " +
                          ob.GetNext());

    Console.WriteLine("\nStarting at 100");
    ob.SetStart(100);
    for(int i=0; i < 5; i++)
      Console.WriteLine("Next value is " +
                          ob.GetNext());
  }
}
```

To compile **ISeriesDemo**, you must include the classes **ISeries**, **ByTwos**, and **ISeriesDemo** in the compilation. The compiler will automatically compile all three files to create the final executable. For example, if you called these files **ISeries.cs**, **ByTwos.cs**, and **ISeriesDemo.cs**, then the following command line will compile the program:

```
>csc ISeries.cs ByTwos.cs ISeriesDemo.cs
```

If you are using the Visual Studio IDE, then simply add all three files to your C# project. One other point: It is perfectly valid to put all three of these classes in the same file, too.

The output from this program is shown here:

```
Next value is 2
Next value is 4
Next value is 6
Next value is 8
Next value is 10

Resetting
Next value is 2
Next value is 4
Next value is 6
Next value is 8
Next value is 10

Starting at 100
Next value is 102
Next value is 104
Next value is 106
Next value is 108
Next value is 110
```

It is both permissible and common for classes that implement interfaces to define additional members of their own. For example, the following version of **ByTwos** adds the method **GetPrevious( )**, which returns the previous value:

```
// Implement ISeries and add GetPrevious().
 class ByTwos : ISeries {
  int start;
  int val;
  int prev;

  public ByTwos() {
    start = 0;
    val = 0;
    prev = -2;
  }

  public int GetNext() {
    prev = val;
    val += 2;
    return val;
  }

  public void Reset() {
    start = 0;
    val = 0;
    prev = -2;
  }

  public void SetStart(int x) {
    start = x;
    val = x;
    prev = x - 2;
  }

  // A method not specified by ISeries.
  int GetPrevious() {                    ◄──────────── Add a method not defined by ISeries.
    return prev;
  }
}
```

Notice that the addition of **GetPrevious( )** required a change to implementations of the methods defined by **ISeries**. However, since the interface to those methods stays the same, the change is seamless and does not break preexisting code. This is one of the advantages of interfaces.

As explained, any number of classes can implement an **interface**. For example, here is a class called **ByThrees** that generates a series of numbers, each three greater than the previous one:

```
// Implement ISeries.
class ByThrees : ISeries {           ◄──────── Implement ISeries a different way.
  int start;
  int val;
```

```
  public ByThrees() {
    start = 0;
    val = 0;
  }

  public int GetNext() {
    val += 3;
    return val;
  }

  public void Reset() {
    start = 0;
    val = 0;
  }

  public void SetStart(int x) {
    start = x;
    val = x;
  }
}
```

Using Interface References

You might be somewhat surprised to learn that you can declare a reference variable of an interface type. In other words, you can create an interface reference variable. Such a variable can refer to any object that implements its interface. When you call a method on an object through an interface reference, it is the version of the method implemented by the object that is executed. This process is similar to using a base class reference to access a derived class object, as described in Chapter 8.

The following example illustrates the use of an interface reference. It uses the same interface reference variable to call methods on objects of both **ByTwos** and **ByThrees**. For clarity, it shows all the pieces assembled into one file.

```
// Demonstrate interface references.
using System;

// Define the interface.
public interface ISeries {
  int GetNext(); // return next number in series
  void Reset();  // restart
  void SetStart(int x); // set starting value
}

// Implement ISeries one way.
class ByTwos : ISeries {
  int start;
  int val;
```

```
  public ByTwos() {
    start = 0;
    val = 0;
  }

  public int GetNext() {
    val += 2;
    return val;
  }

  public void Reset() {
    start = 0;
    val = 0;
  }

  public void SetStart(int x) {
    start = x;
    val = x;
  }
}

// Implement ISeries another way.
class ByThrees : ISeries {
  int start;
  int val;

  public ByThrees() {
    start = 0;
    val = 0;
  }

  public int GetNext() {
    val += 3;
    return val;
  }

  public void Reset() {
    start = 0;
    val = 0;
  }

  public void SetStart(int x) {
    start = x;
    val = x;
  }
}
```

```
class ISeriesDemo2 {
  static void Main() {
    ByTwos twoOb = new ByTwos();
    ByThrees threeOb = new ByThrees();
    ISeries ob;                                          ──────── Declare an interface reference variable.

    for(int i=0; i < 5; i++) {
      ob = twoOb;
      Console.WriteLine("Next ByTwos value is " +
                          ob.GetNext());
      ob = threeOb;                                              Access an object via
      Console.WriteLine("Next ByThrees value is " +              an interface reference.
                          ob.GetNext());
    }
  }
}
```

In **Main( )**, **ob** is declared to be a reference to an **ISeries** interface. This means that it can be used to store references to any object that implements **ISeries**. In this case, it is used to refer to **twoOb** and **threeOb**, which are objects of type **ByTwos** and **ByThrees**, respectively, which both implement **ISeries**. An interface reference variable has knowledge only of the methods declared by its **interface** declaration. Thus, **ob** could not be used to access any other variables or methods that might be supported by the object.

Try This   Create a Queue Interface

To see the power of interfaces in action, we will look at a practical example. In earlier chapters, you developed a class called **Queue** that implemented a simple fixed-size queue for characters. However, there are many ways to implement a queue. For example, the queue can be of a fixed size or it can be "growable." The queue can be *linear,* in which case it can be used up, or it can be *circular,* in which case elements can be put in as long as elements are being taken out. The queue can also be held in an array, a linked list, a binary tree, and so on. No matter how the queue is implemented, the interface to the queue remains the same, and the methods **Put( )** and **Get( )** define the interface to the queue independently of the details of the implementation. Because the interface to a queue is separate from its implementation, it is easy to define a queue interface, leaving it to each implementation to define the specifics.

Here we will create an interface for a character queue and three implementations. All three implementations will use an array to store the characters. One queue will be the **SimpleQueue** class developed earlier. Another will be a circular queue. In a circular queue, when the end of the underlying array is encountered, the get and put indices automatically loop back to the start. Thus, any number of items can be stored in a circular queue as long as items are also being taken out. The final implementation creates a dynamic queue, which grows as necessary when its size is exceeded.

(continued)

Step by Step

1. Create a file called **ICharQ.cs**, and put into that file the following interface definition:

```
// A character queue interface.
public interface ICharQ {
  // Put a character into the queue.
  void Put(char ch);

  // Get a character from the queue.
  char Get();
}
```

As you can see, this interface is very simple, consisting of only two methods. Each class that implements **ICharQ** will need to implement these methods.

2. Create a file called **IQDemo.cs**.

3. Begin creating **IQDemo.cs** by adding the **SimpleQueue** class shown here:

```
// Demonstrate the ICharQ interface.

using System;

// A simple, fixed-size queue class for characters.
 class SimpleQueue : ICharQ {
  char[] q; // this array holds the queue
  int putloc, getloc; // the put and get indices

  // Construct an empty queue given its size.
  public SimpleQueue(int size) {
    q = new char[size+1]; // allocate memory for queue
    putloc = getloc = 0;
  }

  // Put a character into the queue.
  public void Put(char ch) {
    if(putloc==q.Length-1) {
      Console.WriteLine(" -- Queue is full.");
      return;
    }

    putloc++;
    q[putloc] = ch;
  }

  // Get a character from the queue.
  public char Get() {
    if(getloc == putloc) {
      Console.WriteLine(" -- Queue is empty.");
```

```
      return (char) 0;
    }

    getloc++;
    return q[getloc];
  }
}
```

This implementation of **ICharQ** is adapted from the **SimpleQueue** class shown in Chapter 5 and should already be familiar to you.

4. To **IQDemo.cs**, add the **CircularQueue** class shown here. It implements a circular queue for characters.

```
// A circular queue.
class CircularQueue : ICharQ {
  char[] q; // this array holds the queue
  int putloc, getloc; // the put and get indices

  // Construct an empty queue given its size.
  public CircularQueue(int size) {
    q = new char[size+1]; // allocate memory for queue
    putloc = getloc = 0;
  }

  // Put a character into the queue.
  public void Put(char ch) {
    /* Queue is full if either putloc is one less than
       getloc, or if putloc is at the end of the array
       and getloc is at the beginning. */
    if(putloc+1==getloc ||
        ((putloc==q.Length-1) && (getloc==0))) {
      Console.WriteLine(" -- Queue is full.");
      return;
    }

    putloc++;
    if(putloc==q.Length) putloc = 0; // loop back
    q[putloc] = ch;
  }

  // Get a character from the queue.
  public char Get() {
    if(getloc == putloc) {
      Console.WriteLine(" -- Queue is empty.");
      return (char) 0;
    }
```

(continued)

```
    getloc++;
    if(getloc==q.Length) getloc = 0; // loop back
    return q[getloc];
  }
}
```

The circular queue works by reusing space in the array that is freed when elements are retrieved. Thus, it can store an unlimited number of elements as long as elements are also being removed. While conceptually simple—just reset the appropriate index to zero when the end of the array is reached—the boundary conditions are a bit confusing at first. In a circular queue, the queue is full, not when the end of the underlying array is reached, but rather when storing an item would cause an unretrieved item to be overwritten. Thus, **Put( )** must check several conditions in order to determine if the queue is full. As the comments suggest, the queue is full when either **putloc** is one less than **getloc**, or if **putloc** is at the end of the array and **getloc** is at the beginning. As before, the queue is empty when **getloc** and **putloc** are equal.

5. Finally, put into **IQDemo.cs** the **DynQueue** class shown next. It implements a "growable" version of a circular queue that expands its size when space is exhausted.

```
// A dynamic circular queue.
// This implementation automatically doubles the
// size of the queue when it is full.
class DynQueue : ICharQ {
  char[] q; // this array holds the queue
  int putloc, getloc; // the put and get indices

  // Construct an empty queue given its size.
  public DynQueue(int size) {
    q = new char[size+1]; // allocate memory for queue
    putloc = getloc = 0;
  }

  // Put a character into the queue.
  public void Put(char ch) {
    /* If the queue is full, double the size of the
       underlying array. */
    if(putloc+1==getloc ||
      ((putloc==q.Length-1) && (getloc==0))) {

      // Allocate a larger array for the queue.
      char[] t = new char[q.Length * 2];

      // Copy elements into the new array.
      int i;
      for(i=1; putloc != getloc; i++)
        t[i] = Get();
```

```
      // Reset the getloc and putloc indexes.
      getloc = 0;
      putloc = i-1;

      // Make q refer to the new queue.
      q = t;
    }

    putloc++;
    if(putloc==q.Length) putloc = 0; // loop back
    q[putloc] = ch;
  }

  // Get a character from the queue.
  public char Get() {
    if(getloc == putloc) {
      Console.WriteLine(" -- Queue is empty.");
      return (char) 0;
    }

    getloc++;
    if(getloc==q.Length) getloc = 0; // loop back
    return q[getloc];
  }
}
```

In this queue implementation, when the queue is full, an attempt to store another element causes a new underlying array to be allocated that is twice as large as the original, the current contents of the queue are copied into this array, the **putloc** and **getloc** indexes are reset, and a reference to the new array is stored in **q**.

6. To demonstrate the three **ICharQ** implementations, enter the following class into **IQDemo.cs**. It uses an **ICharQ** reference to access all three queues.

```
// Demonstrate the queues.
class IQDemo {
  static void Main() {
    SimpleQueue q1 = new SimpleQueue(10);
    DynQueue q2 = new DynQueue(5);
    CircularQueue q3 = new CircularQueue(10);

    ICharQ iQ;

    char ch;
    int i;

    // Assign iQ a reference to a simple, fixed-size queue.
    iQ = q1;
```

(continued)

```
// Put some characters into queue.
for(i=0; i < 10; i++)
  iQ.Put((char) ('A' + i));

// Show the queue.
Console.Write("Contents of fixed-size queue: ");
for(i=0; i < 10; i++) {
  ch = iQ.Get();
  Console.Write(ch);
}
Console.WriteLine();

// Assign iQ a reference to a dynamic queue.
iQ = q2;

// Put some characters into dynamic queue.
for(i=0; i < 10; i++)
  iQ.Put((char) ('Z' - i));

// Show the queue.
Console.Write("Contents of dynamic queue: ");
for(i=0; i < 10; i++) {
  ch = iQ.Get();
  Console.Write(ch);
}

Console.WriteLine();

// Assign iQ a reference to a circular queue.
iQ = q3;

// Put some characters into circular queue.
for(i=0; i < 10; i++)
  iQ.Put((char) ('A' + i));

// Show the queue.
Console.Write("Contents of circular queue: ");
for(i=0; i < 10; i++) {
  ch = iQ.Get();
  Console.Write(ch);
}

Console.WriteLine();

// Put more characters into circular queue.
for(i=10; i < 20; i++)
  iQ.Put((char) ('A' + i));
```

```
    // Show the queue.
    Console.Write("Contents of circular queue: ");
    for(i=0; i < 10; i++) {
      ch = iQ.Get();
      Console.Write(ch);
    }

    Console.WriteLine("\nStore and consume from" +
                      " circular queue.");

    // Use and consume from circular queue.
    for(i=0; i < 20; i++) {
      iQ.Put((char) ('A' + i));
      ch = iQ.Get();
      Console.Write(ch);
    }

  }
}
```

7. Compile the program by including both **ICharQ.cs** and **IQDemo.cs**.

8. The output from this program is shown here:

```
Contents of fixed queue: ABCDEFGHIJ
Contents of dynamic queue: ZYXWVUTSRQ
Contents of circular queue: ABCDEFGHIJ
Contents of circular queue: KLMNOPQRST
Store and consume from circular queue.
ABCDEFGHIJKLMNOPQRST
```

9. Here are two things to try on your own. Add a **Reset( )** method to **ICharQ** that resets the queue. Create a **static** method that copies the contents of one type of queue into another.

Interface Properties

Like methods, properties are specified in an interface without any body. Here is the general form of a property specification:

```
// interface property
type name {
  get;
  set;
}
```

Of course, only **get** or **set** will be present for read-only or write-only properties, respectively. Although the declaration of a property in an interface looks similar to how an auto-implemented property is declared in a class, the two are not the same. The interface declaration does not cause the property to be auto-implemented. It only specifies the name and type of the property. Implementation is left to each implementing class. Also, no access modifiers are allowed on the accessors when a property is declared in an **interface**. Thus, the **set** accessor, for example, cannot be specified as private in an **interface**.

Here is a rewrite of the **ISeries** interface and the **ByTwos** class that uses a property to obtain and set the next element in the series:

```csharp
// Use a property in an interface.
using System;

public interface ISeries {
  // An interface property.
  int Next {                                    // Declare a property in
    get; // return the next number in series     the ISeries interface.
    set; // set next number
  }
}

// Implement ISeries.
class ByTwos : ISeries {
  int val;

  public ByTwos() {
    val = 0;
  }

  // Get or set value.
  public int Next {                             // Implement the property.
    get {
      val += 2;
      return val;
    }
    set {
      val = value;
    }
  }
}

// Demonstrate an interface property.
class ISeriesDemo3 {
  static void Main() {
    ByTwos ob = new ByTwos();

    // Access series through a property.
    for(int i=0; i < 5; i++)
      Console.WriteLine("Next value is " + ob.Next);
```

```
      Console.WriteLine("\nStarting at 21");
      ob.Next = 21;
      for(int i=0; i < 5; i++)
        Console.WriteLine("Next value is " + ob.Next);
    }
}
```

The output from this program is shown here:

```
Next value is 2
Next value is 4
Next value is 6
Next value is 8
Next value is 10

Starting at 21
Next value is 23
Next value is 25
Next value is 27
Next value is 29
Next value is 31
```

Interface Indexers

An indexer declared in an interface has this general form:

```
// interface indexer
element-type this[int index] {
  get;
  set;
}
```

As before, only **get** or **set** will be present for read-only or write-only indexers, respectively. No access modifiers are allowed on the accessors when an indexer is declared in an **interface**.

Here is another version of **ISeries** that adds a read-only indexer that returns the ith element in the series:

```
// Add an indexer in an interface.
using System;

public interface ISeries {
  // An interface property.
  int Next {
    get; // return the next number in series
    set; // set next number
  }
```

```
    // An interface indexer.
    int this[int index] {                    ─────────── Declare a read-only indexer in ISeries.
      get; // return the specified number in series
    }
}

// Implement ISeries.
class ByTwos : ISeries {
  int val;

  public ByTwos() {
    val = 0;
  }

  // Get or set a value using a property.
  public int Next {
    get {
      val += 2;
      return val;
    }
    set {
      val = value;
    }
  }

  // Get a value using an indexer.
  public int this[int index] {             ─────── Implement the indexer.
    get {
      val = 0;
      for(int i=0; i<index; i++)
        val += 2;
      return val;
    }
  }
}

// Demonstrate an interface indexer.
class ISeriesDemo4 {
  static void Main() {
    ByTwos ob = new ByTwos();

    // Access series through a property.
    for(int i=0; i < 5; i++)
      Console.WriteLine("Next value is " + ob.Next);

    Console.WriteLine("\nStarting at 21");
    ob.Next = 21;
    for(int i=0; i < 5; i++)
```

```
        Console.WriteLine("Next value is " +
                          ob.Next);

    Console.WriteLine("\nResetting to 0");
    ob.Next = 0;

    // Access series through an indexer.
    for(int i=0; i < 5; i++)
      Console.WriteLine("Next value is " + ob[i]);
  }
}
```

The output from this program is shown here:

```
Next value is 2
Next value is 4
Next value is 6
Next value is 8
Next value is 10

Starting at 21
Next value is 23
Next value is 25
Next value is 27
Next value is 29
Next value is 31

Resetting to 0
Next value is 0
Next value is 2
Next value is 4
Next value is 6
Next value is 8
```

Interfaces Can Be Inherited

One interface can inherit another. The syntax is the same as for inheriting classes. When a class implements an interface that inherits another interface, it must provide implementations for all the members defined within the interface inheritance chain. Following is an example:

```
// One interface can inherit another.
using System;

public interface IA {
  void Meth1();
  void Meth2();
}
```

```
// IB now includes Meth1() and Meth2() -- it adds Meth3().
public interface IB : IA {          ◄─────── IB inherits IA.
  void Meth3();
}

// This class must implement all of IA and IB.
class MyClass : IB {
  public void Meth1() {
    Console.WriteLine("Implement Meth1().");
  }

  public void Meth2() {
    Console.WriteLine("Implement Meth2().");
  }

  public void Meth3() {
    Console.WriteLine("Implement Meth3().");
  }
}

class IFExtend {
  static void Main() {
    MyClass ob = new MyClass();

    ob.Meth1();
    ob.Meth2();
    ob.Meth3();
  }
}
```

As an experiment, you might want to try removing the implementation for **Meth1( )** in **MyClass**. This will cause a compile-time error. As stated earlier, any class that implements an interface must implement all methods defined by that interface, including any that are inherited from other interfaces.

Ask the Expert

Q: When one interface inherits another, is it possible to declare a member in the derived interface that hides a member defined by the base interface?

A: Yes. When a member in a derived interface has the same signature as one in the base interface, the base interface name is hidden. As is the case with class inheritance, this hiding will cause a warning message, unless you specify the derived interface member with **new**.

Explicit Implementations

When implementing a member of an interface, it is possible to fully qualify its name with its interface name. Doing this creates an *explicit interface member implementation,* or *explicit implementation,* for short. For example, given

```
interface IMyIF {
  int MyMeth(int x);
}
```

it is legal to implement **IMyIF** as shown here:

```
class MyClass : IMyIF {
  int IMyIF.MyMeth(int x) {          ◄————— A fully qualified name used to
    return x / 3;                            create an explicit implementation.
  }
}
```

As you can see, when the **MyMeth( )** member of **IMyIF** is implemented, its complete name, including its interface name, is specified.

There are two reasons that you might need to create an explicit implementation of an interface member. First, it is possible for a class to implement two interfaces, which both declare methods by the same name and type signature. Qualifying the names with their interfaces removes the ambiguity from this situation. Second, when you implement a method using its fully qualified name, you are providing an implementation that *cannot* be accessed through an object of the class. Thus, an explicit implementation gives you a way to implement an interface method so that it is not a public member of the implementing class. Let's look at an example of each.

The following program contains an interface called **IEven**, which defines two methods, **IsEven( )** and **IsOdd( )**. These methods determine whether a number is even or odd. **MyClass** then implements **IEven**. When it does so, it implements **IsOdd( )** explicitly.

```
// Explicitly implement an interface member.
using System;

interface IEven {
  bool IsOdd(int x);
  bool IsEven(int x);
}

class MyClass : IEven {
  // Explicit implementation.
  bool IEven.IsOdd(int x) {   ◄——————— Explicitly implement IsOdd( ).
    if((x%2) != 0) return true;
    else return false;
  }
```

```
    // Normal implementation.
    public bool IsEven(int x) {
      IEven o = this; // Interface reference to invoking object

      return !o.IsOdd(x);
    }
}

class Demo {
  static void Main() {
    MyClass ob = new MyClass();
    bool result;

    result = ob.IsEven(4);
    if(result) Console.WriteLine("4 is even.");
    else Console.WriteLine("3 is odd.");

    // result = ob.IsOdd(); // Error, not exposed.
  }
}
```

Since **IsOdd( )** is implemented explicitly, it is not exposed as a public member of **MyClass**. Instead, **IsOdd( )** can be accessed only through an interface reference. This is why it is invoked through **o** in the implementation for **IsEven( )**.

Here is an example in which two interfaces are implemented and both interfaces declare a method called **Meth( )**. Explicit implementation is used to eliminate the ambiguity inherent in this situation.

```
// Use explicit implementation to remove ambiguity.
using System;

interface IMyIF_A {
  int Meth(int x); ◄──────────┐
}                              │── The signatures for these two methods are the same.
interface IMyIF_B {           │
  int Meth(int x); ◄──────────┘
}

// MyClass implements both interfaces.
class MyClass : IMyIF_A, IMyIF_B {
  IMyIF_A a_ob;
  IMyIF_B b_ob;

  // Explicitly implement the two Meth()s.
  int IMyIF_A.Meth(int x) { ◄─────── Explicit implementation removes the ambiguity.
    return x + x;
  }
```

```
    int IMyIF_B.Meth(int x) {  ◄──────── Explicit implementation removes the ambiguity.
      return x * x;
    }

    // Call Meth() through an interface reference.
    public int MethA(int x){
      a_ob = this;
      return a_ob.Meth(x); // calls IMyIF_A
    }

    public int MethB(int x){
      b_ob = this;
      return b_ob.Meth(x); // calls IMyIF_B
    }
}

class FQIFNames {
  static void Main() {
    MyClass ob = new MyClass();

    Console.Write("Calling IMyIF_A.Meth(): ");
    Console.WriteLine(ob.MethA(3));

    Console.Write("Calling IMyIF_B.Meth(): ");
    Console.WriteLine(ob.MethB(3));
  }
}
```

The output from this program is shown here:

```
Calling IMyIF_A.Meth(): 6
Calling IMyIF_B.Meth(): 9
```

Looking at the program, first notice that **Meth( )** has the same signature in both **IMyIF_A** and **IMyIF_B**. Thus, when **MyClass** implements both of these interfaces, it explicitly implements each one separately, fully qualifying its name in the process. Since the only way that an explicitly implemented method can be called is on an interface reference, **MyClass** creates two such references, one for **IMyIF_A** and one for **IMyIF_B**. It then calls two of its own methods, which call the interface methods, thereby removing the ambiguity.

Structures

As you know, classes are reference types. This means that class objects are accessed through a reference. This differs from the value types, which are accessed directly. However, there can be times when it would be useful to be able to access an object directly, in the way that value types are. One reason for this is efficiency. Accessing class objects through a reference adds overhead onto every access. It also consumes space. For very small objects, this extra space might be significant. To address these concerns, C# offers the structure. A *structure* is similar to a class, but is a value type, rather than a reference type.

Structures are declared using the keyword **struct** and are syntactically similar to classes. Here is the general form of a **struct**:

struct *name* : *interfaces* {
  // member declarations
}

The name of the structure is specified by *name*.

Structures cannot inherit other structures or classes, or be used as a base for other structures or classes. However, a structure can implement one or more interfaces. These are specified after the structure name using a comma-separated list.

Like classes, structure members include methods, fields, indexers, properties, operator methods, and events. Structures can also define constructors, but not destructors. However, you cannot define a default (parameterless) constructor for a structure. The reason for this is that a default constructor is automatically defined for all structures and this default constructor can't be changed.

A structure object can be created using **new** in the same way as a class object, but it is not required. When **new** is used, the specified constructor is called. When **new** is not used, the object is still created, but it is not initialized. Thus, you will need to perform any initialization manually.

Here is an example that uses a structure:

```
// Demonstrate a structure.
using System;

// Define a structure.
struct Account {  ◄─────────── Define a structure.
  public string name;
  public double balance;

  public Account(string n, double b) {
    name = n;
    balance = b;
  }
}

// Demonstrate Account structure.
class StructDemo {
  static void Main() {
    Account acc1 = new Account("Tom", 1232.22); // explicit constructor
    Account acc2 = new Account(); // default constructor
    Account acc3; // no constructor
```

```
      Console.WriteLine(acc1.name + " has a balance of " + acc1.balance);
      Console.WriteLine();

      if(acc2.name == null) Console.WriteLine("acc2.name is null.");
      Console.WriteLine("acc2.balance is " + acc2.balance);
      Console.WriteLine();

      // Must initialize acc3 prior to use.
      acc3.name = "Mary";
      acc3.balance = 99.33;
      Console.WriteLine(acc3.name + " has a balance of " + acc3.balance);
   }
}
```

The output from this program is shown here:

```
Tom has a balance of 1232.22

acc2.name is null.
acc2.balance is 0

Mary has a balance of 99.33
```

As the program shows, a structure can be initialized either by using **new** to invoke a constructor or by simply declaring an object. If **new** is used, then the fields of the structure will be initialized, either by the default constructor that initializes all fields to their default values or by a user-defined constructor. If **new** is not used, then the object is not initialized and its fields must be set prior to using the object.

Ask the Expert

Q: I know that C++ also has structures and uses the struct **keyword. Are C# and C++ structures the same?**

A: No. In C++, **struct** defines a class type. Thus, in C++, **struct** and **class** are nearly equivalent. (The difference has to do with the default access of their members, which is private for **class** and public for **struct**.) In C#, a **struct** defines a value type, and a **class** defines a reference type.

Enumerations

An *enumeration* is a set of named integer constants. Enumerations are common in everyday life. For example, an enumeration of the coins used in the United States is

penny, nickel, dime, quarter, half-dollar, dollar

The keyword **enum** declares an enumerated type. The general form for an enumeration is

enum *name* { *enumeration list* };

Here, the type name of the enumeration is specified by *name*. The *enumeration list* is a comma-separated list of identifiers. Here is an example that defines an enumeration called **Coin**:

```
enum Coin { Penny, Nickel, Dime, Quarter, HalfDollar, Dollar};
```

A key point to understand about an enumeration is that each of the symbols stands for an integer value. However, no implicit conversions are defined between an **enum** type and the built-in integer types, so an explicit cast must be used. Also, a cast is required when converting between two enumeration types. Since enumerations represent integer values, you can use an enumeration to control a **switch** statement or as the control variable in a **for** loop, for example.

Each enumeration symbol is given a value one greater than the symbol that precedes it. By default, the value of the first enumeration symbol is 0. Therefore, in the **Coin** enumeration, **Penny** is 0, **Nickel** is 1, **Dime** is 2, and so on.

The members of an enumeration are accessed through their type name via the dot operator. For example, this code:

```
Console.WriteLine(Coin.Penny + " " + Coin.Nickel);
```

displays

```
Penny Nickel
```

Here is a program that illustrates the **Coin** enumeration:

```
// Demonstrate an enumeration.
using System;

class EnumDemo {
  enum Coin { Penny, Nickel, Dime, Quarter, HalfDollar, Dollar };

  static void Main() {
    Coin c; // declare an enum variable

    // Use c to cycle through the enum by use of a for loop.
    for(c = Coin.Penny; c <= Coin.Dollar; c++) {          A Coin variable can
      Console.WriteLine(c + " has value of " + (int) c);  control a for loop.

    // Use an enumeration value to control a switch.
    switch(c) {          A Coin value can control a switch.
      case Coin.Nickel:
        Console.WriteLine("A nickel is 5 pennies.");
        break;
      case Coin.Dime:
        Console.WriteLine("A dime is 2 nickels.");
```

```
        break;
      case Coin.Quarter:
        Console.WriteLine("A quarter is 5 nickels.");
        break;
      case Coin.HalfDollar:
        Console.WriteLine("A half-dollar is 5 dimes.");
        break;
      case Coin.Dollar:
        Console.WriteLine("A dollar is 10 dimes.");
        break;
    }
    Console.WriteLine();
  }
 }
}
```

The output from the program is shown here:

```
Penny has value of 0

Nickel has value of 1
A nickel is 5 pennies.

Dime has value of 2
A dime is 2 nickels.

Quarter has value of 3
A quarter is 5 nickels.

HalfDollar has value of 4
A half-dollar is 5 dimes.

Dollar has value of 5
A dollar is 10 dimes.
```

Notice how both the **for** loop and the **switch** statement are controlled by **c**, which is a variable of type **Coin**. As mentioned, a variable of an enumerated type can be used to control a loop or **switch**. Also notice how outputting an enumeration constant via **WriteLine( )** causes its name to be displayed. To obtain its value, a cast to **int** is required.

Initialize an Enumeration

You can specify the value of one or more of the enumeration symbols by using an initializer. Do this by following the symbol with an equal sign and an integer value. Symbols that appear after initializers are assigned values greater than the previous initialization value. For example, the following code assigns the value of 100 to **Quarter**:

```
enum Coin { Penny, Nickel, Dime, Quarter=100, HalfDollar, Dollar};
```

Now, the values of these symbols are

Penny	0
Nickel	1
Dime	2
Quarter	100
HalfDollar	101
Dollar	102

Specifying the Underlying Type of an Enumeration

By default, enumerations are based on type **int**, but you can create an enumeration of any integral type, except for type **char**. To specify a type other than **int**, put the underlying type after the enumeration name, separated by a colon. For example, this statement makes **Coin** an enumeration based on **byte**:

```
enum Coin : byte { Penny, Nickel, Dime, Quarter, HalfDollar, Dollar};
```

Now, **Coin.Penny**, for example, is a **byte** quantity.

Chapter 9 Self Test

1. "One interface, multiple methods" is a key tenet of C#. What feature best exemplifies it?

2. How many classes can implement an interface? How many interfaces can a class implement?

3. Can interfaces be inherited?

4. Must a class implement all of the members of an interface?

5. Can an interface declare a constructor?

6. Create an interface for the **Vehicle** class from Chapter 8. Call the interface **IVehicle**. (Hint: The properties will need to support both read and write operations, and cannot have accessor access modifiers.)

7. Create an interface for safe arrays. Do this by adapting the final fail-soft array example from Chapter 7. (Hint: The **Length** property must be read-only and cannot be auto-implemented.)

8. How does a **struct** differ from a **class**?

9. Show how to create an enumeration for the planets. Call the enumeration **Planets**.

Chapter 10

Exception Handling

Key Skills & Concepts

- Exception handling fundamentals
- **try** and **catch**
- Multiple **catch** clauses
- Nested **try** blocks
- Throw an exception
- The **Exception** class
- **finally**
- The built-in exceptions
- Custom exception classes
- **checked** and **unchecked**

This chapter discusses exception handling. An *exception* is an error that occurs at runtime. Using C#'s exception-handling subsystem, you can handle runtime errors in a structured and controlled manner. A principal advantage of exception handling is that it automates much of the error-handling code that would otherwise have been entered "by hand" into any large program. For example, without the use of exception handling, an error code would be returned by a method when it fails, and this value must be checked manually each time the method is called. This approach is both tedious and error-prone. Exception handling streamlines error handling by allowing your program to define a block of code, called an *exception handler,* that is executed automatically when an error occurs. It is not necessary to manually check the success or failure of each specific operation or method call. If an error occurs, it will be processed by the exception handler.

Another reason that exception handling is important is that C# defines standard exceptions for common program errors, such as divide-by-zero or index-out-of-range. To respond to these errors, your program must watch for and handle these exceptions. In the final analysis, to be a successful C# programmer means that you are fully capable of navigating C#'s exception-handling subsystem.

The System.Exception Class

In C#, exceptions are represented by classes. All exception classes must be derived from the built-in exception class **Exception**, which is part of the **System** namespace. Thus, all exceptions are subclasses of **Exception**.

One very important subclass of **Exception** is **SystemException**. This is the exception class from which all exceptions generated by the C# runtime system (that is, the CLR) are derived. **SystemException** does not add anything to **Exception**. It simply defines the top of the standard exceptions hierarchy.

The .NET Framework defines several built-in exceptions that are derived from **SystemException**. For example, when a division-by-zero is attempted, a **DivideByZeroException** exception is generated. As you will see later in this chapter, you can also create your own exception classes.

Exception-Handling Fundamentals

C# exception handling is managed via four keywords: **try**, **catch**, **throw**, and **finally**. They form an interrelated subsystem in which the use of one implies the use of another. Throughout the course of this chapter, each keyword is examined in detail. However, it is useful at the outset to have a general understanding of the role each plays in exception handling. Briefly, here is how they work.

Program statements that you want to monitor for exceptions are contained within a **try** block. If an exception occurs within the **try** block, it is *thrown*. Your code can catch this exception using **catch** and handle it in some rational manner. System-generated exceptions are automatically thrown by the runtime system. To manually throw an exception, use the keyword **throw**. Any code that absolutely must be executed upon exiting from a **try** block is put in a **finally** block.

Using try and catch

At the core of exception handling are **try** and **catch**. These keywords work together, and you can't have a **catch** without a **try**. Here is the general form of the **try/catch** exception-handling blocks:

```
try {
   // block of code to monitor for errors
}

catch (ExcepType1 exOb) {
   // handler for ExcepType1
}

catch (ExcepType2 exOb) {
   // handler for ExcepType2
}
.
.
.
```

Here, *ExcepType* is the type of exception that has occurred. When an exception is thrown, it is caught by its corresponding **catch** clause, which then processes the exception. As the general form shows, there can be more than one **catch** clause associated with a **try**. The type of the exception determines which **catch** is executed. That is, if the exception type specified by a **catch** matches that of the exception, then the block of code associated with that **catch** clause is executed (and all other **catch** clauses are bypassed). When an exception is caught, the exception variable *exOb* will receive its value.

Actually, specifying *exOb* is optional. If the exception handler does not need access to the exception object (as is often the case), then there is no need to specify *exOb*. For this reason, many of the examples in this chapter will not specify *exOb*.

Here is an important point: If no exception is thrown, then a **try** block ends normally, and all of its **catch** clauses are bypassed. Execution resumes with the first statement following the last **catch**. Thus, a **catch** is executed only if an exception is thrown.

A Simple Exception Example

Here is a simple example that illustrates how to watch for and catch an exception. As you know, it is an error to attempt to index an array beyond its boundaries. When this occurs, the C# runtime system throws an **IndexOutOfRangeException**, which is a standard exception. The following program purposely generates such an exception and then catches it:

```
// Demonstrate exception handling.
using System;

class ExcDemo1 {
  static void Main() {
    int[] nums = new int[4];

    try {
      Console.WriteLine("Before exception is generated.");

      // Generate an index out-of-bounds exception.
      nums[7] = 10;  ◄─────────────────────────── Attempt to index beyond
      Console.WriteLine("this won't be displayed");      nums boundary.
    }
    catch (IndexOutOfRangeException) {  ◄─────────── Catch the exception.
      // catch the exception
      Console.WriteLine("Index out-of-bounds!");
    }
    Console.WriteLine("After catch block.");
  }
}
```

This program displays the following output:

```
Before exception is generated.
Index out-of-bounds!
After catch block.
```

Although quite short, the preceding program illustrates several key points about exception handling. First, the code that you want to monitor for errors is contained within a **try** block. Second, when an exception occurs (in this case, because of the attempt to index **nums** beyond its bounds), the exception is thrown out of the **try** block and caught by the **catch**. At this point, control passes to the **catch** block, and the **try** block is terminated. That is, **catch** is *not* called.

Rather, program execution is transferred to it. Thus, the **WriteLine( )** statement following the out-of-bounds index will never execute. After the **catch** block executes, program control continues with the statements following the **catch**. Thus, it is the job of your exception handler to remedy the problem that caused the exception so that program execution can continue normally.

Notice that no exception variable name is specified in the **catch** clause. Instead, only the type of the exception (**IndexOutOfRangeException** in this case) is required. As mentioned, an exception variable is needed only when access to the exception object is required. In some cases, the value of the exception object can be used by the exception handler to obtain additional information about the error, but in many cases, it is sufficient to simply know that an exception occurred. Thus, it is not unusual for the **catch** exception variable to be absent, as is the case in the preceding program.

As explained, if no exception is thrown by a **try** block, then no **catch** will be executed and program control resumes after the **catch**. To confirm this, in the preceding program, change the line

```
nums[7] = 10;
```

to

```
nums[0] = 10;
```

Now, no exception is generated and the **catch** block is not executed.

A Second Exception Example

It is important to understand that all code within a **try** block is monitored for exceptions. This includes exceptions that might be generated by a method called from within the **try** block. An exception thrown by a method called from within a **try** block can be caught by that **try** block—assuming, of course, that the method itself did not catch the exception. For example, this is a valid program:

```
// An exception can be generated by one method and caught by another.
using System;

class ExcTest {
  // Generate an exception.
  public static void GenException() {
    int[] nums = new int[4];

    Console.WriteLine("Before exception is generated.");

    // Generate an index out-of-bounds exception.
    nums[7] = 10;                                          ◄————————— Exception generated here.
    Console.WriteLine("this won't be displayed");
  }
}
```

```
class ExcDemo2 {
  static void Main() {

    try {
      ExcTest.GenException();
    }
    catch (IndexOutOfRangeException) {    ◄──────────── Exception caught here.
      // Catch the exception.
      Console.WriteLine("Index out-of-bounds!");
    }
    Console.WriteLine("After catch block.");
  }
}
```

This program produces the following output, which is the same as that produced by the first version of the program shown earlier:

```
Before exception is generated.
Index out-of-bounds!
After catch block.
```

Since **GenException( )** is called from within a **try** block, the exception that it generates (and does not catch) is caught by the **catch** in **Main( )**. Understand, however, that if **GenException( )** had caught the exception, it never would have been passed back to **Main( )**.

The Consequences of an Uncaught Exception

Catching one of C#'s standard exceptions, as the preceding program does, has a side benefit: It prevents abnormal program termination. When an exception is thrown, it must be caught by some piece of code somewhere. In general, if your program does not catch an exception, then it will be caught by the runtime system. The trouble is that the runtime system will report an error and terminate the program. For example, in this version of the preceding example, the index out-of-bounds exception is not caught by the program:

```
// Let the runtime system handle the error.
using System;

class NotHandled {
  static void Main() {
    int[] nums = new int[4];

    Console.WriteLine("Before exception is generated.");

    // Generate an index out-of-bounds exception.
    nums[7] = 10;
  }
}
```

When the array index error occurs, execution is halted and the following error message is displayed:

```
Unhandled Exception: System.IndexOutOfRangeException:
        Index was outside the bounds of the array.
   at NotHandled.Main()
```

While such a message is useful for you while debugging, it would not be something that you want the users of your program to see, to say the least! This is why it is important for your program to handle exceptions itself.

As mentioned earlier, the type of the exception must match the type specified in a **catch** clause. If it doesn't, the exception won't be caught. For example, the following program tries to catch an array boundary error with a **catch** that handles **DivideByZeroException** (another built-in exception). When the array boundary is overrun, an **IndexOutOfRangeException** is generated, but it won't be caught by the **catch**. This results in abnormal program termination.

```
// This won't work!
using System;

class ExcTypeMismatch {
  static void Main() {
    int[] nums = new int[4];

    try {
      Console.WriteLine("Before exception is generated.");

      // Generate an index out-of-bounds exception.
      nums[7] = 10;    ◄─────────────────────────────  This throws an
      Console.WriteLine("this won't be displayed");       IndexOutOfRangeException.
    }

    /* Can't catch an array boundary error with a
       DivideByZeroException. */
    catch (DivideByZeroException) {  ◄──────────────   But this tries to catch it with
      Console.WriteLine("Index out-of-bounds!");        a DivideByZeroException.
    }
    Console.WriteLine("After catch block.");
  }
}
```

The output is shown here:

```
Before exception is generated.

Unhandled Exception: System.IndexOutOfRangeException:
        Index was outside the bounds of the array.
   at ExcTypeMismatch.Main()
```

As the output demonstrates, a **catch** for **DivideByZeroException** won't catch an **IndexOutOfRangeException**.

Exceptions Let You Handle Errors Gracefully

One of the key benefits of exception handling is that it enables your program to respond to an error and then continue running. For example, consider the following example that divides the elements of one array by the elements of another. If a division by zero occurs, a **DivideByZeroException** is generated. In the program, this exception is handled by reporting the error and then continuing with execution. Thus, attempting to divide by zero does not cause an abrupt runtime error resulting in the termination of the program. Instead, it is handled gracefully, allowing program execution to continue.

```
// Handle error gracefully and continue.
using System;

class ExcDemo3 {
  static void Main() {
    int[] numer = { 4, 8, 16, 32, 64, 128 };
    int[] denom = { 2, 0, 4, 4, 0, 8 };

    for(int i=0; i < numer.Length; i++) {
      try {
        Console.WriteLine(numer[i] + " / " +
                          denom[i] + " is " +
                          numer[i]/denom[i]);
      }
      catch (DivideByZeroException) {
        Console.WriteLine("Can't divide by Zero!");
      }
    }
  }
}
```

The output from the program is shown here:

```
4 / 2 is 2
Can't divide by Zero!
16 / 4 is 4
32 / 4 is 8
Can't divide by Zero!
128 / 8 is 16
```

This example makes another important point: Once an exception has been handled, it is removed from the system. Therefore, in the program, each pass through the loop enters the **try** block anew—any prior exceptions have been handled. This enables your program to handle repeated errors.

Using Multiple catch Clauses

You can associate more than one **catch** clause with a **try**. In fact, it is common to do so. However, each **catch** must catch a different type of exception. For example, the program shown here catches both array-boundary and divide-by-zero errors:

```
// Use multiple catch clauses.
using System;

class ExcDemo4 {
  static void Main() {
    // Here, numer is longer than denom.
    int[] numer = { 4, 8, 16, 32, 64, 128, 256, 512 };
    int[] denom = { 2, 0, 4, 4, 0, 8 };

    for(int i=0; i < numer.Length; i++) {
      try {
        Console.WriteLine(numer[i] + " / " +
                          denom[i] + " is " +
                          numer[i]/denom[i]);
      }
      catch (DivideByZeroException) {  ◄
        Console.WriteLine("Can't divide by Zero!");
      }                                              Multiple catch clauses.
      catch (IndexOutOfRangeException) {  ◄
        Console.WriteLine("No matching element found.");
      }
    }
  }
}
```

This program produces the following output:

```
4 / 2 is 2
Can't divide by Zero!
16 / 4 is 4
32 / 4 is 8
Can't divide by Zero!
128 / 8 is 16
No matching element found.
No matching element found.
```

As the output confirms, each **catch** clause responds only to its own type of exception.

In general, **catch** clauses are checked in the order in which they occur in a program. Only a matching clause is executed. All others are ignored.

Catching All Exceptions

Sometimes you will want to catch all exceptions, no matter the type. To do this, use a **catch** clause that specifies no exception type at all. This creates a "catch all" handler that is useful when you want to ensure that all exceptions are handled by your program. For example, here the only **catch** is the "catch all," and it catches both the **IndexOutOfRangeException** and the **DivideByZeroException** that is generated by the program:

```
// Use the "catch all" catch.
using System;

class ExcDemo5 {
  static void Main() {
    // Here, numer is longer than denom.
    int[] numer = { 4, 8, 16, 32, 64, 128, 256, 512 };
    int[] denom = { 2, 0, 4, 4, 0, 8 };

    for(int i=0; i < numer.Length; i++) {
      try {
        Console.WriteLine(numer[i] + " / " +
                          denom[i] + " is " +
                          numer[i]/denom[i]);
      }
      catch {                                          This catches all exceptions.
        Console.WriteLine("Some exception occurred.");
      }
    }
  }
}
```

The output is shown here:

```
4 / 2 is 2
Some exception occurred.
16 / 4 is 4
32 / 4 is 8
Some exception occurred.
128 / 8 is 16
Some exception occurred.
Some exception occurred.
```

Try Blocks Can Be Nested

One **try** block can be nested within another. An exception generated within the inner **try** block that is not caught by a **catch** associated with that **try** is propagated to the outer **try** block.

For example, here the **IndexOutOfRangeException** is not caught by the inner **try** block, but by the outer **try**:

```
// Use a nested try block.
using System;

class NestTrys {
  static void Main() {
    // Here, numer is longer than denom.
    int[] numer = { 4, 8, 16, 32, 64, 128, 256, 512 };
    int[] denom = { 2, 0, 4, 4, 0, 8 };

    try { // outer try
      for(int i=0; i < numer.Length; i++) {
        try { // nested try
          Console.WriteLine(numer[i] + " / " +
                            denom[i] + " is " +
                            numer[i]/denom[i]);
        }
        catch (DivideByZeroException) { // catch for inner try
          Console.WriteLine("Can't divide by Zero!");
        }
      }
    }
    catch (IndexOutOfRangeException) { // catch for outer try
      Console.WriteLine("No matching element found.");
      Console.WriteLine("Fatal error -- program terminated.");
    }
  }
}
```

Nested **try** blocks.

The output from the program is shown here:

```
4 / 2 is 2
Can't divide by Zero!
16 / 4 is 4
32 / 4 is 8
Can't divide by Zero!
128 / 8 is 16
No matching element found.
Fatal error -- program terminated.
```

In this example, an exception that can be handled by the inner **try**—in this case, a divide-by-zero error—allows the program to continue. However, an array boundary error is caught by the outer **try**, which causes the program to terminate.

Although certainly not the only reason for nested **try** blocks, the preceding program makes an important point that can be generalized. Often, nested **try** blocks are used to allow different categories of errors to be handled in different ways. Some types of errors are catastrophic and cannot be fixed. Some are minor and can be handled immediately. Many programmers use an outer **try** block to catch the most severe errors, allowing inner **try** blocks to handle less serious ones. You can also use an outer **try** block as a "catch all" block for those errors that are not handled by the inner block.

Throwing an Exception

The preceding examples have been catching exceptions generated automatically by the runtime system. However, it is possible to manually throw an exception by using the **throw** statement. Its general form is shown here:

throw *exceptOb*;

Here, *exceptOb* must be an instance of an exception class derived from **Exception**.

Here is an example that illustrates the **throw** statement by manually throwing a **DivideByZeroException**:

```
// Manually throw an exception.
using System;

class ThrowDemo {
  static void Main() {
    try {
      Console.WriteLine("Before throw.");
      throw new DivideByZeroException();    ◄─────────── Throw an exception.
    }
    catch (DivideByZeroException) {
      Console.WriteLine("Exception caught.");
    }
    Console.WriteLine("After try/catch statement.");
  }
}
```

The output from the program is shown here:

```
Before throw.
Exception caught.
After try/catch statement.
```

Notice how the **DivideByZeroException** was created using **new** in the **throw** statement. Remember, **throw** throws an object. Thus, you must create an object for it to throw. That is, you can't just throw a type. In this case, the default constructor is used to create a **DivideByZeroException** object, but other constructors are available for exceptions (as you will see later).

Ask the Expert

Q: **Why would I want to manually throw an exception?**

A: Most often, the exceptions that you will throw will be instances of exception classes that you created. As you will see later in this chapter, creating your own exception classes allows you to handle errors in your code as part of your program's overall exception-handling strategy.

Rethrowing an Exception

An exception caught by one **catch** clause can be rethrown so that it can be caught by an outer **catch**. The most likely reason for rethrowing an exception is to allow multiple handlers access to the exception. For example, perhaps one exception handler manages one aspect of an exception, and a second handler copes with another aspect. To rethrow an exception, you simply specify **throw**, without specifying an exception. That is, you use this form of **throw**:

throw ;

Remember that when you rethrow an exception, it will not be recaught by the same **catch** clause. It will propagate to an outer **catch** clause.

The following program illustrates rethrowing an exception:

```
// Rethrow an exception.
using System;

class Rethrow {
  public static void GenException() {
    // Here, numer is longer than denom.
    int[] numer = { 4, 8, 16, 32, 64, 128, 256, 512 };
    int[] denom = { 2, 0, 4, 4, 0, 8 };

    for(int i=0; i < numer.Length; i++) {
      try {
        Console.WriteLine(numer[i] + " / " +
                          denom[i] + " is " +
                          numer[i]/denom[i]);
      }
      catch (DivideByZeroException) {
        Console.WriteLine("Can't divide by Zero!");
      }
      catch (IndexOutOfRangeException) {
        Console.WriteLine("No matching element found.");
        throw; // rethrow the exception          ─── Rethrow the exception.
      }
    }
  }
}
```

```
class RethrowDemo {
  static void Main() {
    try {
      Rethrow.GenException();
    }
    catch(IndexOutOfRangeException) {     ◄──────────  Catch the rethrown exception.
      // recatch exception
      Console.WriteLine("Fatal error -- program terminated.");
    }
  }
}
```

In this program, divide-by-zero errors are handled locally by **GenException( )**, but an array boundary error is rethrown. In this case, it is caught by **Main( )**.

Using finally

Sometimes, you will want to define a block of code that will execute when a **try/catch** block is left. For example, an exception might cause an error that terminates the current method, causing its premature return. However, that method may have opened a file or a network connection that needs to be closed. Such types of circumstances are common in programming, and C# provides a convenient way to handle them: **finally**.

To specify a block of code to execute when a **try/catch** block is exited, include a **finally** block at the end of a **try/catch** sequence. The general form of a **try/catch** that includes **finally** is shown here:

try {
  // block of code to monitor for errors
}

catch (*ExcepType1 exOb*) {
  // handler for *ExcepType1*
}

catch (*ExcepType2 exOb*) {
  // handler for *ExcepType2*
}

// ...

finally {
  // finally code
}

The **finally** block will be executed whenever execution leaves a **try/catch** block, no matter what conditions cause it. That is, whether the **try** block ends normally or because of an exception, the last code executed is that defined by **finally**. The **finally** block is also executed if any code within the **try** block or any of its **catch** clauses returns from the method.

Here is an example of **finally**:

```
// Use finally.
using System;

class UseFinally {
  public static void GenException(int what) {
    int t;
    int[] nums = new int[2];

    Console.WriteLine("Receiving " + what);
    try {
      switch(what) {
        case 0:
          t = 10 / what; // generate div-by-zero error
          break;
        case 1:
          nums[4] = 4; // generate array index error.
          break;
        case 2:
          return; // return from try block
      }
    }
    catch (DivideByZeroException) {
      Console.WriteLine("Can't divide by Zero!");
      return; // return from catch
    }
    catch (IndexOutOfRangeException) {
      Console.WriteLine("No matching element found.");
    }
    finally {
      Console.WriteLine("Leaving try.");
    }
  }
}

class FinallyDemo {
  static void Main() {

    for(int i=0; i < 3; i++) {
      UseFinally.GenException(i);
      Console.WriteLine();
    }
  }
}
```

The **finally** block is executed when leaving the **try/catch** blocks.

Here is the output produced by the program:

```
Receiving 0
Can't divide by Zero!
Leaving try.

Receiving 1
No matching element found.
Leaving try.

Receiving 2
Leaving try.
```

As the output shows, no matter how the **try** block is exited, the **finally** block executes.

One other point: Syntactically, when a **finally** block follows a **try** block, no **catch** clauses are technically required. Thus, you can have a **try** followed by a **finally**, with no **catch** clauses. In this case, the **finally** block is executed when the **try** exits, but no exceptions are handled.

A Closer Look at Exception

Up to this point, we have been catching exceptions, but we haven't been doing anything with the exception object itself. As explained earlier, a **catch** clause allows you to specify an exception type *and* a variable. The variable receives a reference to the exception object. Since all exceptions are derived from **Exception**, all exceptions support the members defined by **Exception**. Here we will examine several of its most useful members and constructors, and put the exception variable to use.

Exception defines several properties. Three of the most interesting are **Message**, **StackTrace**, and **TargetSite**. All are read-only. **Message** is a string that describes the nature of the error. **StackTrace** is a string that contains the stack of calls that lead to the exception. **TargetSite** returns an object that specifies the method that generated the exception.

Exception also defines several methods. The one that you will most often use is **ToString( )**, which returns a string that describes the exception. **ToString( )** is automatically called when an exception is displayed via **WriteLine( )**, for example.

The following program demonstrates the properties and method just mentioned:

```
// Using Exception members.
using System;

class ExcTest {
  public static void GenException() {
    int[] nums = new int[4];

    Console.WriteLine("Before exception is generated.");

    // Generate an index out-of-bounds exception.
    nums[7] = 10;
    Console.WriteLine("this won't be displayed");
  }
}
```

```
class UseExcept {
  static void Main() {

    try {
      ExcTest.GenException();
    }
    catch (IndexOutOfRangeException exc) {
      Console.WriteLine("Standard message is: ");
      Console.WriteLine(exc); // calls ToString()
      Console.WriteLine("Stack trace: " + exc.StackTrace);
      Console.WriteLine("Message: " + exc.Message);
      Console.WriteLine("TargetSite: " + exc.TargetSite);
    }
    Console.WriteLine("After catch block.");
  }
}
```

The output from this program is shown here:

```
Before exception is generated.
Standard message is:
System.IndexOutOfRangeException: Index was outside the bounds
                                 of the array.
   at ExcTest.GenException()
   at UseExcept.Main()
Stack trace:     at ExcTest.GenException()
   at UseExcept.Main()
Message: Index was outside the bounds of the array.
TargetSite: Void GenException()
After catch block.
```

Exception defines the following four constructors:

public Exception( )

public Exception(string *str*)

public Exception(string *str*, Exception *inner*)

protected Exception(System.Runtime.Serialization.SerializationInfo *si*,
                  System.Runtime.Serialization.StreamingContext *sc*)

The first is the default constructor. The second specifies the string associated with the **Message** property associated with the exception. The third specifies what is called an *inner exception.* It is used when one exception gives rise to another. In this case, *inner* specifies the first exception, which will be null if no inner exception exists. (The inner exception, if it exists, can be obtained from the **InnerException** property defined by **Exception**.) The last constructor handles exceptions that occur remotely and require deserialization. (Remote execution and serialization are beyond the scope of this book.)

Exception	Meaning
ArrayTypeMismatchException	Type of value being stored is incompatible with the type of the array.
DivideByZeroException	Division by zero attempted.
IndexOutOfRangeException	Array index is out of bounds.
InvalidCastException	A runtime cast is invalid.
OutOfMemoryException	A call to **new** fails because insufficient free memory exists.
OverflowException	An arithmetic overflow occurred.
StackOverflowException	The stack was overrun.

Table 10-1   Commonly Used Exceptions Defined Within the **System** Namespace

One other point: In the fourth **Exception** constructor shown previously, notice that the types **SerializationInfo** and **StreamingContext** are preceded by **System.Runtime.Serialization**. This specifies the namespace in which they are contained. Namespaces are examined in detail in Chapter 14.

Commonly Used Exceptions

The **System** namespace defines several standard, built-in exceptions. All are derived from **SystemException** since they are generated by the CLR when runtime errors occur. Several of the more commonly used standard exceptions are shown in Table 10-1.

Deriving Exception Classes

Although C#'s built-in exceptions handle most common errors, C#'s exception-handling mechanism is not limited to these errors. In fact, part of the power of C#'s approach to exceptions is its ability to handle exceptions that you create. You can use custom exceptions to handle errors in your own code. Creating an exception is easy. Just define a class derived from **Exception**. Your derived classes don't need to actually implement anything—it is their existence in the type system that allows you to use them as exceptions.

NOTE

In the past, custom exceptions were derived from **ApplicationException**, since this is the hierarchy that was originally reserved for application-related exceptions. However, Microsoft no longer recommends this. Instead, at the time of this writing, Microsoft recommends deriving custom exceptions from **Exception**. For this reason, this is the approach used here.

The exception classes that you create will automatically have the properties and methods defined by **Exception** available to them. Of course, you can override one or more of these members in exception classes that you create.

When creating your own exception class, you will generally want your class to support all of the constructors defined by **Exception**. For simple custom exception classes, this is easy to do because you can simply pass along the constructor's arguments to the corresponding **Exception** constructor via **base**. Of course, technically, you only need to provide those constructors actually used by your program.

Here is an example that creates an exception called **NonIntResultException**. In the program, this exception is thrown when the result of dividing two integer values produces a result with a fractional component. For illustration, **NonIntResultException** defines all of the standard constructors, even though most are not used by the example. It also overrides the **ToString( )** method.

```
// Use a custom exception.
using System;

// Create an exception.
class NonIntResultException : Exception {                          A custom exception.
  /* Implement all of the Exception constructors. Notice that
     the constructors simply execute the base class constructor.
     Because NonIntResultException adds nothing to Exception,
     there is no need for any further actions. */
  public NonIntResultException() : base() { }
  public NonIntResultException(string str) : base(str) { }
  public NonIntResultException(string str, Exception inner) :
    base(str, inner) { }
  protected NonIntResultException(
    System.Runtime.Serialization.SerializationInfo si,          Provide the
    System.Runtime.Serialization.StreamingContext sc) :         standard
      base(si, sc) { }                                          constructors.

  // Override ToString for NonIntResultException.
  public override string ToString() {                            Override ToString( ).
    return Message;
  }
}

class CustomExceptDemo {
  static void Main() {

    // Here, numer contains some odd values.
    int[] numer = { 4, 8, 15, 32, 64, 127, 256, 512 };
    int[] denom = { 2, 0, 4, 4, 0, 8 };

    for(int i=0; i < numer.Length; i++) {
      try {
        if((numer[i] % denom[i]) != 0)
          throw new                                              Throw a custom exception.
            NonIntResultException("Outcome of " +
                numer[i] + " / " + denom[i] + " is not even.");
```

```
      Console.WriteLine(numer[i] + " / " +
                        denom[i] + " is " +
                        numer[i]/denom[i]);
    }
    catch (DivideByZeroException) {
      Console.WriteLine("Can't divide by Zero!");
    }
    catch (IndexOutOfRangeException) {
      Console.WriteLine("No matching element found.");
    }
    catch (NonIntResultException exc) {
      Console.WriteLine(exc);
    }
  }
 }
}
```

The output from the program is shown here:

```
4 / 2 is 2
Can't divide by Zero!
Outcome of 15 / 4 is not even.
32 / 4 is 8
Can't divide by Zero!
Outcome of 127 / 8 is not even.
No matching element found.
No matching element found.
```

Notice that none of the constructors provide any statements in their body. Instead, they simply pass their arguments along to **Exception** via **base**. In cases in which your exception class does not add any functionality, you can simply let the **Exception** constructors handle the process. As explained, there is no requirement that your derived classes add anything to what is inherited from **Exception**. It is their existence in the type system that allows you to use them as exceptions.

Before moving on, you might want to experiment with this program a bit. For example, try commenting-out the override of **ToString( )** and observe the results. Also, try creating an exception using the default constructor, and observe what C# generates as its default message.

Catching Derived Class Exceptions

You need to be careful how you order **catch** clauses when trying to catch exception types that involve base and derived classes, because a **catch** clause for a base class will also match any of its derived classes. For example, since the base class of all exceptions is **Exception**, catching **Exception** catches all possible exceptions. Of course, using **catch** without an exception type provides a cleaner way to catch all exceptions, as described earlier. However, the issue of catching derived class exceptions is very important in other contexts, especially when you create exceptions of your own.

If you want to catch exceptions of both a base class type and a derived class type, put the derived class first in the **catch** sequence. This is necessary because a base class **catch** will also catch all derived classes. Fortunately, this rule is self-enforcing because putting the base class first causes a compile-time error.

The following program creates two exception classes called **ExceptA** and **ExceptB**. **ExceptA** is derived from **Exception**. **ExceptB** is derived from **ExceptA**. The program then throws an exception of each type. For brevity, it supplies only one constructor (which takes a string that describes the exception). But remember, in commercial code, your custom exception classes will normally provide all four of the constructors defined by **Exception**.

```
// Derived exceptions must appear before base class exceptions.
using System;

// Create an exception.
class ExceptA : Exception {
  public ExceptA(string str) : base(str) { }

  public override string ToString() {
    return Message;
  }
}

// Create an exception derived from ExceptA
class ExceptB : ExceptA {            ⬅———————— Notice that ExceptB is derived from ExceptA.
  public ExceptB(string str) : base(str) { }

  public override string ToString() {
    return Message;
  }
}

class OrderMatters {
  static void Main() {
    for(int x = 0; x < 3; x++) {
      try {
        if(x==0) throw new ExceptA("Caught an ExceptA exception");
        else if(x==1) throw new ExceptB("Caught an ExceptB exception");
        else throw new Exception();
      }
      catch (ExceptB exc) {      ⬅————————————┐
        Console.WriteLine(exc);                │
      }                                        │
      catch (ExceptA exc) {      ⬅————————————┤———— The order of the catch clauses matters.
        Console.WriteLine(exc);                │
      }                                        │
      catch (Exception exc) {    ⬅————————————┘
        Console.WriteLine(exc);
      }
    }
  }
}
```

The output from the program is shown here:

```
Caught an ExceptA exception
Caught an ExceptB exception
System.Exception: Exception of type 'System.Exception' was thrown.
   at OrderMatters.Main()
```

Notice the order of the **catch** clauses. This is the only order in which they can occur. Since **ExceptB** is derived from **ExceptA**, the **catch** for **ExceptB** must be before the one for **ExceptA**. Similarly, the **catch** for **Exception** (which is the base class for all exceptions) must appear last. To prove this point for yourself, try rearranging the **catch** clauses. Doing so will result in a compile-time error.

Ask the Expert

Q: Since an exception usually indicates a specific error, why would I want to catch a base class exception?

A: A **catch** clause that catches a base class exception allows you to catch an entire category of exceptions, possibly handling them with a single **catch** and avoiding duplicated code. For example, you might create a set of exceptions that describes some sort of device error. If your exception handlers simply tell the user that a device error occurred, then you could use a common **catch** for all exceptions of this type. The handler could simply display the **Message** string. Since the code that accomplishes this is the same for all exceptions, one **catch** can respond to all device exceptions.

Try This Add Exceptions to the Queue Class

In this project, you will create two exception classes that can be used by the queue classes developed in the Try This section in Chapter 9. They will indicate the queue-full and queue-empty error conditions. These exceptions are thrown by the **Put( )** and **Get( )** methods, respectively, when an error occurs. For the sake of simplicity, this example will add these exceptions only to the **SimpleQueue** class, but you can easily incorporate them into the other queue classes. For brevity, the exception classes implement only the constructor that is actually used in the program (which is the one that takes a string argument that describes the exception). You can try adding the others on your own as an exercise.

Step by Step

1. Create a file called **QExcDemo.cs**.

2. Into **QExcDemo.cs**, define the following exceptions:

```
// Add exception handling to the queue classes.

using System;

// An exception for queue-full errors.
class QueueFullException : Exception {
  public QueueFullException(string str) : base(str) { }
  // Add other QueueFullException constructors here, if desired.

  public override string ToString() {
    return "\n" + Message;
  }
}

// An exception for queue-empty errors.
class QueueEmptyException : Exception {
  public QueueEmptyException(string str) : base(str) { }
  // Add other QueueEmptyException constructors here, if desired.

  public override string ToString() {
    return "\n" + Message;
  }
}
```

A **QueueFullException** is generated when an attempt is made to store an item in an already full queue. A **QueueEmptyException** is generated when an attempt is made to remove an element from an empty queue.

3. Modify the **SimpleQueue** class so that it throws an exception when an error occurs, as shown here. Add it to **QExcDemo.cs**.

```
// A simple, fixed-size queue class for characters that uses exceptions.
class SimpleQueue : ICharQ {
  char[] q; // this array holds the queue
  int putloc, getloc; // the put and get indices

  // Construct an empty queue given its size.
  public SimpleQueue(int size) {
    q = new char[size+1]; // allocate memory for queue
    putloc = getloc = 0;
  }

  // Put a character into the queue.
```

(continued)

```
    public void Put(char ch) {
      if(putloc==q.Length-1)
        throw new QueueFullException("Queue Full! Max length is " +
                                       (q.Length-1) + ".");

      putloc++;
      q[putloc] = ch;
    }

    // Get a character from the queue.
    public char Get() {
      if(getloc == putloc)
        throw new QueueEmptyException("Queue is empty.");

      getloc++;
      return q[getloc];
    }
  }
```

The addition of exceptions to **SimpleQueue** allows a queue error to be handled in a rational fashion. You might recall that the previous version of **SimpleQueue** simply reported the error. Throwing an exception is a much better approach because it allows the code that uses **SimpleQueue** to handle the error in an appropriate manner.

4. To try the updated **SimpleQueue** class, add the **QExcDemo** class shown here to **QExcDemo.cs**.

```
// Demonstrate the queue exceptions.

class QExcDemo {
  static void Main() {
    SimpleQueue q = new SimpleQueue(10);
    char ch;
    int i;

    try {
      // Overrun the queue.
      for(i=0; i < 11; i++) {
        Console.Write("Attempting to store : " +
                         (char) ('A' + i));
        q.Put((char) ('A' + i));
        Console.WriteLine(" -- OK");
      }
      Console.WriteLine();
    }
    catch (QueueFullException exc) {
      Console.WriteLine(exc);
    }
    Console.WriteLine();
```

```
    try {
      // Over-empty the queue.
      for(i=0; i < 11; i++) {
        Console.Write("Getting next char: ");
        ch = q.Get();
        Console.WriteLine(ch);
      }
    }
    catch (QueueEmptyException exc) {
      Console.WriteLine(exc);
    }
  }
}
```

5. To create the program, you must compile **QExcDemo.cs** with the **IQChar.cs** file. Recall that **IQChar.cs** contains the queue interface. When you run **QExcDemo**, you will see the following output:

```
Attempting to store : A -- OK
Attempting to store : B -- OK
Attempting to store : C -- OK
Attempting to store : D -- OK
Attempting to store : E -- OK
Attempting to store : F -- OK
Attempting to store : G -- OK
Attempting to store : H -- OK
Attempting to store : I -- OK
Attempting to store : J -- OK
Attempting to store : K
Queue Full! Max length is 10.

Getting next char: A
Getting next char: B
Getting next char: C
Getting next char: D
Getting next char: E
Getting next char: F
Getting next char: G
Getting next char: H
Getting next char: I
Getting next char: J
Getting next char:
Queue is empty.
```

Using checked and unchecked

An arithmetic computation can cause an overflow. For example, consider the following sequence:

```
byte a, b, result;
a = 127;
b = 127;

result = (byte)(a * b);
```

Here, the product of **a** and **b** exceeds the range of a **byte** value. Thus, the result overflows the type of the result.

C# allows you to specify whether your code will raise an exception when overflow occurs using the keywords **checked** and **unchecked**. To specify that an expression be checked for overflow, used **checked**. To specify that overflow be ignored, use **unchecked**. In this case, the result is truncated to fit into the target type of the expression.

The **checked** keyword has these two general forms. One checks a specific expression and is called the *operator form* of **checked**. The other checks a block of statements and is called the *statement form*.

checked (*expr*)

checked {
   // statements to be checked
}

Here, *expr* is the expression being checked. If a checked expression overflows, then an **OverflowException** is thrown.

The **unchecked** keyword also has two general forms. The first is the operator form, which ignores overflow for a specific expression. The other ignores overflow for a block of statements. They are shown here:

unchecked (*expr*)

unchecked {
   // statements for which overflow is ignored
}

Here, *expr* is the expression that is not being checked for overflow. If an unchecked expression overflows, then truncation will occur.

Here is a program that demonstrates both **checked** and **unchecked**.

```
// Using checked and unchecked.
using System;
```

```
class CheckedDemo {
  static void Main() {
    byte a, b;
    byte result;

    a = 127;
    b = 127;

    try {
      result = unchecked((byte)(a * b));
      Console.WriteLine("Unchecked result: " + result);

      result = checked((byte)(a * b)); // this causes exception
      Console.WriteLine("Checked result: " + result); // won't execute
    }
    catch (OverflowException exc) {
      Console.WriteLine(exc);
    }
  }
}
```

The overflow in this expression is truncated.

The overflow here causes an exception.

The output from the program is shown here:

```
Unchecked result: 1
System.OverflowException: Arithmetic operation resulted in an overflow.
   at CheckedDemo.Main()
```

As is evident, the unchecked expression resulted in a truncation. The checked expression caused an exception.

The preceding program demonstrated the use of **checked** and **unchecked** for a single expression. The following program shows how to check and uncheck a block of statements:

```
// Using checked and unchecked with statement blocks.
using System;

class CheckedBlocks {
  static void Main() {
    byte a, b;
    byte result;

    a = 127;
    b = 127;

    try {
      unchecked {
        a = 127;
        b = 127;
```

An unchecked block.

```
     result = (byte)(a * b);
     Console.WriteLine("Unchecked result: " + result);

     a = 125;
     b = 5;
     result = (byte)(a * b);
     Console.WriteLine("Unchecked result: " + result);
  }

  checked {  ◄──────────────── A checked block.
     a = 2;
     b = 7;
     result = (byte)(a * b); // this is OK
     Console.WriteLine("Checked result: " + result);

     a = 127;
     b = 127;
     result = (byte)(a * b); // this causes exception
     Console.WriteLine("Checked result: " + result); // won't execute
  }
}
catch (OverflowException exc) {
  Console.WriteLine(exc);
}
  }
}
```

The output from the program is shown here:

```
Unchecked result: 1
Unchecked result: 113
Checked result: 14
System.OverflowException: Arithmetic operation resulted in an overflow.
   at CheckedBlocks.Main()
```

As you can see, the unchecked block results in the overflow being truncated. When overflow occurred in the checked block, an exception was raised.

One reason that you may need to use **checked** or **unchecked** is that the checked/unchecked status of overflow is determined by the setting of a compiler option and by the execution environment itself. Thus, for some types of programs, it is best to explicitly specify the overflow check status.

Ask the Expert

Q: **When should I use exception handling in a program? When should I create my own custom exception classes?**

A: Since C# extensively uses exceptions to report errors, nearly all real-world programs will make use of exception handling. This is the part of exception handling that most new C# programmers find easy. It is harder to decide when and how to use your own custom-made exceptions. In general, there are two ways errors can be reported: return values and exceptions. When is one approach better than the other? Simply put, in C#, exception handling should be the norm. Certainly, returning an error code is a valid alternative in some cases, but exceptions provide a more powerful, structured way to handle errors. They are the way professional C# programmers handle errors in their code.

Chapter 10 Self Test

1. What class is at the top of the exception hierarchy?

2. Briefly explain how to use **try** and **catch**.

3. What is wrong with this fragment?

```
// ...
vals[18] = 10;
catch (IndexOutOfRangeException exc) {
  // handle error
}
```

4. What happens if an exception is not caught?

5. What is wrong with this fragment?

```
class A : Exception { ...

class B : A { ...

// ...

try {
  // ...
}
catch (A exc) { ... }
catch (B exc) { ... }
```

6. Can an exception caught by an inner **catch** be rethrown to an outer **catch**?

7. The **finally** block is the last bit of code executed before your program ends. True or false? Explain your answer.

8. In Exercise 3 of the Self Test in Chapter 6, you created a **Stack** class. Add custom exceptions to your class that report stack-full and stack-empty conditions. Include all four standard exception class constructors.

9. Explain the purpose of **checked** and **unchecked**.

10. How can all exceptions be caught?

Chapter 11

Using I/O

Key Skills & Concepts

- The stream

- Stream classes

- Console I/O

- File I/O

- Read and write binary data

- Random-access files

- Convert numeric strings

Since the beginning of this book, you have been using parts of the C# I/O system, such as **Console.WriteLine( )**, but you have been doing so without much formal explanation. Because the C# I/O system is built upon a hierarchy of classes, it was not possible to present its theory and details without first discussing classes, inheritance, and exceptions. Now it is time to examine C#'s approach to I/O in detail. As explained in Chapter 1, C# uses the I/O system and classes defined by the .NET Framework. Thus, a discussion of I/O under C# is also a discussion of the .NET I/O system in general.

This chapter examines C#'s approach to both console I/O and file I/O. Be forewarned that the I/O system is quite large. This chapter introduces the most important and commonly used features, but there will be several aspects of I/O that you will want to study on your own. Fortunately, C#'s I/O system is cohesive and consistent; once you understand its fundamentals, the rest of the I/O system is easy to master.

C#'s I/O Is Built Upon Streams

C# programs perform I/O through streams. A *stream* is an abstraction that either produces or consumes information. A stream is linked to a physical device by the I/O system. All streams behave in the same manner, even if the physical devices they are linked to differ. Thus, the I/O classes and methods can be applied to many types of devices. For example, the same methods that you use to write to the console can also be used to write to a disk file.

Byte Streams and Character Streams

At the lowest level, all C# I/O operates on bytes. This makes sense because many devices are byte-oriented when it comes to I/O operations. Frequently, though, we humans prefer to communicate using characters. Recall that in C#, **char** is a 16-bit type and **byte** is an 8-bit type. If you are using the ASCII character set, then it is easy to convert between **char** and **byte**; just ignore the high-order byte of the **char** value. But this won't work for the rest of the Unicode characters, which need both bytes. Thus, byte streams are not perfectly suited to handling character-based I/O. To solve this problem, C# defines several classes that convert a byte stream into a character stream, handling the translation of **byte**-to-**char** and **char**-to-**byte** for you automatically.

The Predefined Streams

Three predefined streams, which are exposed by the properties **Console.In**, **Console.Out**, and **Console.Error**, are available to all programs that use the **System** namespace. **Console.Out** refers to the standard output stream. By default, this is the console. When you call **Console.WriteLine( )**, for example, it automatically sends information to **Console.Out**. **Console.In** refers to standard input, which is, by default, the keyboard. **Console.Error** refers to the standard error stream, which is also the console by default. However, these streams can be redirected to any compatible I/O device. The standard streams are character streams. Thus, these streams read and write characters.

The Stream Classes

The I/O system defines both byte and character stream classes. However, the character stream classes are really just wrappers that convert an underlying byte stream to a character stream, handling any conversion automatically. Thus, the character streams, while logically separate, are built upon byte streams.

All stream classes are defined within the **System.IO** namespace. To use these classes, you will usually include the following statement near the top of your program:

```
using System.IO;
```

The reason that you don't have to specify **System.IO** for console input and output is that the **Console** class is defined in the **System** namespace.

The Stream Class

The core stream class is **System.IO.Stream**. **Stream** represents a byte stream and is a base class for all other stream classes. It is also abstract, which means that you cannot instantiate a **Stream** object directly. **Stream** defines a set of standard stream operations. Table 11-1 shows several commonly used methods defined by **Stream**.

Several of the methods shown in Table 11-1 will throw an **IOException** if an I/O error occurs. If an invalid operation is attempted, such as attempting to write to a stream that is read-only, a **NotSupportedException** is thrown. Other exceptions are possible, depending on the specific method.

Notice that **Stream** defines methods that read and write data. However, not all streams will support both of these operations because it is possible to open read-only or write-only streams. Also, not all streams will support position requests via **Seek( )**. To determine the capabilities of a stream, you will use one or more of **Stream**'s properties. They are shown in Table 11-2. Also shown are the **Length** and **Position** properties, which contain the length of the stream and its current position.

Method	Description
void Close( )	Closes the stream.
void Flush( )	Writes the contents of the stream to the physical device.
int ReadByte( )	Returns an integer representation of the next available byte of input. Returns −1 when the end of the file is encountered.
int Read(byte[ ] *buf*, int *offset*, int *numBytes*)	Attempts to read up to *numBytes* bytes into *buf* starting at *buf*[*offset*], returning the number of bytes successfully read.
long Seek(long *offset*, SeekOrigin *origin*)	Sets the current position in the stream to the specified *offset* from the specified *origin*.
void WriteByte(byte *b*)	Writes a single byte to an output stream.
int Write(byte[ ] *buf*, int *offset*, int *numBytes*)	Writes a subrange of *numBytes* bytes from the array *buf*, beginning at *buf*[*offset*]. The number of bytes written is returned.

Table 11-1   A Sampling of the Methods Defined by **Stream**

The Byte Stream Classes

Several concrete byte streams are derived from **Stream**. Those that are defined in the **System.IO** namespace are shown here.

Stream Class	Description
BufferedStream	Wraps a byte stream and adds buffering. Buffering provides a performance enhancement in many cases.
FileStream	A byte stream designed for file I/O.
MemoryStream	A byte stream that uses memory for storage.
UnmanagedMemoryStream	A byte stream that uses memory for storage, but is not suitable for mixed-language programming.

Several other concrete stream classes that provide support for compressed files, sockets, and pipes, among others, are also supported by the .NET Framework. It is also possible for you to derive your own stream classes. However, for the vast majority of applications, the built-in streams will be sufficient.

The Character Stream Wrapper Classes

To create a character stream, you will wrap a byte stream inside one of the character stream wrappers. At the top of the character-stream hierarchy are the abstract classes **TextReader** and **TextWriter**. The methods defined by these two abstract classes are available to all of their subclasses. Thus, they form a minimal set of I/O functions that all character streams will have.

Property	Description
bool CanRead	This property is true if the stream can be read. This property is read-only.
bool CanSeek	This property is true if the stream supports position requests. This property is read-only.
bool CanTimeout	This property is true if the stream can time out. This property is read-only.
bool CanWrite	This property is true if the stream can be written. This property is read-only.
long Length	This property contains the length of the stream. This property is read-only.
long Position	This property represents the current position of the stream. This property is read/write.
int ReadTimeout	This property represents the length of time before a timeout will occur for read operations. This property is read/write.
int WriteTimeout	This property represents the length of time before a timeout will occur for write operations. This property is read/write.

Table 11-2   The Properties Defined by **Stream**

Table 11-3 shows the input methods in **TextReader**. In general, these methods can throw an **IOException** on error. (Some can also throw other types of exceptions.) Of particular interest is the **ReadLine( )** method, which reads an entire line of text, returning it as a **string**. This method is useful when reading input that contains embedded spaces.

Method	Description
int Peek( )	Obtains the next character from the input stream, but does not remove that character. Returns −1 if no character is available.
int Read( )	Returns an integer representation of the next available character from the input stream. Returns −1 when the end of the stream is encountered.
int Read(char[ ] *buf*, int *offset*, int *numChars*)	Attempts to read up to *numChars* characters into *buf* starting at *buf*[*offset*], returning the number of characters successfully read.
int ReadBlock(char[ ] *buf*, int *offset*, int *numChars*)	Attempts to read up to *numChars* characters into *buf* starting at *buf*[*offset*], returning the number of characters successfully read.
string ReadLine( )	Reads the next line of text and returns it as a string. Null is returned if an attempt is made to read at end-of-file.
string ReadToEnd( )	Returns all of the remaining characters in a stream and returns them as a string.

Table 11-3   The Input Methods Defined by **TextReader**

TextWriter defines versions of **Write( )** and **WriteLine( )** that output all of the built-in types. For example, here are just a few of their overloaded versions:

Method	Description
void Write(int *val*)	Write an **int**.
void Write(double *val*)	Write a **double**.
void Write(bool *val*)	Write a **bool**.
void WriteLine(string *val*)	Write a string followed by a new line.
void WriteLine(uint *val*)	Write a **uint** followed by a new line.
void WriteLine(char *val*)	Write a character followed by a new line.

All throw an **IOException** if an error occurs while writing.

In addition to **Write( )** and **WriteLine( )**, **TextWriter** defines the **Close( )** and **Flush( )** methods shown here:

virtual void Close( )

virtual void Flush( )

Flush( ) causes any data remaining in the output buffer to be written to the physical medium. **Close( )** closes the stream.

The **TextReader** and **TextWriter** classes are implemented by several character-based stream classes, including those shown here. Thus, these streams provide the methods and properties specified by **TextReader** and **TextWriter**.

Stream Class	Description
StreamReader	Read characters from a byte stream. This class wraps a byte input stream.
StreamWriter	Write characters to a byte stream. This class wraps a byte output stream.
StringReader	Read characters from a string.
StringWriter	Write characters to a string.

Binary Streams

In addition to the byte and character streams, there are two binary stream classes, which can be used to read and write binary data directly. These streams are called **BinaryReader** and **BinaryWriter**. We will look closely at these later in this chapter when binary file I/O is discussed.

Now that you understand the general layout of the I/O system, the rest of this chapter will examine its various pieces in detail, beginning with console I/O.

Console I/O

Console I/O is accomplished through the standard streams **Console.In**, **Console.Out**, and **Console.Error**. You have been using console I/O since Chapter 1, so you are already familiar with it. As you will see, it has some additional capabilities.

Before we begin, however, it is important to emphasize a point made earlier in this book: Most real applications of C# will not be text-based, console programs. Rather, they will be graphically oriented programs or components that rely upon a windowed interface for interaction with the user, or they will be sever-side applications. Thus, the portion of the I/O system that relates to console input and output is not widely used. Although text-based programs are excellent as teaching examples and for short utility programs, they are not suitable for most real-world applications.

Reading Console Input

Console.In is an instance of **TextReader**, and you can use the methods and properties defined by **TextReader** to access it. However, you will usually use the methods provided by **Console**, which automatically read from **Console.In**. **Console** defines two input methods: **Read( )** and **ReadLine( )**.

To read a single character, use the **Read( )** method. It is shown here:

static int Read( )

This method was introduced in Chapter 3. It returns the next character read from the console. The character is returned as an **int**, which must be cast to **char**. It returns –1 on error. This method will throw an **IOException** on failure. Recall that **Read( )** is line-buffered, so you must press ENTER before any character that you type will be sent to your program.

To read a string of characters, use the **ReadLine( )** method. It is shown here:

static string ReadLine( )

ReadLine( ) reads characters until you press ENTER and returns them in a **string** object. This method will also throw an **IOException** on failure.

Here is a program that demonstrates reading a line of characters from **Console.In**:

```
// Input from the console using ReadLine().
using System;

class ReadChars {
  static void Main() {
    string str;

    Console.WriteLine("Enter some characters.");
    str = Console.ReadLine(); ◄──────────────── Read a string from the keyboard.
    Console.WriteLine("You entered: " + str);
  }
}
```

Here is a sample run:

```
Enter some characters.
This is a test.
You entered: This is a test.
```

Although the **Console** methods are the easiest way to read from the console, you can call methods on the underlying **TextReader**, which is available through **Console.In**. For example, here is the preceding program rewritten to use the methods defined by **TextReader**:

```
/* Read an array of bytes from the keyboard, using
   Console.In directly. */
using System;

class ReadChars2 {
  static void Main() {
    string str;

    Console.WriteLine("Enter some characters.");

    str = Console.In.ReadLine();          Read from Console.In explicitly.

    Console.WriteLine("You entered: " + str);
  }
}
```

Notice how **ReadLine( )** is now invoked directly on **Console.In**. The key point here is that if you need access to the methods defined by the **TextReader** that underlies **Console.In**, you will invoke those methods as shown in this example.

Writing Console Output

Console.Out and **Console.Error** are objects of type **TextWriter**. Console output is most easily accomplished with **Write( )** and **WriteLine( )**, with which you are already familiar. Versions of these methods exist that handle output for each of the built-in types. **Console** defines its own versions of **Write( )** and **WriteLine( )** so that they can be called directly on **Console**, as you have been doing throughout this book. However, you can invoke these (and other) methods on the **TextWriter** that underlies **Console.Out** and **Console.Error** if you choose.

Here is a program that demonstrates writing to **Console.Out** and **Console.Error**. By default, both write output to the console.

```
// Write to Console.Out and Console.Error.
using System;

class ErrOut {
  static void Main() {
    int a=10, b=0;
    int result;
```

```
   Console.Out.WriteLine("This will generate an exception.");
  try {
    result = a / b; // generate an exception
  } catch(DivideByZeroException exc) {
    Console.Error.WriteLine(exc.Message);
  }
 }
}
```

Write to **Console.Out**.

Write to **Console.Error**.

The output from the program is shown here:

```
This will generate an exception.
Attempted to divide by zero.
```

Sometimes newcomers to programming are confused about when to use **Console.Error**. Since both **Console.Out** and **Console.Error** default to writing their output to the console, why are there two different streams? The answer lies in the fact that the standard streams can be redirected to other devices. For example, **Console.Error** can be redirected to write to a disk file, rather than to the screen. Thus, it is possible to direct error output to a log file, for example, without affecting console output. Conversely, if console output is redirected and error output is not, then error messages will appear on the console, where they can be seen. We will examine redirection later, after file I/O has been described.

Ask the Expert

Q: As you just explained, Read( ) is line-buffered. This means that it buffers keystrokes until I press ENTER. Does C# support an interactive input method that returns as soon as any key is pressed?

A: Yes! Beginning with version 2.0, the .NET Framework has included a method in **Console** that enables you to read individual keystrokes directly from the keyboard in a non-line–buffered manner. This method is called **ReadKey( )**. When it is called, it waits until a key is pressed. When a key is pressed, **ReadKey( )** returns the keystroke immediately. You do not need to press ENTER. Thus, **ReadKey( )** allows keystrokes to be read and processed in real time. **ReadKey( )** has these two forms:

static ConsoleKeyInfo ReadKey( )

static ConsoleKeyInfo ReadKey(bool *noDisplay*)

The first form waits for a key to be pressed. When that occurs, it returns the key and also displays the key on the screen. The second form also waits for and returns a keypress. However, if *noDisplay* is true, then the key is not displayed. If *noDisplay* is false, the key is displayed.

(continued)

ReadKey( ) returns information about the keypress in an object of type **ConsoleKeyInfo**, which is a structure. It contains the following read-only properties:

char KeyChar

ConsoleKey Key

ConsoleModifiers Modifiers

KeyChar contains the **char** equivalent of the character that was pressed. **Key** contains a value from the **ConsoleKey** enumeration, which is an enumeration of all the keys on the keyboard. **Modifiers** describes which, if any, of the keyboard modifiers ALT, CTRL, or SHIFT were pressed when the keystroke was generated. These modifiers are represented by the **ConsoleModifiers** enumeration, which has these values: **Control**, **Shift**, and **Alt**. More than one modifier value might be present in **Modifiers**.

FileStream and Byte-Oriented File I/O

The I/O system provides classes that allow you to read and write files. Of course, the most common type of file is the disk file. At the operating system level, all files are byte-oriented. As you would expect, there are methods that read and write bytes from and to a file. Thus, reading and writing files using byte streams is very common. You can also wrap a byte-oriented file stream within a character-based object. Character-based file operations are useful when text is being stored. Character streams are discussed later in this chapter. Here, byte-oriented I/O is described.

To create a byte-oriented stream attached to a file, you will use the **FileStream** class. **FileStream** is derived from **Stream** and contains all of **Stream**'s functionality.

Remember, the stream classes, including **FileStream**, are defined in **System.IO**. Thus, you will usually include

```
using System.IO;
```

near the top of any program that uses them.

Opening and Closing a File

To create a byte stream linked to a file, create a **FileStream** object. **FileStream** defines several constructors. Perhaps its most commonly used one is shown here:

FileStream(string *filename*, FileMode *mode*)

Here, *filename* specifies the name of the file to open, which can include a full path specification. The *mode* parameter specifies how the file will be opened. It must be one of the values defined by the **FileMode** enumeration. These values are shown in Table 11-4. In general, this

Value	Description
FileMode.Append	Output is appended to the end of the file.
FileMode.Create	Creates a new output file. Any preexisting file by the same name will be destroyed.
FileMode.CreateNew	Creates a new output file. The file must not already exist.
FileMode.Open	Opens a preexisting file.
FileMode.OpenOrCreate	Opens a file if it exists, or creates the file if it does not already exist.
FileMode.Truncate	Opens a preexisting file, but reduces its length to zero.

Table 11-4   The **FileMode** Values

constructor opens a file for read/write access. The exception is when the file is opened using **FileMode.Append**. In this case, the file is write-only.

If a failure occurs when attempting to open the file, an exception will be thrown. If the file cannot be opened because it does not exist, **FileNotFoundException** will be thrown. If the file cannot be opened because of some type of I/O error, **IOException** will be thrown. Other possible exceptions are **ArgumentNullException** (the filename is null), **ArgumentException** (the filename is invalid), **ArgumentOutOfRangeException** (the mode is invalid), **SecurityException** (user does not have access rights), **PathTooLongException** (the filename/ path is too long), **NotSupportedException** (the filename specifies an unsupported device), and **DirectoryNotFoundException** (specified directory is invalid).

The exceptions **PathTooLongException**, **DirectoryNotFoundException**, and **FileNotFoundException** are subclasses of **IOException**. Thus, it is possible to catch all three by catching **IOException**.

The following shows one way to open the file **test.dat** for input:

```
FileStream fin;

try {
  fin = new FileStream("test", FileMode.Open);
}
catch(IOException exc) {
  Console.WriteLine(exc.Message);
  // Handle the error.
}
catch(Exception exc { // catch any other exception.
  Console.WriteLine(exc.Message);
  // Handle the error.
}
```

Here, the first **catch** clause handles situations in which the file is not found, the path is too long, the directory does not exist, or other I/O errors occur. The second **catch**, which is a "catch all" clause for all other types of exceptions, handles the other possible errors (possibly by rethrowing the exception). You could also check for each error individually, reporting more specifically the problem that occurred and taking remedial action specific to that error. For the sake of simplicity, the examples in this book will catch only **IOException**, but your real-world code may need to handle the other possible exceptions, depending upon the circumstances.

NOTE

To keep the code simple, the examples in this chapter catch only **IOException**, but your own code may need to handle other possible exceptions or handle the I/O exceptions individually.

As mentioned, except when **FileMode.Append** is specified, the **FileStream** constructor just described opens a file with read/write access. If you want to restrict access to just reading or just writing, use this constructor instead:

FileStream(string *filename*, FileMode *mode*, FileAccess *how*)

As before, *filename* specifies the name of the file to open, and *mode* specifies how the file will be opened. The value passed in *how* determines how the file can be accessed. It must be one of the values defined by the **FileAccess** enumeration, shown here:

    FileAccess.Read   FileAccess.Write   FileAccess.ReadWrite

For example, this opens a read-only file:

```
FileStream fin = new FileStream("test.dat", FileMode.Open,
                                FileAccess.Read);
```

When you are done with a file, you must close it by calling **Close( )**. Its general form is shown here:

void Close( )

Closing a file releases the system resources allocated to the file, allowing them to be used by another file. As a point of interest, **Close( )** works by calling **Dispose( )**, which actually frees the resources.

NOTE

The **using** statement, described in Chapter 15, offers a way to automatically close a file when it is no longer needed, and this approach is applicable to a variety of situations. However, to clearly illustrate the fundamentals of file handling, this chapter explicitly calls **close( )** in all cases.

Reading Bytes from a FileStream

FileStream defines two methods that read bytes from a file: **ReadByte( )** and **Read( )**. To read a single byte from a file, use **ReadByte( )**, whose general form is shown here:

int ReadByte( )

Each time it is called, it reads a single byte from the file and returns it as an integer value. It returns –1 when the end of the file is encountered. Possible exceptions include **NotSupportedException** (the stream is not opened for input) and **ObjectDisposedException** (the stream is closed).

To read a block of bytes, use **Read( )**, which has this general form:

int Read(byte[ ] *buf*, int *offset*, int *numBytes*)

Read( ) attempts to read up to *numBytes* bytes into *buf* starting at *buf*[*offset*]. It returns the number of bytes successfully read. An **IOException** is thrown if an I/O error occurs. Several other types of exceptions are possible, including **NotSupportedException**, which is thrown if reading is not supported by the stream.

The following program uses **ReadByte( )** to input and display the contents of a file, the name of which is specified as a command-line argument. It casts the values returned by **ReadByte( )** to **char**, allowing them to be displayed as ASCII characters. Note the program handles two errors that might occur when this program is first executed: the specified file not being found or the user forgetting to include the name of the file.

```
/* Display a file.

   To use this program, specify the name
   of the file that you want to see.
   For example, to see a file called TEST.CS,
   use the following command line.

   ShowFile TEST.CS
*/

using System;
using System.IO;

class ShowFile {
  static void Main(string[] args) {
    int i;
    FileStream fin;

    if(args.Length != 1) {
      Console.WriteLine("Usage: ShowFile File");
      return;
    }

    try {
      fin = new FileStream(args[0], FileMode.Open);
    } catch(IOException exc) {
      Console.WriteLine(exc.Message);
      return;
    }
```

```
// Read bytes until EOF is encountered.
do {
  try {
    i = fin.ReadByte();        ←————————— Read from the file.
  } catch(IOException exc) {
    Console.WriteLine(exc.Message);
    break;
  }
  if(i != -1) Console.Write((char) i);
} while(i != -1);              ←—————     When i equals –1, the end of
                                          the file has been reached.

  fin.Close();
  }
}
```

Ask the Expert

Q: I noticed that ReadByte( ) **returns –1 when the end of the file has been reached but that it does not have a special return value for a file error. Why not?**

A: In C#, errors are represented by exceptions. Thus, if **ReadByte( )**, or any other I/O method, does not throw an exception, it means that it has executed without error. This is a much cleaner way of handling I/O errors than is using special error codes.

Writing to a File

To write a byte to a file, use the **WriteByte( )** method. Its simplest form is shown here:

void WriteByte(byte *val*)

This method writes the byte specified by *val* to the file. If the underlying stream is not opened for output, a **NotSupportedException** is thrown. If the stream is closed, **ObjectDisposedException** is thrown.

You can write an array of bytes to a file by calling **Write( )**. It is shown here:

int Write(byte[ ] *buf*, int *offset*, int *numBytes*)

Write( ) writes *numBytes* bytes from the array *buf*, beginning at *buf*[*offset*], to the file. The number of bytes written is returned. If an error occurs during writing, an **IOException** is thrown. If the underlying stream is not opened for output, a **NotSupportedException** is thrown. Other exceptions are possible.

As you may know, when file output is performed, often, that output is not immediately written to the actual physical device. Instead, output is buffered by the operating system until a sizable chunk of data can be written all at once. This improves the efficiency of the system.

For example, disk files are organized by sectors, which might be anywhere from 128 bytes long, on up. Output is usually buffered until an entire sector can be written all at once. However, if you want to cause data to be written to the physical device, whether the buffer is full or not, you can call **Flush( )**, shown here:

void Flush( )

An **IOException** is thrown on failure. If the stream was closed at the time of the call, **ObjectDisposedException** is thrown.

Once you are done with an output file, you must remember to close it using **Close( )**. Doing so ensures that any output remaining in a disk buffer is actually written to the disk. It is not necessary to call **Flush( )** before closing a file.

The following example copies a file. The names of the source and destination files are specified on the command line.

```
/*
   Copy a file.

   To use this program, specify the name
   of the source file and the destination file.
   For example, to copy a file called FIRST.TXT
   to a file called SECOND.TXT, use the following
   command line.

   CopyFile FIRST.TXT SECOND.TXT
*/

using System;
using System.IO;

class CopyFile {
  static void Main(string[] args) {
    int i;
    FileStream fin;
    FileStream fout;

    if(args.Length != 2) {
      Console.WriteLine("Usage: CopyFile From To");
      return;
    }

    // Open input file.
    try {
      fin = new FileStream(args[0], FileMode.Open);
    } catch(IOException exc) {
      Console.WriteLine(exc.Message);
      return;
    }
```

```
      // Open output file.
      try {
        fout = new FileStream(args[1], FileMode.Create);
      } catch(IOException exc) {
        Console.WriteLine(exc.Message);
        fin.Close();
        return;
      }

      // Copy the file.
      try {
        do {
          i = fin.ReadByte();
          if(i != -1) fout.WriteByte((byte)i);
        } while(i != -1);
      } catch(IOException exc) {
        Console.WriteLine(exc.Message);
      }

      fin.Close();
      fout.Close();
    }
}
```

Read bytes from one file and write them to another.

Character-Based File I/O

Although byte-oriented file handling is quite common, it is possible to use character-based streams for this purpose. The advantage to the character streams is that they operate directly on Unicode characters. Thus, if you want to store Unicode text, the character streams are certainly your best option. In general, to perform character-based file operations, you will wrap a **FileStream** inside either a **StreamReader** or a **StreamWriter**. These classes automatically convert a byte stream into a character stream, and vice versa.

Remember, at the operating system level, a file consists of a set of bytes. Using a **StreamReader** or **StreamWriter** does not alter this fact.

StreamWriter is derived from **TextWriter**. **StreamReader** is derived from **TextReader**. Thus, **StreamWriter** and **StreamReader** have access to the methods and properties defined by their base classes.

Using StreamWriter

To create a character-based output stream, wrap a **Stream** object (such as a **FileStream**) inside a **StreamWriter**. **StreamWriter** defines several constructors. One of its most popular is shown here:

StreamWriter(Stream *stream*)

Here, *stream* is the name of an open stream. This constructor throws an **ArgumentException** if the specified stream is not opened for output and an **ArgumentNullException** if *stream* is null. Once created, a **StreamWriter** automatically handles the conversion of characters to bytes.

Here is a simple key-to-disk utility that reads lines of text entered at the keyboard and writes them to a file called **test.txt**. Text is read until the user enters the word "stop." The utility uses a **FileStream** wrapped in a **StreamWriter** to output to the file.

```
// A simple key-to-disk utility that demonstrates a StreamWriter.
using System;
using System.IO;

class KtoD {
  static void Main() {
    string str;
    FileStream fout;

    try {
      fout = new FileStream("test.txt", FileMode.Create);
    }
    catch(IOException exc) {
      Console.WriteLine(exc.Message);
      return ;
    }
    StreamWriter fstr_out = new StreamWriter(fout);   ◄───── Create a
                                                             StreamWriter.
    Console.WriteLine("Enter text ('stop' to quit).");
    do {
      Console.Write(": ");
      str = Console.ReadLine();

      if(str != "stop") {
        str = str + "\r\n"; // add newline
        try {
          fstr_out.Write(str);  ◄───────────── Write strings to the file.
        } catch(IOException exc) {
            Console.WriteLine(exc.Message);
            break;
        }
      }
    } while(str != "stop");

    fstr_out.Close();
  }
}
```

In some cases, you can open a file directly using **StreamWriter**. To do so, use one of these constructors:

StreamWriter(string *filename*)

StreamWriter(string *filename*, bool *appendFlag*)

Here, *filename* specifies the name of the file to open, which can include a full path specifier. In the second form, if *appendFlag* is true, then output is appended to the end of an existing file. Otherwise, output overwrites the specified file. In both cases, if the file does not exist, it is created. Also, both throw an **IOException** if an I/O error occurs. Other exceptions are also possible.

Here is the key-to-disk program rewritten so that it uses **StreamWriter** to open the output file:

```
// Open a file using StreamWriter.
using System;
using System.IO;

class KtoD {
  static void Main() {
    string str;
    StreamWriter fstr_out;

    try {
      fstr_out = new StreamWriter("test.txt");   // Open a file using only
    }                                            //   StreamWriter.
    catch(IOException exc) {
      Console.WriteLine(exc.Message);
      return ;
    }

    Console.WriteLine("Enter text ('stop' to quit).");
    do {
      Console.Write(": ");
      str = Console.ReadLine();

      if(str != "stop") {
        str = str + "\r\n"; // add newline
        try {
          fstr_out.Write(str);
        } catch(IOException exc) {
          Console.WriteLine(exc.Message);
          break;
        }
      }
    } while(str != "stop");

    fstr_out.Close();
  }
}
```

Using a StreamReader

To create a character-based input stream, wrap a byte stream inside a **StreamReader**. **StreamReader** defines several constructors. A frequently used one is shown here:

StreamReader(Stream *stream*)

Here, *stream* is the name of an open stream. This constructor throws an **ArgumentNullException** if *stream* is null and an **ArgumentException** if the stream is not opened for input. Once created, a **StreamReader** will automatically handle the conversion of bytes to characters.

The following program uses **StreamReader** to create a simple disk-to-screen utility that reads line-by-line a text file called **test.txt** and displays its contents on the screen. Thus, it is the complement of the key-to-disk utility shown in the previous section.

```
// A simple disk-to-screen utility that demonstrates a FileReader.

using System;
using System.IO;

class DtoS {
  static void Main() {
    FileStream fin;
    string s;

    try {
      fin = new FileStream("test.txt", FileMode.Open);
    }
    catch(IOException exc) {
      Console.WriteLine(exc.Message);
      return ;
    }

    StreamReader fstr_in = new StreamReader(fin);

    try {
      while((s = fstr_in.ReadLine()) != null) {
        Console.WriteLine(s);
      }
    } catch(IOException exc) {
      Console.WriteLine(exc.Message);
    }

    fstr_in.Close();
  }
}
```

Read lines from the file and display them on the screen.

Notice how the end of the file is determined. When the reference returned by **ReadLine( )** is null, the end of the file has been reached.

As with **StreamWriter**, in some cases, you can open a file directly using **StreamReader**. To do so, use this constructor:

StreamReader(string *filename*)

Here, *filename* specifies the name of the file to open, which can include a full path specifier. The file must exist. If it doesn't, a **FileNotFoundException** is thrown. If *filename* is null, then an **ArgumentNullException** is thrown. If *filename* is an empty string, **ArgumentException** is thrown. **IOException** and **DirectoryNotFoundException** are also possible.

Ask the Expert

Q: I have heard that I can specify a "character encoding" when opening a StreamReader or StreamWriter. What is a character encoding and when should I use one?

A: **StreamReader** and **StreamWriter** convert bytes to characters and vice versa based upon a *character encoding* that specifies how the translation occurs. By default, C# uses the UTF-8 encoding, which is compatible with ASCII. To specify another encoding, you will use overloaded versions of the **StreamReader** or **StreamWriter** constructors that include an encoding parameter. In general, you will need to specify a character encoding only under unusual circumstances.

Redirecting the Standard Streams

As mentioned earlier, the standard streams, such as **Console.In**, can be redirected. By far, the most common redirection is to a file. When a standard stream is redirected, input or output is automatically directed to the new stream, bypassing the default devices. By redirecting the standard streams, your program can read commands from a disk file, create log files, or even read input from a network connection.

Redirection of the standard streams can be accomplished in two ways. First, when you execute a program on the command line, you can use the < and > operators to redirect **Console.In** and **Console.Out**, respectively. For example, given this program:

```
using System;

class Test {
  static void Main() {
    Console.WriteLine("This is a test.");
  }
}
```

Executing the program like this:

Test > log

will cause the line "This is a test." to be written to a file called **log**. Input can be redirected in the same way. The thing to remember when input is redirected is that you must make sure that what you specify as an input source contains sufficient input to satisfy the demands of the program. If it doesn't, the program will hang.

The < and > command-line redirection operators are not part of C#, but are provided by the operating system. Thus, if your environment supports I/O redirection (as is the case with Windows), you can redirect standard input and standard output without making any changes to your program. However, there is a second way that you can redirect the standard streams that is under program control. To do so, you will use the **SetIn( )**, **SetOut( )**, and **SetError( )** methods, shown here, which are members of **Console**:

static void SetIn(TextReader *input*)

static void SetOut(TextWriter *output*)

static void SetError(TextWriter *output*)

Thus, to redirect input, call **SetIn( )**, specifying the desired stream. You can use any input stream as long as it is derived from **TextReader**. To redirect output, specify any stream derived from **TextWriter**. For example, to redirect output to a file, use a **StreamWriter**. The following program shows an example:

```
// Redirect Console.Out.

using System;
using System.IO;

class Redirect {
  static void Main() {
    StreamWriter log_out;

    try {
      log_out = new StreamWriter("logfile.txt");
    }
    catch(IOException exc) {
      Console.WriteLine(exc.Message);
      return ;
    }

    // Redirect standard out to logfile.txt.
    Console.SetOut(log_out);  ◄─────────────── Redirect Console.Out.

    try {
      Console.WriteLine("This is the start of the log file.");

      for(int i=0; i<10; i++) Console.WriteLine(i);

      Console.WriteLine("This is the end of the log file.");
```

```
    } catch(IOException exc) {
        Console.WriteLine(exc.Message);
    }

    log_out.Close();
  }
}
```

When you run this program, you won't see any output on the screen. However, the file **logfile.txt** will contain the following:

```
This is the start of the log file.
0
1
2
3
4
5
6
7
8
9
This is the end of the log file.
```

On your own, you might want to experiment with redirecting the other built-in streams.

Try This **Create a File Comparison Utility**

This example develops a simple, yet useful, file comparison utility. It works by opening both files to be compared and then reading and comparing each corresponding set of bytes. If a mismatch is found, the files differ. If the end of each file is reached at the same time and no mismatches have been found, then the files are the same.

Step by Step

1. Create a file called **CompFiles.cs**.

2. Into **CompFiles.cs**, add the following program:

```
/*
    Compare two files.

    To use this program, specify the names
    of the files to be compared on the command line.

    For example:
        CompFile FIRST.TXT SECOND.TXT
*/
```

```
using System;
using System.IO;

class CompFiles {
  static void Main(string[] args) {
    int i=0, j=0;
    FileStream f1;
    FileStream f2;

    if(args.Length != 2) {
      Console.WriteLine("Usage: CompFiles F1 F2");
      return;
    }

    // Open the first file.
    try {
      f1 = new FileStream(args[0], FileMode.Open);
    } catch(IOException exc) {
      Console.WriteLine(exc.Message);
      return;
    }

    // Open the second file.
    try {
      f2 = new FileStream(args[1], FileMode.Open);
    } catch(IOException exc) {
      Console.WriteLine(exc.Message);
      f1.Close();
      return;
    }

    // Compare the files.
    try {
      do {
        i = f1.ReadByte();
        j = f2.ReadByte();
        if(i != j) break;
      } while(i != -1 && j != -1);

      if(i != j)
        Console.WriteLine("Files differ.");
      else
        Console.WriteLine("Files are the same.");
    } catch(IOException exc) {
      Console.WriteLine(exc.Message);
    }
```

(continued)

```
        f1.Close();
        f2.Close();
    }
}
```

3. To try **CompFiles**, first copy **CompFiles.cs** to a file called **temp**. Then, try this command line:

CompFiles CompFiles.cs temp

4. The program will report that the files are the same. Next, compare **CompFiles.cs** to **CopyFile.cs** (shown earlier) using this command line:

CompFiles CompFiles.cs CopyFile.cs

These files differ, and **CompFiles** will report this fact.

5. On your own, try enhancing **CompFiles** with various options. For example, add an option that ignores the case of letters. Another idea is to have **CompFiles** display the position within the file where the files differ.

Reading and Writing Binary Data

So far, we have just been reading and writing bytes or characters, but it is possible—indeed, common—to read and write other types of data. For example, you might want to create a file that contains **int**s, **double**s, or **short**s. To read and write binary values of the C# built-in types, you will use **BinaryReader** and **BinaryWriter**. When using these streams, it is important to understand that this data is read and written using its internal, binary format, not its human-readable text form.

BinaryWriter

A **BinaryWriter** is a wrapper around a byte stream that manages the writing of binary data. Its most commonly used constructor is shown here:

BinaryWriter(Stream *outputStream*)

Here, *outputStream* is the stream to which data is written. To write output to a file, you can use the object created by **FileStream** for this parameter. If *outputStream* is null, then an **ArgumentNullException** is thrown. If *outputStream* has not been opened for writing, **ArgumentException** is thrown.

  BinaryWriter defines methods that can write all of C#'s built-in types. Several are shown in Table 11-5. **BinaryWriter** also defines the standard **Close( )** and **Flush( )** methods that work as described earlier.

Method	Description
void Write(sbyte *val*)	Writes a signed byte.
void Write(byte *val*)	Writes an unsigned byte.
void Write(byte[ ] *buf*)	Writes an array of bytes.
void Write(short *val*)	Writes a short integer.
void Write(ushort *val*)	Writes an unsigned short integer.
void Write(int *val*)	Writes an integer.
void Write(uint *val*)	Writes an unsigned integer.
void Write(long *val*)	Writes a long integer.
void Write(ulong *val*)	Writes an unsigned long integer.
void Write(float *val*)	Writes a **float**.
void Write(double *val*)	Writes a **double**.
void Write(char *val*)	Writes a character.
void Write(char[ ] *buf*)	Writes an array of characters.
void Write(string *val*)	Writes a string.

Table 11-5 Commonly Used Output Methods Defined by **BinaryWriter**

BinaryReader

A **BinaryReader** is a wrapper around a byte stream that handles the reading of binary data. Its most commonly used constructor is shown here:

BinaryReader(Stream *inputStream*)

Here, *inputStream* is the stream from which data is read. To read from a file, you can use the object created by **FileStream** for this parameter. If *inputStream* has not been opened for input or is otherwise invalid, an **ArgumentException** is thrown.

    BinaryReader provides methods for reading all of C#'s built-in types. The most commonly used are shown in Table 11-6. **BinaryReader** also defines three versions of **Read( )**, which are shown here:

int Read( )	Returns an integer representation of the next available character from the invoking input stream. Returns −1 when attempting to read at the end of the file.
int Read(byte[ ] *buf*, int *offset*, int *num*)	Attempts to read up to *num* bytes into *buf*, starting at *buf*[*offset*], and returns the number of bytes successfully read.
int Read(char[ ] *buf*, int *offset*, int *num*)	Attempts to read up to *num* characters into *buf*, starting at *buf*[*offset*], and returns the number of characters successfully read.

These methods will throw an **IOException** on failure. Other exceptions are also possible. Also defined is the standard **Close( )** method.

Method	Description
bool ReadBoolean( )	Reads a **bool**.
byte ReadByte( )	Reads a **byte**.
sbyte ReadSByte( )	Reads an **sbyte**.
byte[ ] ReadBytes(int *num*)	Reads *num* bytes and returns them as an array.
char ReadChar( )	Reads a **char**.
char[ ] ReadChars(int *num*)	Reads *num* characters and returns them as an array.
double ReadDouble( )	Reads a **double**.
float ReadSingle( )	Reads a **float**.
short ReadInt16( )	Reads a **short**.
int ReadInt32( )	Reads an **int**.
long ReadInt64( )	Reads a **long**.
ushort ReadUInt16( )	Reads a **ushort**.
uint ReadUInt32( )	Reads a **uint**.
ulong ReadUInt64( )	Reads a **ulong**.
string ReadString( )	Reads a string.

Table 11-6 Commonly Used Input Methods Defined by **BinaryReader**

Demonstrating Binary I/O

Here is a program that demonstrates **BinaryReader** and **BinaryWriter**. It writes and then reads back various types of data to and from a file.

```
// Write and then read back binary data.
using System;
using System.IO;

class RWData {
  static void Main() {
    BinaryWriter dataOut;
    BinaryReader dataIn;

    int i = 10;
    double d = 1023.56;
    bool b = true;

    try {
      dataOut = new
        BinaryWriter(new FileStream("testdata", FileMode.Create));
    }
```

```
  catch(IOException exc) {
    Console.WriteLine(exc.Message);
    return;
  }

  // Write data to a file.
  try {
    Console.WriteLine("Writing " + i);
    dataOut.Write(i);

    Console.WriteLine("Writing " + d);
    dataOut.Write(d);

    Console.WriteLine("Writing " + b);
    dataOut.Write(b);

    Console.WriteLine("Writing " + 12.2 * 7.4);
    dataOut.Write(12.2 * 7.4);
  }
  catch(IOException exc) {
    Console.WriteLine(exc.Message);
  }

  dataOut.Close();

  Console.WriteLine();

  // Now, read the data.
  try {
    dataIn = new
        BinaryReader(new FileStream("testdata", FileMode.Open));
  }
  catch(IOException exc) {
    Console.WriteLine(exc.Message);
    return;
  }

  try {
    i = dataIn.ReadInt32();
    Console.WriteLine("Reading " + i);

    d = dataIn.ReadDouble();
    Console.WriteLine("Reading " + d);

    b = dataIn.ReadBoolean();
    Console.WriteLine("Reading " + b);

    d = dataIn.ReadDouble();
    Console.WriteLine("Reading " + d);
  }
```

Write binary data.

Read binary data.

```
    catch(IOException exc) {
      Console.WriteLine(exc.Message);
    }

    dataIn.Close();
  }
}
```

The output from the program is shown here:

```
Writing 10
Writing 1023.56
Writing True
Writing 90.28

Reading 10
Reading 1023.56
Reading True
Reading 90.28
```

Random Access Files

Up to this point, we have been using *sequential files,* which are files that are accessed in a strictly linear fashion, one byte after another. However, you can also access the contents of a file in random order. To do this, you will use the **Seek( )** method defined by **FileStream**. This method allows you to set the *file position indicator* (also called the *file pointer*) to any point within a file.

The method **Seek( )** is shown here:

long Seek(long *newPos*, SeekOrigin *origin*)

Here, *newPos* specifies the new position, in bytes, of the file pointer from the location specified by *origin*. The origin will be one of these values, which are defined by the **SeekOrigin** enumeration:

Value	Meaning
Begin	Seek from the beginning of the file.
Current	Seek from the current location.
End	Seek from the end of the file.

After a call to **Seek( )**, the next read or write operation will occur at the new file position. If an error occurs while seeking, an **IOException** is thrown. If the underlying stream does not support position requests, a **NotSupportedException** is thrown. Other exceptions are possible.

Here is an example that demonstrates random access I/O. It writes the uppercase alphabet to a file and then reads it back in nonsequential order.

```csharp
// Demonstrate random access.
using System;
using System.IO;

class RandomAccessDemo {
  static void Main() {
    FileStream f;
    char ch;

    try {
      f = new FileStream("random.dat", FileMode.Create);
    }
    catch(IOException exc) {
      Console.WriteLine(exc.Message);
      return ;
    }

    // Write the alphabet.
    for(int i=0; i < 26; i++) {
      try {
        f.WriteByte((byte)('A'+i));
      }
      catch(IOException exc) {
        Console.WriteLine(exc.Message);
        f.Close();
        return ;
      }
    }

    try {
      // Now, read back specific values.
      f.Seek(0, SeekOrigin.Begin); // seek to first byte
      ch = (char) f.ReadByte();
      Console.WriteLine("First value is " + ch);

      f.Seek(1, SeekOrigin.Begin); // seek to second byte
      ch = (char) f.ReadByte();
      Console.WriteLine("Second value is " + ch);

      f.Seek(4, SeekOrigin.Begin); // seek to 5th byte
      ch = (char) f.ReadByte();
      Console.WriteLine("Fifth value is " + ch);

      Console.WriteLine();

      // Now, read every other value.
      Console.WriteLine("Here is every other value: ");
```

Use **Seek( )** to move the file pointer.

```
    for(int i=0; i < 26; i += 2) {
      f.Seek(i, SeekOrigin.Begin); // seek to ith character
      ch = (char) f.ReadByte();
      Console.Write(ch + " ");
    }
  }
  catch(IOException exc) {
    Console.WriteLine(exc.Message);
  }

  Console.WriteLine();
  f.Close();
  }
}
```

The output from the program is shown here:

```
First value is A
Second value is B
Fifth value is E

Here is every other value:
A C E G I K M O Q S U W Y
```

Converting Numeric Strings to Their Internal Representation

Before leaving the topic of I/O, we will examine a technique useful when reading numeric strings. As you know, **WriteLine( )** provides a convenient way to output various types of data to the console, including numeric values of the built-in types, such as **int** and **double**. Thus, **WriteLine( )** automatically converts numeric values into their human-readable form. However, there is no parallel input method that reads and converts strings containing numeric values into their internal, binary format. For example, there is no version of **Read( )** that reads from the keyboard a string such as "100" and then automatically converts it into its corresponding binary value that can be stored in an **int** variable. Instead, there are other ways to accomplish this task. Perhaps the easiest is to use a method that is defined for all of the built-in numeric types: **Parse( )**.

Before we begin, it is necessary to state an important fact: All of C#'s built-in types, such as **int** and **double**, are actually just aliases (that is, other names) for structures defined by the .NET Framework. In fact, the C# type and .NET structure type are indistinguishable. One is just another name for the other. Because C#'s value types are supported by structures, the value types have members defined for them.

For the C# numeric value types, the .NET structure names and their C# keyword equivalents are shown here:

.NET Structure Name	C# Name
Decimal	decimal
Double	double
Single	float
Int16	short
Int32	int
Int64	long
UInt16	ushort
UInt32	uint
UInt64	ulong
Byte	byte
SByte	sbyte

These structures are defined inside the **System** namespace. Thus, the fully qualified name for **Int32** is **System.Int32**. These structures offer a wide array of methods that help fully integrate the value types into C#'s object hierarchy. As a side benefit, the numeric structures also define static methods that convert a numeric string into its corresponding binary equivalent. These conversion methods are shown here. Each returns a binary value that corresponds to the string.

Structure	Conversion Method
Decimal	static decimal Parse(string *str*)
Double	static double Parse(string *str*)
Single	static float Parse(string *str*)
Int64	static long Parse(string *str*)
Int32	static int Parse(string *str*)
Int16	static short Parse(string *str*)
UInt64	static ulong Parse(string *str*)
UInt32	static uint Parse(string *str*)
UInt16	static ushort Parse(string *str*)
Byte	static byte Parse(string *str*)
SByte	static sbyte Parse(string *str*)

The **Parse( )** methods will throw a **FormatException** if *str* does not contain a valid number as defined by the invoking type. **ArgumentNullException** is thrown if *str* is null, and **OverflowException** is thrown if the value in *str* exceeds the bounds of the invoking type.

The parsing methods give you an easy way to convert a numeric value, read as a string from the keyboard or from a text file, into its proper internal format. For example, the following program averages a list of numbers entered by the user. It first asks the user for the number of values to be averaged. It then reads that number using **ReadLine( )** and uses **Int32.Parse( )** to convert the string into an integer. Next, it inputs the values, using **Double.Parse( )** to convert the strings into their **double** equivalents.

```
// This program averages a list of numbers entered by the user.
using System;
using System.IO;

class AvgNums {
  static void Main() {
    string str;
    int n;
    double sum = 0.0;
    double avg, t;

    Console.Write("How many numbers will you enter: ");
    str = Console.ReadLine();
    try {
      n = Int32.Parse(str);  ◄─────────── Convert a string to an int.
    } catch(FormatException exc) {
      Console.WriteLine(exc.Message);
      return;
    } catch(OverflowException exc) {
      Console.WriteLine(exc.Message);
      return;
    }

    Console.WriteLine("Enter " + n + " values.");
    for(int i=0; i < n ; i++)  {
      Console.Write(": ");
      str = Console.ReadLine();
      try {
        t = Double.Parse(str);  ◄─────────── Convert a string to a double.
      } catch(FormatException exc) {
        Console.WriteLine(exc.Message);
        t = 0.0;
      } catch(OverflowException exc) {
        Console.WriteLine(exc.Message);
        t = 0;
      }
      sum += t;
```

```
      }
      avg = sum / n;
      Console.WriteLine("Average is " + avg);
    }
}
```

Here is a sample run:

```
How many numbers will you enter: 5
Enter 5 values.
: 1.1
: 2.2
: 3.3
: 4.4
: 5.5
Average is 3.3
```

You can put the **Parse( )** methods to good use by improving the loan payment calculator developed in Chapter 2. In that version, the loan principal, interest, and so on were "hard-coded" into the program. The program would be much more useful if the user were prompted for these values. Here is an improved version of the loan calculator that does this:

```
// Compute the regular payments for a loan, improved.

using System;

class RegPay {
  static void Main() {
    decimal Principal;     // original principal
    decimal IntRate;       // interest rate as a decimal, such as 0.075
    decimal PayPerYear;    // number of payments per year
    decimal NumYears;      // number of years
    decimal Payment;       // the regular payment
    decimal numer, denom;  // temporary work variables
    double b, e;           // base and exponent for call to Pow()

    string str;

    try {
      Console.Write("Enter principal: ");
      str = Console.ReadLine();
      Principal = Decimal.Parse(str);

      Console.Write("Enter interest rate (such as 0.085): ");
      str = Console.ReadLine();

      IntRate = Decimal.Parse(str);
```

```
    Console.Write("Enter number of years: ");
    str = Console.ReadLine();
    NumYears = Decimal.Parse(str);

    Console.Write("Enter number of payments per year: ");
    str = Console.ReadLine();
    PayPerYear = Decimal.Parse(str);
  } catch(FormatException exc) {
    Console.WriteLine(exc.Message);
    return;
  } catch(OverflowException exc) {
    Console.WriteLine(exc.Message);
    return;
  }

  numer = IntRate * Principal / PayPerYear;

  e = (double) -(PayPerYear * NumYears);
  b = (double) (IntRate / PayPerYear) + 1;

  denom = 1 - (decimal) Math.Pow(b, e);

  Payment = numer / denom;

  Console.WriteLine("Payment is {0:C}", Payment);
  }
}
```

A sample run is shown here:

```
Enter principal: 10000
Enter interest rate (0.085): 0.075
Enter number of years: 5
Enter number of payments per year: 12
Payment is $200.38
```

Ask the Expert

Q: What else can the numeric value-type structures, such as Int32 or Double, do?

A: The numeric value-type structures provide a number of methods that help integrate the C# built-in types into the object hierarchy. For example, all of the structures have methods called **CompareTo( )**, which compare the values contained within the wrapper; **Equals( )**, which tests two values for equality; and methods that return the value of the object in various forms. The numeric structures also include the fields **MinValue** and **MaxValue**, which contain the minimum and maximum values that can be stored by an object of its type.

Try This Create a Disk-Based Help System

In the Try This section in Chapter 4, you created a **Help** class that displayed information about C#'s control statements. In that implementation, the help information was stored within the class itself, and the user selected help from a menu of numbered options. Although this approach was fully functional, it is certainly not the ideal way of creating a Help system. For example, to add to or change the help information, the source code of the program must be modified. Also, the selection of the topic by number rather than by name is tedious and not suitable for long lists of topics. Here, we will remedy these shortcomings by creating a disk-based Help system.

The disk-based Help system stores help information in a help file. The help file is a standard text file, which can be changed or expanded at will, without changing the Help program. The user obtains help about a topic by typing in its name. The Help system searches the help file for the topic. If it is found, information about the topic is displayed.

Step by Step

1. You must create the help file that will be used by the Help system. The help file is a standard text file that is organized like this:

   ```
   #topic-name1
   topic info

   #topic-name2
   topic info

        .
        .
        .

   #topic-nameN
   topic info
   ```

   The name of each topic must be preceded by a #, and the topic name must be on a line of its own. By preceding each topic name with a #, it allows the program to quickly find the start of each topic. After the topic name is any number of information lines about the topic. However, there must be a blank line between the end of one topic's information and the start of the next topic. Also, there *must be no trailing spaces* at the end of any lines.

   Here is a simple help file that you can use to try the disk-based Help system. It stores information about C#'s control statements.

   ```
   #if
   if(condition) statement;
   else statement;
   ```

   (continued)

```
#switch
switch(expression) {
  case constant:
    statement sequence
    break;
    // ...
  }

#for
for(init; condition; iteration) statement;

#while
while(condition) statement;

#do
do {
  statement;
} while (condition);

#break
break; or break label;

#continue
continue; or continue label;

#goto
goto label;
```

Call this file **helpfile.txt**.

2. Create a file called **FileHelp.cs**.

3. Begin creating the new **Help** class with these lines of code:

```
class Help {
  string helpfile; // name of help file

  public Help(string fname) {
    helpfile = fname;
  }
```

The name of the help file is passed to the **Help** constructor and stored in the instance variable **helpfile**. Since each instance of **Help** will have its own copy of **helpfile**, each instance can use a different file. Thus, you can create different sets of help files for different sets of topics.

4. Add the **HelpOn( )** method shown here to the **Help** class. This method retrieves help on the specified topic.

```
// Display help on a topic.
public bool HelpOn(string what) {
  StreamReader helpRdr;
  int ch;
  string topic, info;

  try {
    helpRdr = new StreamReader(helpfile);
  }
  catch(IOException exc) {
    Console.WriteLine(exc.Message);
    return false;
  }

  try {
    do {
      // Read characters until a # is found.
      ch = helpRdr.Read();

      // Now, see if topics match.
      if(ch == '#') {
        topic = helpRdr.ReadLine();
        if(what == topic) { // found topic
          do {
            info = helpRdr.ReadLine();
            if(info != null) Console.WriteLine(info);
          } while((info != null) && (info != ""));
          helpRdr.Close();
          return true;
        }
      }
    } while(ch != -1);
  }
  catch(IOException exc) {
    Console.WriteLine(exc.Message);
  }
  helpRdr.Close();
  return false; // topic not found
}
```

The help file is opened using a **StreamReader**. Since the help file contains text, using a character stream allows the Help system to be more efficiently internationalized.

The **HelpOn( )** method works like this: A string containing the name of the topic is passed in the **what** parameter. The help file is then opened. Then, the file is searched, looking for a match between **what** and a topic in the file. Remember, in the file, each topic is preceded by a #, so the search loop scans the file for #s. When it finds one, it then checks to see if the topic following that # matches the one passed in **what**. If it does, the information associated with that topic is displayed. If a match is found, **HelpOn( )** returns **true**. Otherwise, it returns **false**.

(continued)

5. The Help class also provides a method called **GetSelection( )**, shown next. It prompts the user for a topic and returns the topic string entered by the user.

```
// Get a Help topic.
public string GetSelection() {
  string topic = "";

  Console.Write("Enter topic: ");
  topic = Console.ReadLine();
  return topic;
}
```

6. The entire disk-based Help system is shown here:

```
// A help program that uses a disk file to store help information.

using System;
using System.IO;

/* The Help class opens a help file,
   searches for a topic, and then displays
   the information associated with that topic. */
class Help {
  string helpfile; // name of help file

  public Help(string fname) {
    helpfile = fname;
  }

  // Display help on a topic.
  public bool HelpOn(string what) {
    StreamReader helpRdr;
    int ch;
    string topic, info;

    try {
      helpRdr = new StreamReader(helpfile);
    }
    catch(IOException exc) {
      Console.WriteLine(exc.Message);
      return false;
    }

    try {
      do {
        // Read characters until a # is found.
        ch = helpRdr.Read();

        // Now, see if topics match.
        if(ch == '#') {
```

```
        topic = helpRdr.ReadLine();
        if(what == topic) { // found topic
          do {
            info = helpRdr.ReadLine();
            if(info != null) Console.WriteLine(info);
          } while((info != null) && (info != ""));
          helpRdr.Close();
          return true;
        }
      }
    } while(ch != -1);
  }
  catch(IOException exc) {
    Console.WriteLine(exc.Message);
  }
  helpRdr.Close();
  return false; // topic not found
}

// Get a Help topic.
public string GetSelection() {
  string topic = "";

  Console.Write("Enter topic: ");
  topic = Console.ReadLine();
  return topic;
}
}

// Demonstrate the file-based Help system.
class FileHelp {
  static void Main() {
    Help hlpobj = new Help("helpfile.txt");
    string topic;

    Console.WriteLine("Try the help system. " +
                      "Enter 'stop' to end.");
    for(;;) {
      topic = hlpobj.GetSelection();

      if(topic == "stop") break;

      if(!hlpobj.HelpOn(topic))
        Console.WriteLine("Topic not found.\n");

    }
  }
}
```

Ask the Expert

Q: Earlier in this chapter, you mentioned the stream class MemoryStream, **which uses memory for storage. How can this stream be used?**

A: **MemoryStream** is an implementation of **Stream** that uses an array of bytes for input or output. Here is one of the constructors that it defines:

MemoryStream(byte[ ] *buf*)

Here, *buf* is an array of bytes that will be used for the source or target of I/O requests. It must be large enough to hold whatever output you will be directing to it. The stream created by this constructor can be written or read, and supports **Seek( )**.

Memory-based streams are quite useful in programming. For example, you can construct complicated output in advance, storing it in the array until it is needed. This technique is especially useful when programming for a GUI environment, such as Windows. You can also redirect a standard stream to read from an array. This might be useful for feeding test information into a program, for example.

One last point: To create a memory-based character stream, use **StringReader** or **StringWriter**.

Chapter 11 Self Test

1. Why does C# define both byte and character streams?

2. What class is at the top of the stream hierarchy?

3. Show how to open a file for reading bytes.

4. Show how to open a file for reading characters.

5. What does **Seek( )** do?

6. What classes support binary I/O for the built-in types?

7. What methods are used to redirect the standard streams under program control?

8. How do you convert a numeric string such as "123.23" into its binary equivalent?

9. Write a program that copies a text file. In the process, have it convert all spaces into hyphens. Use the byte stream file classes.

10. Rewrite the program in question 9 so that it uses the character stream classes.

Chapter 12

Delegates, Events, and Namespaces

Key Skills & Concepts

- Delegates
- Use instance methods with delegates
- Multicast delegates
- Anonymous methods
- Events
- Use anonymous methods with events
- Multicast events
- Namespaces
- The **using** directive
- Add namespaces
- Nest namespaces

The preceding eleven chapters have introduced what might be described as the core of C#. They covered foundational topics, such as data types, control statements, classes, methods, and objects. They also discussed several key concepts, such as inheritance, interfaces, structures, indexers, properties, overloading, exceptions, and I/O. At this point in your study, you can begin to write useful programs. However, there is much more to C#. The remainder of this book introduces some of the most sophisticated, or (in some cases) the most advanced, features of C#. Now is a good time to pause and review. You will want to be on a solid footing before continuing.

This chapter examines three important C# topics: delegates, events, and namespaces. Delegates are, essentially, objects that can refer to executable code. Events are built on delegates. An event is a notification that some action occurred. Namespaces help organize your code. Collectively, these features add greatly to the expressive power of C# and are used extensively in commercial code.

NOTE

This and the remaining chapters of this book introduce some of the most sophisticated and powerful features in C# programming. Several of these features support options and techniques that are beyond the scope of this beginner's guide. As you progress in your knowledge of C#, you will want to learn more about these features. One good place to start is my book *C# 3.0: The Complete Reference*.

Delegates

Newcomers to C# are sometimes intimidated by the delegate, but there is nothing to fear. Delegates are no more difficult to understand or use than any other C# feature, as long as you bear in mind precisely what a delegate is. Simply put, a *delegate* is an object that can refer to a method. Thus, when you create a delegate, you are creating an object that can hold a reference to a method. Furthermore, the method can be called through this reference. Thus, a delegate can invoke the method to which it refers.

Once a delegate refers to a method, the method can be called through that delegate. Furthermore, the same delegate can be used to call a different method by simply changing the method to which the delegate refers. The principal advantage of a delegate is that it allows you to specify a call to a method, but the method actually invoked is determined at runtime, not at compile time.

NOTE

If you are familiar with C/C++, it will help to know that a delegate in C# is similar to a function pointer in C/C++.

A delegate type is declared using the keyword **delegate**. The general form of a delegate declaration is shown here:

delegate *ret-type name*(*parameter-list*);

Here, *ret-type* is the type of value returned by the methods that the delegate will be calling. The name of the delegate is specified by *name*. The parameters required by the methods called through the delegate are specified in the *parameter-list*. Once created, a delegate instance can refer to and call only methods whose return type and parameter list match those specified by the delegate declaration.

A key point to understand is that a delegate can be used to call *any* method that agrees with its signature and return type. Furthermore, the method can be specified at runtime by simply assigning to the delegate a reference to a compatible method. The method invoked can be an instance method associated with an object or a static method associated with a class. All that matters is that the signature and return type of the method agree with that of the delegate.

To see delegates in action, let's begin with the simple example shown here:

```
// A simple delegate example.
using System;

// Declare a delegate.
delegate string StrMod(string str);              A delegate called StrMod.

class DelegateTest {
  // Replaces spaces with hyphens.
  static string ReplaceSpaces(string a) {
```

```
      Console.WriteLine("Replaces spaces with hyphens.");
      return a.Replace(' ', '-');
    }

    // Remove spaces.
    static string RemoveSpaces(string a) {
      string temp = "";
      int i;

      Console.WriteLine("Removing spaces.");
      for(i=0; i < a.Length; i++)
        if(a[i] != ' ') temp += a[i];

      return temp;
    }

    // Reverse a string.
    static string Reverse(string a) {
      string temp = "";
      int i, j;

      Console.WriteLine("Reversing string.");
      for(j=0, i=a.Length-1; i >= 0; i--, j++)
        temp += a[i];

      return temp;
    }

    static void Main() {
      // Construct a delegate.
      StrMod strOp = ReplaceSpaces;          ◄──────────  Construct a delegate instance.
      string str;

      // Call methods through the delegate.
      str = strOp("This is a test.");        ◄──────────  Call a method through a delegate.
      Console.WriteLine("Resulting string: " + str);
      Console.WriteLine();

      strOp = RemoveSpaces;
      str = strOp("This is a test.");
      Console.WriteLine("Resulting string: " + str);
      Console.WriteLine();

      strOp = Reverse;
      str = strOp("This is a test.");
      Console.WriteLine("Resulting string: " + str);
    }
}
```

The output from the program is shown here:

```
Replaces spaces with hyphens.
Resulting string: This-is-a-test.

Removing spaces.
Resulting string: Thisisatest.

Reversing string.
Resulting string: .tset a si sihT
```

Let's examine this program closely. The program declares a delegate called **StrMod** that takes one **string** parameter and returns a **string**. In **DelegateTest**, three static methods are declared, each with a matching signature. These methods perform some type of string modification. Notice that **ReplaceSpaces( )** uses one of **string**'s methods, called **Replace( )**, to replace spaces with hyphens.

In **Main( )**, a **StrMod** reference called **strOp** is created and assigned a reference to **ReplaceSpaces( )**. Pay close attention to this line:

```
StrMod strOp = ReplaceSpaces;
```

Notice how the method **ReplaceSpaces( )** is assigned to **strOp**. Only its name is used; no parameters are specified. This syntax can be generalized to any situation in which a method is assigned to a delegate. This syntax works because C# automatically provides a conversion from the method to the delegate type. This is called a *method group conversion* and is a feature that was added by C# 2.0. This conversion is really just shorthand for this longer form:

```
StrMod strOp = new StrMod(ReplaceSpaces);
```

In this form, a new delegate is explicitly instantiated using **new**. Although you will still find this longer form in use in some code, the previous approach is far simpler and is more widely used. With either approach, the method's signature must match that of the delegate's declaration. If it doesn't, a compile-time error will result.

Next, **ReplaceSpaces( )** is called through the delegate instance **strOp**, as shown here:

```
str = strOp("This is a test.");
```

Because **strOp** refers to **ReplaceSpaces( )**, it is **ReplaceSpaces( )** that is invoked.

Next, **strOp** is assigned a reference to **RemoveSpaces( )**, and then **strOp** is called again. This time, **RemoveSpaces( )** is invoked.

Finally, **strOp** is assigned a reference to **Reverse( )** and **strOp** is called. This results in **Reverse( )** being called.

The key point of the example is that the invocation of **strOp** results in a call to the method referred to by **strOp** at the time at which the invocation occurred. Thus, the method to call is resolved at runtime, not at compile time.

Use Instance Methods as Delegates

Although the preceding example used static methods, a delegate can also refer to instance methods. It must do so, however, through an object reference. For example, here is a rewrite of the previous example, which encapsulates the string operations inside a class called **StringOps**:

```
// Delegates can refer to instance methods, too.
using System;

// Declare a delegate type.
delegate string StrMod(string str);

class StringOps {
  // Replaces spaces with hyphens.
  public string ReplaceSpaces(string a) {
    Console.WriteLine("Replaces spaces with hyphens.");
    return a.Replace(' ', '-');
  }

  // Remove spaces.
  public string RemoveSpaces(string a) {
    string temp = "";
    int i;

    Console.WriteLine("Removing spaces.");
    for(i=0; i < a.Length; i++)
      if(a[i] != ' ') temp += a[i];

    return temp;
  }

  // Reverse a string.
  public string Reverse(string a) {
    string temp = "";
    int i, j;

    Console.WriteLine("Reversing string.");
    for(j=0, i=a.Length-1; i >= 0; i--, j++)
      temp += a[i];

    return temp;
  }
}

class DelegateTest {
  static void Main() {
    StringOps so = new StringOps();
```

```
    // Construct a delegate.
    StrMod strOp = so.ReplaceSpaces;          Create a delegate using
    string str;                               an instance method.

    // Call methods through a delegate.
    str = strOp("This is a test.");
    Console.WriteLine("Resulting string: " + str);
    Console.WriteLine();

    strOp = so.RemoveSpaces;
    str = strOp("This is a test.");
    Console.WriteLine("Resulting string: " + str);
    Console.WriteLine();

    strOp = so.Reverse;
    str = strOp("This is a test.");
    Console.WriteLine("Resulting string: " + str);
  }
}
```

This program produces the same output as the first, but in this case, the delegate refers to methods on an instance of **StringOps**.

Multicasting

One of the most exciting features of a delegate is its support for *multicasting*. In simple terms, multicasting is the ability to create a chain of methods that will be called automatically when a delegate is invoked. Such a chain is very easy to create. Simply instantiate a delegate, and then use the **+** or **+=** operator to add methods to the chain. To remove a method, use **–** or **– =**. If the delegate returns a value, then the value returned by the last method in the list becomes the return value of the entire delegate invocation. For this reason, a delegate that will make use of multicasting will often have a **void** return type.

Here is an example of multicasting. It reworks the preceding examples by changing the string manipulation methods' return type to **void** and using a **ref** parameter to return the altered string to the caller.

```
    // Demonstrate multicasting.
    using System;

    // Declare a delegate type.
    delegate void StrMod(ref string str);

    class StringOps {
      // Replaces spaces with hyphens.
      static void ReplaceSpaces(ref string a) {
        Console.WriteLine("Replaces spaces with hyphens.");
        a = a.Replace(' ', '-');
      }
```

```
// Remove spaces.
static void RemoveSpaces(ref string a) {
  string temp = "";
  int i;

  Console.WriteLine("Removing spaces.");
  for(i=0; i < a.Length; i++)
    if(a[i] != ' ') temp += a[i];

  a = temp;
}

// Reverse a string.
static void Reverse(ref string a) {
  string temp = "";
  int i, j;

  Console.WriteLine("Reversing string.");
  for(j=0, i=a.Length-1; i >= 0; i--, j++)
    temp += a[i];

  a = temp;
}

static void Main() {
  // Construct a delegate.
  StrMod strOp;
  StrMod replaceSp = ReplaceSpaces;
  StrMod removeSp = RemoveSpaces;
  StrMod reverseStr = Reverse;
  string str = "This is a test";

  // Set up the multicast.
  strOp = replaceSp;
  strOp += reverseStr;          ◄───────────────────── Create a multicast.

  // Invoke multicast.
  strOp(ref str);
  Console.WriteLine("Resulting string: " + str);
  Console.WriteLine();

  // Remove replaceSp and add removeSp.
  strOp -= replaceSp;           ◄───────────────────── Create a different multicast.
  strOp += removeSp;

  str = "This is a test."; // reset string
```

```
        // Invoke multicast.
        strOp(ref str);
        Console.WriteLine("Resulting string: " + str);
        Console.WriteLine();
    }
}
```

Here is the output:

```
Replaces spaces with hyphens.
Reversing string.
Resulting string: tset-a-si-sihT

Reversing string.
Removing spaces.
Resulting string: .tsetasisihT
```

In **Main( )**, four delegate instances are created. One, **strOp**, is null. The other three refer to specific string modification methods. Next, a multicast is created that calls **ReplaceSpaces( )** and **Reverse( )**. This is accomplished via the following lines:

```
strOp = replaceSp;
strOp += reverseStr;
```

First, **strOp** is assigned a reference to **replaceSp**. Next, using **+=**, **reverseStr** is added. When **strOp** is invoked, both methods are invoked, replacing spaces with hyphens and reversing the string, as the output illustrates.

Next, **replaceSp** is removed from the chain using this line:

```
strOp -= replaceSp;
```

and **removeSp** is added using this line:

```
strOp += removeSp;
```

Then, **StrOp** is again invoked. This time, spaces are removed and the string is reversed.

Why Delegates

Although the preceding examples show the "how" behind delegates, they don't really illustrate the "why." In general, delegates are useful for two main reasons. First, as you will soon see, delegates support events. Second, delegates give your program a way to execute methods at runtime without having to specify what that method is at compile time. This ability is quite useful when you want to create a framework that allows components to be plugged in. For example, imagine a drawing program (a bit like the standard Windows Paint accessory). Using a delegate, you could allow the user to plug in special color filters or image analyzers. Furthermore, the user could create a sequence of these filters or analyzers. Such a scheme would be easily handled using a delegate.

Anonymous Methods

When working with delegates, you will often find that the method referred to by a delegate is used only for that purpose. In other words, the only reason for the method is so that it can be invoked via a delegate. The method is never called on its own. In such a case, you can avoid the need to create a separate method by the use of an *anonymous method*. An anonymous method is, essentially, a block of code that is passed to a delegate constructor. One advantage to using an anonymous method is simplicity. There is no need to declare a separate method whose only purpose is to be passed to a delegate.

Before continuing, an important point needs to be made. C# 3.0 adds a new feature, the lambda expression, that (in many cases) improves on the concept of the anonymous method. A discussion of lambda expressions is found in Chapter 14. Although lambda expressions are often a better option, they are not applicable to all situations. Also, anonymous methods are widely used in existing C# code. Therefore, it is still important that you understand how they work and see them in action.

Here is a simple example that uses an anonymous method:

```
// Demonstrate an anonymous method.
using System;

// Declare a delegate.
delegate void CountIt();

class AnonMethDemo {

  static void Main() {

    // Here, the code for counting is passed
    // as an anonymous method.
    CountIt count = delegate {
      // This is the block of code passed to the delegate.
      for(int i=0; i <= 5; i++)
        Console.Write(i + " ");
    }; // notice the semicolon

    count();
    Console.WriteLine();
  }
}
```

An anonymous method.

The output from the program is shown here:

```
0 1 2 3 4 5
```

This program first declares a delegate type called **CountIt** that has no parameters and returns **void**. Inside **Main( )**, a **CountIt** delegate called **count** is created, and it is passed the block of code that follows the **delegate** keyword. This block of code is the anonymous method that will be executed when **count** is called. Notice that the block of code is followed by a semicolon, which terminates the declaration statement.

It is possible to pass one or more arguments to an anonymous method. To do so, follow the **delegate** keyword with a parenthesized parameter list. Then, pass the argument(s) to the delegate instance when it is called. For example, here is the preceding program rewritten so that the ending value for the count is passed:

```
// Demonstrate an anonymous method that takes an argument.
using System;

// Notice that CountIt now has a parameter.
delegate void CountIt(int end);

class AnonMethDemo2 {

  static void Main() {

    // Here, the ending value for the count
    // is passed to the anonymous method.
    CountIt count = delegate (int end) {       ◄———————  Use a parameter with
      for(int i=0; i <= end; i++)                          an anonymous method.
        Console.Write(i + " ");
    };

    count(3);
    Console.WriteLine();
    count(5);
    Console.WriteLine();
  }
}
```

In this version, **CountIt** now takes an integer argument. Notice how the parameter list is specified after the **delegate** keyword when the anonymous method is created. In this case, the only parameter is **end**, which is an **int**. The code inside the anonymous method has access to the parameter **end** in just the same way it would if a "normal" method were being created. The output from this program is shown here.

```
0 1 2 3
0 1 2 3 4 5
```

As you can see, the value of the argument to **count( )** is received by **end**, and this value is used as the stopping point for the count.

An anonymous method can return a value. The value is returned by use of the **return** statement, which works the same in an anonymous method as it does in a named method. As you would expect, the type of the return value must be compatible with the return type specified by the delegate.

The following example demonstrates an anonymous method that returns a value. It changes the countdown code so that it returns the summation of the count.

```
// Demonstrate an anonymous method that returns a value.
using System;

// This delegate returns a value.
delegate int CountIt(int end);

class AnonMethDemo3 {

  static void Main() {
    int result;

    // Here, the ending value for the count
    // is passed to the anonymous method.
    // A summation of the count is returned.
    CountIt count = delegate (int end) {
      int sum = 0;

      for(int i=0; i <= end; i++) {
        Console.Write(i + " ");
        sum += i;
      }
      return sum; // return a value from an anonymous method
    };

    result = count(3);
    Console.WriteLine("\nSummation of 3 is " + result);
    Console.WriteLine();

    result = count(5);
    Console.WriteLine("\nSummation of 5 is " + result);
    Console.WriteLine();
  }
}
```

———— An anonymous method can return a value.

In this version, the value of **sum** is returned by the code block that is associated with the **count** delegate instance. Notice that the return statement is used in the anonymous method in just the same way that it is used in a "normal" method. The output is shown here:

```
0 1 2 3
Summation of 3 is 6

0 1 2 3 4 5
Summation of 5 is 15
```

Perhaps the most important use of anonymous methods is with events. As you will see later in this chapter, often an anonymous method is the most efficient means of coding an event handler.

Ask the Expert

Q: I have heard the term *outer variables* used in a discussion of anonymous methods. To what does it refer?

A: A local variable or parameter whose scope includes an anonymous method is called an *outer variable.* An anonymous method has access to and can use these outer variables. When an outer variable is used by an anonymous method, that variable is said to be *captured.* A captured variable will stay in existence at least until the delegate that captured it is subject to garbage collection. Thus, even though a local variable will normally cease to exist when its block is exited, if that local variable is being used by an anonymous method, then that variable will stay in existence at least until the delegate referring to that method is destroyed.

Events

Another important C# feature is the *event.* An event is, essentially, an automatic notification that some action has occurred. Events are widely used in real-world code because they are used to represent things such as keystrokes, mouse clicks, repaint requests, and incoming data. Events are built upon the foundation of the delegate. Thus, an understanding of delegates is required to use events.

Events work like this: An object that has an interest in an event registers an event handler for that event. When the event occurs, all registered handlers are called. Event handlers are represented by delegates. The event handler responds to the event by taking appropriate action. For example, an event handler for keystrokes might respond by echoing the character to the screen. As a general rule, an event should respond quickly and then return. It should not maintain control of the CPU for an extended period of time. Because events are normally used to handle real-time activities, an event that dominates the CPU may negatively impact the overall performance and responsiveness of the program.

Events are members of a class and are declared using the **event** keyword. Its general form is shown here:

event *event-delegate event-name*;

Here, *event-delegate* is the name of the delegate used to support the event, and *event-name* is the name of the specific event being declared.

Let's begin with a very simple example:

```
// A very simple event demonstration.
using System;

// Declare a delegate type for an event.
delegate void MyEventHandler();            ◄——————————— Create a delegate for the event.

// Declare a class that contains an event.
class MyEvent {
  public event MyEventHandler SomeEvent;   ◄——————— Declare an event.

  // This is called to fire the event.
  public void Fire() {
    if(SomeEvent != null)
      SomeEvent();                         ◄——————————————— Fire the event.
  }
}

class EventDemo {
  static void Handler() {                  ◄——————————— An event handler.
    Console.WriteLine("Event occurred");
  }

  static void Main() {
    MyEvent evt = new MyEvent();           ◄——————————— Create event instance.

    // Add Handler() to the event list.
    evt.SomeEvent += Handler;              ◄——————————— Add handler to the event chain.

    // Fire the event.
    evt.Fire();                            ◄——————————— Generate the event.
  }
}
```

This program displays the following output:

```
Event occurred
```

Although simple, this program contains all the elements essential to proper event handling. Let's look at it carefully.

The program begins by declaring a delegate type for the event handler, as shown here:

```
delegate void MyEventHandler();
```

All events are activated through a delegate. Thus, the event delegate type defines the return type and signature for the event. In this case, there are no parameters, but event parameters are allowed.

Next, an event class, called **MyEvent**, is created. Inside the class, an event called **SomeEvent** is declared, using this line:

```
public event MyEventHandler SomeEvent;
```

Notice the syntax. The keyword **event** tells the compiler than an event is being declared.

Also declared inside **MyEvent** is the method **Fire( )**, which is the method that a program will call to signal (or "fire") an event. It calls an event handler through the **SomeEvent** delegate, as shown here:

```
if(SomeEvent != null)
  SomeEvent();
```

Notice that a handler is called if and only if **SomeEvent** is not **null**. Since other parts of your program must register an interest in an event in order to receive event notifications, it is possible that **Fire( )** could be called before any event handler has been registered. To prevent calling on a **null** reference, the event delegate must be tested to ensure that it is not **null**.

Inside **EventDemo**, an event handler called **Handler( )** is created. In this simple example, the event handler just displays a message, but handlers usually perform more meaningful actions. In **Main( )**, a **MyEvent** object is created and **Handler( )** is registered as a handler for this event, as shown here:

```
MyEvent evt = new MyEvent();

// Add Handler() to the event list.
evt.SomeEvent += Handler;
```

Notice that the handler is added using the **+=** operator. Events support only **+=** and **– =** for adding or removing handlers.

Finally, the event is fired, as shown here:

```
// Fire the event.
evt.Fire();
```

Calling **Fire( )** causes all registered event handlers to be called. In this case, there is only one registered handler, but there could be more, as the next section explains.

A Multicast Event Example

Events can be multicast. This enables multiple objects to respond to an event notification. Here is an event multicast example:

```
// An event multicast demonstration.
using System;

// Declare a delegate type for an event.
delegate void MyEventHandler();
```

```csharp
// Declare a class that contains an event.
class MyEvent {
  public event MyEventHandler SomeEvent;

  // This is called to fire the event.
  public void Fire() {
    if(SomeEvent != null)
      SomeEvent();
  }
}

class X {
  public void Xhandler() {
    Console.WriteLine("Event received by X object");
  }
}

class Y {
  public void Yhandler() {
    Console.WriteLine("Event received by Y object");
  }
}

class EventDemo {
  static void Handler() {
    Console.WriteLine("Event received by EventDemo");
  }

  static void Main() {
    MyEvent evt = new MyEvent();
    X xOb = new X();
    Y yOb = new Y();

    // Add the handlers to the event list.
    evt.SomeEvent += Handler;
    evt.SomeEvent += xOb.Xhandler;     ◄──────  Create a multicast chain for the event.
    evt.SomeEvent += yOb.Yhandler;

    // Fire the event.
    evt.Fire();
    Console.WriteLine();

    // Remove a handler.
    evt.SomeEvent -= xOb.Xhandler;
    Console.WriteLine("After removing xOb.Xhandler");
    evt.Fire();
  }
}
```

The output from the program is shown here:

```
Event received by EventDemo
Event received by X object
Event received by Y object

After removing xOb.Xhandler
Event received by EventDemo
Event received by Y object
```

This example creates two additional classes, called **X** and **Y**, which also define event handlers compatible with **MyEventHandler**. Thus, these handlers can also become part of the event chain. Notice that the handlers in **X** and **Y** are not static. This means that objects of each must be created, and the handler linked to an object instance is added to the event chain. When the event is fired, those handlers in the event chain are called. Therefore, if the contents of the event chain change, different handlers are called. This is illustrated by the program when it removes **xOb.Xhandler**.

Understand that events are sent to specific object instances, not generically to a class. Thus, each object of a class must register to receive an event notification. For example, the following program multicasts an event to three objects of type **X**:

```
// Objects, not classes, receive events.
using System;

// Declare a delegate type for an event.
delegate void MyEventHandler();

// Declare a class that contains an event.
class MyEvent {
  public event MyEventHandler SomeEvent;

  // This is called to fire the event.
  public void Fire() {
    if(SomeEvent != null)
      SomeEvent();
  }
}

class X {
  int id;

  public X(int x) { id = x; }

  public void Xhandler() {
    Console.WriteLine("Event received by object " + id);
  }
}
```

```
class EventDemo {
  static void Main() {
    MyEvent evt = new MyEvent();
    X o1 = new X(1);
    X o2 = new X(2);
    X o3 = new X(3);

    evt.SomeEvent += o1.Xhandler;
    evt.SomeEvent += o2.Xhandler;
    evt.SomeEvent += o3.Xhandler;

    // Fire the event.
    evt.Fire();
  }
}
```

Each object that wants to receive an event must add its own handler to the chain.

The output from this program is shown here:

```
Event received by object 1
Event received by object 2
Event received by object 3
```

As the output shows, each object registers its interest in an event separately, and each receives a separate notification.

Use Anonymous Methods with Events

Anonymous methods are especially useful when working with events because an anonymous method can serve as an event handler. This eliminates the need to declare a separate method, which can significantly streamline event-handling code. Here is an example that uses an anonymous event handler:

```
// Use an anonymous method as an event handler.
using System;

// Declare a delegate type for an event.
delegate void MyEventHandler();

// Declare a class that contains an event.
class MyEvent {
  public event MyEventHandler SomeEvent;

  // This is called to fire the event.
  public void Fire() {
    if(SomeEvent != null)
      SomeEvent();
  }
}

class AnonMethHandler {
  static void Main() {
    MyEvent evt = new MyEvent();
```

```
      // Use an anonymous method as an event handler.
   evt.SomeEvent += delegate {
     // This is the event handler.
     Console.WriteLine("Event received.");
   };

      // Fire the event twice.
   evt.Fire();
   evt.Fire();
  }
}
```

An anonymous method used as an event handler.

The output is shown here.

```
Event received.
Event received.
```

In the program, pay special attention to the way the anonymous event handler is added to the event by the following code sequence:

```
// Use an anonymous method as an event handler.
evt.SomeEvent += delegate {
  // This is the event handler.
  Console.WriteLine("Event received.");
};
```

The syntax for using an anonymous event handler is the same as that for using an anonymous method with any other type of delegate.

Anonymous event handlers are especially useful, because often, the event handler is not called by any code other than the event handling mechanism. Thus, there is usually no reason for a stand-alone method. As mentioned earlier in this chapter, C# 3.0 adds lambda expressions, which improve on the concept of the anonymous method. In many cases, lambda expressions will offer the best way to implement an event handler (see Chapter 14).

Ask the Expert

Q: Are there any special techniques that I must use to create events and event handlers that are compatible with the types of events used by the .NET Framework?

A: Yes. Although C# allows you to write any type of event that you desire, for component compatibility with the .NET Framework, you must follow Microsoft's guidelines in this regard. At the core of these guidelines is the requirement that event handlers have two parameters. The first is a reference to the object that generated the event. The second is a parameter of type **EventArgs** that contains any other information required by the handler. For simple events in which the **EventArgs** parameter is unused, the delegate type can be **EventHandler**. This is a predefined type that can be used to declare events that provide no extra information. Consult Microsoft's guidelines for details. Also, information on writing events compatible with the .NET Framework is found in my book *C# 3.0: The Complete Reference*.

Namespaces

The namespace was mentioned briefly in Chapter 1 because it is a concept fundamental to C#. In fact, every C# program makes use of a namespace in one way or another. We have not needed to examine the namespace in detail prior to now because C# automatically provides a default "global" namespace for your program.

Let's begin by reviewing what you already know about namespaces. A *namespace* defines a declarative region that provides a way to keep one set of names separate from another. Names declared in one namespace will not conflict with the same names declared in another. The namespace used by the .NET Framework library (which is the C# library) is **System**. This is why you have included

```
using System;
```

near the top of every program. As you saw in Chapter 11, the I/O classes are defined within a namespace subordinate to **System** called **System.IO**. There are many other namespaces subordinate to **System** that hold other parts of the C# library.

Namespaces are important because there has been an explosion of variable, method, property, and class names over the past few years. These include library routines, third-party code, and your own code. Without namespaces, all of these names would compete for slots in the global namespace and conflicts would arise. For example, if your program defined a class called **Finder**, it could conflict with another class called **Finder** supplied by a third-party library that your program uses. Fortunately, namespaces prevent this type of problem because a namespace restricts the visibility of names declared within it.

Declare a Namespace

A namespace is declared using the **namespace** keyword. The general form of **namespace** is shown here:

```
namespace name {
  // members
}
```

Here, *name* is the name of the namespace. A namespace declaration defines a scope. Anything declared immediately inside the namespace is in scope throughout the namespace. Within a namespace, you can declare classes, structures, delegates, enumerations, interfaces, or another namespace.

Here is an example of a **namespace** that creates a namespace called **Counter**. It localizes the name used to implement a simple countdown counter class called **CountDown**.

```
// Declare a namespace for counters.
namespace Counter {                           Declare the Counter namespace.

  // A simple countdown counter.
  class CountDown {
    int val;
```

```
  public CountDown(int n) { val = n; }

  public void Reset(int n) {
    val = n;
  }

  public int Count() {
    if(val > 0) return val--;
    else return 0;
  }
}
```

```
} // This marks the end of the Counter namespace.
```

Here, the class **CountDown** is declared within the scope defined by the **Counter** namespace. To follow along with the example, put this code into a file called **Counter.cs**.

Here is a program that demonstrates the use of the **Counter** namespace:

```
// Demonstrate the Counter namespace.
using System;

class NSDemo {
  static void Main() {
    Counter.CountDown cd1 = new Counter.CountDown(10);   ◄─────┐
    int i;                                                     │

    do {                                          Here, Counter qualifies
      i = cd1.Count();                            CountDown.
      Console.Write(i + " ");
    } while(i > 0);
    Console.WriteLine();

    Counter.CountDown cd2 = new Counter.CountDown(20);

    do {
      i = cd2.Count();
      Console.Write(i + " ");
    } while(i > 0);
    Console.WriteLine();

    cd2.Reset(4);
    do {
      i = cd2.Count();
      Console.Write(i + " ");
    } while(i > 0);
    Console.WriteLine();
  }
}
```

To compile this program, you must include both the preceding code and the code contained in the **Counter** namespace. Assuming that you called the preceding code **NSDemo.cs** and put the source code for the **Counter** namespace into a file called **Counter.cs**, as mentioned earlier, then you can use this command line to compile the program.

```
csc NSDemo.cs Counter.cs
```

When run, the program produces the following result:

```
10 9 8 7 6 5 4 3 2 1 0
20 19 18 17 16 15 14 13 12 11 10 9 8 7 6 5 4 3 2 1 0
4 3 2 1 0
```

Some important aspects of this program warrant close examination. First, since **CountDown** is declared within the **Counter** namespace, when an object is created, **CountDown** must be qualified with **Counter**, as shown here:

```
Counter.CountDown cd1 = new Counter.CountDown(10);
```

This rule can be generalized. Whenever you use a member of a namespace, you must qualify it with the namespace name. If you don't, the member of the namespace won't be found by the compiler.

Second, once an object of type **Counter** has been created, it is not necessary to further qualify it or any of its members with the namespace. Thus, **cd1.Count( )** can be called directly without namespace qualification, as this line shows:

```
i = cd1.Count();
```

Third, although this example used two separate files, one to hold the **Counter** namespace and the other to hold the **NSDemo** program, both could have been contained in the same file. When a named namespace ends, the outer namespace resumes, which in this case, is the global namespace. Furthermore, a single file can contain two or more named namespaces. This situation is similar to the way that a file can contain two or more separate classes. Each namespace defines its own declarative region.

using

As explained in Chapter 1, if your program includes frequent references to the members of a namespace, having to specify the namespace each time you need to refer to one quickly becomes tedious. The **using** directive alleviates this problem. Throughout this book, you have been using **using** to bring the **System** namespace into view, so you are already familiar with it. As you would expect, **using** can also be used to bring namespaces that you create into view.

There are two forms of the **using** directive. The first is shown here:

using *name*;

Here, *name* specifies the name of the namespace you want to access. This is the form of **using** that you have already seen. All of the members defined within the specified namespace are brought into view and can be used without qualification. A **using** directive must be specified at the top of each file, prior to any other declarations, or at the start of a namespace body.

The following program reworks the counter example from the previous section to show how you can employ **using** to bring a namespace that you create into view:

```
// Demonstrate a namespace.
using System;

// Bring Counter into view.
using Counter;                                              using brings Counter into view.

class NSDemo {
  static void Main() {
    // now, CountDown can be used directly.
    CountDown cd1 = new CountDown(10);                   Refer to CountDown directly.
    int i;

    do {
      i = cd1.Count();
      Console.Write(i + " ");
    } while(i > 0);
    Console.WriteLine();

    CountDown cd2 = new CountDown(20);

    do {
      i = cd2.Count();
      Console.Write(i + " ");
    } while(i > 0);
    Console.WriteLine();

    cd2.Reset(4);
    do {
      i = cd2.Count();
      Console.Write(i + " ");
    } while(i > 0);
    Console.WriteLine();
  }
}
```

As before, to compile this program, you must include both the preceding code and the code contained in the **Counter** namespace.

The program illustrates one other important point: Using one namespace does not override another. When you bring a namespace into view, it simply lets you use its names without qualification. Thus, in the example, both **System** and **Counter** have been brought into view.

A Second Form of using

The **using** directive has a second form which creates another name, called an alias, for a namespace or a type. This form is shown here:

using *alias* = *name*;

Here, *alias* becomes another name for the type (such as a class type) or namespace specified by *name*. Once the alias has been created, it can be used in place of the original name.

The counting program is reworked once again here so that an alias for **Counter .CountDown** called **MyCounter** is created.

```
// Demonstrate a using alias.
using System;

// Create an alias for Counter.CountDown.
using MyCounter = Counter.CountDown;              Create an alias for
                                                  Counter.CountDown.

class NSDemo {
  static void Main() {
    MyCounter cd1 = new MyCounter(10);            Use the alias.
    int i;

    do {
      i = cd1.Count();
      Console.Write(i + " ");
    } while(i > 0);
    Console.WriteLine();

    MyCounter cd2 = new MyCounter(20);

    do {
      i = cd2.Count();
      Console.Write(i + " ");
    } while(i > 0);
    Console.WriteLine();

    cd2.Reset(4);
    do {
      i = cd2.Count();
      Console.Write(i + " ");
    } while(i > 0);
    Console.WriteLine();
  }
}
```

In this case, **MyCounter** is an alias for the type **Counter.CountDown**. Once **MyCounter** has been specified as an alias, it can be used to declare objects without any further namespace qualification. For example, in the program, this line

```
MyCounter cd1 = new MyCounter(10);
```

creates a **CountDown** object.

Namespaces Are Additive

There can be more than one namespace declaration of the same name. This allows a namespace to be split over several files or even separated within the same file. For example, the following code also specifies the **Counter** namespace. It adds a class called **CountUp**, which counts up, rather than down.

```
// Here is another part of the Counter namespace.
namespace Counter {                                          Add to the Counter namespace.
  // A simple count-up counter.
  class CountUp {
    int val;
    int target;

    public int Target { get{ return target; } }

    public CountUp(int n) { target = n; val = 0; }

    public void Reset(int n) {
      target = n;
      val = 0;
    }

    public int Count() {
      if(val < target) return val++;
      else return target;
    }
  }
}
```

To follow along, put this code into a file called **Counter2.cs**.

The following program demonstrates the additive effect of namespaces by using both **CountDown** and **CountUp**:

```
// Namespaces are additive.
using System;

// Bring the entire Counter namespace into view.
using Counter;
```

```
class NSDemo {
  static void Main() {
    CountDown cd = new CountDown(10);
    CountUp cu = new CountUp(8);
    int i;

    do {
      i = cd.Count();
      Console.Write(i + " ");
    } while(i > 0);
    Console.WriteLine();

    do {
      i = cu.Count();
      Console.Write(i + " ");
    } while(i < cu.Target);

  }
}
```

To compile this program, you must include the preceding code and both files that contain the **Counter** namespace. Assuming that you called the preceding code **NSDemo.cs** and that the **Counter** namespace files are called **Counter.cs** and **Counter2.cs**, you can use this command line to compile the program:

```
csc NSDemo.cs Counter.cs Counter2.cs
```

This program produces the following output:

```
10 9 8 7 6 5 4 3 2 1 0
0 1 2 3 4 5 6 7 8
```

Notice one other thing: the directive

```
using Counter;
```

brings into view the entire contents of the **Counter** namespace. Thus, both **CountDown** and **CountUp** can be referred to directly, without namespace qualification. It doesn't matter that the **Counter** namespace was split into two parts.

Namespaces Can Be Nested

One namespace can be nested within another. When referring to a nested namespace from code outside the nested namespaces, both the outer namespace and the inner namespace must be specified, with the two separated by a period. To understand the process, consider this program:

```
// Namespaces can be nested.
using System;
```

```
namespace NS1 {
  class ClassA {
    public ClassA() {
      Console.WriteLine("constructing ClassA");
    }
  }
  namespace NS2 { // a nested namespace          ◄——————————— Nest NS2 inside NS1.
    class ClassB {
      public ClassB() {
        Console.WriteLine("constructing ClassB");
      }
    }
  }
}

class NestedNSDemo {
  static void Main() {
    NS1.ClassA a= new NS1.ClassA();

 // NS2.ClassB b = new NS2.ClassB(); // Error!!! NS2 is not in view

    NS1.NS2.ClassB b = new NS1.NS2.ClassB(); // this is right
  }
}
```

This program produces the following output:

```
constructing ClassA
constructing ClassB
```

In the program, the namespace **NS2** is nested within **NS1**. Thus, to refer to **ClassB** from code that is outside both **NS1** and **NS2**, you must qualify it with both the **NS1** and **NS2** names. **NS2** by itself is insufficient. As explained, the namespace names are separated by a period. Therefore, to refer to **ClassB** within **Main( )**, you must use **NS1.NS2.ClassB**.

Namespaces can be nested by more than two levels. When this is the case, a member in a nested namespace must be qualified with all of the enclosing namespace names.

You can specify a nested namespace using a single **namespace** statement by separating each namespace with a period. For example:

```
namespace OuterNS {
  namespace InnerNS {
    // ...
  }
}
```

can also be specified like this:

```
namespace OuterNS.InnerNS {
  // ...
}
```

The Global Namespace

If you don't declare a namespace for your program, the default global namespace is used. This is why you have not needed to use **namespace** for the programs in the preceding chapters. While the global namespace is convenient for the short, sample programs found in this book, most real-world code will be contained within a declared namespace. The main reason for encapsulating your code within a declared namespace is that it prevents name conflicts. Namespaces are another tool that you have to help you organize programs and make them viable in today's complex, networked environment.

Ask the Expert

Q: I was reading through the C# documentation that came with Visual C# Express Edition and I saw a feature called a namespace alias qualifier. What is this?

A: Although namespaces help prevent name conflicts, they do not completely eliminate them. One way that a conflict can still occur is when the same name is declared within two different namespaces, and you then try to bring both namespaces into view. For example, assume that you have two namespaces: one called **Alpha** and one called **Beta**. Further assume that each contains a class called **MyClass**. If you attempt to bring these two namespaces into view via **using** statements, **MyClass** in the **Alpha** namespace will conflict with **MyClass** in the **Beta** namespace, causing an ambiguity error. In this situation, you can use the **::** *namespace alias qualifier* to explicitly specify which namespace is intended.

The :: operator has this general form:

namespace-alias::*identifier*

Here, *namespace-alias* is the name of a namespace alias and *identifier* is the name of a member of that namespace. For example, assuming the namespaces **Alpha** and **Beta** just described, the following **using** statement creates an alias called **alpha** for the **Alpha** namespace:

```
using alpha = Alpha;
```

After this statement has been compiled, the following refers to the version of **MyClass** within the **Alpha** namespace, not the one within the **Beta** namespace:

```
alpha::MyClass
```

Thus, the namespace alias qualifier disambiguated the situation.

One last point: You can use the **::** qualifier to refer to the global namespace by using the predefined identifier **global**, as in

```
global::Test
```

Try This Put Set into a Namespace

In *Try This: Create a Set Class* in Chapter 7, you created a class that implemented a set type called **Set**. This is precisely the type of class that you should consider putting into its own namespace. One reason for this is that the name **Set** could easily conflict with other classes of the same name. By putting **Set** into its own namespace, you can avoid potential name conflicts. This example shows the process.

Step by Step

1. Using the code from **SetDemo.cs** shown in Chapter 7, move the entire **Set** class into a file called **Set.cs**. In the process, enclose the **Set** code inside the namespace **MyTypes**, as shown here:

```
// Put the Set class into its own namespace.
using System;

namespace MyTypes {
  class Set {
    char[] members; // this array holds the set

    // An auto-implemented, read-only Length property.
    public int Length { get; private set; }

    // Construct a null set.
    public Set() {
      Length = 0;
    }

    // Construct an empty set of a given size.
    public Set(int size) {
      members = new char[size]; // allocate memory for set
      Length = 0; // no members when constructed
    }

    // Construct a set from another set.
    public Set(Set s) {
      members = new char[s.Length]; // allocate memory for set
      for(int i=0; i < s.Length; i++) members[i] = s[i];
      Length = s.Length; // number of members
    }

    // Implement read-only indexer.
    public char this[int idx]{
      get {
```

(continued)

```
    if(idx >= 0 & idx < Length) return members[idx];
    else return (char)0;
  }
}

/* See if an element is in the set.
   Return the index of the element or -1 if not found. */
int find(char ch) {
  int i;

  for(i=0; i < Length; i++)
    if(members[i] == ch) return i;

  return -1;
}

// Add a unique element to a set.
public static Set operator +(Set ob, char ch) {

  // If ch is already in the set, return a copy of the
  // original set.
  if(ob.find(ch) != -1) {

    // Return a copy of the original set.
    return new Set(ob);

  } else { // Return a new set that contains the new element.

    // Make the new set one element larger than the original.
    Set newset = new Set(ob.Length+1);

    // Copy elements into the new set.
    for(int i=0; i < ob.Length; i++)
      newset.members[i] = ob.members[i];

    // Set the Length property.
    newset.Length = ob.Length+1;

    // Add new element to new set.
    newset.members[newset.Length-1] = ch;

    return newset; // return the new set
  }
}
```

```
// Remove an element from the set.
public static Set operator -(Set ob, char ch) {
  Set newset = new Set();
  int i = ob.find(ch); // i will be -1 if element not found

  // Copy and compress the remaining elements.
  for(int j=0; j < ob.Length; j++)
    if(j != i) newset = newset + ob.members[j];

  return newset;
}

// Set union.
public static Set operator +(Set ob1, Set ob2) {
  Set newset = new Set(ob1); // copy the first set

  // Add unique elements from second set.
  for(int i=0; i < ob2.Length; i++)
    newset = newset + ob2[i];

  return newset; // return updated set
}

// Set difference.
public static Set operator -(Set ob1, Set ob2) {
  Set newset = new Set(ob1); // copy the first set

  // Subtract elements from second set
  for(int i=0; i < ob2.Length; i++)
    newset = newset - ob2[i];

  return newset; // return updated set
  }
 }
} // The end of MyTypes namespace.
```

2. After putting **Set** into the **MyTypes** namespace, you will need to include the **MyTypes** namespace in any program that uses **Set**, as shown here:

```
using MyTypes;
```

3. Alternatively, you can fully qualify references to **Set**, as shown in this example:

```
MyTypes.Set s1 = new MyTypes.Set();
```

Chapter 12 Self Test

1. Show how to declare a delegate called **Filter** that returns a **double** and takes one **int** argument.

2. How is multicasting accomplished using a delegate?

3. What is an anonymous method?

4. Can an anonymous method have parameters? Can it return a value?

5. How are delegates and events related?

6. What keyword declares an event?

7. Can an event be multicast?

8. Is an event sent to an instance or to a class?

9. What is the main benefit of namespaces?

10. Show the alias form of **using**.

11. Show another way to declare this namespace:

```
namespace X {
  namespace Y {
    // ...
  }
}
```

Chapter 13

Generics

Key Skills & Concepts

- Generics fundamentals
- The base class constraint
- The interface constraint
- The constructor constraint
- The reference type constraint
- The value type constraint
- The **default** operator
- Generic structures
- Generic methods
- Generic delegates
- Generic interfaces

An extremely important event occurred in the lifecycle of C# when version 2.0 was released. This was the addition of *generics*. Not only did generics add a new syntactic element to C#, it also resulted in many changes and upgrades to the .NET library. Although it has been a few years since generics were added, its effects still reverberate throughout C# 3.0. Generics have become an indispensable part of C# programming.

The generics feature makes it possible to create classes, interfaces, methods, and delegates that work in a type-safe manner with various kinds of data. As you may know, many algorithms are logically the same, no matter what type of data they are being applied to. For example, the mechanism that supports a queue is the same whether the queue is storing items of type **int**, **string**, **object**, or a user-defined class. Prior to generics, you might have created several different versions of the same algorithm to handle different types of data. Through the use of generics, you can define a solution once, independently of any specific type of data, and then apply that solution to a wide variety of data types without any additional effort.

Before beginning, it is necessary to state that the generics feature is one of C#'s most sophisticated and, at times, most complicated. Furthermore, the topic of generics is quite large. It is not possible in this beginner's guide to detail all aspects of this powerful subsystem. Instead, this chapter introduces the theory behind generics, describes its syntax, and then shows several examples that put it into action. After completing this chapter, you will be able to begin writing your own generic code and make use of the generic features in the .NET library. You will also have the knowledge needed to move on to its more advanced features.

What Are Generics?

At its core, the term *generics* means *parameterized types.* Parameterized types are important because they enable you to create classes, structures, interfaces, methods, and delegates in which the type of data upon which they operate is specified as a parameter. Using generics, it is possible to create a single class, for example, that automatically works with different types of data. A class, structure, interface, method, or delegate that operates on a parameterized type is called *generic,* as in *generic class* or *generic method.*

It is important to understand that C# has always given you the ability to create generalized classes, structures, interfaces, methods, and delegates by operating through references of type **object**. Because **object** is the base class of all other types, an **object** reference can refer to any type of object. Thus, in pre-generics code, generalized code used **object** references to operate on a variety of different kinds of objects. The problem was that it could not do so with type safety because casts were needed to convert between the **object** type and the actual type of the data. Generics add the type safety that was lacking because it is no longer necessary to employ a cast to translate between **object** and the actual data type. This streamlines your code. It also expands your ability to reuse code.

Generics Fundamentals

Although the generics feature can be applied to several C# constructs, its primary use is to create a generic class. Thus, it is there that we will begin our discussion. Let's start with a simple example. The following program defines two classes. The first is the generic class **MyGenClass**, and the second is **GenericsDemo**, which uses **MyGenClass**.

```
// A simple generic class.
using System;

// Here, MyGenClass is a generic class that has one type
// parameter called T. T will be replaced by a real type
// when a MyGenClass object is constructed.
class MyGenClass<T> {                              ──────── Declare a generic class.
  T ob; // declare a variable of type T ◄─┐

  // Notice that this constructor has a parameter │ of type T.
  public MyGenClass(T o) { ◄─────────────┤
    ob = o;                              │──── Notice the use of the
  }                                      │     T type parameter.
                                         │
  // Return ob, which is of type T.      │
  public T GetOb() { ◄───────────────────┘
    return ob;
  }
}
```

```
// Demonstrate the generic class.
class GenericsDemo {
  static void Main() {
    // Declare a MyGenClass reference for int.
    MyGenClass<int> iOb;

    // Create a MyGenClass<int> object.
    iOb = new MyGenClass<int>(88);

    // Get the value in iOb.
    int v = iOb.GetOb();
    Console.WriteLine("iOb is an instance of MyGenClass<int>.\n" +
                "The value returned by GetOb(): " + v + "\n");

    // Create a MyGenClass object for strings.
    MyGenClass<string> strOb = new MyGenClass<string>("Generics Demo");

    // Get the value in strOb.
    string str = strOb.GetOb();
    Console.WriteLine("strOb is an instance of MyGenClass<string>.\n" +
                "The value returned by GetOb(): " + str + "\n");
  }
}
```

Create a **MyGenClass** reference, passing **int** to **T**.

Create a **MyGenClass** object, again passing **int** to **T**.

Create a **MyGenClass** reference and object that uses **string**.

The output produced by the program is shown here:

```
iOb is an instance of MyGenClass<int>.
The value returned by GetOb(): 88

strOb is an instance of MyGenClass<string>.
The value returned by GetOb(): Generics Demo
```

Let's examine this program carefully. First, notice how **MyGenClass** is declared by the following line:

```
class MyGenClass<T> {
```

Here, **T** is the name of a *type parameter*. This name is used as a placeholder for the actual type that will be specified when a **MyGenClass** object is created. Thus, **T** is used within **MyGenClass** whenever the type parameter is needed. Notice that **T** is contained within < >. This syntax can be generalized. Whenever a type parameter is being declared, it is specified within angle brackets. Because **MyGenClass** uses a type parameter, **MyGenClass** is a *generic class*.

In the declaration of **MyGenClass**, there is no special significance to the name **T**. Any valid identifier could have been used, but **T** is traditional. Other commonly used type parameter names include **V** and **E**. Of course, you can also use descriptive names for type parameters, such as **TValue** or **TKey**. When using a descriptive name, it is common practice to use **T** as the first letter.

Next, **T** is used to declare a variable called **ob**, as shown here:

```
T ob; // declare a variable of type T
```

As explained, **T** is a placeholder for the actual type that will be specified when a **MyGenClass** object is created. Thus, **ob** will be a variable of the type *bound to* **T** when a **MyGenClass** object is instantiated. For example, if type **string** is specified for **T**, then in that instance, **ob** will be of type **string**.

Now consider **MyGenClass**'s constructor.

```
public MyGenClass(T o) {
  ob = o;
}
```

Notice that its parameter, **o**, is of type **T**. This means that the actual type of **o** is determined by the type to which **T** is bound when a **MyGenClass** object is created. Also, because both the parameter **o** and the instance variable **ob** are of type **T**, they will both be of the same actual type when a **MyGenClass** object is created.

The type parameter **T** can also be used to specify the return type of a method, as is the case with the **GetOb( )** method, shown here:

```
public T GetOb() {
  return ob;
}
```

Because **ob** is also of type **T**, its type is compatible with the return type specified by **GetOb( )**.

The **GenericsDemo** class demonstrates the generic **MyGenClass** class. It first creates a version of **MyGenClass** for type **int**, as shown here:

```
MyGenClass<int> iOb;
```

Look closely at this declaration. First, notice that the type **int** is specified within the angle brackets after **MyGenClass**. In this case, **int** is a *type argument* that is bound to **MyGenClass**'s type parameter, **T**. This creates a version of **MyGenClass** in which all uses of **T** are replaced by **int**. Thus, for this declaration, **ob** is of type **int**, and the return type of **GetOb( )** is of type **int**.

When you specify a type argument such as **int** or **string** for **MyGenClass**, you are creating what is referred to in C# as a *closed constructed type*. Thus, **MyGenClass<int>** is a closed constructed type. In essence, a generic type, such as **MyGenClass<T>**, is an abstraction. It is only after a specific version, such as **MyGenClass<int>**, has been constructed that a concrete type has been created. In C# terminology, a construct such as **MyGenClass<T>** is called an *open constructed type*, because **T** (rather than an actual type such as **int**) is specified.

The next line assigns to **iOb** a reference to an instance of an **int** version of the **MyGenClass** class.

```
iOb = new MyGenClass<int>(88);
```

Notice that when the **MyGenClass** constructor is called, the type argument **int** is also specified. This is necessary because the type of the variable (in this case, **iOb**) to which the reference is being assigned is of type **MyGenClass<int>**. Thus, the reference returned by **new** must also be of type **MyGenClass<int>**. If it isn't, a compile-time error will result. For example, the following assignment will cause a compile-time error.

```
iOb = new MyGenClass<byte>(16); // Error! Wrong Type!
```

Because **iOb** is of type **MyGenClass<int>**, it can't be used to refer to an object of **MyGenClass<byte>**. This type-checking is one of the main benefits of generics because it ensures type safety.

Next, the program obtains the value of **ob** by use of the following line:

```
int v = iOb.GetOb();
```

Because the return type of **GetOb( )** is **T**, which was replaced by **int** when **iOb** was declared, the return type of this call to **GetOb( )** is also **int**. Thus, this value can be assigned to an **int** variable.

Next, **GenericsDemo** declares an object of type **MyGenClass<string>**.

```
MyGenClass<string> strOb = new MyGenClass<string>("Generics Demo.");
```

Because the type argument is **string**, **string** is substituted for **T** inside **MyGenClass**. This creates a **string** version of **MyGenClass**, as the remaining lines in the program demonstrate.

Generic Types Differ Based on Their Type Arguments

A key point to understand about generic types is that a reference of one specific version of a generic type is not type-compatible with another version of the same generic type. For example, assuming the program just shown, the following line of code is in error and will not compile.

```
iOb = strOb; // Wrong!
```

Even though both **iOb** and **strOb** are of type **MyGenClass<T>**, they are references to different types because their type arguments differ.

Generics Improve Type Safety

At this point, you might be asking yourself the following question. Given that the same functionality found in the generic **MyGenClass** class can be achieved without generics, by simply specifying **object** as the data type and employing the proper casts, what is the benefit of making **MyGenClass** generic? The answer is that generics automatically ensure the type safety of all operations involving **MyGenClass**. In the process, generics eliminate the need for you to use casts and to type-check code by hand.

To understand the benefits of generics, first consider the following program that creates a non-generic equivalent of **MyGenClass** called **NotGeneric**:

```
// NotGeneric is functionally equivalent to MyGenClass but does
// not use generics.
using System;
```

```
class NotGeneric {
  object ob; // ob is now of type object ◄─────── Use an object reference.

  // Pass the constructor a reference of type object.
  public NotGeneric(object o) {
    ob = o;
  }

  // Return type object.
  public object GetOb() {
    return ob;
  }
}

// Demonstrate the non-generic class.
class NonGenDemo {
  static void Main() {
    NotGeneric iOb;

    // Create NotGeneric object.
    iOb = new NotGeneric(88);

    // Get the value in iOb.
    // This time, a cast is necessary.
    int v = (int) iOb.GetOb(); ◄─────── Cast needed.
    Console.WriteLine("iOb is an instance of NotGeneric.\n" +
                      "Therefore, the value returned by GetOb() " +
                      "is object.\nIt must be cast to int: " +
                      v + "\n");

    // Create another NotGeneric object and store a string in it.
    NotGeneric strOb = new NotGeneric("Non-Generic class");

    // Get the value of strOb.
    // Again, notice that a cast is necessary.
    String str = (string) strOb.GetOb(); ◄─────── Cast needed.
    Console.WriteLine("strOb is an instance of NotGeneric.\n" +
                      "Therefore, the value returned by GetOb() " +
                      "is also object.\nIt must be cast to string: " +
                      str + "\n");

    // This compiles, but is conceptually wrong!
    iOb = strOb;

    // The following line results in a runtime exception.
    // v = (int) iOb.GetOb(); // runtime error! ◄─────── Runtime type mismatch.
  }
}
```

This program produces the following output:

```
iOb is an instance of NotGeneric.
Therefore, the value returned by GetOb() is object.
It must be cast to int: 88

strOb is an instance of NotGeneric.
Therefore, the value returned by GetOb() is also object.

It must be cast to string: Non-Generic class
```

There are several things of interest in this version. First, notice that **NotGeneric** replaces all uses of **T** with **object**. This makes **NotGeneric** able to store any type of object, as can the generic version. However, this is bad for two reasons. First, explicit casts must be employed to retrieve the stored data. Second, many kinds of type mismatch errors cannot be found until runtime. Let's look closely at each problem.

First, notice this line:

```
int v = (int) iOb.GetOb();
```

Because the return type of **GetOb( )** is now **object**, the cast to **int** is necessary to enable the value returned by **GetOb( )** to be unboxed and stored in **v**. If you remove the cast, the program will not compile. In the generic version of the program, this cast was not needed because **int** was specified as a type argument when **iOb** was constructed. In the non-generic version, the cast must be employed. This is not only an inconvenience, but a potential source of error.

Now, consider the following sequence from near the end of the program.

```
// This compiles, but is conceptually wrong!
iOb = strOb;

// The following line results in a runtime exception.
// v = (int) iOb.GetOb(); // runtime error!
```

Here, **strOb** is assigned to **iOb**. However, **strOb** refers to an object that contains a string, not an integer. This assignment is syntactically valid because all **NotGeneric** references are of the same type. Thus, any **NotGeneric** reference can refer to any **NotGeneric** object. However, the statement is semantically wrong, as the commented-out line shows. In that line, the return type of **GetOb( )** is cast to **int** and then an attempt is made to assign this value to **v**. The trouble is that **iOb** now refers to an object that stores a **string**, not an **int**. Unfortunately, without the use of generics, the compiler won't catch this error. Instead, a runtime exception will occur when the cast to **int** is attempted. To see this for yourself, try removing the comment symbol from the start of the line, and then compiling and running the program. A runtime error will occur.

The preceding sequence can't occur when generics are used. If this sequence were attempted in the generic version of the program, the compiler would catch it and report an error, thus preventing a serious bug that results in a runtime exception. The ability to create type-safe code in which type-mismatch errors are caught at compile time is a key advantage of generics. Although using **object** references to create "generic" code has always been possible in C#, that code was not type-safe and its misuse could result in runtime exceptions. Generics prevent this from occurring. In essence, through generics, what were once runtime errors have become compile-time errors. This is a major advantage.

A Generic Class with Two Type Parameters

You can declare more than one type parameter in a generic type. To specify two or more type parameters, simply use a comma-separated list. For example, the following **TwoGen** class is a variation of the **MyGenClass** class that has two type parameters:

```
// A simple generic class with two type parameters: T and V.
using System;

// TwoGen has two type parameters, T and V.
class TwoGen<T, V> {                                          Use two type parameters.
  T ob1;
  V ob2;

  // Notice that this constructor uses the two type parameters, T and V.
  public TwoGen(T o1, V o2) {
    ob1 = o1;
    ob2 = o2;
  }

  public T GetOb1() {
    return ob1;
  }

  public V GetOb2() {
    return ob2;
  }
}

// Demonstrate two generic type parameters.
class SimpGen {
  static void Main() {

    Console.WriteLine("Constructing a TwoGen<int, string> object.");
    TwoGen<int, string> tgObj =
       new TwoGen<int, string>(1024, "Using two type parameters");

    // Obtain and show values.
    int v = tgObj.GetOb1();                        Pass two type arguments.
    Console.WriteLine("The value of ob1: " + v);

    string str = tgObj.GetOb2();
    Console.WriteLine("The value of ob2: " + str);
  }
}
```

The output from this program is shown here:

```
Constructing a TwoGen<int, string> object.
The value of ob1: 1024
The value of ob2: Using two type parameters
```

Notice how **TwoGen** is declared:

```
class TwoGen<T, V> {
```

It specifies two type parameters, **T** and **V**, separated by a comma. Because it has two type parameters, two type arguments must be specified for **TwoGen** when an object is created, as shown next:

```
TwoGen<int, string> tgObj =
  new TwoGen<int, string>(1024, "Using two type parameters");
```

In this case, **int** is substituted for **T** and **string** is substituted for **V**.

Although the two type arguments differ in this example, it is possible for both types to be the same. For example, the following line of code is valid:

```
TwoGen<double, double> x = new TwoGen<double, double>(98.6, 102.4);
```

In this case, both **T** and **V** are of type **double**. Of course, if the type arguments were always the same, then two type parameters would be unnecessary.

The generics syntax shown in the preceding examples can be generalized. Here is the syntax for declaring a generic class:

```
class class-name<type-param-list> { // ...
```

Here is the syntax for declaring a reference to a generic class and giving it an initial value:

```
class-name<type-arg-list> var-name =
    new class-name<type-arg-list>(cons-arg-list);
```

Ask the Expert

Q: You say that classes, structures, methods, interfaces, and delegates can be generic. What about properties, operators, indexers, and events?

A: Properties, operators, indexers, and events cannot declare type parameters. Thus, they cannot be made generic. However, they can be used in a generic class and make use of the type parameters defined by that class.

Constrained Types

In the preceding examples, the type parameters could be replaced by any type. For example, given this declaration:

```
class MyGenClass<T> {
```

any type can be specified for **T**. Thus, it is legal to create **MyGenClass** objects in which **T** is replaced by **int**, **double**, **string**, **FileStream**, or any other type. Although having no restrictions on the type argument is fine for many purposes, sometimes it is useful to limit the types that can be bound to a type parameter. For example, you might want to create a method that operates on the contents of a stream, including a **FileStream** or **MemoryStream**. This situation seems perfect for generics, but you need some way to ensure that only stream types are used as type arguments. You don't want to allow a type argument of **int**, for example. You also need some way to tell the compiler that the methods defined by a stream will be available for use. For example, your generic code needs some way to know that it can call the **Read( )** method.

To handle such situations, C# provides *constrained types*. When specifying a type parameter, you can specify a constraint that the type parameter must satisfy. This is accomplished through the use of a **where** clause when specifying the type parameter, as shown here:

class *class-name<type-param>* where *type-param* : *constraints* { // ...

Here, *constraints* is a comma-separated list of constraints.

C# defines the following types of constraints:

1. You can require that a certain base class be present in a type argument by using a *base class constraint*. This constraint is specified by naming the desired base class. There is a variation of this constraint, called a *naked type constraint*, in which the base class is specified as a type parameter rather than an actual type. This enables you to establish a relationship between two type parameters.

2. You can require that one or more interfaces be implemented by a type argument by using an *interface constraint*. This constraint is specified by naming the desired interface.

3. You can require that the type argument supply a parameterless constructor. This is called a *constructor constraint*. It is specified by **new( )**.

4. You can specify that a type argument must be a reference type by specifying the *reference type constraint*: **class**.

5. You can specify that the type argument be a value type by specifying the *value type constraint*: **struct**.

Of these constraints, the base class constraint and the interface constraint are probably the most often used, but all are important. Each of the constraints is examined in the following sections.

Use a Base Class Constraint

The base class constraint enables you to specify a base class that a type argument must inherit. A base class constraint serves two important purposes. First, it lets you use the members of the base class specified by the constraint within the generic class. For example, you can call a method or use a property of the base class. Without a base class constraint, the compiler has no way to know what type of members a type argument might have. By supplying a base class constraint, you are letting the compiler know that all type arguments will have the members defined by the base class constraint.

The second purpose of a base class constraint is to ensure that only type arguments that support the specified base class can be used. This means that for any given base class constraint, the type argument must be either the base class itself or a class derived from that base class. If you attempt to use a type argument that does not match or inherit the specified base class, a compile-time error will result.

The base class constraint uses this form of the **where** clause:

where *T* : *base-class-name*

Here, *T* is the name of the type parameter, and *base-class-name* is the name of the base class. Only one base class can be specified.

Here is a simple example that demonstrates the base class constraint mechanism. It creates a base class called **MyStrMethods**, which defines a public method called **ReverseStr( )** that returns a reversed version of its string argument. Therefore, any class that inherits **MyStrMethods** will have access to this method.

```
// A simple demonstration of a base class constraint.
using System;

class MyStrMethods {

  // Reverse a string and return the result.
  public string ReverseStr(string str) {
    string result = "";

    foreach(char ch in str)
      result = ch + result;

    return result;
  }

  // ...
}

// Class MyClass inherits MyStrMethods.
class MyClass : MyStrMethods { }

// Class MyClass2 does not inherit MyStrMethods.
class MyClass2 { }
```

```
// Because of the base class constraint, all type arguments
// specified for Test must have MyStrMethods as a base class.
class Test<T> where T : MyStrMethods {
```
◄─────────── Use a base class constraint.

```
  T obj;

  public Test(T o) {
    obj = o;
  }

  public void ShowReverse(string str) {
    // OK to call ReverseStr() on obj because it's declared by
    // the base class MyStrMethods.
    string revStr = obj.ReverseStr(str);
    Console.WriteLine(revStr);
  }
}

class BaseClassConstraintDemo {
  static void Main() {
    MyStrMethods objA = new MyStrMethods();
    MyClass objB = new MyClass();
    MyClass2 objC = new MyClass2();

    // The following is valid because MyStrMethods is
    // the specified base class.
    Test<MyStrMethods> t1 = new Test<MyStrMethods>(objA);

    t1.ShowReverse("This is a test.");

    // The following is valid because MyClass inherits MyStrMethods.
    Test<MyClass> t2 = new Test<MyClass>(objB);
```
◄─────── OK because **MyClass**
inherits **MyStrMethods**.

```
    t2.ShowReverse("More testing.");

    // The following is invalid because MyClass2 DOES NOT
    // inherit MyStrMethods.
//    Test<MyClass2> t3 = new Test<MyClass2>(objC); // Error!
//    t3.ShowReverse("Error!");
  }
}
```
↑
This won't work because **MyClass2**
does not inherit **MyStrMethods**.

In this program, the class **MyStrMethods** is inherited by **MyClass**, but not by **MyClass2**. As mentioned, **MyStrMethods** declares a method called **ReverseStr( )**, which reverses a string and returns the result. Next, notice that **Test** is a generic class that is declared like this:

```
class Test<T> where T : MyStrMethods {
```

The **where** clause stipulates that any type argument specified for **T** must have **MyStrMethods** as a base class.

Test defines an instance variable called **obj**, which is of type **T**, and one constructor. These are shown here:

```
T obj;

public Test(T o) {
  obj = o;
}
```

As you can see, the object passed to **Test( )** is stored in **obj**.

Now notice that **Test** declares the method **ShowReverse( )**, shown next:

```
public void ShowReverse(string str) {
  // OK to call ReverseStr() on obj because it's declared by
  // the base class MyStrMethods.
  string revStr = obj.ReverseStr(str);
  Console.WriteLine(revStr);
}
```

This method calls **ReverseStr( )** on **obj**, which is a **T** object, and then displays the reversed string. The key point is that the only reason that **ReverseStr( )** can be called is because the base class constraint requires that any type argument bound to **T** will inherit **MyStrMethods**, which declares **ReverseStr( )**. If the base class constraint had not been used, the compiler wouldn't know that a method called **ReverseStr( )** can be called on an object of type **T**. You can prove this for yourself by removing the **where** clause. The program will no longer compile because the **ReverseStr( )** method will be unknown.

In addition to enabling access to members of the base class, the base class constraint enforces that only types that inherit the base class can be used as type arguments. This is why the following two lines are commented-out:

```
//    Test<MyClass2> t3 = new Test<MyClass2>(objC); // Error!
//    t3.ShowReverse("Error!");
```

Because **MyClass2** does not inherit **MyStrMethods**, it can't be used as a type argument when constructing a **Test** object. You can prove this by removing the comment symbols and trying to recompile.

Before continuing, let's review the two effects of a base class constraint: A base class constraint enables a generic class to access the members of the base class. It also ensures that only those type arguments that fulfill this constraint are valid, thus preserving type-safety.

Use a Constraint to Establish a Relationship Between Two Type Parameters

There is a variation of the base class constraint that allows you to establish a relationship between two type parameters. For example, consider the following generic class declaration:

```
class MyGenClass<T, V> where V : T {
```

In this declaration, the **where** clause tells the compiler that the type argument bound to **V** must be identical to or inherit from the type argument bound to **T**. If this relationship is not present, a compile-time error will result. A constraint that uses a type parameter such as that just shown is called a *naked type constraint*. The following example illustrates this constraint:

```
// Create a relationship between two type parameters.
using System;

class A {
  //...
}

class B : A {
  // ...
}

// Here, V must inherit T.
class MyGenClass<T, V> where V : T {
  // ...
}

class NakedConstraintDemo {
  static void Main() {

    // This declaration is OK because B inherits A.
    MyGenClass<A, B> x = new MyGenClass<A, B>();

    // This declaration is in error because A does not inherit B.
//    MyGenClass<B, A> y = new MyGenClass<B, A>();
  }
}
```

This constraint requires that the type argument passed to **T** must be a base class of the type argument passed to **V**.

First, notice that class **B** inherits class **A**. Next, examine the two **MyGenClass** declarations in **Main( )**. As the comments explain, the first declaration:

```
MyGenClass<A, B> x = new MyGenClass<A, B>();
```

is legal because **B** inherits **A**. However, the second declaration:

```
//    MyGenClass<B, A> y = new MyGenClass<B, A>();
```

is illegal because **A** does not inherit **B**.

Use an Interface Constraint

The interface constraint enables you to specify an interface that a type argument must implement. The interface constraint serves the same two purposes as the base class constraint. First, it lets you use the members of the interface within the generic class. Second, it ensures that only type arguments that implement the specified interface are used. This means that for any given interface constraint, the type argument must be either the interface or a type that implements that interface.

The interface constraint uses this form of the **where** clause:

where *T* : *interface-name*

Here, *T* is the name of the type parameter, and *interface-name* is the name of the interface. More than one interface can be specified by using a comma-separated list. If a constraint includes both a base class and interface, then the base class must be listed first.

The following program illustrates the interface constraint:

```
// A simple demonstration of an interface constraint.
using System;

// A simple interface.
interface IMyInterface {
  void Start();
  void Stop();
}

// Class MyClass implements IMyInterface.
class MyClass : IMyInterface {
  public void Start() {
    Console.WriteLine("Starting...");
  }

  public void Stop() {
    Console.WriteLine("Stopping...");
  }
}

// Class MyClass2 does not implement IMyInterface.
class MyClass2 { }

// Because of the interface constraint, all type arguments
// specified for Test must implement IMyInterface.
class Test<T> where T : IMyInterface {      ◄——— Require the all type arguments passed
                                                  to T implement IMyInterface.
  T obj;

  public Test(T o) {
    obj = o;
  }

  public void Activate() {
    // OK to call Start() and Stop() because they are
    // declared by IMyInterface.
```

```
      obj.Start();          These calls are legal because
      obj.Stop();           T implements IMyInterface.
    }
}

class InterfaceConstraintDemo {
  static void Main() {
    MyClass objA = new MyClass();
    MyClass2 objB = new MyClass2();

    // The following is valid because MyClass implements IMyInterface.
    Test<MyClass> t1 = new Test<MyClass>(objA);

    t1.Activate();

    // The following is invalid because MyClass2 DOES NOT
    // implement IMyInterface.
//    Test<MyClass2> t2 = new Test<MyClass2>(objB);
//    t2.Activate();
  }
}
```

First, the program creates an interface called **IMyInterface**. It defines two methods, called **Start( )** and **Stop( )**. The program then defines three classes. The first class, **MyClass**, implements **IMyInterface**. The second class, **MyClass2**, does not. The third is the generic **Test** class. Notice that **Test** uses an interface constraint to require that **T** implement the interface **IMyInterface**. Also notice that an object of type **T** is passed to **Test**'s constructor and stored in **obj**. **Test** defines a method called **Activate( )**, which uses **obj** to call the **Start( )** and **Stop( )** methods declared by **IMyInterface**.

In **Main( )**, the program creates objects of **MyClass** and **MyClass2**, called **objA** and **objB**, respectively. It then creates a **Test** object called **t1**, using **MyClass** as a type argument. This works because **MyClass** implements **IMyInterface**, thus satisfying the interface constraint. However, an attempt to create a **Test** object called **t2** using **MyClass2** as a type argument will fail because **MyClass2** does not implement **IMyInterface**. You can prove this by uncommenting the last two lines.

Use the new( ) Constructor Constraint

The **new( )** constructor constraint enables you to instantiate an object of a generic type. Normally, you cannot create an instance of a generic type parameter. However, the **new( )** constraint changes this because it requires that a type argument supply a parameterless constructor. (This parameterless constructor can be the default constructor provided automatically when no explicit constructors are declared.) With the **new( )** constraint in place, you can invoke the parameterless constructor to create an object of the generic type.

Here is a simple example that illustrates the use of **new( )**:

```
// Demonstrate a new() constructor constraint.
using System;

class MyClass {

  public MyClass() {
    Console.WriteLine("Creating a MyClass instance.");
    // ...
  }

  //...
}

class Test<T> where T : new() {
  T obj;

  public Test() {
    Console.WriteLine("Creating a Test instance.");

    // The following works because of the new() constraint.
    obj = new T(); // create a T object
  }

  // ...
}

class ConsConstraintDemo {
  static void Main() {

    Test<MyClass> t = new Test<MyClass>();

  }
}
```

Require that all type arguments passed to **T** provide a default constructor.

This program produces the following output:

```
Creating a Test instance.
Creating a MyClass instance.
```

First, notice the declaration of the **Test** class, shown here:

```
class Test<T> where T : new() {
```

Because of the **new( )** constraint, any type argument must supply a parameterless constructor. As explained, this can be the default constructor or one that you create.

Next, examine the **Test** constructor, shown here:

```
public Test() {
  Console.WriteLine("Creating a Test instance.");

  // The following works because of the new() constraint.
  obj = new T(); // create a T object
}
```

A new object of type **T** is created, and a reference to it is assigned to **obj**. This statement is valid only because the **new( )** constraint ensures that a constructor will be available. To prove this, try removing the **new( )** constraint and then attempt to recompile the program. As you will see, an error will be reported.

In **Main( )**, an object of type **Test** is instantiated, as shown here:

```
Test<MyClass> x = new Test<MyClass>();
```

Notice that the type argument is **MyClass** and that **MyClass** defines a parameterless constructor. Thus, it is valid for use as a type argument for **Test**. It must be pointed out that it was not necessary for **MyClass** to explicitly declare a parameterless constructor. Its default constructor would also satisfy the constraint. However, if a class needs other constructors in addition to a parameterless one, then it would be necessary to also explicitly declare a parameterless version.

Here are three important points about using **new( )**. First, it can be used with other constraints, but it must be the last constraint in the list. Second, **new( )** allows you to construct an object using only the parameterless constructor, even when other constructors are available. In other words, it is not permissible to pass arguments to the constructor of a type parameter. Third, you cannot use **new( )** in conjunction with a value type constraint, described next.

The Reference Type and Value Type Constraints

The next two constraints enable you to indicate that a type argument must be either a reference type or a value type. These are useful in the few cases in which the difference between reference and value types is important to generic code. Here is the general form of the reference type constraint:

where *T* : class

In this form of the **where** clause, the keyword **class** specifies that *T* must be a reference type. Thus, an attempt to use a value type, such as **int** or **bool**, for *T* will result in a compilation error. Here is the general form of the value type constraint:

where *T* : struct

In this case, the keyword **struct** specifies that *T* must be a value type. (Recall that structures are value types.) Thus, an attempt to use a reference type, such as **string**, for *T* will result in a compilation error. In both cases, when additional constraints are present, **class** or **struct** must be the first constraint in the list.

Here is an example that demonstrates the reference type constraint:

```
// Demonstrate a reference constraint.
using System;

class MyClass {
  //...
}

// Use a reference constraint.
class Test<T> where T : class {          Only reference types can be passed to T.
  T obj;

  public Test() {
    // The following statement is legal only because
    // T is guaranteed to be a reference type, which
    // can be assigned the value null.
    obj = null;
  }

  // ...
}

class ClassConstraintDemo {
  static void Main() {

    // The following is OK because MyClass is a class.
    Test<MyClass> x = new Test<MyClass>();

    // The next line is in error because int is a value type.
//    Test<int> y = new Test<int>();
  }
}
```

First, notice how **Test** is declared:

```
class Test<T> where T : class {
```

The **class** constraint requires that any type argument for **T** be a reference type. In this program, this is necessary because of what occurs inside the **Test** constructor:

```
public Test() {
  // The following statement is legal only
  // because T is guaranteed to be a reference
  // type, which can be assigned the value null.
  obj = null;
}
```

Here, **obj** (which is of type **T**) is assigned the value **null**. This assignment is valid only for reference types. As a general rule, you cannot assign **null** to a value type. (The exception to this rule is the *nullable type,* which is a special structure type that encapsulates a value type and allows the value null. See Chapter 14 for details.) Therefore, without the constraint, the assignment would not have been valid and the compile would have failed. This is one case in which the difference between value types and reference types might be important to a generic routine.

The value type constraint is the complement of the reference type constraint. It simply ensures that any type argument is a value type, including a **struct** or an **enum**. (In this context, a nullable type is not considered a value type.) Here is an example:

```
// Demonstrate a value type constraint.
using System;

struct MyStruct {
  //...
}

class MyClass {
  // ...
}

class Test<T> where T : struct {          ◄———————— Only value types can be passed to T.
  T obj;

  public Test(T x) {
    obj = x;
  }

  // ...
}

class ValueConstraintDemo {
  static void Main() {

    // Both of these declarations are legal.
    Test<MyStruct> x = new Test<MyStruct>(new MyStruct());
    Test<int> y = new Test<int>(10);

    // But, the following declaration is illegal!
//    Test<MyClass> z = new Test<MyClass>(new MyClass());
  }
}
```

In this program, **Test** is declared as shown here:

```
class Test<T> where T : struct {
```

Because **T** of **Test** now has the **struct** constraint, **T** can be bound to only value type arguments. This means that **Test<MyStruct>** and **Test<int>** are valid, but **Test<MyClass>** is not. To prove this, try removing the comment symbols from the start of the last line in the program and recompiling. An error will be reported.

Use Multiple Constraints

There can be more than one constraint associated with a parameter. When this is the case, use a comma-separated list of constraints. In this list, the first constraint must be **class** or **struct** (if present), or the base class (if one is specified). It is illegal to specify both a **class** or **struct** constraint and a base class constraint. Next must be any interface constraints. The **new( )** constraint must be last. For example, this is a valid declaration:

```
class MyGenClass<T> where T : MyClass, IMyInterface, new() { // ...
```

In this case, **T** must be replaced by a type argument that inherits **MyClass**, implements **IMyInterface**, and has a parameterless constructor.

When using two or more type parameters, you can specify a constraint for each parameter by using a separate **where** clause. For example,

```
// Use multiple where clauses.
using System;

// TwoWheres has two type arguments and both have a where clause.
class TwoWheres<T, V> where T : class
                      where V : struct {
```
⟵ Two **where** clauses. One for **T** and one for **V**.

```
  T ob1;
  V ob2;

  public TwoWheres(T t, V v) {
    ob1 = t;
    ob2 = v;
  }
}

class TwoWheresDemo {
  static void Main() {
    // This is OK because string is a class and int is a value type.
    TwoWheres<string, int> obj =
            new TwoWheres<string, int>("test", 11);

    // The following is wrong because bool is not a reference type.
//    TwoWheres<bool, int> obj2 =
//            new TwoWheres<bool, int>(true, 11);
  }
}
```

In this example, **TwoWheres** takes two type arguments and both have a **where** clause. Pay special attention to its declaration:

```
class TwoWheres<T, V> where T : class
                    where V : struct {
```

Notice that the only thing that separates the first **where** clause from the second is whitespace. No other punctuation is required or valid.

Create a Default Value of a Type Parameter

When writing generic code, there will be times when the difference between value types and parameter types is an issue. One such situation occurs when you want to give a variable of a type parameter a default value. For reference types, the default value is **null**. For non-**struct** value types, the default value is 0. The default value for a **struct** is an object of that **struct** with all fields set to their defaults. Thus, trouble occurs if you want to give a variable of a type parameter a default value. What value would you use: **null**, 0, or something else?

For example, given a generic class called **Test** declared like this:

```
class Test<T> {
  T obj;
  // ...
```

If you want to give **obj** a default value, would you use

```
obj = null; // works only for reference types
```

or

```
obj = 0; // works only for numeric types and enums, but not structs
```

The solution to this problem is to use another form of **default**, shown here:

default(*type*)

This is the operator form of **default**, and it produces a default value of the specified *type,* no matter what type is used. Thus, continuing with the example, to assign **obj** a default value of type **T**, you would use this statement:

```
obj = default(T);
```

This will work for all type arguments, whether they are value or reference types.

Here is a short program that demonstrates **default**:

```
// Demonstrate the default operator.
using System;

class MyClass {
  //...
}
```

```
// Construct a default value of T.
class Test<T> {
  public T obj;

  public Test() {
    // The following statement will work only for reference types.
//    obj = null; // can't use

    // The following statement will work only for numeric value types.
//    obj = 0; // can't use

    // This statement works for both reference and value types.
    obj = default(T); ◄──────── Create a default value for any T.
  }
}

class DefaultDemo {
  static void Main() {

    // Construct Test using a reference type.
    Test<MyClass> x = new Test<MyClass>();
```

Ask the Expert

Q: Some of the declarations that involve generic types are *very long*. Is there a way to make them shorter?

A: The new C# 3.0 implicitly typed variable feature can shorten a long declaration that includes an initializer. As you know from Chapter 2, in a **var** declaration, the type of the variable is determined by the type of the initializer. Therefore, a declaration such as

```
SomeClass<String, bool> someObj =
        new SomeClass<string, bool>("testing", false);
```

can be more compactly written as

```
var someObj = new SomeClass<string, bool>("testing", false);
```

Although the use of **var** does shorten the code in this case, its primary use is with anonymous types, which are described in Chapter 14. Furthermore, because implicitly typed variables are new to C#, it's not clear (at the time of this writing) that the preceding use of **var** will be considered a "best practice" by all C# practitioners. Also, the coding standards used in your workplace may preclude such use.

```
    if(x.obj == null)
      Console.WriteLine("x.obj is null.");

    // Construct Test using a value type.
    Test<int> y = new Test<int>();

    if(y.obj == 0)
      Console.WriteLine("y.obj is 0.");
  }
}
```

The output is shown here:

```
x.obj is null.
y.obj is 0.
```

Generic Structures

You can create a structure that takes type parameters. The syntax for a generic structure is the same as for generic classes. For example, in the following program, the **KeyValue** structure, which stores key/value pairs, is generic:

```
// Demonstrate a generic struct.
using System;

// This structure is generic.
struct KeyValue<TKey, TValue> {         ◄─────── A generic structure.
  public TKey key;
  public TValue val;

  public KeyValue(TKey a, TValue b) {
    key = a;
    val = b;
  }
}

class GenStructDemo {
  static void Main() {
    KeyValue<string, int> kv =
        new KeyValue<string, int>("Tom", 20);

    KeyValue<string, bool> kv2 =
        new KeyValue<string, bool>("Fan On", false);

    Console.WriteLine(kv.key + " is " + kv.val + " years old.");

    Console.WriteLine(kv2.key + " is " + kv2.val );
  }
}
```

The output is shown here:

```
Tom is 20 years old.
Fan On is False
```

Like generic classes, generic structures can have constraints. For example, this version of **KeyValue** restricts **TValue** to value types:

```
struct KeyValue<TKey, TValue> where TValue : struct {
// ...
```

Generic Methods

As the preceding examples have shown, methods inside a generic class can make use of a class' type parameter and are, therefore, automatically generic relative to the type parameter. However, it is possible to declare a generic method that uses one or more type parameters of its own. Furthermore, it is possible to create a generic method that is enclosed within a non-generic class.

Let's begin with an example. The following program declares a non-generic class called **ArrayUtils** and a static generic method within that class called **CopyInsert( )**. The **CopyInsert( )** method copies the contents of one array to another, inserting a new element at a specified location in the process. It can be used with any type of array.

```
// Demonstrate a generic method.
using System;

// A class of array utilities.  Notice that this is not
// a generic class.
class ArrayUtils {

  // Copy an array, inserting a new element in the process.
  // This is a generic method.
  public static bool CopyInsert<T>(T e, int idx,          ◄——— A generic method.
                        T[] src, T[] target) {

    // See if target array is big enough.
    if(target.Length < src.Length+1)
      return false;

    // Copy src to target, inserting e at idx in the process.
    for(int i=0, j=0; i < src.Length; i++, j++) {
      if(i == idx) {
        target[j] = e;
        j++;
      }
      target[j] = src[i];
    }
```

```
      return true;
    }
    // ...
}

class GenMethDemo {
  static void Main() {
    int[] nums = { 1, 2, 3 };
    int[] nums2 = new int[4];

    // Display contents of nums.
    Console.Write("Contents of nums: ");
    foreach(int x in nums)
      Console.Write(x + " ");

    Console.WriteLine();

    // Operate on an int array.
    ArrayUtils.CopyInsert(99, 2, nums, nums2);
```

Invoke the generic method. The type of **T** is determined by inference. In this case, the type is **int**.

```
    // Display contents of nums2.
    Console.Write("Contents of nums2: ");
    foreach(int x in nums2)
      Console.Write(x + " ");

    Console.WriteLine();


    // Now, use CopyInsert on an array of strings.
    string[] strs = { "Generics", "are", "powerful."};
    string[] strs2 = new string[4];

    // Display contents of strs.
    Console.Write("Contents of strs: ");
    foreach(string s in strs)
      Console.Write(s + " ");

    Console.WriteLine();

    // Insert into a string array.
    ArrayUtils.CopyInsert("in C#", 1, strs, strs2);
```

The type of **T** here is **string**.

```
    // Display contents of strs2.
    Console.Write("Contents of strs2: ");
    foreach(string s in strs2)
      Console.Write(s + " ");

    Console.WriteLine();
```

```
    // This call is invalid because the first argument
    // is of type double, and the third and fourth arguments
    // have element types of int.
//    ArrayUtils.CopyInsert(0.01, 2, nums, nums2);
  }
}
```

The output from the program is shown here:

```
Contents of nums: 1 2 3
Contents of nums2: 1 2 99 3
Contents of strs: Generics are powerful.
Contents of strs2: Generics in C# are powerful.
```

Let's examine **CopyInsert( )** closely. First, notice how it is declared by this line:

```
public static bool CopyInsert<T>(T e, int idx,
                                 T[] src, T[] target) {
```

The type parameters are declared *after* the method name, but before the parameter list. Also notice that **CopyInsert( )** is static, enabling it to be called independently of any object. Understand, though, that generic methods can be either static or non-static. There is no restriction in this regard.

Now, notice how **CopyInsert( )** is called within **Main( )** by use of the normal call syntax, without the need to specify type arguments. This is because the types of the type arguments are automatically discerned based on the type of data used to call **CopyInsert( )**. Based on this information, the type of **T** is adjusted accordingly. This process is called *type inference*. For example, in the first call:

```
ArrayUtils.CopyInsert(99, 2, nums, nums2);
```

the type of **T** becomes **int** because 99 is an **int**, and the element types of **nums** and **nums2** are **int**. In the second call, **string** types are used, and **T** is replaced by **string**.

Now, notice the commented-out code, shown here:

```
//    ArrayUtils.CopyInsert(0.01, 2, nums, nums2);
```

If you remove the comment symbols and then try to compile the program, you will receive an error. The reason is that the type of the first argument is **double**, but the element types of **nums** and **nums2** are **int**. However, all three types must be substituted for the same type parameter, **T**. This causes a type-mismatch, which results in a compile-time error. This ability to enforce type safety is one of the most important advantages of generic methods.

The syntax used to create **CopyInsert( )** can be generalized. Here is the general form of a generic method:

ret-type meth-name<type-parameter-list>(param-list) { // ...

In all cases, *type-parameter-list* is a comma-separated list of type parameters. Notice that for a generic method, the type parameter list follows the method name.

Using Explicit Type Arguments to Call a Generic Method

Although implicit type inference is adequate for most invocations of a generic method, it is possible to explicitly specify the type argument. To do so, specify the type argument after the method name when calling the method. For example, here **CopyInsert( )** is explicitly specified as type **string**:

```
ArrayUtils.CopyInsert<string>("in C#", 1, strs, strs2);
```

You will need to explicitly specify the type when the compiler cannot infer the type of a type parameter.

Using a Constraint with a Generic Method

You can add constraints to the type arguments of a generic method by specifying them after the parameter list. For example, the following version of **CopyInsert( )** will work only with reference types:

```
public static bool CopyInsert<T>(T e, int idx,
                                 T[] src, T[] target) where T : class {
```

If you were to try this version in the program shown earlier, the following call to **CopyInsert( )** would not compile because **int** is a value type, not a reference type:

```
// Now wrong because T must be a reference type!
ArrayUtils.CopyInsert(99, 2, nums, nums2); // Now illegal!
```

Ask the Expert

Q: You mentioned that there are cases in which the compiler cannot infer the type to use for a type parameter when a generic method is called and the type will need to be explicitly specified. Can you give an example?

A: Yes. Among others, this situation can occur when a generic method has no parameters. For example, consider this generic method:

```
class SomeClass {
  public static T SomeMeth<T>() where T: new() {
    return new T();
  }
  // ...
```

(continued)

When this method is invoked, there are no arguments from which the type of **T** can be inferred. The return type of **T** is not sufficient for the inference to take place. Therefore, this won't work:

```
someObj = SomeClass.SomeMeth(); // won't work
```

Instead, it must be invoked with an explicit type specified. For example:

```
someObj = SomeClass.SomeMeth<MyClass>(); // fixed
```

Generic Delegates

Like methods, delegates can also be generic. To declare a generic delegate, use this general form:

delegate *ret-type delegate-name<type-parameter-list>(arg-list)*;

Notice the placement of the type parameter list. It immediately follows the delegate's name. The advantage of generic delegates is that they let you define, in a type-safe manner, a generalized form that can then be matched to any compatible method.

The following program demonstrates a generic delegate called **Invert** that has one type parameter called **T**. It returns type **T** and takes an argument of type **T**.

```
// Demonstrate a generic delegate.
using System;

// Declare a generic delegate.
delegate T Invert<T>(T v);  ◄——————— A generic delegate.

class GenDelegateDemo {

  // Return the reciprocal of a double.
  static double Recip(double v) {
    return 1 / v;
  }

  // Reverse a string and return the result.
  static string ReverseStr(string str) {
    string result = "";

    foreach(char ch in str)
      result = ch + result;

    return result;
  }
```

```
static void Main() {

    // Construct two Invert delegates.
    Invert<double> invDel = Recip;
    Invert<string> invDel2 = ReverseStr;

    Console.WriteLine("The reciprocal of 4 is " + invDel(4.0));

    Console.WriteLine();

    string str = "ABCDEFG";
    Console.WriteLine("Original string: " + str);
    str = invDel2(str);
    Console.WriteLine("Reversed string: " + str);
  }
}
```

Create **double** and **string** instances of **Invert**.

The output is shown here.

```
The reciprocal of 4 is 0.25

Original string: ABCDEFG
Reversed string: GFEDCBA
```

Let's look closely at this program. First, notice how the **Invert** delegate is declared:

```
delegate T Invert<T>(T v);
```

Notice that **T** can be used as the return type even though the type parameter **T** is specified after the name **Invert**.

Inside **GenDelegateDemo**, the methods **Recip( )** and **ReverseStr( )** are declared, as shown here:

```
static double Recip(double v) {

static string ReverseStr(string str) {
```

The **Recip( )** method returns the reciprocal of the **double** value passed as an argument. The **ReverseStr( )** method, which is adapted from an earlier example, reverses a string and returns the result.

Inside **Main( )**, a delegate called **invDel** is instantiated and assigned a reference to **Recip( )**.

```
Invert<double> invDel = Recip;
```

Because **Recip( )** takes a **double** argument and returns a **double** value, **Recip( )** is compatible with a **double** instance of **Invert**.

In a similar fashion, the delegate **invDel2** is created and assigned a reference to **ReverseStr( )**.

```
Invert<string> invDel2 = ReverseStr;
```

Because **ReverseStr( )** takes a string argument and returns a string result, it is compatible with the string version of **Invert**.

Because of the type-safety inherent in generics, you cannot assign incompatible methods to delegates. For example, assuming the preceding program, the following statement would be in error:

```
Invert<int> invDel = ReverseStr; // Error!
```

Because **ReverseStr( )** takes a string argument and returns a string result, it cannot be assigned to an **int** version of **Invert**.

Generic Interfaces

Generic interfaces are specified just like generic classes. Here is an example. It creates a generic interface called **ITwoDCoord** that defines methods that get and set X and Y coordinate values. Therefore, any class that implements this interface will support X and Y coordinates. The data type of the coordinates is specified by a type parameter. **ITwoDCoord** is then implemented by two different classes.

```
// Demonstrate a generic interface.
using System;

// This interface is generic. It defines methods that support
// two-dimensional coordinates.
public interface ITwoDCoord<T> {          ◄——————— A generic interface.

  T GetX();
  void SetX(T x);

  T GetY();
  void SetY(T y);
}

// A class that encapsulates two-dimensional coordinates.
class XYCoord<T> : ITwoDCoord<T> {        ◄——————— Implement a generic interface.
  T X;
  T Y;

  public XYCoord(T x, T y) {
    X = x;
    Y = y;
  }

  public T GetX() { return X; }
  public void SetX(T x) { X = x; }

  public T GetY() { return X; }
  public void SetY(T y) { Y = y; }
}
```

```
// A class that encapsulates three-dimensional coordinates.
class XYZCoord<T> : ITwoDCoord<T> {          ◄———————— Implement a generic interface.
  T X;
  T Y;
  T Z;

  public XYZCoord(T x, T y, T z) {
    X = x;
    Y = y;
    Z = z;
  }

  public T GetX() { return X; }
  public void SetX(T x) { X = x; }

  public T GetY() { return Y; }
  public void SetY(T y) { Y = y; }

  public T GetZ() { return Z; }
  public void SetZ(T z) { Z = z; }
}

class GenInterfaceDemo {

  // A generic method that can display the X,Y coordinates associated
  // with any object that implements the generic interface ITwoDCoord.
  static void ShowXY<T>(ITwoDCoord<T> xy) {
    Console.WriteLine(xy.GetX() + ", " + xy.GetY());   ◄——  Use methods specified
  }                                                          by ITwoDCoord.

  static void Main() {

    XYCoord<int> xyObj = new XYCoord<int>(10, 20);
    Console.Write("The X,Y values in xyObj: ");
    ShowXY(xyObj);

    XYZCoord<double> xyzObj = new XYZCoord<double>(-1.1, 2.2, 3.1416);
    Console.Write("The X,Y component of xyzObj: ");
    ShowXY(xyzObj);
  }
}
```

The output is shown here:

```
The X,Y values in xyObj: 10, 10
The X,Y component of xyzObj: -1.1, 2.2
```

There are several things of interest in the preceding example. First, notice how **ITwoDCoord** is declared:

```
public interface ITwoDCoord<T> {
```

As mentioned, a generic interface uses a syntax similar to that of a generic class.

Now, notice how **XYCoord**, which implements **ITwoDCoord**, is declared:

```
class XYCoord<T> : ITwoDCoord<T> {
```

The type parameter **T** is specified by **XYCoord** and is also specified in **ITwoDCoord**. This is important. A class that implements a generic version of a generic interface must, itself, be generic. For example, the following declaration would be illegal because **T** is not defined:

```
class XYCoord : ITwoDCoord<T> { // Wrong!
```

The type parameter required by **ITwoDCoord** must be specified by the implementing class, which is **XYCoord** in this case. Otherwise, there is no way for the interface to receive the type argument.

Next, **XYCoord** declares two variables called **X** and **Y** that hold the coordinates. These are, as one would expect, objects of the generic type **T**. Finally, the methods defined by **ITwoDCoord** are implemented.

ITwoDCoord is also implemented by the class **XYZCoord**. It encapsulates three-dimensional (X,Y,Z) coordinates. It implements the methods defined by **ITwoDCoord** and adds methods to access the Z coordinate.

In **GenInterfaceDemo**, a generic method called **ShowXY( )** is defined. It displays the X,Y coordinates of the object that it is passed. Notice that the type of its parameter is **ITwoDCoord**. This means that it can operate on any object that implements the **ITwoDCoord** interface. In this case, it means that objects of type **XYCoord** and **XYZCoord** can be used as arguments. This fact is illustrated by **Main( )**.

A type parameter for a generic interface can have constraints in the same way as it can for a generic class. For example, this version of **ITwoDCoord** restricts its use to value types:

```
public interface ITwoDCoord<T> where T : struct {
```

When this version is implemented, the implementing class must also specify the same constraint for **T**, as shown here:

```
class XYCoord<T> : ITwoDCoord<T> where T : struct {
```

Because of the value type constraint, this version of **XYCoord** cannot be used on class types, for example. Thus, the following declaration would be disallowed:

```
// Now, this won't work.
XYCoord<string> xyObj = new XYCoord<string>("10", "20");
```

Because **string** is not a value type, its use with **XYCoord** is illegal.

Although a class that implements a generic version of a generic interface must, itself, be generic, as explained earlier, a non-generic class *can* implement a specific version of a generic interface. For example, here, **XYCoordInt** explicitly implements **ITwoDCoord<int>**:

```
class XYCoordInt : ITwoDCoord<int> {
  int X;
  int Y;

  public XYCoordInt(int x, int y) {
    X = x;
    Y = y;
  }

  public int GetX() { return X; }
  public void SetX(int x) { X = x; }

  public int GetY() { return X; }
  public void SetY(int y) { Y = y; }
}
```

Notice that **ITwoDCoord** is specified with an explicit **int** type. Therefore, **XYCoordInt** does not need to take a type argument because it does not pass it along to **ITwoDCoord**.

One other point: Although a property declaration cannot, itself, specify a type parameter, a property declared in a generic class can use a type parameter that is declared by the generic class. Therefore, the methods **GetX( )**, **GetY( )**, and so on in the preceding example can be made into properties that use the type parameter **T**. This is left to the reader as an exercise in the Self Test section at the end of this chapter.

Ask the Expert

Q: Can I compare two instances of a type parameter using the = = or ! = operators

A: The answer has two parts. First, if the type parameter specifies a reference or a base class constraint, then = = and ! = are allowed, but they only test for reference equality. For example, the following method will not compile:

```
public static bool SameValue<T>(T a, T b) {
  if(a == b) return true; // Won't work
  return false;
}
```

Because **T** is a generic type, the compiler has no way to know precisely how two objects should be compared for equality. Should a bitwise comparison be done? Should only certain fields be compared? Should reference equality be used? The compiler has no way to answer these questions.

(continued)

At first glance, this seems to be a serious problem. Fortunately, it isn't because C# provides a mechanism by which you can determine if two instances of a type parameter are the same. To enable two objects of a generic type parameter to be compared, use the **CompareTo( )** method defined by one of the standard interfaces: **IComparable**. This interface has both a generic and a non-generic form. **IComparable** is implemented by all of C#'s built-in types, including **int**, **string**, and **double**. It is also easy to implement for classes that you create.

The **IComparable** interface defines only the **CompareTo( )** method. Its generic form is shown here:

int CompareTo(T *obj*)

It compares the invoking object to *obj*. It returns zero if the two objects are equal, a positive value if the invoking object is greater than *obj*, and a negative value if the invoking object is less than *obj*.

To use **CompareTo( )**, you must specify a constraint that requires every type argument to implement the **IComparable** interface. Then, when you need to compare two objects of the type parameter, simply call **CompareTo( )**. For example, here is a corrected version of **SameValue( )**:

```
// Require IComparable interface.
public static bool SameValue<T>(T a, T b) where T : IComparable<T> {
  if(a.CompareTo(b) == 0) return true; // fixed
  return false;
}
```

Because the interface constraint requires that **T** implement **IComparable<T>**, the **CompareTo( )** method can be used to determine equality. Of course, this means that the only instances of classes that implement **IComparable<T>** can be passed to **SameValue( )**.

Try This Create a Generic Queue

In previous chapters, you created and enhanced a queue class. In those chapters, the type of data operated on by the queue is hardcoded as **char**. Through the use of generics, you can easily convert the queue class into a form that can operate on any type of data. This is the subject of this example. Since the queue code has been modified and enhanced throughout several chapters, for clarity, all pieces of the code will be shown here, even if they aren't affected by the change to generics.

Step by Step

1. Create a generic interface called **IQ** that takes a type parameter that specifies the type of data that the queue will store. It is shown here:

```
// A generic queue interface.
// Here, T specifies the type of data stored in the queue.
```

```
public interface IQ<T> {
  // Put an object into the queue.
  void Put(T obj);

  // Get an object from the queue.
  T Get();
}
```

This interface is similar to the **ICharQ** interface developed in *Try This: Create a Queue Interface* in Chapter 9, but it is generic.

2. Include the exception classes developed in *Try This: Add Exceptions to the Queue Class* in Chapter 10. These are unaffected by the change to generics. They are shown here:

```
// An exception for queue-full errors.
class QueueFullException : Exception {
  public QueueFullException(string str) : base(str) { }
  // Add other QueueFullException constructors here, if desired.

  public override string ToString() {
    return "\n" + Message;
  }
}

// An exception for queue-empty errors.
class QueueEmptyException : Exception {
  public QueueEmptyException(string str) : base(str) { }
  // Add other QueueEmptyException constructors here, if desired.

  public override string ToString() {
    return "\n" + Message;
  }
}
```

3. Change the queue classes so that they implement the **IQ** interface. For brevity, we will only update the **SimpleQueue** class, but you should have no trouble updating the other two queue implementations. The generic version of **SimpleQueue** is shown here:

```
// A generic, fixed-size queue class.
// This class implements the generic IQ interface.
class SimpleQueue<T> : IQ<T> {
  T[] q; // this array holds the queue
  int putloc, getloc; // the put and get indices

  // Construct an empty queue given its size.
  public SimpleQueue(int size) {
    q = new T[size+1]; // allocate memory for queue
    putloc = getloc = 0;
  }
```

(continued)

```
    // Put an item into the queue.
    public void Put(T obj) {
      if(putloc==q.Length-1)
        throw new QueueFullException("Queue Full! Max length is " +
                                     (q.Length-1) + ".");

      putloc++;
      q[putloc] = obj;
    }

    // Get an item from the queue.
    public T Get() {
      if(getloc == putloc)
        throw new QueueEmptyException("Queue is empty.");

      getloc++;
      return q[getloc];
    }
  }
```

As you can see, the type of data stored in the queue is specified by the type parameter **T**. This means that **SimpleQueue** can be used to store any type of data.

4. The following program assembles all the pieces and shows the generic queue in action:

```
// A generic Queue class.

using System;

// A generic queue interface.
// Here, T specifies the type of data stored in the queue.
public interface IQ<T> {
  // Put an object into the queue.
  void Put(T obj);

  // Get an object from the queue.
  T Get();
}

// An exception for queue-full errors.
class QueueFullException : Exception {
  public QueueFullException(string str) : base(str) { }
  // Add other QueueFullException constructors here, if desired.

  public override string ToString() {
    return "\n" + Message;
  }
}
```

```csharp
// An exception for queue-empty errors.
class QueueEmptyException : Exception {
  public QueueEmptyException(string str) : base(str) { }
  // Add other QueueEmptyException constructors here, if desired.

  public override string ToString() {
    return "\n" + Message;
  }
}

// A generic, fixed-size queue class.
// This class implements the generic IQ interface.
class SimpleQueue<T> : IQ<T> {
  T[] q; // this array holds the queue
  int putloc, getloc; // the put and get indices

  // Construct an empty queue given its size.
  public SimpleQueue(int size) {
    q = new T[size+1]; // allocate memory for queue
    putloc = getloc = 0;
  }

  // Put an item into the queue.
  public void Put(T obj) {
    if(putloc==q.Length-1)
      throw new QueueFullException("Queue Full! Max length is " +
                                    (q.Length-1) + ".");

    putloc++;
    q[putloc] = obj;
  }

  // Get an item from the queue.
  public T Get() {
    if(getloc == putloc)
      throw new QueueEmptyException("Queue is empty.");

    getloc++;
    return q[getloc];
  }
}

// Demonstrate the generic queue.
class GenQueueDemo {
  static void Main() {
```

(continued)

```
// Create a queue for chars and a queue for doubles.
SimpleQueue<char> charQ = new SimpleQueue<char>(10);
SimpleQueue<double> doubleQ = new SimpleQueue<double>(5);

char ch;
double d;
int i;

try {
  // Use a char queue.
  for(i=0; i < 10; i++) {
    Console.WriteLine("Storing: " + (char) ('A' + i));
    charQ.Put((char) ('A' + i));
  }
  Console.WriteLine();

  for(i=0; i < 10; i++) {
    Console.Write("Getting next char: ");
    ch = charQ.Get();
    Console.WriteLine(ch);
  }
}
catch (QueueFullException exc) {
  Console.WriteLine(exc);
}
Console.WriteLine();

try {
  // Use a double queue.
  for(i=1; i <= 5; i++) {
    Console.WriteLine("Storing: " + i * 3.1416 );
    doubleQ.Put(i * 3.1416);
  }

  Console.WriteLine();

  for(i=0; i < 5; i++) {
    Console.Write("Getting next double: ");
    d = doubleQ.Get();
    Console.WriteLine(d);
  }
}
catch (QueueEmptyException exc) {
  Console.WriteLine(exc);
}
  }
}
```

The output is shown here:

```
Storing: A
Storing: B
Storing: C
Storing: D
Storing: E
Storing: F
Storing: G
Storing: H
Storing: I
Storing: J

Getting next char: A
Getting next char: B
Getting next char: C
Getting next char: D
Getting next char: E
Getting next char: F
Getting next char: G
Getting next char: H
Getting next char: I
Getting next char: J

Storing: 3.1416
Storing: 6.2832
Storing: 9.4248
Storing: 12.5664
Storing: 15.708

Getting next double: 3.1416
Getting next double: 6.2832
Getting next double: 9.4248
Getting next double: 12.5664
Getting next double: 15.708
```

Chapter 13 Self Test

1. Generics streamline the creation of classes that work with various kinds of data in a type-safe manner. True or False?

2. What is a type parameter?

3. What is a type argument?

4. As explained, generalized code was possible in C# prior to the addition of generics through the use of **object** references. One problem with this approach is the tedium and the possibility of errors associated with supplying the required casts. What is the other problem?

5. What does a base class constraint do? What does a value type constraint do?

6. Can interfaces be generic?

7. How do you create a default value for a type?

8. When creating a generic method, where is the type parameter list specified?

9. Can generic methods use type constraints?

10. As mentioned, although generic properties cannot be created, a property can use a type parameter from its enclosing scope. Rework the **ITwoDCoord** interface and the **XYCoord** class shown in the chapter so that they convert methods such as **GetX( )** and **GetY( )** into properties.

Chapter 14

Introducing LINQ

Key Skills & Concepts

- LINQ fundamentals

- Type correspondence in a query

- Filter values with **where**

- Sort results with **orderby**

- Select values with **select**

- Group results with **group**

- Use **into** to create a continuation

- Join two sequences with **join**

- Anonymous types and object initializers

- Create a group join

- Use **let** to create a variable in a query

- The query methods

- Deferred VS immediate query execution

- Lambda expressions

- Extension methods

If the addition of generics in the 2.0 release had a profound effect on C# (which it did), then the addition of LINQ in version 3.0 is nothing short of earth-shaking! Without question, LINQ is the single most important new feature in C# 3.0. It adds an entirely new syntactic element, several new keywords, and a powerful new capability. The inclusion of LINQ has significantly increased the scope of the language, expanding the range of tasks to which C# can be applied. Simply put, with the inclusion of LINQ, C# has set a new standard, which will affect the course of language development well into the future. LINQ *is* that important.

NOTE

As was the case with generics described in the preceding chapter, the subject of LINQ is quite large, involving many features, options, and alternatives. It is not possible to cover all of its aspects in this beginner's guide. (In fact, a complete description of LINQ requires an entire book of its own!) This chapter explains its theory, core concepts, and basic syntax. It also shows several examples that illustrate LINQ's use. After completing this chapter, you will be able to begin using LINQ in your programs. However, it is a subsystem that you will almost certainly want to explore in greater detail.

What Is LINQ?

LINQ stands for language-integrated query. It encompasses a set of features that lets you retrieve information from a data source. As you may know, the retrieval of data constitutes an important part of many programs. For example, a program might obtain information from a customer list, look up product information in a catalog, or access an employee's record. In many cases, such data is stored in a database that is separate from the application. For example, a product catalog might be stored in a relational database. In the past, interacting with such a database would involve generating queries using SQL (Structured Query Language). Other sources of data, such as XML, required their own approaches. Therefore, prior to C# 3.0, support for such queries was not built into C#. LINQ changes this.

LINQ adds to C# the ability to generate queries for any LINQ-compatible data source. Furthermore, the syntax used for the query is the same, no matter what data source is used. This means that the syntax used to query data in a relational database is the same as that used to query data stored in an array, for example. It is no longer necessary to use SQL or any other non-C# mechanism. The query capability is fully integrated into the C# language.

In addition to using LINQ with SQL, LINQ can be used with XML files and ADO.NET datasets. Perhaps equally important, it can also be used with C# arrays and collections (described in Chapter 15). Therefore, LINQ gives you a uniform way to access data. This is a powerful, innovative concept. It is not only changing the way that data is accessed, it also offers a new way to think about and approach old problems. In the future, many types of programming solutions will be crafted in terms of LINQ. Its effects will not be limited to just database access.

LINQ is supported by a set of interrelated features, including the query syntax added to the C# language, lambda expressions, anonymous types, and extension methods. All are examined in this chapter.

LINQ Fundamentals

At the core of LINQ is the *query*. A query specifies what data will be obtained from a data source. For example, a query on a customer mailing list might request the addresses of all customers that reside in a specific city, such as Chicago or Tokyo. A query on an inventory database might request a list of out-of-stock items. A query on a log of Internet usage could ask for a list of the websites with the highest hit counts. Although these queries differ in their specifics, all can be expressed using the same LINQ syntactic elements.

After a query has been created, it can be executed. One way this is done is by using the query in a **foreach** loop. Executing a query causes its results to be obtained. Thus, using a query involves two key steps. First, the form of the query is created. Second, the query is executed. Therefore, the query defines *what* to retrieve from a data source. Executing the query actually *obtains the results*.

In order for a source of data to be used by LINQ, it must implement the **IEnumerable** interface. There are two forms of this interface: one generic, one not. In general, it is easier if the data source implements the generic version, **IEnumerable<T>**, where **T** specifies the type of data being enumerated. The rest of the chapter assumes that a data source implements **IEnumerable<T>**. This interface is declared in **System.Collections.Generic**. A class that implements **IEnumerable<T>** supports enumeration, which means that its contents can be obtained one at a time in sequence. All C# arrays support **IEnumerable<T>**. Thus, we can use arrays to demonstrate the central concepts of LINQ. Understand, however, that LINQ is not limited to arrays.

A Simple Query

Before going into any more theory, let's work through a simple LINQ example. The following program uses a query to obtain the positive values contained in an array of integers:

```
// Create a simple LINQ query.
using System;
using System.Linq;

class SimpQuery {
  static void Main() {

    int[] nums =  { 1, -2, 3, 0, -4, 5 };

    // Create a query that obtains only positive numbers.
    var posNums = from n in nums
                  where n > 0            ◄──────── Create a query.
                  select n;

    Console.WriteLine("The positive values in nums:");

    // Execute the query and display the results.
    foreach(int i in posNums) Console.WriteLine(i);  ◄──────── Execute the query.
  }
}
```

This program produces the following output:

```
The positive values in nums:
1
3
5
```

As you can see, only the positive values in the **nums** array are displayed. Although quite simple, this program demonstrates the key features of LINQ. Let's examine it closely.

The first thing to notice in the program is the **using** directive:

```
using System.Linq;
```

To use the LINQ features, you must include the **System.Linq** namespace.

Next, an array of **int** called **nums** is declared. All arrays in C# are implicitly convertible to **IEnumerable<T>**. This makes any C# array usable as a LINQ data source.

Next, a query is declared that retrieves those elements in **nums** that are positive. It is shown here:

```
var posNums = from n in nums
              where n > 0
              select n;
```

The variable **posNums** is called the *query variable.* It refers to the set of rules defined by the query. Notice that it uses **var** to implicitly declare **posNums**. As you know, this makes **posNums** an implicitly typed variable. In queries, it is often convenient to use implicitly typed variables, although you can also explicitly declare the type, which must be some form of **IEnumerable<T>**. The variable **posNums** is then assigned the query expression.

All queries begin with **from**. This clause specifies two items. The first is the *range variable,* which will receive elements obtained from the data source. In this case, the range variable is **n**. The second item is the data source, which, in this case, is the **nums** array. The type of the range variable is inferred from the data source. In this case, the type of **n** is **int**. Generalizing, here is the syntax of the **from** clause:

from *range-variable* in *data-source*

The next clause in the query is **where**. It specifies a condition that an element in the data source must meet in order to be obtained by the query. Its general form is shown here:

where *boolean-expression*

The *boolean-expression* must produce a **bool** result. (This expression is also called a *predicate.*) There can be more than one **where** clause in a query. In the program, this **where** clause is used:

```
where n > 0
```

It will be true only for an element whose value is greater than zero. This expression will be evaluated for every **n** in **nums** when the query executes. Only those values that satisfy this condition will be obtained. In other words, a **where** clause acts as a filter on the data source, allowing only certain items through.

All queries end with either a **select** clause or a **group** clause. In this example, the **select** clause is used. It specifies precisely what is obtained by the query. For simple queries, such as in this example, the range value is selected. Therefore, it returns those integers from **nums** that satisfy the **where** clause. In more sophisticated situations, it is possible to finely tune what is selected. For example, when querying a mailing list, you might return just the last name of each recipient, rather than the entire address. Notice that the **select** clause ends with a semicolon. Because **select** ends a query, it ends the statement and requires a semicolon. Notice, however, that the other clauses in the query do not end with a semicolon.

At this point, a query variable called **posNums** has been created, but no results have been obtained. It is important to understand that a query simply defines a set of rules. It is not until the query is executed that results are obtained. Furthermore, the same query can be executed two or more times, with the possibility of differing results if the underlying data source changes between executions. Therefore, simply declaring the query **posNums** does not mean that it contains the results of the query.

To execute the query, the program uses the **foreach** loop shown here:

```
foreach(int i in posNums) Console.WriteLine(i);
```

Notice that **posNums** is specified as the collection being iterated over. When the **foreach** executes, the rules defined by the query specified by **posNums** are executed. With each pass through the loop, the next element returned by the query is obtained. The process ends when there are no more elements to retrieve. In this case, the type of the iteration variable **i** is explicitly specified as **int** because this is the type of the elements retrieved by the query. Explicitly specifying the type of the iteration variable is fine in this situation, since it is easy to know the type of the value selected by the query. However, in more complicated situations, it will be easier (or, in some cases, necessary) to implicitly specify the type of the iteration variable by using **var**.

A Query Can Be Executed More Than Once

Because a query defines a set of rules that is used to retrieve data, but does not, itself, produce results, the same query can be run multiple times. If the data source changes between runs, then the results of the query may differ. Therefore, once you define a query, executing it will always produce the most current results. Here is an example. In the following version of the preceding program, the contents of the **nums** array are changed between two executions of **posNums**:

```
// Create a simple query.
using System;
using System.Linq;
using System.Collections.Generic;

class SimpQuery {
  static void Main() {

    int[] nums = { 1, -2, 3, 0, -4, 5 };

    // Create a query that obtains only positive numbers.
    var posNums = from n in nums
                  where n > 0
                  select n;
```

```
      Console.WriteLine("The positive values in nums:");

      // Execute the query and display the results.
      foreach(int i in posNums) Console.WriteLine(i);

      // Change nums.
      Console.WriteLine("\nSetting nums[1] to 99.");
      nums[1] = 99;

      Console.WriteLine("The positive values in nums:");

      // Execute the query a second time.
      foreach(int i in posNums) Console.WriteLine(i);
   }
}
```

These produce
different results.

The following output is produced:

```
The positive values in nums:
1
3
5

Setting nums[1] to 99.
The positive values in nums:
1
99
3
5
```

As the output confirms, after the value in **nums[1]** was changed from –2 to 99, the result
of re-running the query reflects the change. This is a key point that must be emphasized. Each
execution of a query produces its own results, which are obtained by enumerating the current
contents of the data source. Therefore, if the data source changes, so, too, might the results of
executing a query. The benefits of this approach are quite significant. For example, if you are
obtaining a list of pending orders for an online store, then you want each execution of your
query to produce all orders, including those just entered.

How the Data Types in a Query Relate

As the preceding examples have shown, a query involves variables whose types relate to one
another. These are the query variable, the range variable, and the data source. Because the
correspondence between these types is both important and a bit confusing at first, they merit
a closer look.

The type of the range variable must agree with the type of the elements stored in the data
source. Thus, the type of the range variable is dependent upon the type of the data source. In
many cases, C# can infer the type of the range variable. As long as the data source implements
IEnumerable<T>, the type inference can be made, because **T** describes the type of the

elements in the data source. (As mentioned, all arrays implement **IEnumerable<T>**, as do many other data sources.) However, if the data source implements the non-generic version of **IEnumerable**, then you will need to explicitly specify the type of the range variable. This is done by specifying its type in the **from** clause. For example, assuming the preceding examples, this shows how to explicitly declare **n** to be an **int**:

```
var posNums = from int n in nums
  // ...
```

Of course, the explicit type specification is not needed here, because all arrays are implicitly convertible to **IEnumerable<T>**, which enables the type of the range variable to be inferred.

The type of object returned by a query is an instance of **IEnumerable<T>**, where **T** is the type of the elements. Thus, the type of the query variable must be an instance of **IEnumerable<T>**. The value of **T** is determined by the type of the value specified by the **select** clause. In the case of the preceding example, **T** is **int** because **n** is an **int**. (As explained, **n** is an **int** because **int** is the type of elements stored in **nums**.) Therefore, the query could have been written like this, with the type explicitly specified as **IEnumerable <int>**:

```
IEnumerable<int> posNums = from n in nums
                          where n > 0
                          select n;
```

The key point is that the type of the item selected by **select** must agree with the type argument passed to **IEnumerable<T>** used to declare the query variable. Often, query variables use **var** rather than explicitly specifying the type because this lets the compiler infer the proper type from the **select** clause. As you will see, this approach is particularly useful when **select** returns something other than an element from the data source.

When a query is executed by the **foreach** loop, the type of the iteration variable must be the same as the type of the range variable. In the preceding examples, this type was explicitly specified as **int**, but you can let the compiler infer the type by specifying this variable as **var**. As you will see, there are also some cases in which **var** must be used because the type name of the data is unknown.

The General Form of a Query

All queries share a general form, which is based on a set of contextual keywords, shown here:

ascending	descending	equals	from
group	in	into	join
let	on	orderby	select
where			

Of these, the following begin query clauses:

from	group	join	let
orderby	select	where	

As mentioned, a query must begin with the keyword **from** and end with either a **select** or **group** clause. The **select** clause determines what type of value is enumerated by the query. The **group** clause returns the data by groups, with each group able to be enumerated individually. As the preceding examples have shown, the **where** clause specifies criteria that an item must meet in order for it to be returned. The remaining clauses help you fine-tune a query. The following sections examine each query clause.

Filter Values with where

As explained, **where** is used to filter the data returned by a query. The preceding examples have shown only its simplest form, in which a single condition is used. A key point to understand is that you can use **where** to filter data based on more than one condition. One way to do this is through the use of multiple **where** clauses. For example, consider the following program that displays only those values in the array that are both positive and less than 10.

```
// Use multiple where clauses.
using System;
using System.Linq;

class TwoWheres {
  static void Main() {

    int[] nums =  { 1, -2, 3, -3, 0, -8, 12, 19, 6, 9, 10 };

    // Create a query that obtains positive values less than 10:
    var posNums = from n in nums
                  where n > 0          ◄——————— Use two where clauses.
                  where n < 10
                  select n;

    Console.WriteLine("The positive values less than 10:");

    // Execute the query and display the results.
    foreach(int i in posNums) Console.WriteLine(i);
  }
}
```

The output is shown here:

```
The positive values less than 10:
1
3
6
9
```

As you can see, only positive values less than 10 are retrieved.

Although it is not wrong to use two **where** clauses as just shown, the same effect can be achieved in a more compact manner by using a single **where** in which both tests are combined into a single expression. Here is the query rewritten to use this approach:

```
var posNums = from n in nums
              where n > 0 && n < 10
              select n;
```

In general, a **where** condition can use any valid C# expression that evaluates to a Boolean result. For example, the following program defines an array of **string**s. Several of the strings are Internet addresses. The query **netAddrs** retrieves only those strings that have more than four characters and that end with ".net." Thus, it finds those strings that contain Internet addresses that use the **.net** domain name.

```
// Demonstrate another where clause.
using System;
using System.Linq;

class WhereDemo2 {

  static void Main() {

    string[] strs = { ".com", ".net", "hsNameA.com", "hsNameB.net",
                      "test", ".network", "hsNameC.net", "hsNameD.com" };

    // Create a query that obtains Internet addresses that
    // end with .net.
    var netAddrs = from addr in strs
                   where addr.Length > 4 && addr.EndsWith(".net")
                   select addr;

    // Execute the query and display the results.
    foreach(var str in netAddrs) Console.WriteLine(str);
  }
}
```

A more complicated **where** expression.

The output is shown here:

```
hsNameB.net
hsNameC.net
```

Notice that the program makes use of another of **string**'s method called **EndsWith( )**. It returns true if the invoking string ends with the character sequence specified as an argument.

Sort Results with orderby

Often you will want the results of a query to be sorted. For example, you might want to obtain a list of past-due accounts, in order of the remaining balance, from greatest to least. Or, you might want to obtain a customer list, alphabetized by name. Whatever the purpose, LINQ gives you an easy way to produce sorted results: the **orderby** clause.

The general form of **orderby** is shown here:

orderby *sort-on how*

The item on which to sort is specified by *sort-on*. This can be as inclusive as the entire element stored in the data source or as restricted as a portion of a single field within the element. The value of *how* determines if the sort is ascending or descending, and it must be either **ascending** or **descending**. The default direction is ascending, so you won't normally specify **ascending**.

Here is an example that uses **orderby** to retrieve the values in an **int** array in ascending order:

```
// Demonstrate orderby.
using System;
using System.Linq;

class OrderbyDemo {

  static void Main() {

    int[] nums = { 10, -19, 4, 7, 2, -5, 0 };

    // Create a query that obtains the values in sorted order.
    var sNums = from n in nums
                orderby n  ◄──────── Sort the result.
                select n;

    Console.Write("Values in ascending order: ");

    // Execute the query and display the results.
    foreach(int i in sNums) Console.Write(i + " ");

    Console.WriteLine();
  }
}
```

The output is shown here:

```
Values in ascending order: -19 -5 0 2 4 7 10
```

To change the order to descending, simply specify the **descending** option, as shown here:

```
var sNums = from n in nums
            orderby n descending
            select n;
```

If you try this, you will see that the order of the values is reversed.

A Closer Look at select

The **select** clause determines what types of elements are obtained by a query. Its general form is shown here:

select *expression*

So far, we have been using **select** to return the range variable. Thus, *expression* has simply named the range variable. However, **select** is not limited to this simple action. It can return a specific portion of the range variable, the result of applying some operation or transformation to the range variable, or even a new type of object that is constructed from pieces of the information obtained from the range variable. This is called *projecting*.

To begin examining the other capabilities of **select**, consider the following program. It displays the square roots of the positive values contained in an array of **double** values.

```
// Use select to return the square root of all positive values
// in an array of doubles.
using System;
using System.Linq;

class SelectDemo {

  static void Main() {

    double[] nums =  { -10.0, 16.4, 12.125, 100.85, -2.2, 25.25, -3.5 } ;

    // Create a query that returns the square roots of the
    // positive values in nums.
    var sqrRoots = from n in nums
                   where n > 0
                   select Math.Sqrt(n);
```
Return a sequence that contains the square roots of **n**.
```
    Console.WriteLine("The square roots of the positive values" +
                      " rounded to two decimal places:");

    // Execute the query and display the results.
    foreach(double r in sqrRoots) Console.WriteLine("{0:#.##}", r);
  }
}
```

The output is shown here:

```
The square roots of the positive values rounded to two decimal places:
4.05
3.48
10.04
5.02
```

In the program, pay special attention to the **select** clause:

```
select Math.Sqrt(n);
```

It returns the square root of the range variable. It does this by obtaining the result of passing the range variable to **Math.Sqrt( )**, which returns the square root of its argument. This means that the sequence obtained when the query is executed will contain the square roots of the positive values in **nums**. If you generalize this concept, the power of **select** becomes apparent. You can use **select** to generate any type of sequence you need, based on the values obtained from the data source.

Here is a program that shows another way to use **select**. It creates a class called **EmailAddress** that contains two properties. The first holds a person's name. The second contains an e-mail address. The program then creates an array that contains several **EmailAddress** entries. The program uses a query to obtain a list of just the e-mail addresses by themselves.

```
// Return a portion of the range variable.
using System;
using System.Linq;

class EmailAddress {
  public string Name { get; set; }
  public string Address { get; set; }

  public EmailAddress(string n, string a) {
    Name = n;
    Address = a;
  }
}

class SelectDemo2 {
  static void Main() {

    EmailAddress[] addrs = {
        new EmailAddress("Herb", "Herb@HerbSchildt.com"),
        new EmailAddress("Tom", "Tom@HerbSchildt.com"),
        new EmailAddress("Sara", "Sara@HerbSchildt.com")
    };

    // Create a query that selects e-mail addresses.
    var eAddrs = from entry in addrs
                 select entry.Address;

    Console.WriteLine("The e-mail addresses are");

    // Execute the query and display the results.
    foreach(string s in eAddrs) Console.WriteLine("  " + s);
  }
}
```

Use just the **Address** portion of the elements in **addrs**.

The output is shown here:

```
The e-mail addresses are
  Herb@HerbSchildt.com
  Tom@HerbSchildt.com
  Sara@HerbSchildt.com
```

Pay special attention to the **select** clause:

```
select entry.Address;
```

Instead of returning the entire range variable, it returns only the **Address** portion. This fact is evidenced by the output. This means that the query returns a sequence of strings, not a sequence of **EmailAddress** objects. This is why the **foreach** loop specifies **s** as a **string**. As explained, the type of sequence returned by a query is determined by the type of value returned by the **select** clause.

One of the more powerful features of **select** is its ability to return a sequence that contains elements created during the execution of the query. For example, consider the following program. It defines a class called **ContactInfo**, which stores a name, e-mail address, and telephone number. It also defines the **EmailAddress** class used by the preceding example. Inside **Main( )**, an array of **ContactInfo** is created. Then, a query is declared in which the data source is an array of **ContactInfo**, but the sequence returned contains **EmailAddress** objects. Thus, the type of the sequence returned by **select** is not **ContactInfo**, but rather **EmailAddress**, and these objects are created during the execution of the query.

```
// Use a query to obtain a sequence of EmailAddresses
// from a list of ContactInfo.
using System;
using System.Linq;

class ContactInfo {
  public string Name { get; set; }
  public string Email { get; set; }
  public string Phone { get; set; }

  public ContactInfo(string n, string a, string p) {
    Name = n;
    Email = a;
    Phone = p;
  }
}

class EmailAddress {
  public string Name { get; set; }
  public string Address { get; set; }

  public EmailAddress(string n, string a) {
    Name = n;
```

```
        Address = a;
    }
}

class SelectDemo3 {
  static void Main() {

    ContactInfo[] contacts = {
        new ContactInfo("Herb", "Herb@HerbSchildt.com", "555-1010"),
        new ContactInfo("Tom", "Tom@HerbSchildt.com", "555-1101"),
        new ContactInfo("Sara", "Sara@HerbSchildt.com", "555-0110")
    };

    // Create a query that creates a list of EmailAddress objects.
    var emailList = from entry in contacts
                    select new EmailAddress(entry.Name, entry.Email);

    Console.WriteLine("The e-mail list is");

    // Execute the query and display the results.
    foreach(EmailAddress e in emailList)
      Console.WriteLine("  {0}: {1}", e.Name, e.Address );
  }
}
```

From an array of **ContactInfo**, produce a list of **EmailAddress** objects.

The output is shown here:

```
The e-mail list is
  Herb: Herb@HerbSchildt.com
  Tom: Tom@HerbSchildt.com
  Sara: Sara@HerbSchildt.com
```

The key point of this example is that the type of sequence generated by a query can consist of objects created by the query.

Group Results with group

One of the most powerful query features is provided by the **group** clause because it enables you to create results that are grouped by keys. Using the sequence obtained from a group, you can easily access all of the data associated with a key. This makes **group** an easy and effective way to retrieve data that is organized into sequences of related items. The **group** clause is one of only two clauses that can end a query. (The other is **select**.)

The **group** clause has the following general form:

group *range-variable* by *key*

It returns data grouped into sequences, with each sequence sharing the key specified by *key*.

The result of **group** is a sequence that contains elements of type **IGrouping<TKey, TElement>**, which is declared in the **System.Linq** namespace. It defines a collection of objects that share a common key. The type of query variable in a query that returns a group is **IEnumerable<IGrouping<TKey, TElement>>**. **IGrouping** defines a read-only property called **Key**, which returns the key associated with each sequence.

Here is an example that illustrates the use of **group**. It declares an array that contains a list of websites. It then creates a query that groups the list by top-level domain name, such as **.org** or **.com**.

```
// Demonstrate the group clause.
using System;
using System.Linq;

class GroupDemo {

  static void Main() {

    string[] websites = { "hsNameA.com", "hsNameB.net", "hsNameC.net",
                          "hsNameD.com", "hsNameE.org", "hsNameF.org",
                          "hsNameG.tv", "hsNameH.net", "hsNameI.tv" };

    // Create a query that groups websites by top-level domain name.
    var webAddrs = from addr in websites
                   where addr.LastIndexOf(".") != -1
                   group addr by addr.Substring(addr.LastIndexOf("."));

    // Execute the query and display the results.
    foreach(var sites in webAddrs) {
      Console.WriteLine("Websites grouped by " + sites.Key);
      foreach(var site in sites)
        Console.WriteLine("  " + site);
      Console.WriteLine();
    }
  }
}
```

Group results by domain name.

The output is shown here:

```
Websites grouped by .com
  hsNameA.com
  hsNameD.com

Websites grouped by .net
  hsNameB.net
  hsNameC.net
  hsNameH.net

Websites grouped by .org
```

```
hsNameE.org
hsNameF.org

Websites grouped by .tv
  hsNameG.tv
  hsNameI.tv
```

As the output shows, the data is grouped based on the top-level domain name of a website. Notice how this is achieved by the **group** clause:

```
var webAddrs = from addr in websites
               where addr.LastIndexOf(".") != -1
               group addr by addr.Substring(addr.LastIndexOf("."));
```

The key is obtained by use of the **LastIndexOf( )** and **Substring( )** methods defined by **string**. (These are described in Chapter 5. The version of **Substring( )** used here returns the substring that starts at the specified index and runs to the end of the invoking string.) The index of the last period in a website name is found using **LastIndexOf( )**. Using this index, the **Substring( )** method obtains the remainder of the string, which is the part of the website name that contains the top-level domain name. One other point: Notice the use of the **where** clause to filter out any strings that don't contain a period. The **LastIndex( )** method returns –1 if the specified string is not contained in the invoking string.

Because the sequence obtained when **webAddrs** is executed is a list of groups, you will need to use two **foreach** loops to access the members of each group. The outer loop obtains each group. The inner loop enumerates the members within the group. The iteration variable of the outer **foreach** loop must be an **IGrouping** instance compatible with the key and element type. In the example, both the keys and elements are **string**. Therefore, the type of **sites** iteration variable of the outer loop is **IGrouping<string, string>**. The type of the iteration variable of the inner loop is **string**. For brevity, the example implicitly declares these variables, but they could have been explicitly declared as shown here:

```
foreach(IGrouping<string, string> sites in webAddrs) {
  Console.WriteLine("Websites grouped by " + sites.Key);
  foreach(string site in sites)
    Console.WriteLine("   " + site);
  Console.WriteLine();
}
```

Use into to Create a Continuation

When using **select** or **group**, you will sometimes want to generate a temporary result that will be used by a subsequent part of the query to produce the final result. This is called a *query continuation* (or just a *continuation* for short), and it is accomplished through the use of **into** with a **select** or **group** clause. It has the following general form:

into *name query-body*

where *name* is the name of the range variable that iterates over the temporary result and is used by the continuing query, specified by *query-body*. This is why **into** is called a query continuation when used with **select** or **group**—it continues the query. In essence, a query continuation embodies the concept of building a new query that queries the results of the preceding query.

NOTE

There is also a form of **into** that can be used with **join**, which creates a *group join*. This is described later in this chapter.

Here is an example that uses **into** with **group**. The following program reworks the **GroupDemo** example shown earlier, which creates a list of websites grouped by top-level domain name. In this case, the initial results are queried by a range variable called **ws**. This result is then filtered to remove all groups that have fewer than three elements.

```
// Use into with group.
using System;
using System.Linq;

class IntoDemo {

  static void Main() {

    string[] websites = { "hsNameA.com", "hsNameB.net", "hsNameC.net",
                          "hsNameD.com", "hsNameE.org", "hsNameF.org",
                          "hsNameG.tv",  "hsNameH.net", "hsNameI.tv" };

    // Create a query that groups websites by top-level domain name,
    // but select only those groups that have more than two members.
    // Here, ws is the range variable over the set of groups
    // returned when the first half of the query is executed.
    var webAddrs = from addr in websites
                   where addr.LastIndexOf(".") != -1
                   group addr by addr.Substring(addr.LastIndexOf("."))
                   into ws           ←——————— Put temporary results into ws.
                   where ws.Count() > 2
                   select ws;        ↑
                              Filter ws.
    // Execute the query and display the results.
    Console.WriteLine("Top-level domains with more than 2 members.\n");

    foreach(var sites in webAddrs) {
      Console.WriteLine("Contents of " + sites.Key + " domain:");
      foreach(var site in sites)
        Console.WriteLine("   " + site);
      Console.WriteLine();
    }
  }
}
```

The following output is produced:

```
Top-level domains with more than 2 members.

Contents of .net domain:
  hsNameB.net
  hsNameC.net
  hsNameH.net
```

As the output shows, only the **.net** group is returned because it is the only group that has more than two elements.

In the program, pay special attention to this sequence of clauses in the query:

```
group addr by addr.Substring(addr.LastIndexOf(".", addr.Length))
          into ws
where ws.Count() > 2
select ws;
```

First, the results of the **group** clause are stored (creating a temporary result) and a new query begins, which operates on the stored results. The range variable of the new query is **ws**. At this point, **ws** will range over each group returned by the first query. (It ranges over groups because the first query results in a sequence of groups.) Next, the **where** clause filters the query so that the final result contains only those groups that contain more than two members. This determination is made by calling **Count( )**, which is an *extension method* that is implemented for all **IEnumerable<T>** objects. It returns the number of elements in a sequence. (You'll learn more about extension methods later in this chapter.) The resulting sequence of groups is returned by the **select** clause.

Use let to Create a Variable in a Query

In a query, you will sometimes want to temporarily retain a value. For example, you might want to create an enumerable variable that can, itself, be queried. Or, you might want to store a value that will be used later on in a **where** clause. Whatever the purpose, these types of actions can be accomplished through the use of **let**.

The **let** clause has this general form:

let *name* = *expression*

Here, *name* is an identifier that is assigned the value of *expression*. The type of *name* is inferred from the type of the expression.

Here is an example that shows how **let** can be used to create another enumerable data source. The query takes as input an array of strings. It then converts those strings into **char** arrays. This is accomplished by use of another **string** method called **ToCharArray( )**, which returns an array containing the characters in the string. The result is assigned to a variable called **chrArray**, which is then used by another **from** clause to obtain the individual characters in the array. The query then sorts the characters and returns the resulting sequence.

```
// Use a let clause and a nested from clause.
using System;
using System.Linq;

class LetDemo {

  static void Main() {

    string[] strs = { "alpha", "beta", "gamma" };

    // Create a query that obtains the characters in the
    // strings, returned in sorted order. Notice the use
    // of a nested from clause.
    var chrs = from str in strs
               let chrArray = str.ToCharArray()
               from ch in chrArray
               orderby ch
               select ch;

    Console.WriteLine("The individual characters in sorted order:");

    // Execute the query and display the results.
    foreach(char c in chrs) Console.Write(c + " ");

    Console.WriteLine();
  }
}
```

chrArray refers to an array of characters obtained from str.

The output is shown here:

```
The individual characters in sorted order:
a a a a a b e g h l m m p t
```

In the program, notice how the **let** clause assigns to **chrArray** a reference to the array returned by **str.ToCharArray( )**:

```
let chrArray = str.ToCharArray()
```

After the **let** clause, other clauses can make use of **chrArray**. Furthermore, because all arrays in C# implement **IEnumerable<T>**, **chrArray** can be used as a data source for a second, nested **from** clause. This is what happens in the example. It uses the nested **from** to enumerate the individual characters in the array, sorting them into ascending sequence and returning the result.

You can also use a **let** clause to hold a non-enumerable value. For example, the following is a more efficient way to write the query used in the **IntoDemo** program shown in the preceding section.

```
var webAddrs = from addr in websites
               let idx = addr.LastIndexOf(".")
               where idx != -1
```

*Call **LastIndexOf( )** only once, storing the result in **idx**.*

```
        group addr by addr.Substring(idx)
                into ws
        where ws.Count() > 2
        select ws;
```

In this version, the index of the last occurrence of a period is assigned to **idx**. This value is then used by **Substring( )**. This prevents the search for the period from having to be conducted twice.

Join Two Sequences with join

When working with databases, it is common to want to create a sequence that correlates data from two different data sources. For example, an online store might have one database that associates the name of an item with its item number and a second database that associates the item number with its in-stock status. Given this situation, you might want to generate a list that shows the in-stock status of items by name, rather than by item number. You can do this by correlating the data in the two databases. Such an action is easy to accomplish in LINQ through the use of the **join** clause.

The general form of **join** is shown here (in context with the **from** clause):

from *range-varA* in *data-sourceA*
   join *range-varB* in *data-sourceB*
      on *range-varA.property* equals *range-varB.property*

The key to using **join** is to understand that each data source must contain data in common and that data can be compared for equality. Thus, in the general form, *data-sourceA* and *data-sourceB* must have something in common that can be compared. The items being compared are specified by the **on** section. Thus, when *range-varA.property* is equal to *range-varB.property,* the correlation succeeds. In essence, **join** acts like a filter, allowing only those elements that share a common value to pass through.

When using **join**, often the sequence returned is a composite of portions of the two data sources. Thus, **join** lets you generate a new list that contains elements from two different data sources. This enables you to organize data in a new way.

The following program creates a class called **Item**, which encapsulates an item's name with its number. It creates another class called **InStockStatus**, which links an item number with a Boolean property that indicates whether or not the item is in stock. It also creates a class called **Temp**, which has two fields, one **string** and one **bool**. Objects of this class will hold the result of the query. The query uses **join** to produce a list in which an item's name is associated with its in-stock status.

```
// Demonstrate join.
using System;
using System.Linq;

// A class that links an item name with its number.
class Item {
```

```csharp
    public string Name { get; set; }
    public int ItemNumber { get; set; }

  public Item(string n, int inum) {
    Name = n;
    ItemNumber = inum;
  }
}

// A class that links an item number with its in-stock status.
class InStockStatus {
  public int ItemNumber { get; set; }
  public bool InStock { get; set; }

  public InStockStatus(int n, bool b) {
    ItemNumber = n;
    InStock = b;
  }
}

// A class that encapsulates a name with its status.
class Temp {
  public string Name { get; set; }
  public bool InStock { get; set; }

  public Temp(string n, bool b) {
    Name = n;
    InStock  = b;
  }
}

class JoinDemo {
  static void Main() {

    Item[] items = {
        new Item("Pliers", 1424),
        new Item("Hammer", 7892),
        new Item("Wrench", 8534),
        new Item("Saw", 6411)
    };

    InStockStatus[] statusList = {
        new InStockStatus(1424, true),
        new InStockStatus(7892, false),
        new InStockStatus(8534, true),
        new InStockStatus(6411, true)
    };
```

```
// Create a query that joins Item with InStockStatus to
// produce a list of item names and availability. Notice
// that a sequence of Temp objects is produced.
var inStockList = from item in items
                  join entry in statusList
                       on item.ItemNumber equals entry.ItemNumber
                  select new Temp(item.Name, entry.InStock);

Console.WriteLine("Item\tAvailable\n");

// Execute the query and display the results.
foreach(Temp t in inStockList)
   Console.WriteLine("{0}\t{1}", t.Name, t.InStock);
  }
}
```

Return a **Temp** object
that contains the
result of the join.

Join two lists based
on **ItemNumber**.

The output is shown here:

```
Item    Available

Pliers  True
Hammer  False
Wrench  True
Saw     True
```

To understand how **join** works, let's walk through each line in the query. The query begins in the normal fashion with this **from** clause:

```
var inStockList = from item in items
```

This clause specifies that **item** is the range variable for the data source specified by **items**. The **items** array contains objects of type **Item**, which encapsulate a name and a number for an inventory item.

Next comes the **join** clause, shown here:

```
join entry in statusList
  on item.ItemNumber equals entry.ItemNumber
```

It specifies that **entry** is the range variable for the **statusList** data source. The **statusList** array contains objects of type **InStockStatus**, which link an item number with its status. Thus, **items** and **statusList** have a property in common: the item number. This is used by the **on/equals** portion of the **join** clause to describe the correlation. Thus, **join** matches items from the two data sources when their item numbers are equal.

Finally, the **select** clause returns a **Temp** object that contains an item's name along with its in-stock status:

```
select new Temp(item.Name, entry.InStock);
```

Therefore, the sequence obtained by the query consists of **Temp** objects.

Although the preceding example is fairly straightforward, **join** supports substantially more sophisticated operations. For example, you can use **into** with **join** to create a *group join,* which creates a result that consists of an element from the first sequence and a group of all matching elements from the second sequence. (You'll see an example of this a bit later in this chapter.) In general, the time and effort needed to fully master **join** are well worth the investment because it gives you the ability to reorganize data at runtime. This is a powerful capability. It is made even more powerful by the use of anonymous types, described in the next section.

Anonymous Types and Object Initializers

C# 3.0 adds a new feature called the *anonymous type* that directly relates to LINQ. As the name implies, an anonymous type is a class that has no name. Its primary use is to create an object returned by the **select** clause. Often, the outcome of a query is a sequence of objects that either is a composite of two (or more) data sources (such as in the case of **join**) or includes a subset of the members of one data source. In either case, the type being returned is often needed only because of the query and is not used elsewhere in the program. In this case, using an anonymous type eliminates the need to declare a class that will be used simply to hold the outcome of the query.

An anonymous type is created through the use of this general form:

```
new { nameA = valueA, nameB = valueB, ... }
```

Here, the names specify identifiers that translate into read-only properties, which are initialized by the values. For example,

```
new { Count = 10, Max = 100, Min = 0 }
```

This creates a class type that has three public read-only properties: **Count**, **Max**, and **Min**. These are given the values 10, 100, and 0, respectively. These properties can be referred to by name by other code. This syntax is called *object initialization.* It is another new feature of C# 3.0. It provides a way to initialize an object without explicitly invoking a constructor. This is necessary in the case of anonymous types because there is no way to explicitly call a constructor. (Recall that constructors have the same name as their class. In the case of an anonymous class, there is no name. So, how would you invoke the constructor?)

Because an anonymous type has no name, you must use an implicitly typed variable to refer to it. This lets the compiler infer the proper type. For example,

```
var myOb = new { Count = 10, Max = 100, Min = 0 }
```

creates a variable called **myOb** that is assigned a reference to the object created by the anonymous type expression. This means that the following statements are legal:

```
Console.WriteLine("Count is " + myOb.Count);

if(i <= myOb.Max && i >= myOb.Min) // ...
```

Remember, when an anonymous type is created, the identifiers that you specify become read-only public properties. Thus, they can be used by other parts of your code.

Although the term *anonymous type* is used, it's not quite completely true! The type is anonymous relative to you, the programmer. However, the compiler does give it an internal name. Thus, anonymous types do not violate C#'s strong type-checking rules.

To fully understand the value of anonymous types, consider this rewrite of the previous program that demonstrated **join**. Recall that in the previous version, a class called **Temp** was needed to encapsulate the result of the **join**. Through the use of an anonymous type, this "placeholder" class is no longer needed and no longer clutters the source code to the program. The output from the program is unchanged from before.

```csharp
// Use an anonymous type to improve the join demo program.
using System;
using System.Linq;

// A class that links an item name with its number.
class Item {
  public string Name { get; set; } ,
  public int ItemNumber { get; set; }

  public Item(string n, int inum) {
    Name = n;
    ItemNumber = inum;
  }
}

// A class that links an item number with its in-stock status.
class InStockStatus {
  public int ItemNumber { get; set; }
  public bool InStock { get; set; }

  public InStockStatus(int n, bool b) {
    ItemNumber = n;
    InStock = b;
  }
}

class AnonTypeDemo {
  static void Main() {

    Item[] items = {
        new Item("Pliers", 1424),
        new Item("Hammer", 7892),
        new Item("Wrench", 8534),
        new Item("Saw", 6411)
    };
```

```
InStockStatus[] statusList = {
    new InStockStatus(1424, true),
    new InStockStatus(7892, false),
    new InStockStatus(8534, true),
    new InStockStatus(6411, true)
};

// Create a query that joins Item with InStockStatus to
// produce a list of item names and availability.
// Now, an anonymous type is used.
var inStockList = from item in items
                  join entry in statusList
                    on item.ItemNumber equals entry.ItemNumber
                  select new { Name = item.Name,
                               InStock =  entry.InStock };

Console.WriteLine("Item\tAvailable\n");
```

Return an anonymous type.

```
// Execute the query and display the results.
foreach(var t in inStockList)
    Console.WriteLine("{0}\t{1}", t.Name, t.InStock);
  }
}
```

Pay special attention to the select clause:

```
select new { Name = item.Name,
             InStock =  entry.InStock };
```

It returns an object of an anonymous type that has two read-only properties, **Name** and **InStock**. These are given the values specified by the item's name and availability. Because of the anonymous type, there is no longer any need for the **Temp** class.

One other point. Notice the **foreach** loop. It now uses **var** to declare the iteration variable. This is necessary because the type of the object contained in **inStockList** has no name. This situation is one of the reasons that C# 3.0 added implicitly typed variables. They are needed to support anonymous types.

Before moving on, there is one more aspect of anonymous types that warrants a mention. In some cases, including the one just shown, you can simplify the syntax of the anonymous type through the use of a *projection initializer*. In this case, you simply specify the name of the initializer by itself. This name automatically becomes the name of the property. For example, here is another way to code the **select** clause used by the preceding program:

```
select new { item.Name, entry.InStock };
```

Here, the property names are still **Name** and **InStock**, just as before. The compiler automatically "projects" the identifiers **Name** and **InStock**, making them the property names of the anonymous type. Also, as before, the properties are given the values specified by **item.Name** and **entry.InStock**.

Ask the Expert

Q: Can the object initialization syntax used by an anonymous type also be used for named types?

A: Yes! The object initialization syntax can also be used with named types. For example, given this class:

```
class MyClass {
  public int Alpha { get; set; }
  public int Beta { get; set; }
}
```

The following declaration is legal:

```
var myOb = new MyClass { Alpha = 10, Beta = 20 };
```

After this statement executes, the line

```
Console.WriteLine("Alpha: {0}, Beta {1}", myOb.Alpha, myOb.Beta);
```

displays

```
Alpha: 10, Beta 20
```

Although object initializers can be used with named classes, their primary use is with anonymous types. Therefore, normally, you should explicitly call a constructor when working with named classes.

Create a Group Join

As explained earlier, you can use **into** with **join** to create a *group join,* which creates a sequence in which each entry in the result consists of an entry from the first sequence and a group of all matching elements from the second sequence. No example was presented earlier because often a group join makes use of an anonymous type. Now that anonymous types have been covered, an example of a simple group join can be given.

The following example uses a group join to create a list in which various transports, such as cars, boats, and planes, are organized by their general transportation category, which is land, sea, or air. The program first creates a class called **Transport** that links a transport type with its classification. Inside **Main( )**, it creates two input sequences. The first is an array of strings that contains the names of the general means by which one travels: land, sea, and air. The second is an array of **Transport** that encapsulates various means of transportation. It then uses a group join to produce a list of transports that are organized by their category.

```
// Demonstrate a simple group join.
using System;
using System.Linq;

// This class links the name of a transport, such as Train,
// with its general classification, such as land, sea, or air.
class Transport {
  public string Name { get; set; }
  public string How { get; set; }

  public Transport(string n, string h) {
    Name = n;
    How = h;
  }
}

class GroupJoinDemo {
  static void Main() {

    // An array of transport classifications.
    string[] travelTypes = {
        "Air",
        "Sea",
        "Land",
    };

    // An array of transports.
    Transport[] transports = {
        new Transport("Bicycle", "Land"),
        new Transport("Balloon", "Air"),
        new Transport("Boat", "Sea"),
        new Transport("Jet", "Air"),
        new Transport("Canoe", "Sea"),
        new Transport("Biplane", "Air"),
        new Transport("Car", "Land"),
        new Transport("Cargo Ship", "Sea"),
        new Transport("Train", "Land")
    };

    // Create a query that uses a group join to produce
    // a list of item names and IDs organized by category.
    var byHow = from how in travelTypes
                join trans in transports
                on how equals trans.How         ←——— Create a
                into lst                              group join.
                select new { How = how, Tlist = lst };
```

```
    // Execute the query and display the results.
    foreach(var t in byHow) {
      Console.WriteLine("{0} transportation includes:", t.How);

      foreach(var m in t.Tlist)
        Console.WriteLine("   " + m.Name);

      Console.WriteLine();
    }

  }
}


Air transportation includes:
  Balloon
  Jet
  Biplane

Sea transportation includes:
  Boat
  Canoe
  Cargo Ship

Land transportation includes:
  Bicycle
  Car
  Train
```

The key part of the program is, of course, the query, which is shown here:

```
var byHow = from how in travelTypes
                join trans in transports
                on how equals trans.How
                into lst
                select new { How = how, Tlist = lst };
```

Here is how it works. The **from** statement uses **how** to range over the **travelTypes** array. Recall that **travelTypes** contains an array of the general travel classifications, air, land, and sea. The **join** clause joins each travel type with those transports that use that type. For example, the type Land is joined with Bicycle, Car, and Train. However, because of the **into** clause, for each travel type, the **join** produces a list of the transports that use that type. This list is represented by **lst**. Finally, **select** returns an anonymous type that encapsulates each value of **how** (the travel type) with a list of transports. This is why two **foreach** loops are needed to display the results of the query. The outer loop obtains an object that contains the name of the travel type and a list of the transports for that type. The inner loop displays the individual transports.

There are many options and nuances associated with group joins. In fact, the group join is one of the most sophisticated query techniques, and it is one feature that you will want to explore thoroughly. One of the best ways is to experiment with simple examples, making sure that you thoroughly understand what is occurring in each step.

The Query Methods and Lambda Expressions

The query syntax described in the preceding sections is the way you will probably write most queries in C#. It is convenient, powerful, and compact. It is, however, not the only way to write a query. The other way is to use the *query methods*. These methods can be called on any enumerable object, such as an array. Many of the query methods require the use of another new C# 3.0 feature: the lambda expression. Because the query methods and lambda expressions are intertwined, both are introduced here.

The Basic Query Methods

The query methods are defined by **System.Linq.Enumerable** and are implemented as extension methods that extend the functionality of **IEnumerable<T>**. (Query methods are also defined by **System.Linq.Queryable**, which extends the functionality of **IQueryable<T>**, but this interface is not used in this chapter.) An extension method adds functionality to another class, but without the use of inheritance. Support for extension methods was added by C# 3.0, and we will look more closely at them later in this chapter. For now, it is sufficient to understand that query methods can be called only on an object that implements **IEnumerable<T>**.

The **Enumerable** class provides many query methods, but at the core are those that correspond to the query keywords described earlier. These methods are shown here, along with the keywords to which they relate. Understand that these methods have overloaded forms and only their simplest form is shown. However, this is also the form that you will usually use.

Query Keyword	Equivalent Query Method
select	Select(*arg*)
where	Where(*arg*)
order	OrderBy(*arg*) or OrderByDescending(*arg*)
join	Join(*seq2, key1, key2, result*)
group	GroupBy(*arg*)

Except for **Join( )**, the other methods take one argument, *arg,* which is an object of type **Func<T, TResult>**, as a parameter. This is a delegate type defined by LINQ. It is declared like this:

delegate TResult Func<T, TResult>(T *arg*)

Here, **TResult** specifies the result of the delegate and **T** specifies the parameter type. In the query methods, *arg* determines what action the query method takes. For example, in the case of **Where( )**, *arg* determines how the query filters the data. Each of these query methods returns an enumerable object. Thus, the result of one can be used to execute a call on another, allowing the methods to be chained together.

The **Join( )** method takes four arguments. The first is a reference to the second sequence to be joined. The first sequence is the one on which **Join( )** is called. The key selector for the first sequence is passed via *key1,* and the key selector for the second sequence is passed via *key2*. The result of the join is described by *result*. The type of *key1* is **Func<TOuter, TKey>**, and the type of *key2* is **Func<TInner, TKey>**. The *result* argument is of type **Func<TOuter, TInner, TResult>**. Here, **TOuter** is the element type of the invoking sequence, **TInner** is the element type of the passed sequence, and **TResult** is the type of the resulting elements. An enumerable object is returned that contains the result of the join.

Before looking at any examples that use the query methods, you need to know about lambda expressions.

Lambda Expressions

Although an argument to a query method such as **Where( )** must be of type **Func<T, TResult>**, it does not need to be an explicitly declared method. In fact, most often it won't be. Instead, you will usually use a *lambda expression*. A lambda expression is a new syntactic feature provided by C# 3.0. It offers a streamlined, yet powerful way to define what is, essentially, an anonymous method. The C# compiler automatically converts a lambda expression into a form that can be passed to a **Func<T, TResult>** parameter.

Although we will examine the lambda expression in greater detail later in this section, here is a general overview. All lambda expressions use the new *lambda operator,* which is =>. This operator divides a lambda expression into two parts. On the left is specified the input parameter (or parameters). On the right is one of two things: an expression or a statement block. If the right side is an expression, then an *expression lambda* is being created. If the right side is a block of statements, then it is a *statement lambda*. For the purposes of this section, we will be using only expression lambdas.

In an expression lambda, the expression on the right side of the => acts on the parameter (or parameters) specified by the left side. The result of the expression becomes the result of the lambda operator. Here is the general form of a lambda expression that takes only one parameter:

param => expr

When more than one parameter is required, then the following form is used:

(param-list) => expr

Therefore, when two or more parameters are needed, they must be enclosed by parentheses. If no parameters are needed, then empty parentheses must be used.

Here is a simple lambda expression:

n => n > 0

For any **n**, this expression determines if **n** is greater than zero and returns the result. Here is another example:

count => count + 2

In this case, the result is the value of **count** increased by two.

Create Queries by Using the Query Methods

Using the query methods in conjunction with lambda expressions, it is possible to create queries that do not use the C# query syntax. Instead, the query methods are called. Let's begin with a simple example. It reworks the first program in this chapter so that it uses calls to **Where( )** and **Select( )** rather than the query keywords.

```
// Use the query methods to create a simple query.
// This is a reworked version of the first program
// in this chapter.
using System;
using System.Linq;

class SimpQuery {
  static void Main() {

    int[] nums =  { 1, -2, 3, 0, -4, 5 };

    // Use Where() and Select() to create a simple query.
    var posNums = nums.Where(n => n > 0).Select(r => r);

    Console.WriteLine("The positive values in nums:");

    // Execute the query and display the results.
    foreach(int i in posNums) Console.WriteLine(i);
  }
}
```

Use query methods, not query syntax.

The output, shown here, is the same as the original version:

```
The positive values in nums:
1
3
5
```

In the program, pay special attention to this line:

```
var posNums = nums.Where(n => n > 0).Select(r => r);
```

This creates a query called **posNums** that creates a sequence of the positive values in **nums**. It does this by use of the **Where( )** method to filter the values and **Select( )** to select the values. The **Where( )** method can be invoked on **nums** because all arrays implement **IEnumerable<T>**, which supports the query extension methods.

Technically, the **Select( )** method in the preceding example is not necessary, because in this simple case, the sequence returned by **Where( )** already contains the result. However, you can use more sophisticated selection criteria, just as you did with the query syntax. For example, this query returns the positive values in **nums** increased by an order of magnitude:

```
var posNums = nums.Where(n => n > 0).Select(r => r * 10);
```

As you might expect, you can chain together other operations. For example, this query selects the positive values, sorts them into descending order, and returns the resulting sequence:

```
var posNums = nums.Where(n => n > 0).OrderByDescending(j => j);
```

Here, the expression **j => j** specifies that the ordering is dependent on the input parameter, which is an element from the sequence obtained from **Where( )**.

Here is an example that demonstrates the **GroupBy( )** method. It reworks the **group** example shown earlier.

```
// Demonstrate the GroupBy() query method.
// This program reworks the earlier version that used
// the query syntax.
using System;
using System.Linq;

class GroupByDemo {

  static void Main() {

    string[] websites = { "hsNameA.com", "hsNameB.net", "hsNameC.net",
                          "hsNameD.com", "hsNameE.org", "hsNameF.org",
                          "hsNameG.tv",  "hsNameH.net", "hsNameI.tv" };

    // Use query methods to group websites by top-level domain name.
    var webAddrs = websites.Where(w => w.LastIndexOf(".") != 1).
        GroupBy(x => x.Substring(x.LastIndexOf(".", x.Length)));

    // Execute the query and display the results.
    foreach(var sites in webAddrs) {
      Console.WriteLine("Websites grouped by " + sites.Key);
      foreach(var site in sites)
        Console.WriteLine("  " + site);
      Console.WriteLine();
    }
  }
}
```

This version produces the same output as before. The only difference is how the query is created. In this version, the query methods are used.

Here is another example. Recall the **join** query used in the **JoinDemo** example shown earlier:

```
var inStockList = from item in items
                  join entry in statusList
                    on item.ItemNumber equals entry.ItemNumber
                  select new Temp(item.Name, entry.InStock);
```

This query produces a sequence that contains objects that encapsulate the name and the in-stock status of an inventory item. This information is synthesized from joining the two lists called **items** and **statusList**. The following version reworks this query so that it uses the **Join( )** method rather than the C# query syntax:

```
// Use Join() to produce a list of item names and status.
var inStockList = items.Join(statusList,
                 k1 => k1.ItemNumber,
                 k2 => k2.ItemNumber,
                 (k1, k2) => new Temp(k1.Name, k2.InStock) );
```

Although this version uses the named class called **Temp** to hold the resulting object, an anonymous type could have been used instead. This approach is shown next:

```
var inStockList = items.Join(statusList,
                 k1 => k1.ItemNumber,
                 k2 => k2.ItemNumber,
                 (k1, k2) => new { k1.Name, k2.InStock} );
```

Ask the Expert

Q: I have heard the term *expression tree* used in the context of lambda expressions. What is this?

A: An expression tree is a representation of a lambda expression as data. Thus, an expression tree, itself, cannot be executed. It can, however, be converted into an executable form. Expression trees are encapsulated by the **System.Linq.Expressions.Expression<T>** class. Expression trees are useful in situations in which a query will be executed by something outside the program, such as a database that uses SQL. By representing the query as data, the query can be converted into a format understood by the database. This process is used by the LINQ-to-SQL feature provided by Visual C#, for example. Thus, expression trees help C# support a variety of data sources.

You can obtain an executable form of an expression tree by calling the **Compile( )** method defined by **Expression**. It returns a reference that can be assigned to a delegate and then executed. Expression trees have one key restriction: Only expression lambdas can be represented by expression trees. They cannot be used to represent statement lambdas. Although we won't be making explicit use of expression trees in this chapter, they are something that you may find quite interesting.

More Query-Related Extension Methods

In addition to the methods that correspond to the query keywords, there are several other query-related methods defined for **IEnumerable<T>** by **Enumerable**. Here is a sampling of several commonly used methods. Because many of the methods are overloaded, only their general form is shown

Method	Description
All(*condition*)	Returns true if all elements in a sequence satisfy a specified condition.
Any(*condition*)	Returns true if any element in a sequence satisfies a specified condition.
Average( )	Returns the average of the values in a numeric sequence.
Contains(*obj*)	Returns true if the sequence contains the specified object.
Count( )	Returns the length of a sequence. This is the number of elements that it contains.
First( )	Returns the first element in a sequence.
Last( )	Returns the last element in a sequence.
Max( )	Returns the maximum value in a sequence.
Min( )	Returns the minimum value in a sequence.
Sum( )	Returns the summation of the values in a numeric sequence.

You have already seen **Count( )** in action earlier in this chapter. Here is a program that demonstrates the others:

```
// Use several of the extension methods defined by Enumerable.
using System;
using System.Linq;

class ExtMethods {
  static void Main() {

    int[] nums = { 3, 1, 2, 5, 4 };

    Console.WriteLine("The minimum value is " + nums.Min());
    Console.WriteLine("The maximum value is " + nums.Max());

    Console.WriteLine("The first value is " + nums.First());
    Console.WriteLine("The last value is " + nums.Last());

    Console.WriteLine("The sum is " + nums.Sum());
    Console.WriteLine("The average is " + nums.Average());

    if(nums.All(n => n > 0))
      Console.WriteLine("All values are greater than zero.");

    if(nums.Any(n => (n % 2) == 0))
      Console.WriteLine("At least one value is even.");
```

```
      if(nums.Contains(3))
        Console.WriteLine("The array contains 3.");
    }
}
```

The output is shown here:

```
The minimum value is 1
The maximum value is 5
The first value is 3
The last value is 4
The sum is 15
The average is 3
All values are greater than zero.
At least one value is even.
The array contains 3.
```

You can also use these extension methods within a query based on the C# query syntax. For example, this program uses **Average( )** to obtain a sequence that contains only those values that are less than the average of the values in an array.

```
// Use Average() with the query syntax.
using System;
using System.Linq;

class ExtMethods2 {
  static void Main() {

    int[] nums = { 1, 2, 4, 8, 6, 9, 10, 3, 6, 7 };

    var ltAvg = from n in nums
                let x = nums.Average()          Use a query method with
                where n < x                     the query syntax.
                select n;

    Console.WriteLine("The average is " + nums.Average());

    Console.WriteLine("These values are less than the average:");

    // Execute the query and display the results.
    foreach(int i in ltAvg) Console.WriteLine(i);
  }
}
```

The output is shown here:

```
The average is 5.6
These values are less than the average:
1
2
4
3
```

Deferred vs. Immediate Query Execution

Before moving on, there is one more concept that needs to be presented. In LINQ, queries have two different modes of execution: immediate and deferred. In general, a query defines a set of rules that are not actually executed until a **foreach** statement executes. This is called *deferred execution.*

However, if you use one of the extension methods that produce a non-sequence result, then the query must be executed to obtain that result. For example, consider the **Count( )** method. In order for **Count( )** to return the number of elements in the sequence, the query must be executed, and this is done automatically when **Count( )** is called. In this case, *immediate execution* takes place, with the query being executed automatically in order to obtain the result. Therefore, even though you don't explicitly use the query in a **foreach** loop, the query is still executed.

Here is a simple example. It obtains the number of positive elements in the sequence.

```
// Use immediate execution.
using System;
using System.Linq;

class ImmediateExec {
  static void Main() {

    int[] nums = { 1, -2, 3, 0, -4, 5 };

    // Create a query that obtains the number of positive
    // values in nums.
    int len = (from n in nums          This query executes immediately,
               where n > 0      ◄────  returning the count.
               select n).Count();

    Console.WriteLine("The number of positive values in nums: " + len);
  }
}
```

The output is shown here:

```
The number of positive values in nums: 3
```

In the program, notice that no explicit **foreach** loop is specified. Instead, the query automatically executes because of the call to **Count( )**.

As a point of interest, the query in the preceding program could also have been written like this:

```
var posNums = from n in nums
              where n > 0
              select n;

int len = posNums.Count(); // query executes here
```

In this case, **Count( )** is called on the query variable. At that point, the query is executed to obtain the count.

Ask the Expert

Q: Why does C# have two ways of creating queries, the query syntax and the query methods?

A: Actually, aside from the syntax involved, it really only has one way. Why? Because the query syntax is compiled into calls to the query methods! Thus, when you write something like:

```
where x < 10
```

the compiler translates it into

```
Where(x => x < 10)
```

Thus, the two approaches to creating a query ultimately lead to the same place.

This, then, leads to a second question: Which approach should be used in a C# program? In general, you will want to use the query syntax. It is cleaner and is fully integrated into the C# language.

A Closer Look at Extension Methods

Extension methods provide a means by which functionality can be added to a class without using the normal inheritance mechanism. Although you won't often create your own extension methods (because the inheritance mechanism offers a better solution in many cases), it is still important that you understand how they work because of their integral importance to LINQ.

An extension method is a static method that must be contained within a static, non-generic class. The type of its first parameter determines the type of objects on which the extension method can be called. Furthermore, the first parameter must be modified by **this**. The object on which the method is invoked is passed automatically to the first parameter. It is not explicitly passed in the argument list. A key point is that even though an extension method is declared **static**, it can still be called on an object, just as if it were an instance method.

Here is the general form of an extension method:

static *ret-type name*(this *invoked-on-type ob*, *param-list*)

Of course, if there are no arguments other than the one passed implicitly to *ob,* then *param-list* will be empty. Remember, the first parameter is automatically passed the object on which the method is invoked. In general, an extension method will be a public member of its class.

Here is an example that creates three simple extension methods:

```
// Create and use some extension methods.
using System;

static class MyExtMeths {

  // Return the reciprocal of a double.
  public static double Reciprocal(this double v) {
    return 1.0 / v;
  }

  // Reverse the case of letters within a string and
  // return the result.
  public static string RevCase(this string str) {
    string temp = "";

    foreach(char ch in str) {
      if(Char.IsLower(ch)) temp += Char.ToUpper(ch);
      else temp += Char.ToLower(ch);
    }
    return temp;
  }

  // Return the absolute value of n / d.
  public static double AbsDivideBy(this double n, double d) {
    return Math.Abs(n / d);
  }
}
```

Extension methods. Notice the use of **this**.

```
class ExtDemo {
  static void Main() {
    double val = 8.0;
    string str = "Alpha Beta Gamma";

    // Call the Recip() extension method.
    Console.WriteLine("Reciprocal of {0} is {1}",
                      val, val.Reciprocal());

    // Call the RevCase() extension method.
```

```
        Console.WriteLine(str + " after reversing case is " +
                          str.RevCase());

        // Use AbsDivideBy();
        Console.WriteLine("Result of val.AbsDivideBy(-2): " +
                          val.AbsDivideBy(-2));
    }
}
```

The output is shown here:

```
Reciprocal of 8 is 0.125
Alpha Beta Gamma after reversing case is aLPHA bETA gAMMA
Result of val.AbsDivideBy(-2): 4
```

In the program, notice that each extension method is contained in a static class called **MyExtMeths**. As explained, an extension method must be declared within a static class. Furthermore, this class must be in scope in order for the extension methods that it contains to be used. (This is why you need to include the **System.Linq** namespace when using LINQ.) Next, notice the calls to the extension methods. They are invoked on an object in just the same way that an instance method is called. The main difference is that the invoking object is passed to the first parameter of the extension method. Therefore, when the expression

```
val.AbsDivideBy(-2))
```

executes, **val** is passed to the **n** parameter of **AbsDivideBy( )** and –2 is passed to the **d** parameter.

As a point of interest, because the methods **Reciprocal( )** and **AbsDivideBy( )** are defined for **double**, it is legal to invoke them on a **double** literal, as shown here:

```
8.0.Reciprocal()
8.0.AbsDivideBy(-1)
```

Furthermore, **RevCase( )** can be invoked like this:

```
"AbCDe".RevCase()
```

Here, the reversed-case version of a string literal is returned.

A Closer Look at Lambda Expressions

Although a principal use of lambda expressions is with LINQ, they are a feature that can be used with other aspects of C#. The reason is that a lambda expression creates another type of anonymous function. (The other type of anonymous function is the anonymous method, described earlier in this book.) Thus, a lambda expression can be assigned to (or passed to) a delegate. Because a lambda expression is usually more streamlined than the equivalent anonymous method, lambda expressions are now the recommended approach in most cases.

As mentioned earlier, C# supports two types of lambda expressions. The first is called the *expression lambda,* and it is the type of lambda expression that you have been using up to this point. The body of an expression lambda is freestanding—that is, it is not enclosed between braces. The second is the *statement lambda.* In a statement lambda, the body is enclosed by braces.

A statement lambda can include other C# statements, such as loops, method calls, and **if** statements. Both kinds of lambdas are examined here.

Expression Lambdas

The body of an expression lambda consists solely of the expression on the right side of the =>. Thus, whatever action an expression lambda performs, it must take place within a single expression. Expression lambdas are typically used with queries, as the preceding examples have shown, but they can be used whenever a delegate requires a method that can be expressed in a single expression.

To use a lambda with a delegate involves two steps. First, you must declare the delegate type itself. Second, when you declare an instance of the delegate, assign to it the lambda expression. Once this has been done, the lambda expression can be executed by calling the delegate instance.

The following example illustrates the use of an expression lambda with a delegate. It declares two delegate types. It then assigns lambda expressions to instances of those delegates. Finally, it executes the lambda expressions through the delegate instances.

```
// Demonstrate the expression lambda.
using System;

// First, declare two delegate types.

// The Transform delegate takes one double argument and
// returns a double value.
delegate double Transform(double v);

// The TestInts delegate takes two int arguments and
// returns a bool result.
delegate bool TestInts(int w, int v);

class ExpressionLambdaDemo {

  static void Main() {

    // Create a lambda expression that returns the
    // reciprocal of a value.
    Transform reciprocal = n => 1.0 / n;          ◄──── Assign an expression
                                                        lambda to a delegate.
    Console.WriteLine("The reciprocal of 4 is " + reciprocal(4.0));
    Console.WriteLine("The reciprocal of 10 is " + reciprocal(10.0));

    Console.WriteLine();

    // Create a lambda expression that determines if one
    // integer is a factor of another.
    TestInts isFactor = (n, d) => n % d == 0;     ◄──────┘
```

```
        Console.WriteLine("Is 3 a factor of 9? " + isFactor(9, 3));
        Console.WriteLine("Is 3 a factor of 10? " + isFactor(10, 3));
    }
}
```

The output is shown here:

```
The reciprocal of 4 is 0.25
The reciprocal of 10 is 0.1

Is 3 a factor of 9? True
Is 3 a factor of 10? False
```

In the program, first notice how the delegates are declared. The **Transform** delegate takes a **double** argument and returns a **double** result. The **TestInts** delegate takes two **int** arguments and returns a **bool** result. Next, pay special attention to these declarations:

```
Transform reciprocal = n => 1.0 / n;
TestInts isFactor = (n, d) => n % d == 0;
```

The first assigns to **reciprocal** a lambda expression that returns the reciprocal of the value that it is passed. This expression can be assigned to a **Transform** delegate because it is compatible with **Transform**'s declaration. The argument used in the call to reciprocal is passed to **n**. The value returned is the result of the expression **1.0 / n**.

The second statement assigns to **isFactor** an expression that returns true if the second argument is a factor of the first. This lambda takes two arguments, and it returns true if the first can be evenly divided by the second. Thus, it is compatible with the **TestInts** declaration. The two arguments passed to **isFactor( )** when it is called are automatically passed to **n** and **d**, in that order. One other point: The parentheses around the parameters **n** and **d** are necessary. The parentheses are optional only when one parameter is used.

Statement Lambdas

A statement lambda expands the types of operations that can be handled directly within a lambda expression. For example, using a statement lambda, you can use loops, **if** statements, declare variables, and so on. A statement lambda is easy to create. Simply enclose the body of the lambda expression within braces.

Here is an example that uses a statement lambda to compute and return the factorial of an **int** value:

```
// Demonstrate a statement lambda.
using System;

// IntOp takes one int argument and returns an int result.
delegate int IntOp(int end);

class StatementLambdaDemo {
```

```
static void Main() {

  // A statement lambda that returns the factorial
  // of the value it is passed.
  IntOp fact = n => {
                  int r = 1;
                  for(int i=1; i <= n; i++)        ◄── This is a statement
                    r = i * r;                          lambda.
                  return r;
                };

  Console.WriteLine("The factorial of 3 is " + fact(3));
  Console.WriteLine("The factorial of 5 is " + fact(5));
  }
}
```

The output is shown here:

```
The factorial of 3 is 6
The factorial of 5 is 120
```

In the program, notice that the statement lambda declares a variable called **r**, uses a **for** loop, and has a **return** statement. These are legal inside a statement lambda. In essence, a statement lambda closely parallels an anonymous method. Therefore, many anonymous methods will be converted to statement lambdas when updating legacy code. One other point: When a **return** statement occurs within a lambda expression, it simply causes a return from the lambda. It does not cause the enclosing method to return.

Try This Use Lambda Expressions to Implement Event Handlers

Since lambda expressions can be assigned to delegates, they can also be used as event handlers. In this capacity, lambda expressions can be used in place of an anonymous method in many cases. The example developed here illustrates the use of both an expression lambda and a statement lambda as an event handler.

Step by Step

1. Create an event delegate called **MyEventHandler** and an event class called **MyEvent**, as shown here:

```
// Declare a delegate type for an event.
delegate void MyEventHandler();

// Declare a class with an event.
class MyEvent {
```

(continued)

```
public event MyEventHandler SomeEvent;

// This is called to fire the event.
public void Fire() {
  if(SomeEvent != null)
    SomeEvent();
}
}
```

2. Begin creating a class called **LambdaEventHandlers** that will generate and handle events, as shown here:

```
class LambdaEventHandlers {
  static void Main() {
    MyEvent evt = new MyEvent();
    int count = 0;
```

Notice that **Main( )** creates an event referred to by **evt** and declares **count** as an integer variable that is initialized to zero.

3. Add an event handler that increments **count** to **evt**'s event chain, as shown here:

```
// This expression lambda increments count when
// the event occurs.
evt.SomeEvent += () => count++;
```

This uses an expression lambda as the event handler. Notice that it can use the outer variable **count**. The same rules regarding the use of outer variables that apply to anonymous methods (described in Chapter 12) also apply to lambda expressions.

4. Add an event handler to **evt** that displays the value of **count**, as shown next:

```
// This statement lambda displays the value of count.
// If count is greater than 3, it is reset to 0.
evt.SomeEvent += () => {
                        if(count > 3) count = 0;
                        Console.WriteLine("Count is " + count);
                      };
```

This uses a statement lambda to display the current value of **count**. Before doing so, it tests the value of **count**. If it is greater than 3, it is reset to zero.

5. Complete **LambdaEventHandlers** by invoking the event five times:

```
// Fire the event five times.
evt.Fire();
evt.Fire();
evt.Fire();
evt.Fire();
evt.Fire();
}
}
```

6. Here is the entire example:

```
// Use lambda expressions as event handlers.
using System;

// Declare a delegate type for an event.
delegate void MyEventHandler();

// Declare a class with an event.
class MyEvent {
  public event MyEventHandler SomeEvent;

  // This is called to fire the event.
  public void Fire() {
    if(SomeEvent != null)
      SomeEvent();
  }
}

class LambdaEventHandlers {
  static void Main() {
    MyEvent evt = new MyEvent();
    int count = 0;

    // Use lambda expressions to define event handlers.

    // This expression lambda increments count when
    // the event occurs.
    evt.SomeEvent += () => count++;

    // This statement lambda displays the value of count.
    // If count is greater than 3, it is reset to 0.
    evt.SomeEvent += () => {
                           if(count > 3) count = 0;
                           Console.WriteLine("Count is " + count);
                         };

    // Fire the event five times.
    evt.Fire();
    evt.Fire();
    evt.Fire();
    evt.Fire();
    evt.Fire();
  }
}
```

(continued)

The output is shown here:

```
Count is 1
Count is 2
Count is 3
Count is 0
Count is 1
```

Ask the Expert

Q: Okay, I'm convinced! LINQ is incredibly powerful. What's the best way to begin learning more about it?

A: Begin by exploring the contents of **System.Linq**. Pay special attention to the capabilities of the extension methods defined by **Enumerable**. Next, expand your knowledge and expertise in writing lambda expressions. They are expected to play an increasingly important role in C# programming. Also, study the collections in **System.Collections** and **System.Collections.Generic**. An introduction to collections is presented in Chapter 15, but there is much more to learn. Although quite new, LINQ is already an important part of C#, and its use is expected to increase with time. Simply put, LINQ will be a part of every C# programmer's future. The effort you put forth today will be repaid several times over.

Chapter 14 Self Test

1. What does LINQ stand for? In general terms, what is its purpose?

2. As it relates to LINQ, what interface must a data source implement?

3. What are the query keywords that begin query clauses?

4. Assuming a data source called **myDataList**, show how to create a query that returns a sequence of those objects. Call the query variable **allData**.

5. Assuming that **myDataList** contains **MyData** objects and that **MyData** defines a property called **Height**, rewrite the query for question 4 so that it returns a sequence of the **Height** property, rather than the entire **MyData** object.

6. What query keyword is used to filter a sequence? Use it to rewrite your answer to question 5 so that it returns only those **MyData** objects whose **Height** property is less than 100.

7. What query keyword orders a sequence? Using your answer for question 6, sort the results into descending order based on the **Height** property.

8. What query keyword groups the result of a query organized into sequences? (In other words, what keyword returns a sequence of sequences?) Show its general form.

9. What keyword joins two sequences? Show its general form in the context of a **from** clause.

10. When using **select** or **group**, what keyword creates a continuation?

11. What keyword creates a variable that holds a value?

12. Show how to create an instance of an anonymous type that has two **string** properties called **Title** and **Author**.

13. What is the lambda operator?

14. A lambda expression is one form of anonymous function. True or False?

15. What is the query method that corresponds to the **where** keyword?

16. What is an extension method? How must the first parameter be declared?

17. Why are extension methods important to LINQ?

Chapter 15

The Preprocessor, RTTI, Nullable Types, and Other Advanced Topics

Key Skills & Concepts

- Preprocessor

- Runtime type identification

- Nullable types

- Unsafe code

- Attributes

- Conversion operators

- Collections

- Additional keywords

You have come a long way since the start of this book. This, the final chapter, examines several C# topics, such as the preprocessor, runtime type ID, and nullable types, that don't fit easily into any of the preceding chapters. It also introduces collections, gives an overview of unsafe code, and shows how to create a conversion operator. The chapter concludes with a brief look at the remaining C# keywords that are not covered elsewhere. Many of the topics in this chapter apply to advanced uses of C#, and detailed discussions of these topics are outside the scope of this book. They are introduced here so that you will have a full picture of what is available in C#.

The Preprocessor

C# defines several *preprocessor directives,* which affect the way that your program's source file is interpreted by the compiler. These directives affect the text of the source file in which they occur, prior to the translation of the program into object code. The term *preprocessor directive* comes from the fact that these instructions were traditionally handled by a separate compilation phase called the *preprocessor.* Today's modern compiler technology no longer requires a separate preprocessing stage to handle the directives, but the name has stuck.

C# defines the following preprocessor directives:

#define	#elif	#else	#endif
#endregion	#error	#if	#line
#pragma	#region	#undef	#warning

All preprocessor directives begin with a # sign. In addition, each preprocessing directive must be on its own line.

Given C#'s modern, object-oriented architecture, there is not as much need for the preprocessor directives as there is in older languages. Nevertheless, they can be of value from time to time, especially for conditional compilation. Each directive is examined in turn.

#define

The **#define** directive defines a character sequence called a *symbol*. The existence or nonexistence of a symbol can be determined by **#if** or **#elif**, and is used to control compilation.

#define *symbol*

Notice that there is no semicolon in this statement. There may be any number of spaces between **#define** and the symbol, but once the symbol begins, it is terminated only by a newline character. For example, to define the symbol **EXPERIMENTAL**, use this directive:

```
#define EXPERIMENTAL
```

#if and #endif

The **#if** and **#endif** directives allow you to conditionally compile a sequence of code based upon whether an expression involving one or more symbols evaluates to true. A symbol is true if it has been defined. It is false otherwise. Thus, if a symbol has been defined by a **#define** directive, it will evaluate as true.

The general form of **#if** is

#if *symbol-expression*
   statement sequence
#endif

If the expression following **#if** is true, the code that is between it and **#endif** is compiled. Otherwise, the intervening code is skipped. The **#endif** directive marks the end of an **#if** block.

A symbol expression can be as simple as just the name of a symbol. You can also use these operators in a symbol expression: **!**, **= =**, **!=**, **&&**, and **||**. Parentheses are also allowed.

Here is a simple example that demonstrates condition compilation:

```
// Demonstrate #if, #endif, and #define.
#define EXPERIMENTAL

using System;

class Test {
  static void Main() {

    #if EXPERIMENTAL
      Console.WriteLine("Compiled for experimental version.");
    #endif

    Console.WriteLine("This is in all versions.");
  }
}
```

Compiled only if EXPERIMENTAL is defined.

This program displays the following:

```
Compiled for experimental version.
This is in all versions.
```

The program defines the symbol **EXPERIMENTAL**. Thus, when the **#if** is encountered, the symbol expression evaluates to true, and the first **WriteLine( )** statement is compiled. If you remove the definition of **EXPERIMENTAL** and recompile the program, the first **WriteLine( )** statement will not be compiled because the **#if** will evaluate to false. In all cases, the second **WriteLine( )** statement is compiled because it is not part of the **#if** block.

As explained, you can use a symbol expression in an **#if**. For example:

```
// Use a symbol expression.
#define EXPERIMENTAL
#define TRIAL

using System;

class Test {
  static void Main() {

    #if EXPERIMENTAL
      Console.WriteLine("Compiled for experimental version.");
    #endif

    #if EXPERIMENTAL && TRIAL   ◄──────── A symbol expression.
      Console.Error.WriteLine("Testing experimental trial version.");
    #endif

    Console.WriteLine("This is in all versions.");
  }
}
```

The output from this program is shown here:

```
Compiled for experimental version.
Testing experimental trial version.
This is in all versions.
```

In this example, two symbols are defined, **EXPERIMENTAL** and **TRIAL**. The second **WriteLine( )** statement is compiled only if both are defined.

You can use the ! to compile code when a symbol is not defined. For example,

```
#if !QC_PASSED
  Console.WriteLine("Code has not passed quality control.");
#endif
```

The call to **WriteLine( )** will be compiled only if **QC_PASSED** *has not* been defined.

#else and #elif

The **#else** directive works much like the **else** that is part of the C# language: It establishes an alternative if **#if** fails. Here is an example:

```
// Demonstrate #else.

#define EXPERIMENTAL

using System;

class Test {
  static void Main() {

    #if EXPERIMENTAL
      Console.WriteLine("Compiled for experimental version.");
    #else
      Console.WriteLine("Compiled for release.");
    #endif

    #if EXPERIMENTAL && TRIAL
      Console.Error.WriteLine("Testing experimental trial version.");
    #else
      Console.Error.WriteLine("Not experimental trial version.");
    #endif

    Console.WriteLine("This is in all versions.");
  }
}
```

Use the **#else**.

The output is shown here:

```
Compiled for experimental version.
Not experimental trial version.
This is in all versions.
```

Since **TRIAL** is not defined, the **#else** portion of the second conditional code sequence is used.

Notice that **#else** marks both the end of the **#if** block and the beginning of the **#else** block. This is necessary, because there can only be one **#endif** associated with any **#if**. Furthermore, there can be only one **#else** associated with any **#if**.

The **#elif** directive means "else if" and establishes an if-else-if chain for multiple compilation options. **#elif** is followed by a symbol expression. If the expression is true, that block of code is compiled and no other **#elif** expressions are tested. Otherwise, the next block in the series is checked. If no **#elif** succeeds, then if there is an **#else**, the code sequence associated with the **#else** is compiled. Otherwise, no code in the entire **#if** is compiled.

Here is an example that demonstrates **#elif**:

```
// Demonstrate #elif.
#define RELEASE

using System;

class Test {
  static void Main() {

    #if EXPERIMENTAL
      Console.WriteLine("Compiled for experimental version.");
    #elif RELEASE            Use #elif.
      Console.WriteLine("Compiled for release.");
    #else
      Console.WriteLine("Compiled for internal testing.");
    #endif

    #if TRIAL && !RELEASE
        Console.WriteLine("Trial version.");
    #endif

    Console.WriteLine("This is in all versions.");
  }
}
```

The output is shown here:

```
Compiled for release.
This is in all versions.
```

Putting together all the pieces, here is the general form of **#if/#else/#elif/#endif** directives:

```
#if symbol-expression
  statement sequence
#elif symbol-expression
  statement sequence
#elif symbol-expression
  statement sequence

  .
  .
  .

#else symbol-expression
  statement sequence
#endif
```

#undef

The **#undef** directive removes a previously defined symbol. That is, it "undefines" a symbol. The general form for **#undef** is

#undef *symbol*

For example:

```
#define MOBILE_DEVICE

#if MOBILE_DEVICE
  // ...
#undef MOBILE_DEVICE
// At this point MOBILE_DEVICE is undefined.
```

After the **#undef** directive, **MOBILE_DEVICE** is no longer defined.

   #undef is used principally to allow symbols to be localized to only those sections of code that need them.

Ask the Expert

Q: I notice that the C# preprocessor directives have many similarities with the preprocessor directives supported by C and C++. Furthermore, in C/C++, I know that you can use *#define* to perform textual substitutions, such as defining a name for a value, and to create function-like macros. Does C# support these uses of *#define*?

A: No. In C#, **#define** is used only to define a symbol.

#error

The **#error** directive forces the compiler to stop compilation. It is used for debugging. The general form of the **#error** directive is

#error *error-message*

When the **#error** directive is encountered, the error message is displayed. For example, when the compiler encounters this line:

```
#error Debug code still being compiled!
```

compilation stops and the error message "Debug code still being compiled!" is displayed.

#warning

The **#warning** directive is similar to **#error**, except that a warning rather than an error is produced. Thus, compilation is not stopped. The general form of the **#warning** directive is

#warning *warning-message*

#line

The **#line** directive sets the line number and filename for the file that contains the **#line** directive. The number and the name are used when errors or warnings are output during compilation. The general form for **#line** is

#line *number "filename"*

where *number* is any positive integer and becomes the newline number, and the optional *filename* is any valid file identifier, which becomes the new filename.

    #line allows two options. The first is **default**, which returns the line numbering to its original condition. It is used like this:

```
#line default
```

The second is **hidden**. When stepping through a program, the **hidden** option allows a debugger to bypass lines between a

```
#line hidden
```

directive and the next **#line** directive that does not include the **hidden** option.

#region and #endregion

The **#region** and **#endregion** directives let you define a region that will be expanded or collapsed by the Visual Studio IDE when using the outlining feature. The general form is shown here:

```
#region
  // code sequence
#endregion
```

#pragma

The **#pragma** directive gives instructions to the compiler, such as specifying an option. It has this general form:

#pragma *option*

Here, *option* is the instruction passed to the compiler.

    In C# 3.0, there are two options supported by **#pragma**. The first is **warning**, which is used to enable or disable specific compiler warnings. It has these two forms:

#pragma warning disable *warnings*

#pragma warning restore *warnings*

Here, *warnings* is a comma-separated list of warning numbers. To disable a warning, use the **disable** option. To enable a warning, use the **restore** option.

For example, this **#pragma** statement disables warning 168, which indicates when a variable is declared but not used:

```
#pragma warning disable 168
```

The second **#pragma** option is **checksum**. It is used to generate checksums for ASP.NET projects. It has this general form:

#pragma checksum "*filename*" "*{GUID}*" "*check-sum*"

Here, *filename* is the name of the file, *GUID* is the globally unique identifier associated with *filename,* and *check-sum* is a hexadecimal number that contains the checksum. This string must contain an even number of digits.

Runtime Type Identification

In C#, it is possible to determine the type of an object at runtime. In fact, C# includes three keywords that support runtime type identification: **is**, **as**, and **typeof**. Although runtime type identification is one of C#'s more advanced features, it is important to have a general understanding of it.

Testing a Type with is

You can determine if an object is of a certain type by using the **is** operator. Its general form is shown here:

obj is *type*

Here, *obj* is an expression that describes an object whose type is being tested against *type*. If the type of *obj* is the same as, or compatible with, *type,* then the outcome of this operation is true. Otherwise, it is false. Thus, if the outcome is true, *obj* can be cast to *type*. Here is an example:

```
// Demonstrate is.
using System;

class A {}
class B : A {}

class UseIs {
  static void Main() {
    A a = new A();
    B b = new B();

    if(a is A) Console.WriteLine("a is an A");
    if(b is A)  ◄──────────── This is true because b is an A.
      Console.WriteLine("b is an A because it is derived from A");
```

```
    if(a is B) ◄───────────── This is false because a is not a B.
      Console.WriteLine("This won't display -- a not derived from B");

    if(b is B) Console.WriteLine("b is a B");
    if(a is object) Console.WriteLine("a is an Object");
  }
}
```

The output is shown here:

```
a is an A
b is an A because it is derived from A
b is a B
a is an Object
```

Most of the **is** expressions are self-explanatory, but two warrant a closer look. First, notice this statement:

```
if(b is A)
  Console.WriteLine("b is an A because it is derived from A");
```

The **if** succeeds because **b** is an object of type **B**, which is derived from type **A**. Thus, **b** is compatible with **A**. However, the reverse is not true. When this line is executed:

```
if(a is B)
  Console.WriteLine("This won't display -- a not derived from B");
```

the **if** does not succeed because **a** is of type **A**, which is not derived from **B**. Thus, they are not compatible.

Using as

Sometimes you will want to try a conversion at runtime but not throw an exception if the conversion fails (which is the case when a cast is used). To do this, use the **as** operator, which has this general form:

expr as *type*

Here, *expr* is the expression being converted to *type*. If the conversion succeeds, then a reference to *type* is returned. Otherwise, a null reference is returned. The **as** operator can only be used to perform reference, boxing, unboxing, or identity conversions.

Using typeof

You can obtain type information about a given type by using **typeof**, which has this general form:

typeof(*type*)

Here, *type* is the type being obtained. It returns an instance of **System.Type**, which is a class that describes the information associated with a type. Using this instance, you can retrieve information about the type. For example, this program displays the complete name for the **StreamReader** class:

```
// Demonstrate typeof.
using System;
using System.IO;

class UseTypeof {
  static void Main() {
    Type t = typeof(StreamReader);
    Console.WriteLine(t.FullName);
  }
}
```

This program outputs the following:

```
System.IO.StreamReader
```

System.Type contains many methods, fields, and properties that describe a type. You will want to explore it on your own.

Nullable Types

Beginning with version 2.0, C# has included a feature that provides an elegant solution to what is both a common and an irritating problem. The feature is the *nullable type*. The problem is how to recognize and handle fields that do not contain values (in other words, unassigned fields). To understand the problem, consider a simple customer database that keeps a record of the customer's name, address, customer ID, invoice number, and current balance. In such a situation, it is possible to create a customer entry in which one or more of those fields would be unassigned. For example, a customer may simply request a catalog. In this case, no invoice number would be needed and the field would be unused.

Prior to nullable types, handling the possibility of unused fields required either the use of placeholder values or an extra field that simply indicated whether a field was used or not. Of course, placeholder values could only work if there was a value that would otherwise not be valid, which won't be the case in all situations. Adding an extra field to indicate if a field was in use works in all cases, but having to manually create and manage such a field is an annoyance. The nullable type solves both problems.

A nullable type is a special version of a value type that is represented by a structure. In addition to the values defined by the underlying type, a nullable type can store the value **null**. Thus, a nullable type has the same range and characteristics as its underlying type. It simply adds the ability to represent a value that indicates that a variable of that type is unassigned. Nullable types are objects of **System.Nullable<T>**, where **T** must be a non-nullable value type.

A nullable type can be specified in two different ways. First, you can explicitly use the type **Nullable<T>**. For example, this declares variables of **int** and **bool** nullable types:

```
Nullable<int> count;
Nullable<bool> done;
```

The second way to specify a nullable type is much shorter and is more commonly used. Simply follow the underlying type name with a **?**. For example, the following shows the more common way to declare variables of the nullable **int** and **bool** types:

```
int? count;
bool? done;
```

When using nullable types, you will often see a nullable object created like this:

```
int? count = null;
```

This explicitly initializes **count** to **null**. This satisfies the constraint that a variable must be given a value before it is used. In this case, the value simply means undefined.

You can assign a value to a nullable variable in the normal way because a conversion from the underlying type to the nullable type is predefined. For example, this assigns **count** the value 100:

```
count = 100;
```

There are two ways to determine whether a variable of a nullable type is **null** or contains a value. First, you can test its value against **null**. For example, using **count** declared by the preceding statement, the following determines if it has a value:

```
if(count != null) // has a value
```

If **count** is not **null**, then it contains a value.

The second way to determine if a nullable type contains a value is to use the **HasValue** read-only property defined by **Nullable<T>**. It is shown here:

bool HasValue

HasValue will return true if the instance on which it is called contains a value. It will return false otherwise. Using the **HasValue** property, here is the second way to determine if the nullable object **count** has a value:

```
if(count.HasValue) // has a value
```

Assuming that a nullable object contains a value, you can obtain its value by using the **Value** read-only property defined by **Nullable<T>**, which is shown here:

T Value

It returns the value of the nullable instance on which it is called. If you try to obtain a value from a variable that is **null**, a **System.InvalidOperationException** will be thrown. It is also possible to obtain the value of a nullable instance by casting it into its underlying type.

The following program puts together the pieces and demonstrates the basic mechanism that handles a nullable type:

```
// Demonstrate a nullable type.

using System;

class NullableDemo {
  static void Main() {
    int? count = null;                              Declare a nullable type for int.

    if(count.HasValue)
      Console.WriteLine("count has this value: " + count.Value);
    else
      Console.WriteLine("count has no value");

    count = 100;

    if(count.HasValue)
      Console.WriteLine("count has this value: " + count.Value);
    else
      Console.WriteLine("count has no value");
                                                    Use HasValue to determine
  }                                                 if count has a value.
}
```

The output is shown here:

```
count has no value
count has this value: 100
```

The ?? Operator

If you attempt to use a cast to convert a nullable object to its underlying type, a **System.InvalidOperationException** will be thrown if the nullable object contains a **null** value. This can occur, for example, when you use a cast to assign the value of a nullable object to a variable of its underlying type. You can avoid the possibility of this exception begin thrown by using the **??** operator, which is called the *null coalescing operator.* It lets you specify a default value that will be used when the nullable object contains **null**. It also eliminates the need for the cast.

The **??** operator has this general form:

nullable-object **??** *default-value*

If *nullable-object* contains a value, then the value of the **??** is that value. Otherwise, the value of the **??** operation is *default-value*.

For example, in the following code, **balance** is **null**. This causes **currentBalance** to be assigned the value 0.0 and no exception will be thrown.

```
double? balance = null;
double currentBalance;

currentBalance = balance ?? 0.0;
```

In the next sequence, **balance** is given the value 123.75.

```
double? balance = 123.75;
double currentBalance;

currentBalance = balance ?? 0.0;
```

Now, **currentBalance** will contain the value of **balance**, which is 123.75.

One other point: The right-hand expression of the **??** is evaluated only if the left-hand expression does not contain a value.

Nullable Objects and the Relational and Logical Operators

Nullable objects can be used in relational expressions in just the same way as their corresponding non-nullable types. However, there is one additional rule that applies. When two nullable objects are compared using the **<**, **>**, **<=**, or **>=** operator, the result is false if either of the objects is **null**. For example, consider this sequence:

```
byte? lower = 16;
byte? upper = null;

// Here, lower is defined, but upper isn't.
if(lower < upper) // false
```

Here, the result of the test for less than is false. However, somewhat counterintuitively, so is the inverse comparison:

```
if(lower > upper) // .. also false!
```

Thus, when one (or both) of the nullable objects used in a comparison is **null**, the result of that comparison is always false. Thus, **null** does not participate in an ordering relationship.

You can test whether a nullable object contains **null**, however, by using the **==** or **!=** operator. For example, this is a valid test that will result in a true outcome:

```
if(upper == null) // ...
```

When a logical expression involves two **bool?** objects, the outcome of that expression will be one of three values: **true**, **false**, or **null** (undefined). Here are the entries that are added to the truth table for the **&** and **|** operators that apply to **bool?**:

P	Q	P | Q	P & Q
true	null	true	null
false	null	null	false
null	true	true	null
null	false	null	false

One other point: When the **!** operator is applied to a **bool?** value that is **null**, the outcome is **null**.

Unsafe Code

C# allows you to write what is called "unsafe" code! While this might sound like a name for code that contains mistakes, it isn't. Unsafe code is not code that is poorly written; it is code that does not execute under the full management of the Common Language Runtime (CLR). As explained in Chapter 1, C# is normally used to create managed code. It is possible, however, to write code that does not execute under the full control of the CLR. Since this unmanaged code is not subject to the same controls and constraints as managed code, it is called "unsafe" because it is impossible to verify that it won't perform some type of harmful action. Thus, the term *unsafe* does not mean that the code is inherently flawed. It just means that it is possible for the code to perform actions that are not subject to the supervision of the managed context.

Managed code, while beneficial for the most part, prevents the use of *pointers*. If you are familiar with C or C++, then you know that pointers are variables that hold the addresses of other objects. Thus, conceptually, pointers are a bit like references in C#. The main difference is that a pointer can point anywhere in memory; a reference always refers to an object of its type. Since a pointer can point anywhere in memory, it is possible to misuse a pointer. It is also easy to introduce a coding error when using pointers. This is why C# does not support pointers when creating managed code. Pointers are, however, both useful and necessary for some types of programming (such as when writing code that interacts with a device), and C# does allow you to create and use pointers. All pointer operations must be marked as unsafe, since they execute outside the managed environment.

As a point of interest, the declaration and use of pointers in C# parallels that of C/C++; if you know how to use pointers in C/C++, then you can use them in C#. But remember, the point of C# is to create managed code. Its ability to support unmanaged code allows it to be applied to a special class of problems. It is not for normal C# programming. In fact, to compile unmanaged code, you must use the **/unsafe** compiler option. In general, if you need to create large amounts of code that execute outside of the CLR, then you are probably better off using C++.

Working with unmanaged code is an advanced topic, and a detailed discussion is well beyond the scope of this book. That said, we will briefly examine pointers and the two keywords that support unmanaged code: **unsafe** and **fixed**.

A Brief Look at Pointers

A pointer is a variable that holds the address of some other object. For example, if **p** contains the address of **y**, then **p** is said to "point to" **y**. Pointer variables must be declared as such. The general form of a pointer variable declaration is

*type** *var-name*;

Here, *type* is the type of object to which the pointer will point, and it must be a non-reference type. *var-name* is the name of the pointer variable. For example, to declare **ip** to be a pointer to an **int**, use this declaration:

```
int* ip;
```

For a **float** pointer, use

```
float* fp;
```

In general, in a declaration statement, following a type name with an * creates a pointer type.

The type of data that a pointer will point to is determined by its *referent type,* which is also commonly referred to as the pointer's base type. Thus, in the preceding examples, **ip** can be used to point to an **int**, and **fp** can be used to point to a **float**. Understand, however, that there is nothing that actually prevents a pointer from pointing to something else. This is why pointers are potentially unsafe.

Remember that a pointer type can be declared only for non-reference types. This means that the referent type of a pointer can be any of the simple types, such as **int**, **double**, and **char**; an enumeration type; or a **struct** (as long as its fields are all non-reference types).

There are two key pointer operators: * and **&**. The **&** is a unary operator that returns the memory address of its operand. (Recall that a unary operator requires only one operand.) For example:

```
int* ip;
int num = 10;

ip = &num;
```

puts into **ip** the memory address of the variable **num**. This address is the location of the variable in the computer's internal memory. It has *nothing* to do with the *value* of **num**. Thus, **ip** *does not* contain the value 10 (**num**'s initial value). It contains the address at which **num** is stored. The operation of **&** can be remembered as returning "the address of" the variable it precedes. Therefore, the above assignment statement could be verbalized as "**ip** receives the address of **num**."

The second operator is *, and it is the complement of **&**. It is a unary operator that *dereferences* the pointer. In other words, it evaluates to the variable located at the address specified by its operand. Continuing with the same example, if **ip** contains the memory address of the variable **num**, then

```
int val;
val = *ip;
```

will place into **val** the value 10, which is the value of **num** (which is pointed to by **ip**). The operation of * can be remembered as "at address." In this case, then, the statement could be read as "**val** receives the value at address **ip**."

Pointers can also be used with structures. When you access a member of a structure through a pointer, you must use the –> operator rather than the dot (.) operator. The –> is informally called the *arrow operator*. For example, given this structure:

```
struct MyStruct {
  public int x;
  public int y;
  public int sum() { return x + y; }
}
```

here is how you would access its members through a pointer:

```
MyStruct o = new MyStruct();
MyStruct* p; // declare a pointer

p = &o;
p->x = 10;
p->y = 20;

Console.WriteLine("Sum is " + p->sum());
```

Pointers can have simple arithmetic operations performed on them. For example, you can increment or decrement a pointer. Doing so causes it to point to the next or previous object of its referent type. You can also add or subtract integer values to or from a pointer. You can subtract one pointer from another (which yields the number of elements of the referent type separating the two), but you can't add pointers.

Ask the Expert

Q: I know that when declaring a pointer in C++, the * is not distributive over a list of variables in a declaration. Thus, in C++, this statement,

```
int* p, q;
```

declares an integer pointer called p and an integer called q. It is equivalent to the following two declarations:

```
int* p;
int q;
```

Is the same also true for C#?

A: No. In C#, the * *is* distributive and the declaration

```
int* p, q;
```

creates two pointer variables. Thus, it is the same as these two declarations:

```
int* p;
int* q;
```

This is an important difference to be aware of when porting C++ code to C#.

The unsafe Keyword

Any code that uses pointers must be marked as unsafe by using the **unsafe** keyword. You can mark types (such as classes and structures), members (such as methods and operators), or individual blocks of code as unsafe. For example, here is a program that uses pointers inside **Main( )**, which is marked unsafe:

```
// Demonstrate pointers and unsafe.
// You need to compile this program by use of the /unsafe option.
using System;

class UnsafeCode {
  // Mark Main as unsafe.
  unsafe static void Main() {         Main( ) is marked unsafe
    int count = 99;                   because it uses a pointer.
    int* p; // create an int pointer

    p = &count; // put address of count into p

    Console.WriteLine("Initial value of count is " + *p);

    *p = 10; // assign to count via p

    Console.WriteLine("New value of count is " + *p);
  }
}
```

The output of this program is shown here:

```
Initial value of count is 99
New value of count is 10
```

This program uses the pointer **p** to obtain the value contained in **count**, which is the object that **p** points to. Because of the pointer operations, it must be marked unsafe in order for it to be compiled.

Using fixed

The **fixed** keyword has two uses. The first is to prevent a managed object from being moved by the garbage collector. This is needed when a pointer refers to a field within such an object, for example. Since the pointer has no knowledge of the actions of the garbage collector, if the object is moved, the pointer will point to the wrong location. Here is the general form of **fixed**:

```
fixed (type* p = &fixedVar) {
  // use fixed object
}
```

Here, *p* is a pointer that is being assigned the address of a variable. The variable will remain in its current memory location until the block of code has executed. You can also use a single statement for the target of a **fixed** statement. The **fixed** keyword can be used only in an unsafe context.

Here is an example of **fixed**:

```
// Demonstrate fixed.
using System;

class Test {
  public int num;
  public Test(int i) { num = i; }
}

class UseFixed {
  // Mark Main as unsafe.
  unsafe static void Main() {
    Test o = new Test(19);
```

Use **fixed** to fix the location of **o**.

```
    fixed (int* p = &o.num) { // use fixed to put address of o.num into p

      Console.WriteLine("Initial value of o.num is " + *p);

      *p = 10; // assign to o.num via p

      Console.WriteLine("New value of o.num is " + *p);
    }
  }
}
```

The output from this program is shown here:

```
Initial value of o.num is 19
New value of o.num is 10
```

Here, **fixed** prevents **o** from being moved. This is required because **p** points to **o.num**. If **o** moved, then **o.num** would also move. This would cause **p** to point to an invalid location. The use of **fixed** prevents this.

The second use of **fixed** is to create fixed-sized, single-dimensional arrays. These are referred to as *fixed-size buffers*. A fixed-size buffer is always a member of a **struct**. The purpose of a fixed-size buffer is to allow the creation of a **struct** in which the array elements that make up the buffer are contained within the **struct**. Normally, when you include an array member in a **struct**, only a reference to the array is actually held within the **struct**. By using a fixed-size buffer, you cause the entire array to be contained within the **struct**. This results in a structure that can be used in situations in which the size of a **struct** is important, such as in mixed-language programming, interfacing to data not created by a C# program, or whenever a non-managed **struct** containing an array is required. Fixed-size buffers can be used only within an unsafe context.

To create a fixed-size buffer, use this form of **fixed**:

fixed *type buf-name*[*size*];

Here, *type* is the data type of the array, *buf-name* is the name of the fixed-size buffer, and *size* is the number of elements in the buffer. Fixed-size buffers can be specified only inside a **struct**.

As stated at the outset of this section, the creation and use of unsafe code is an advanced topic, and there are more issues involved with its creation than are discussed here. If writing unsafe code will be a part of your programming future, then you will need to study it further.

Attributes

C# allows you to add declarative information to a program in the form of an *attribute*. An attribute defines additional information that is associated with a class, structure, method, and so on. For example, you might define an attribute that determines the type of button that a class will display.

Attributes are specified between square brackets, preceding the item they apply to. You can define your own attribute or use attributes defined by C#. Although creating your own attributes is a topic that is beyond the scope of this book, it is quite easy to use two of C#'s built-in attributes: **Conditional** and **Obsolete**. They are examined in the following sections.

The Conditional Attribute

The attribute **Conditional** is perhaps C#'s most interesting attribute. It allows you to create *conditional methods*. A conditional method is invoked only when a specific symbol has been defined via **#define**. Otherwise, the method is bypassed. Thus, a conditional method offers an alternative to conditional compilation using **#if**. To use the **Conditional** attribute, you must include the **System.Diagnostics** namespace.

Let's begin with an example:

```
// Demonstrate the Conditional attribute.
#define TRIAL

using System;
using System.Diagnostics;

class Test {

  [Conditional("TRIAL")]
  void Trial() {                   ◄——————— Trial( ) is executed only if TRIAL is defined.
    Console.WriteLine("Trial version, not for distribution.");
  }

  [Conditional("RELEASE")]
  void Release() {                 ◄——————— Release( ) is executed only if RELEASE is defined.
    Console.WriteLine("Final release version.");
  }
```

```
    static void Main() {
      Test t = new Test();

      t.Trial(); // call only if TRIAL is defined
      t.Release(); // called only if RELEASE is defined
    }
}
```

The output from this program is shown here:

```
Trial version, not for distribution.
```

Let's look closely at this program to understand why this output is produced. First notice that the program defines the symbol **TRIAL**. Next, notice how the methods **Trial( )** and **Release( )** are coded. They are both preceded with the **Conditional** attribute, which has this general form:

[Conditional *symbol*]

where *symbol* is the symbol that determines whether the method will be executed. This attribute can be used only on methods. If the symbol is defined, then when the method is called, it will be executed. If the symbol is not defined, then the method is not executed.

Inside **Main( )**, both **Trial( )** and **Release( )** are called. However, only **TRIAL** is defined. Thus, **Trial( )** is executed. The call to **Release( )** is ignored. If you define **RELEASE**, then **Release( )** will also be called. If you remove the definition for **TRIAL**, then **Trial( )** will not be called.

Conditional methods have a few restrictions: They must return **void**; they must be members of a class or structure, not an interface; and they cannot be preceded with the **override** keyword.

The Obsolete Attribute

The **System.Obsolete** attribute lets you mark a program element as obsolete. It has two basic forms. The first is:

[Obsolete "*message*"]

Here, *message* is displayed when that program element is compiled. Here is a short example:

```
// Demonstrate the Obsolete attribute.
using System;

public class Test {

  [Obsolete("Use MyMeth2, instead.")]  ◄──────  Display a warning if MyMeth( ) is used.
  public static int MyMeth(int a, int b) {
    return a / b;
  }
```

```
// Improved version of MyMeth.
public static int MyMeth2(int a, int b) {
  return b == 0 ? 0 : a /b;
}

static void Main() {
 // Warning displayed for this.
  Console.WriteLine("4 / 3 is " + Test.MyMeth(4, 3));

 // No warning here.
  Console.WriteLine("4 / 3 is " + Test.MyMeth2(4, 3));
 }
}
```

When the call to **MyMeth( )** is encountered in **Main( )** during program compilation, a warning will be generated that tells the user to use **MyMeth2( )** instead.

A second form of **Obsolete** is shown here:

[Obsolete("*message*", *error*)]

Here, *error* is a Boolean value. If it is true, then the use of the obsolete item generates a compilation error rather than a warning. The difference is, of course, that a program containing an error cannot be compiled into an executable program.

Conversion Operators

In some situations, you will want to use an object of a class in an expression involving other types of data. Sometimes, overloading one or more operators can provide the means of doing this. However, in other cases, what you want is a simple type conversion from the class type to the target type. To handle these cases, C# allows you to create a *conversion operator.* A conversion operator converts an object of your class into another type.

There are two forms of conversion operators: implicit and explicit. The general form for each is shown here:

public static operator implicit *target-type*(*source-type v*) { return *value*; }

public static operator explicit *target-type*(*source-type v*) { return *value*; }

Here, *target-type* is the target type that you are converting to, *source-type* is the type you are converting from, and *value* is the value of the class after conversion. The conversion operators return data of type *target-type,* and no other return-type specifier is allowed.

If the conversion operator specifies **implicit**, then the conversion is invoked automatically, such as when an object is used in an expression with the target type. When the conversion operator specifies **explicit**, the conversion is invoked when a cast is used. You cannot define both an implicit and an explicit conversion operator for the same target and source types.

To illustrate a conversion operator, we will use the **ThreeD** class that we created in Chapter 7. Recall that **ThreeD** stores three-dimensional coordinates. Suppose you want to convert an object of type **ThreeD** into a numeric value so it can be used in a numeric expression. Further more, the conversion will take place by computing the distance from the point to the origin, which will be represented as a **double**. To accomplish this, you can use an implicit conversion operator that looks like this:

```
public static implicit operator double(ThreeD op1)
{
  return Math.Sqrt(op1.x * op1.x + op1.y * op1.y + op1.z * op1.z);
}
```

It takes a **ThreeD** object and returns its distance to the origin as a **double** value.

Here is a program that illustrates this conversion operator:

```
// An example that uses an implicit conversion operator.
using System;

// A three-dimensional coordinate class.
class ThreeD {
  int x, y, z; // 3-D coordinates

  public ThreeD() { x = y = z = 0; }
  public ThreeD(int i, int j, int k) { x = i; y = j; z = k; }

  // Overload binary +.
  public static ThreeD operator +(ThreeD op1, ThreeD op2)
  {
    ThreeD result = new ThreeD();

    result.x = op1.x + op2.x;
    result.y = op1.y + op2.y;
    result.z = op1.z + op2.z;

    return result;
  }

  // An implicit conversion from ThreeD to double.
  // It returns the distance from the origin to the
  // specified point.
  public static implicit operator double(ThreeD op1)    ◄──── A conversion operator
  {                                                            from ThreeD to double.
    return Math.Sqrt(op1.x * op1.x + op1.y * op1.y + op1.z * op1.z);
  }

  // Show X, Y, Z coordinates.
  public void Show()
  {
    Console.WriteLine(x + ", " + y + ", " + z);
  }
}
```

```
class ConversionOpDemo {
  static void Main() {
    ThreeD alpha = new ThreeD(12, 3, 4);
    ThreeD beta = new ThreeD(10, 10, 10);
    ThreeD gamma = new ThreeD();
    double dist;

    Console.Write("Here is alpha: ");
    alpha.Show();
    Console.WriteLine();
    Console.Write("Here is beta: ");
    beta.Show();
    Console.WriteLine();

    // Add alpha and beta together. This does NOT invoke
    // the conversion operator because no conversion to
    // double is needed.
    gamma = alpha + beta;
    Console.Write("Result of alpha + beta: ");
    gamma.Show();
    Console.WriteLine();

    // The following statement invokes the conversion
    // operator because the value of a is assigned
    // to dist, which is a double.
    dist = alpha; // convert to double
    Console.WriteLine("Result of dist = alpha: " + dist);
    Console.WriteLine();

    // This also invokes the conversion operator
    // because the expression requires a double value.
    if(beta > dist)
      Console.WriteLine("beta is farther from the origin");
  }
}
```

Conversion operator invoked.

This program displays the output:

```
Here is alpha: 12, 3, 4

Here is beta: 10, 10, 10

Result of alpha + beta: 22, 13, 14

Result of dist = alpha: 13

beta is farther from the origin
```

As the program illustrates, when a **ThreeD** object is used in a **double** expression, such as **dist = alpha**, the conversion is applied to the object. In this specific case, the conversion returns the value 13, which is **alpha's** distance from the origin. However, when an expression does not require a conversion to **double**, the conversion operator is not called. This is why **gamma = alpha + beta** does not invoke **operator double( )**.

Remember that you can create different conversion operators to meet different needs. You could define one that converts to **long**, for example. Each conversion is applied automatically and independently.

An implicit conversion operator is used automatically when a conversion is required in an expression, when passing an object to a method, in an assignment, and also when an explicit cast to the target type is used. Alternatively, you can create an explicit conversion operator that is invoked only when an explicit cast is used. An explicit conversion operator is not invoked automatically. For example, here is the conversion operator in the previous program reworked as an explicit conversion:

```
// This is now explicit.
public static explicit operator double(ThreeD op1)
{
  return Math.Sqrt(op1.x * op1.x + op1.y * op1.y + op1.z * op1.z);
}
```

Now, this statement from the previous example

```
dist = alpha;
```

must be recoded to use an explicit cast, as shown here:

```
dist = (double) alpha;
```

Furthermore, this statement:

```
if(beta > dist)
  Console.WriteLine("beta is farther from the origin");
```

must be reworked like this:

```
if((double) beta > dist)
  Console.WriteLine("beta is farther from the origin");
```

Because the conversion operator is now marked as explicit, conversion to **double** must be explicitly cast in all cases.

There are a few restrictions to conversion operators:

- You cannot create a conversion from a built-in type to another built-in type. For example, you cannot redefine the conversion from **double** to **int**.

- You cannot define a conversion to or from **object**.

- You cannot define both an implicit and an explicit conversion for the same source and target types.

- You cannot define a conversion from a base class to a derived class.

- You cannot define a conversion from or to an interface.

Ask the Expert

Q: Since implicit conversions are invoked automatically, without the need for a cast, why would I want to create an explicit conversion?

A: Although convenient, implicit conversions should be used only in situations in which the conversion is inherently error-free. To ensure this, implicit conversions should be created only when two conditions are met. The first is that no loss of information, such as truncation, overflow, or loss of sign, occurs. The second is that the conversion does not throw an exception. If the conversion cannot meet these two requirements, then you should use an explicit conversion.

A Brief Introduction to Collections

One of the most important parts of the .NET Framework is collections. As it relates to C#, a *collection* is a group of objects. The .NET Framework contains a large number of interfaces and classes that define and implement various types of collections. Collections simplify many programming tasks because they supply off-the-shelf solutions to several common, but sometimes tedious-to-develop, data structures. For example, there are built-in collections that support dynamic arrays, linked lists, stacks, queues, and hash tables.

Containing both generic and non-generic collection classes, the Collections API is very large. It isn't possible to fully describe its contents or illustrate its use here. However, because collections are an increasingly important part of C# programming, they are a feature that you need to be aware of. Towards this end, this section provides a brief introduction to this important subsystem. As you advance in your study of C#, collections are definitely a feature that you will want to study further.

Collection Basics

The principal benefit of collections is that they standardize the way groups of objects are handled by a program. All collections are designed around a set of cleanly defined interfaces. Several built-in implementations of these interfaces are provided, which you can use as-is. You can also implement your own collection, but you will seldom need to.

As mentioned, the .NET Framework defines both generic and non-generic collections. The original 1.0 release contained only non-generic collections, but the generic collections were added by the 2.0 release. Although both are still used, new code should focus on the generic collections because they are type-safe. (The original, non-generic collections store object references, which makes them vulnerable to type mismatch errors.) The non-generic collection classes and interfaces are declared in **System.Collections**. Generic collections are declared in **System.Collections.Generic**. Since the generic collections have largely superseded the non-generic collections, they are the only type of collections described here.

The basic functionality of the collections is defined by the interfaces that they implement. For generic collections, the foundation is the **ICollection<T>** interface, which is implemented by all generic collections. It inherits **IEnumerable<T>** (which extends **IEnumerable**) and defines the methods shown here:

Method	Description
void Add(T *obj*)	Adds *obj* to the invoking collection.
void Clear( )	Deletes all elements from the invoking collection.
bool Contains(T *obj*)	Returns **true** if the invoking collection contains the object passed in *obj* and **false** otherwise.
void CopyTo(T[ ] *target*, int *startIdx*)	Copies the contents of the invoking collection to the array specified by *target*, beginning at the index specified by *startIdx*.
IEnumerator<T> GetEnumerator( )	Returns the enumerator for the collection. (Specified by **IEnumerable<T>**.)
IEnumerator GetEnumerator( )	Returns the non-generic enumerator for the collection. (Specified by **IEnumerable**.)
bool Remove(T *obj*)	Removes the first occurrence of *obj* from the invoking collection. Returns **true** if *obj* was removed and **false** if it was not found in the invoking collection.

Methods that modify a collection will throw **NotsupportedException** if the collection is read-only.

ICollection<T> also defines the following properties:

int Count { get; }

bool IsReadOnly { get; }

Count contains the number of items currently held in the collection. **IsReadOnly** is true if the collection is read-only. It is false if the collection is read/write.

Because **ICollection<T>** inherits the **IEnumerable<T>** interface, it ensures that all of the collections classes can be enumerated (cycled through one element at a time). Furthermore, inheriting **IEnumerable<T>** allows a collection to be used as a data source for queries or iterated by the **foreach** loop. (Recall that only instances of objects that implement **IEnumerable** or **IEnumerable<T>** can be used as a data source for a query.) Because collections implement **IEnumerable<T>**, they also support the extension methods defined for **IEnumerable<T>** (see Chapter 14).

The Collections API defines several other interfaces that add functionality. For example, **IList<T>** extends **ICollection<T>**, adding support for collections whose elements can be accessed through an index. The **IDictionary<TK, TV>** extends **ICollection<T>** to support the storage of key/value pairs.

The Collections API provides several implementations of the collections interfaces. For example, the generic **List<T>** collection implements a type-safe dynamic array, which is an array that grows as needed. There are classes that implement stacks and queues, such as **Stack<T>** and **Queue<T>**. Other classes, such as **Dictionary<TK, TV>**, store key/value pairs.

Although an in-depth look at each collection interface and class is not possible, a case study is presented that will give you an idea of their power and illustrate the general way in which they are used. It uses the **List<T>** collection.

A Collections Case Study: Create a Dynamic Array

Perhaps the most widely used collection is **List<T>**, which implements a generic, dynamic array. It has the constructors shown here:

public List( )
public List(IEnumerable<T> *c*)
public List(int *capacity*)

The first constructor builds an empty list with a default initial capacity. The second constructor builds a list that is initialized with the elements of the collection specified by *c* and with an initial capacity equal to the number of elements. The third constructor builds a list that has the specified initial *capacity*. The capacity grows automatically as elements are added to a **List<T>**. Each time the list must be enlarged, its capacity is increased.

List<T> implements several interfaces, including **IList<T>**. The **IList<T>** interface extends **ICollection<T>**, **IEnumerable<T>**, and **IEnumerable**. The **IList<T>** interface defines the behavior of a generic collection that allows elements to be accessed via a zero-based index. In addition to the methods specified by the interfaces that it extends, **IList<T>** adds the methods shown here. If the collection is read-only, then the **Insert( )** and **RemoveAt( )** methods will throw a **NotSupportedException**.

Method	Description
int IndexOf(T *obj*)	Returns the index of *obj* if *obj* is contained within the invoking collection. If *obj* is not found, −1 is returned.
void Insert(int *idx*, T *obj*)	Inserts *obj* at the index specified by *idx*.
void RemoveAt(int *idx*)	Removes the object at the index specified by *idx* from the invoking collection.

IList<T> defines the following indexer:

T this[int *idx*] { get; set; }

This indexer sets or gets the value of the element at the index specified by *idx*.

In addition to the functionality defined by the interfaces that it implements, **List\<T>** provides much of its own. For example, it supplies methods that sort a list, perform a binary search, and convert a list into an array. **List\<T>** also defines a property called **Capacity** that gets or sets the capacity of the invoking list. The capacity is the number of elements that can be held before the list must be enlarged. (It is not the number of elements currently in the list.) Because a list grows automatically, it is not necessary to set the capacity manually. However, for efficiency reasons, you might want to set the capacity when you know in advance how many elements the list will contain. This prevents the overhead associated with the allocation of more memory.

Here is a program that demonstrates the basic usage of **List\<T>**. It creates a dynamic array of type **int**. Notice that the list automatically expands and contracts, based on the number of elements that it contains.

```
// Demonstrate List<T>.

using System;
using System.Collections.Generic;

class ListDemo {
  static void Main() {
    // Create a list of integers.
    List<int> lst = new List<int>();     ◄────── Create an instance of List for int.

    Console.WriteLine("Initial number of elements: " +  lst.Count);

    Console.WriteLine();

    Console.WriteLine("Adding 5 elements");
    // Add elements to the array list.
    lst.Add(1);
    lst.Add(-2);
    lst.Add(14);    ◄────── Add elements to the list.
    lst.Add(9);
    lst.Add(88);

    Console.WriteLine("Number of elements: " +  lst.Count);

    // Display the array list using array indexing.
    Console.Write("Contents: ");
    for(int i=0; i < lst.Count; i++)
      Console.Write(lst[i] + " ");    ◄────── Index the list.
    Console.WriteLine("\n");

    Console.WriteLine("Removing 2 elements");
    // Remove elements from the array list.
    lst.Remove(-2);
    lst.Remove(88);    ◄────── Remove elements from the list.

    Console.WriteLine("Number of elements: " +  lst.Count);
```

```
    // Use foreach loop to display the list.
    Console.Write("Contents: ");
    foreach(int i in lst)          ◄——————— Cycle through the list via a foreach loop.
      Console.Write(i + " ");
    Console.WriteLine("\n");

    Console.WriteLine("Adding 10 elements");
    // Add enough elements to force lst to grow.
    for(int i=0; i < 10; i++)      ◄——————— Expand the list.
      lst.Add(i);

    Console.WriteLine("Number of elements after adding 10: " +
                      lst.Count);
    Console.Write("Contents: ");
    foreach(int i in lst)
      Console.Write(i + " ");
    Console.WriteLine("\n");

    // Change contents using array indexing.
    Console.WriteLine("Change first three elements");
    lst[0] = -10;
    lst[1] = -lst[1];              ◄——————— Change the list.
    lst[2] = 99;

    Console.Write("Contents: ");
    foreach(int i in lst)
      Console.Write(i + " ");
    Console.WriteLine();
  }
}
```

The output is shown here:

```
Initial number of elements: 0

Adding 5 elements
Number of elements: 5
Contents: 1 -2 14 9 88

Removing 2 elements
Number of elements: 3
Contents: 1 14 9

Adding 10 elements
Number of elements after adding 10: 13
Contents: 1 14 9 0 1 2 3 4 5 6 7 8 9

Change first three elements
Contents: -10 -14 99 0 1 2 3 4 5 6 7 8 9
```

The program begins by creating an instance of **List<int>** called **lst**. This collection is initially empty. Notice how its size grows as elements are added. As explained, **List<T>** creates a dynamic array, which grows as needed to accommodate the number of elements that it must hold. Also notice how **lst** can be indexed, using the same syntax as that used to index an array.

Because the **List<T>** collection creates an indexable, dynamic array, it is often used in place of an array. The principal advantage is that you don't need to know how many elements will be stored in the list at compile time. Of course, arrays offer a bit better runtime efficiency, so using **List<T>** trades speed for convenience.

Try This   Use the Queue<T> Collection

In the preceding chapters, several Try This examples have developed and evolved a queue class as a means of illustrating several fundamental C# programming concepts, such as encapsulation, properties, exceptions, and so on. Although creating your own data structures, such as a queue, is a good way to learn about C#, it is not something that you will normally need to do. Instead, you will usually use one of the standard collections. In the case of a queue, this is **Queue<T>**. It provides a high-performance implementation that is fully integrated into the overall Collections framework. In this section, the final Try This in the book, you will see how to put **Queue<T>** into action. It creates a short program that simulates using a queue to grant users access to a network.

Queue<T> is a dynamic collection that grows as needed to accommodate the elements it must store. **Queue<T>** defines the following constructors:

```
public Queue( )
public Queue (int capacity)
public Queue (IEnumerable<T> c)
```

The first form creates an empty queue with an initial default capacity. The second form creates an empty queue with the initial capacity specified by *capacity*. The third form creates a queue that contains the elements of the collection specified by *c*.

In addition to the functionality defined by the collection interfaces that it implements, **Queue<T>** defines the methods shown here. To put an object in the queue, call **Enqueue( )**. To remove and return the object at the front of the queue, call **Dequeue( )**. An **InvalidOperationException** is thrown if you call **Dequeue( )** when the invoking queue is empty. You can use **Peek( )** to return, but not remove, the next object.

(continued)

Method	Description
public T Dequeue( )	Returns the object at the front of the invoking queue. The object is removed in the process.
public void Enqueue(T v)	Adds v to the end of the queue.
public T Peek( )	Returns the object at the front of the invoking queue, but does not remove it.
public T[ ] ToArray( )	Returns an array that contains copies of the elements of the invoking queue.
public void TrimExcess( )	Removes the excess capacity of the invoking queue if its size is less than 90 percent of its capacity.

This example uses a queue to simulate scheduling access to a network by a collection of users. It doesn't actually do any real scheduling. Instead, it simply fills a queue with the names of the users and then grants the users access based on the order in which they are entered into the queue. Of course, since this is a simulation, the program simply displays the user's name when a user is granted access.

Step by Step

1. Begin creating the simulation as shown here:

```
// Use the Queue<T> class to simulate scheduling user access to a network.

using System;
using System.Collections.Generic;

class QueueDemo {
  static void Main() {
    Queue<string> userQ = new Queue<string>();
```

Notice that a **Queue** called **userQ** is created that can hold references to objects of type **string**.

2. Add the following code that puts user names into the queue:

```
Console.WriteLine("Adding users to the network user queue.\n");

userQ.Enqueue("Eric");
userQ.Enqueue("Tom");
userQ.Enqueue("Ralph");
userQ.Enqueue("Ken");
```

3. Add the code that removes one name at a time, which simulates granting access to the network.

```
Console.WriteLine("Granting network access in queue order.\n");

while(userQ.Count > 0) {
  Console.WriteLine("Granting network access to: " + userQ.Dequeue());
}
```

4. Finish the program.

```
      Console.WriteLine("\nUser queue is exhausted.");
   }
}
```

5. Here is the complete program that uses **Queue\<T>** to simulate scheduling users' access to a network:

```
// Use the Queue<T> class to simulate scheduling access to a network.

using System;
using System.Collections.Generic;

class QueueDemo {
  static void Main() {
    Queue<string> userQ = new Queue<string>();

    Console.WriteLine("Adding users to the network user queue.\n");

    userQ.Enqueue("Eric");
    userQ.Enqueue("Tom");
    userQ.Enqueue("Ralph");
    userQ.Enqueue("Ken");

    Console.WriteLine("Granting network access in queue order.\n");

    while(userQ.Count > 0) {
      Console.WriteLine("Granting network access to: " + userQ.Dequeue());
    }

    Console.WriteLine("\nUser queue is exhausted.");
  }
}
```

The output is shown here:

```
Adding users to the network user queue.

Granting network access in queue order.

Granting network access to: Eric
Granting network access to: Tom
Granting network access to: Ralph
Granting network access to: Ken

User queue is exhausted.
```

(continued)

A key point about this example is how little code is needed to implement the simulation. If you had to actually develop the queue yourself (as previous Try This examples did), the code would be much larger. Furthermore, the standard **Queue<T>** class offers a solution that all C# programmers will instantly recognize, thus making your programs easier to maintain.

Other Keywords

To conclude this book, the few remaining keywords defined by C# that have not been described elsewhere are briefly discussed.

The internal Access Modifier

In addition to the access modifiers **public**, **private**, and **protected**, which we have been using throughout this book, C# also defines **internal**. Mentioned briefly in Chapter 6, **internal** declares that a member is known throughout all files in an assembly, but unknown outside that assembly. An *assembly* is a file (or files) that contains all deployment and version information for a program. Thus, in simplified terms, a member marked as **internal** is known throughout a program, but not elsewhere.

sizeof

Occasionally, you might find it useful to know the size, in bytes, of one of C#'s value types. To obtain this information, use the **sizeof** operator. It has this general form:

sizeof(*type*)

Here, *type* is the type whose size is being obtained. Thus, it is intended primarily for special-case situations, especially when working with a blend of managed and unmanaged code.

lock

The **lock** keyword is used when working with *multiple threads*. In C#, a program can contain two or more *threads of execution*. When this is the case, pieces of the program are multitasked. Thus, pieces of the program execute independently and simultaneously. This raises the prospect of a special type of problem: What if two threads try to use a resource that can be used by only one thread at a time? To solve this problem, you can create a *critical code section* that will be executed by one and only one thread at a time. This is accomplished by **lock**. Its general form is shown here:

```
lock(obj) {
  // critical section
}
```

Here, *obj* is the object on which the lock is synchronized. If one thread has already entered the critical section, then a second thread will wait until the first thread exits the critical section.

When the first thread leaves the critical section, the lock is released and the second thread can be granted the lock, at which point the second thread can execute the critical section.

readonly

You can create a read-only field in a class by declaring it as **readonly**. A **readonly** field can be given a value only by using an initializer when it is declared, or by assigning it a value within a constructor. Once the value has been set, it can't be changed outside the constructor. Thus, **readonly** fields are a good way to create constants, such as array dimensions, that are used throughout a program. Both static and non-static **readonly** fields are allowed.

Here is an example that creates and uses a **readonly** field:

```
// Demonstrate readonly.
using System;

class MyClass {
  public static readonly int SIZE = 10;    ◄──────  This essentially declares a constant.
}

class DemoReadOnly {
  static void Main() {
    int[] nums = new int[MyClass.SIZE];

    for(int i=0; i < MyClass.SIZE; i++)
      nums[i] = i;

    foreach(int i in nums)
      Console.Write(i + " ");

    // MyClass.SIZE = 100; // Error!!! can't change
  }
}
```

Here, **MyClass.SIZE** is initialized to 10. After that, it can be used, but not changed. To prove this, try removing the comment symbol from before the last line and then compiling the program. As you will see, an error will result.

stackalloc

You can allocate memory from the stack by using **stackalloc**. It can be used only when initializing local variables and has this general form:

type * *p* = stackalloc *type*[*size*]

Here, *p* is a pointer that receives the address of the memory that is large enough to hold *size* number of objects of *type*. **stackalloc** must be used in an unsafe context.

Normally, memory for objects is allocated from the *heap,* which is a region of free memory. Allocating memory from the stack is the exception. Variables allocated on the stack are not garbage-collected. Rather, they exist only while the block in which they are declared is executing. The only advantage to using **stackalloc** is that you don't need to worry about the variables being moved about by the garbage collector.

The using Statement

In addition to the **using** *directive* discussed earlier, **using** has a second form that is called the **using** *statement*. It has these general forms:

using (*obj*) {
  // use *obj*
}

using (*type obj = initializer*) {
  // use *obj*
}

Here, *obj* is an expression that must evaluate to an object that implements the **System.IDisposable** interface. It specifies a variable that will be used inside the **using** block. In the first form, the object is declared outside the **using** statement. In the second form, the object is declared within the **using** statement. When the block concludes, the **Dispose( )** method (defined by the **System.IDisposable** interface) will be called on *obj*. Thus, a **using** statement provides a means by which objects are automatically disposed when they are no longer needed. Remember, the **using** statement applies only to objects that implement the **System.IDisposable** interface.

Here is an example of each form of the **using** statement:

```
// Demonstrate using statement.

using System;
using System.IO;

class UsingDemo {
  static void Main() {
    StreamReader sr = new StreamReader("test.txt");

    // Use object inside using statement.
    using(sr) {
      // ...
    }

    // Create StreamReader inside the using statement.
    using(StreamReader sr2 = new StreamReader("test.txt")) {
      // ...
    }
  }
}
```

The class **StreamReader** implements the **IDisposable** interface (through its base class **TextReader**). Thus, it can be used in a **using** statement. When the **using** statement ends, **Dispose( )** is automatically called on the stream variables, thus closing the stream.

const and volatile

The **const** modifier is used to declare fields or local variables that cannot be changed. These variables must be given initial values when they are declared. Thus, a **const** variable is essentially a constant. For example,

```
const int i = 10;
```

creates a **const** variable called **i** that has the value 10.

The **volatile** modifier tells the compiler that a field's value may be changed by two or more concurrently executing threads. In this situation, one thread may not know when the field has been changed by another thread. This is important, because the C# compiler will automatically perform certain optimizations that work only when a field is accessed by a single thread of execution. To prevent these optimizations from being applied to a shared field, declare it **volatile**. This tells the compiler that it must obtain the value of this field each time it is accessed.

The partial Modifier

The **partial** modifier has two uses. First, it can be used to allow a class, structure, or interface definition to be broken into two or more pieces, with each piece residing in a separate file. When your program is compiled, the pieces of the class, structure, or interface are united, forming the complete type. Second, in a partial class or structure, **partial** can be used to allow the declaration of a method to be separate from its implementation. Each use is described here.

Partial Types

When used to create a partial type, the **partial** modifier has this general form:

partial class *typename* { // ...

Here, *typename* is the name of the class, structure, or interface that is being split into pieces. Each part of a partial type must be modified by **partial**.

Here is an example that divides a simple XY coordinate class into three separate files. The first file is shown here:

```
partial class XY {
  public XY(int a, int b) {
    X = a;
    Y = b;
  }
}
```

The second file is shown next:

```
partial class XY {
  public int X { get; set; }
}
```

The third file is

```
partial class XY {
  public int Y { get; set; }
}
```

The following file demonstrates the use of **XY**:

```
// Demonstrate partial class definitions.
using System;

class Test {
  static void Main() {
    XY xy = new XY(1, 2);


    Console.WriteLine(xy.X + "," + xy.Y);
  }
}
```

To use **XY**, all files must be included in the compile. For example, assuming the XY files are called **xy1.cs**, **xy2.cs**, and **xy3.cs**, and that the **Test** class is contained in a file called **test.cs**, then to compile **Test**, use the following command line:

```
csc test.cs xy1.cs xy2.cs xy3.cs
```

One last point: It is legal to have partial generic classes. However, the type parameters of each partial declaration must match the other parts.

Partial Methods

Within a partial type that is a class or a structure, you can use **partial** to create a partial method. A partial method has its declaration in one part and its implementation in another part. Partial methods were added by C# 3.0.

The key aspect of a partial method is that the implementation is not required! When the partial method is not implemented by another part of the class or structure, then all calls to the partial method are silently ignored. This makes it possible for a class to specify, but not require, optional functionality. If that functionality is not implemented, then it is simply ignored.

Here is an expanded version of the preceding program that creates a partial method called **Show( )**. It is called by another method called **ShowXY( )**.

```
// Demonstrate a partial method.
using System;
```

```
partial class XY {
  public XY(int a, int b) {
    X = a;
    Y = b;
  }

  // Declare a partial method.
  partial void Show();
}

partial class XY {
  public int X { get; set; }

  // Implement a partial method.
  partial void Show() {
    Console.WriteLine("{0}, {1}", X, Y);
  }
}

partial class XY {
  public int Y { get; set; }

  // Call a partial method.
  public void ShowXY() {
    Show();
  }
}

class Test {
  static void Main() {
    XY xy = new XY(1, 2);

    xy.ShowXY();
  }
}
```

Notice that **Show( )** is declared in one part of **XY** and implemented by another part. The implementation displays the values of **X** and **Y**. This means that when **Show( )** is called by **ShowXY( )**, the call has effect and it will, indeed, display **X** and **Y**. However, if you comment-out the implementation of **Show( )**, then the call to **Show( )** within **ShowXY( )** does nothing.

Partial methods have several restrictions, including these: They must be void; they cannot have access modifiers; they cannot be virtual; and they cannot use **out** parameters.

yield

The yield contextual keyword is used with an iterator, which is a method, operator, or accessor that returns the members of a set of objects, one element at a time, in sequence. Iterators are most often used with collections.

extern

The **extern** keyword has two uses. First, it indicates that a method is provided by external code, which is usually unmanaged code. Second, it is used to create an alias for an external assembly.

What Next?

Congratulations! If you have read and worked through all the 15 chapters, then you can call yourself a C# programmer. Of course, there are still many, many things to learn about C#, its libraries, and subsystems, but you now have a solid foundation upon which you can build your knowledge and expertise. Here are a few of the topics that you will want to learn more about:

- Creating multithreaded applications

- Using Windows forms

- Using the collection classes

- Networking with C# and .NET

To continue your study of C#, I recommend my book *C# 3.0: The Complete Reference* (McGraw-Hill).

Chapter 15 Self Test

1. Name the preprocessor directives that are used for conditional compilation.

2. What does **#elif** do?

3. How can you obtain a **System.Type** instance that represents the type of an object at runtime?

4. What does **is** do?

5. What benefit does **as** provide?

6. Show how to declare a nullable **int** called **count** that is initialized to **null**.

7. A nullable type can represent all values of its underlying type, plus the **null** value. True or False?

8. What is the **??** operator called and what does it do?

9. What is unsafe code?

10. Show how to declare a pointer to a **double**. Call the pointer **ptr**.

11. Show the attribute syntax.

12. What are the two kinds of conversion operators? Show their general forms.

13. What is a collection? What namespace are the generic collections in?

14. What interface is implemented by all generic collections?

15. What keyword is used to declare a partial class? What keyword is used to declare a partial method?

16. On your own, continue to explore and experiment with C#.

Appendix A

Answers to Self Tests

Chapter 1: C# Fundamentals

1. **MSIL stands for Microsoft Intermediate Language. It is an optimized, portable set of assembly language instructions that is compiled into executable code by a JIT compiler. MSIL helps C# achieve portability, security, and mixed-language compatibility.**

2. **The Common Language Runtime (CLR) is the part of .NET that manages the execution of C# and other .NET-compatible programs.**

3. **Encapsulation, polymorphism, and inheritance.**

4. **C# programs begin execution at** Main( ).

5. **A variable is a named memory location. The contents of a variable can be changed during the execution of a program. A namespace is a declarative region. Namespaces help keep one set of names separate from another.**

6. **The invalid variables are B and D. Variable names cannot begin with a $ or a digit.**

7. **A single-line comment begins with // and ends at the end of the line. A multiline comment begins with /* and ends with */.**

8. **The general form of the** if**:**

   if(*condition*) *statement*;

   The general form of the **for**:

   for(*initialization*; *condition*; *iteration*) *statement*;

9. **A block of code begins with a { and ends with a }.**

10. **No,** using System **is not necessary, but leaving it out means that you must fully qualify members of the** System **namespace by putting** System **in front of them.**

11.
```
//   Compute your weight on the moon.

using System;

class Moon {
  static void Main() {
    double earthweight; // weight on earth
    double moonweight;  // weight on moon

    earthweight = 165.0;

    moonweight = earthweight * 0.17;

    Console.WriteLine(earthweight + " earth-pounds is equivalent to " +
                      moonweight + " moon-pounds.");

  }
}
```

12.
```csharp
/*
    This program displays a conversion
    table of inches to meters.
*/

using System;

class InchToMeterTable {
  static void Main() {
    double inches, meters;
    int counter;

    counter = 0;
    for(inches = 1.0; inches <= 144.0; inches++) {

      // Convert to meters.
      meters = inches / 39.37;

      Console.WriteLine(inches + " inches is " + meters + " meters.");

      counter++;

      // Every 12th line, print a blank line.
      if(counter == 12) {
        Console.WriteLine();
        counter = 0; // reset the line counter
      }
    }
  }
}
```

Chapter 2: Introducing Data Types and Operators

1. C# strictly specifies the range and behavior of its simple types to ensure portability and interoperability in a mixed-language environment.

2. C#'s character type is char. C# characters are Unicode rather than ASCII, which is used by many other computer languages.

3. False. A bool value must be either true or false.

4. `Console.WriteLine("One\nTwo\nThree");`

5. There are three fundamental flaws in the fragment. First, sum is created each time the block created by the for loop is entered and is destroyed on exit. Thus, it will not hold its value between iterations. Attempting to use sum to hold a running sum of the iterations is pointless. Second, sum will not be known outside of the block in which it is declared. Thus, the reference to it in the WriteLine( ) statement is invalid. Third, sum has not been given an initial value.

6. When the increment operator precedes its operand, C# will increment the operand prior to obtaining its value. If the operator follows its operand, then C# will first obtain the operand's value. Then, its value will be incremented.

7. `if((b != 0) && (val / b))` ...

8. In an expression, byte and short are promoted to int.

9. A.

10. A cast is needed when converting between incompatible types or when a narrowing conversion is occurring.

11. Here is one way to find the primes between 2 and 100. There are, of course, other solutions.

```
// Find prime numbers between 2 and 100.

using System;

class Prime {
  static void Main() {
    int i, j;
    bool isprime;

    for(i=2; i < 100; i++) {
      isprime = true;

      // See if the number is evenly divisible.
      for(j=2; j <= i/j; j++)
        // If i is evenly divisible, then it's not prime.
        if((i%j) == 0) isprime = false;

      if(isprime)
        Console.WriteLine(i + " is prime.");
    }
  }
}
```

Chapter 3: Program Control Statements

1.
```
// Count spaces.

using System;

class Spaces {
  static void Main() {
    char ch;
    int spaces = 0;

    Console.WriteLine("Enter a period to stop.");
```

```
      do {
        ch = (char) Console.Read();
        if(ch == ' ') spaces++;
      } while(ch != '.');

      Console.WriteLine("Spaces: " + spaces);
    }
}
```

2. No. The "no fall through" rule states that the code sequence from one case label must not continue on into the next. Case labels can be "stacked," however.

3. if(*condition*)
  statement;
else if(*condition*)
  statement;
else if(*condition*)
  statement;

  .

  .

  .

else
  statement;

4. The last else associates with the outer if, which is the nearest if at the same level as the else.

5. for(int i = 1000; i >= 0; i -= 2) // ...

6. No, i is not known outside of the for loop in which it is declared.

7. A break causes termination of its immediately enclosing loop or switch statement.

8. After break executes, "after while" is displayed.

9. 0 1
  2 3
  4 5
  6 7
  8 9

10. /* Use a for loop to generate the progression

     1 2 4 8 16, ...
  */

  using System;

  class Progress {
    static void Main() {
```
```

```
      for(int i = 1; i < 100; i += i)
        Console.Write(i + " ");
    }
  }
```

11. `// Change case.`

```
using System;

class CaseChg {
  static void Main() {
    char ch;
    int changes = 0;

    Console.WriteLine("Enter period to stop.");

    do {
      ch = (char) Console.Read();
      if(ch >= 'a' && ch <= 'z') {
        ch -= (char) 32;
        changes++;
        Console.WriteLine(ch);
      }
      else if(ch >= 'A' && ch <= 'Z') {
        ch += (char) 32;
        changes++;
        Console.WriteLine(ch);
      }
    } while(ch != '.');
    Console.WriteLine("Case changes: " + changes);
  }
}
```

Chapter 4: Introducing Classes, Objects, and Methods

1. **A class is a logical abstraction that describes the form and behavior of an object. An object is a physical instance of the class.**

2. **A class is defined by using the keyword** class. **Inside the** class **statement, you specify the code and data that comprise the class.**

3. **Each object of a class has its own copy of the class' instance variables.**

4. ```
MyCounter counter;
counter = new MyCounter();
```

5. `double MyMeth(int a, int b) { // ...`
```

6. A method that returns a value must return via the return statement, passing back the return value in the process.

7. A constructor has the same name as its class.

8. The new operator allocates memory for an object and initializes it using the object's constructor.

9. Garbage collection is the mechanism that recycles unused objects so that their memory can be reused. A destructor is a method that is called just prior to an object being recycled.

10. For a method, the this keyword is a reference to the object on which a method is invoked. For a constructor, this is a reference to the object being constructed.

Chapter 5: More Data Types and Operators

1. `double[] x = new double[12];`

2. `int[,] nums = new int[4, 5];`

3. `int [][] nums = new int[5][];`

4. `int[] x = { 1, 2, 3, 4, 5 };`

5. The foreach loop cycles through a collection, obtaining each element in turn. Its general form is shown here:

   foreach(*type var-name* in *collection*) *statement*;

6. ```
// Average 10 double values.

using System;

class Avg {
  static void Main() {
    double[] nums = { 1.1, 2.2, 3.3, 4.4, 5.5,
                      6.6, 7.7, 8.8, 9.9, 10.1 };
    double sum = 0;

    for(int i=0; i < nums.Length; i++)
      sum += nums[i];

    Console.WriteLine("Average: " + sum / nums.Length);
  }
}
```

7. ```
// Demonstrate the bubble sort with strings.

using System;

class StrBubble {
  static void Main() {
```

```
            string[] strs = {
                              "this", "is", "a", "test",
                              "of", "a", "string", "sort"
                            };
            int a, b;
            string t;
            int size;

            size = strs.Length; // number of elements to sort

            // Display original array.
            Console.Write("Original array is:");
            for(int i=0; i < size; i++)
              Console.Write(" " + strs[i]);
            Console.WriteLine();

            // This is the bubble sort for strings.
            for(a=1; a < size; a++)
              for(b=size-1; b >= a; b--) {
                if(strs[b-1].CompareTo(strs[b]) > 0) {
                  // Exchange out of order elements.
                  t = strs[b-1];
                  strs[b-1] = strs[b];
                  strs[b] = t;
                }
              }

            // display sorted array
            Console.Write("Sorted array is:");
            for(int i=0; i < size; i++)
              Console.Write(" " + strs[i]);
            Console.WriteLine();
      }
}
```

8. The IndexOf( ) **method finds the first occurrence of the specified substring.** LastIndexOf( ) **finds the last occurrence.**

9.
```
// An improved XOR cipher.

using System;

class Encode {
    static void Main() {
        string msg = "This is a test";
        string encmsg = "";
        string decmsg = "";
        string key = "abcdefgi";
        int j;
```

```
      Console.Write("Original message: ");
      Console.WriteLine(msg);

      // Encode the message.
      j = 0;
      for(int i=0; i < msg.Length; i++) {
        encmsg = encmsg + (char) (msg[i] ^ key[j]);
        j++;
        if(j==8) j = 0;
      }

      Console.Write("Encoded message: ");
      Console.WriteLine(encmsg);

      // Decode the message.
      j = 0;
      for(int i=0; i < msg.Length; i++) {
        decmsg = decmsg + (char) (encmsg[i] ^ key[j]);
        j++;
        if(j==8) j = 0;
      }

      Console.Write("Decoded message: ");
      Console.WriteLine(decmsg);
    }
  }
```

10. No.

11. y = x < 0 ? 10 : 20;

12. It is a logical operator because the operands are of type bool.

Chapter 6: A Closer Look at Methods and Classes

1. No, a private member cannot be accessed outside of its class. As explained, when no access specifier is present, a class member defaults to private access.

2. precede

3.
```
// A stack class for characters.

using System;

class Stack {
  char[] stck; // this array holds the stack
  int tos;     // top of stack

  // Construct an empty Stack given its size.
```

```csharp
public Stack(int size) {
  stck = new char[size]; // allocate memory for stack
  tos = 0;
}

// Construct a Stack from a Stack.
public Stack(Stack ob) {
  tos = ob.tos;
  stck = new char[ob.stck.Length];

  // Copy elements.
  for(int i=0; i < tos; i++)
    stck[i] = ob.stck[i];
}

// Construct a stack with initial values.
public Stack(char[] a) {
  stck = new char[a.Length];

  for(int i = 0; i < a.Length; i++) {
    Push(a[i]);
  }
}


// Push characters onto the stack.
public void Push(char ch) {
  if(tos==stck.Length) {
    Console.WriteLine(" -- Stack is full.");
    return;
  }

  stck[tos] = ch;
  tos++;
}

// Pop a character from the stack.
public char Pop() {
  if(tos==0) {
    Console.WriteLine(" -- Stack is empty.");
    return (char) 0;
  }

  tos--;
  return stck[tos];
}
}
```

```
// Demonstrate the Stack class.
class SDemo {
  static void Main() {
    // construct 10-element empty stack
    Stack stk1 = new Stack(10);

    char[] name = {'T', 'o', 'm'};

    // Construct stack from array.
    Stack stk2 = new Stack(name);

    char ch;
    int i;

    // Put some characters into stk1.
    for(i=0; i < 10; i++)
      stk1.Push((char) ('A' + i));

    // Construct stack from another stack.
    Stack stk3 = new Stack(stk1);

    //Show the stacks.
    Console.Write("Contents of stk1: ");
    for(i=0; i < 10; i++) {
      ch = stk1.Pop();
      Console.Write(ch);
    }

    Console.WriteLine("\n");

    Console.Write("Contents of stk2: ");
    for(i=0; i < 3; i++) {
      ch = stk2.Pop();
      Console.Write(ch);
    }

    Console.WriteLine("\n");

    Console.Write("Contents of stk3: ");
    for(i=0; i < 10; i++) {
      ch = stk3.Pop();
      Console.Write(ch);
    }
  }
}
```

Here is the output from the program:

```
Contents of stk1: JIHGFEDCBA

Contents of stk2: moT

Contents of stk3: JIHGFEDCBA
```

4.
```
void Swap(Test ob1, Test ob2) {
    int t;

    t = ob1.a;
    ob1.a = ob2.a;
    ob2.a = t;
}
```

5. No. Overloaded methods can have different return types, but they do not play a role in overload resolution. Overloaded methods *must* have different parameter lists.

6.
```
// Display a string backwards using recursion.

using System;

class Backwards {
    string str;

    public Backwards(string s) {
        str = s;
    }

    public void Backward(int idx) {
        if(idx != str.Length-1) Backward(idx+1);

        Console.Write(str[idx]);
    }
}

class BWDemo {
    static void Main() {
        Backwards s = new Backwards("This is a test");

        s.Backward(0);
    }
}
```

7. Shared variables are declared as static.

8. The ref modifier causes an argument to be passed by reference. This allows a method to modify the contents of the argument. A ref parameter can receive information passed into the method. The out modifier is the same as ref, except that it cannot be used to pass a value into a method.

9.
```
static void Main()
static void Main(string[] args)
static int Main()
static int Main(string[] args)
```

10. They are all legal.

Chapter 7: Operator Overloading, Indexers, and Properties

1. public static *ret-type* operator *op(param-type operand)*

   {

     // operations

   }

The operand must be of the same type as the class for which the operator is being overloaded.

2. To allow the full mixing of a class type with a built-in type, you must overload an operator two ways. One way has the class type as the first operand and the built-in type as the second operand. The second way has the built-in type as the first operand and the class type as the second operand.

3. No, the ? cannot be overloaded. No, you cannot change the precedence of an operator.

4. An indexer provides array-like accessing of an object.

   element-type this[int *index*] {

     // The get accessor.

     get {

       // Return the value specified by index.

     }

     // The set accessor.

     set {

       // Set the value specified by index.

     }

   }

5. The get and set accessors get the value specified by the index or set the value specified by an index, respectively.

6. A property provides controlled access to a value.

   type name {

     get {

       // Get accessor code.

     }

     set {

       // Set accessor code.

     }

   }

7. No, a property does not define a storage location. It manages access to a separately defined field. Thus, you must declare a field that will be managed by the property or use an auto-implemented property, in which the compiler provides the field.

8. No, a property cannot be passed as a ref or out parameter.

9. An auto-implemented property is a property in which the compiler automatically supplies an anonymous variable, called a backing field, to hold the value. It is indicated by specifying only get; and set; without any bodies.

10.
```
// Determine if one set is a subset of another.
public static bool operator <(Set ob1, Set ob2) {
  if(ob1.Length > ob2.Length) return false; // ob1 has more elements

  for(int i=0; i < ob1.Length; i++)
    if(ob2.find(ob1[i]) == -1) return false;

  return true;
}

// Determine if one set is a superset of another.
public static bool operator >(Set ob1, Set ob2) {
  if(ob1.Length < ob2.Length) return false; // ob1 has fewer elements

  for(int i=0; i < ob2.Length; i++)
    if(ob1.find(ob2[i]) == -1) return false;

  return true;
}
```

11.
```
// Set intersection.
public static Set operator &(Set ob1, Set ob2) {
  Set newset = new Set();

  // Add elements common to both sets.
  for(int i=0; i < ob1.Length; i++)
    if(ob2.find(ob1[i]) != -1)
      // Add the element if it is a member of both sets.
      newset = newset + ob1[i];

  return newset; // return intersection
}
```

Chapter 8: Inheritance

1. No, a base class has no knowledge of its derived classes. Yes, a derived class has access to all non-private members of its base class.

2.
```
// A subclass of TwoDShape for circles.
class Circle : TwoDShape {
  // Construct Circle
  public Circle(double x) : base(x, "circle") { }

  // Construct a copy of an object.
  public Circle(Circle ob) : base(ob) { }

  public override double Area() {
    return (Width / 2) * (Width / 2) * 3.1416;
  }
}
```

3. To prevent a derived class from having access to a base class member, declare that member as private.

4. The base keyword has two forms. The first is used to call a base class constructor. The general form of this usage is

   base(*param-list*)

   The second form of base is used to access a base class member. It has this general form:

   base.*member*

5. Constructors are always called in order of derivation. Thus, when a Gamma object is created, the order is Alpha, Beta, Gamma.

6. When a virtual method is called through a base class reference, it is the type of the object being referred to that determines which version of the method is called.

7. An abstract class contains at least one abstract method.

8. To prevent a class from being inherited, declare it as sealed.

9. Inheritance, virtual methods, and abstract classes support polymorphism by enabling you to create a generalized class structure that can be implemented by a variety of classes. Thus, the abstract class defines a consistent interface, which is shared by all implemented classes. This embodies the concept of "one interface, multiple methods."

10. object

11. Boxing is the process of storing a value type in an object. Boxing occurs automatically when you assign a value to an object reference.

12. A protected member is available for use by derived classes, but is otherwise private to its class.

Chapter 9: Interfaces, Structures, and Enumerations

1. The interface best exemplifies the "one interface, multiple methods" principle of OOP.

2. An interface can be implemented by an unlimited number of classes. A class can implement as many interfaces as it chooses.

3. Yes, interfaces can be inherited.

4. Yes, a class must implement all members defined by an interface.

5. No, an interface cannot define a constructor.

6.
```csharp
interface IVehicle {
    int Range();

    double FuelNeeded(int miles);

    int Passengers {
      get;
      set;
    }

    int FuelCap {
      get;
      set;
    }

    int Mpg {
      get;
      set;
    }
}
```

7.
```csharp
// Create a fail-soft interface.
using System;

// This is the fail-soft interface.
public interface IFailSoft {
  // This specifies the length property interface.
  int Length {
    get;
  }

  // This specifies the indexer interface.
  int this[int index] {
    get;
    set;
  }
}
```

```
// Now, implement IFailSoft.
class FailSoftArray : IFailSoft {
  int[] a; // reference to array
  int len; // backing variable for length property

  public bool ErrFlag; // indicates outcome of last operation

  // Construct array given its size.
  public FailSoftArray(int size) {
    a = new int[size];
    len = size;
  }

  // A read-only Length property.
  public int Length { get{ return len; } }

  // This is the indexer for FailSoftArray.
  public int this[int index] {
    // This is the get accessor.
    get {
      if(ok(index)) {
        ErrFlag = false;
        return a[index];
      } else {
        ErrFlag = true;
        return 0;
      }
    }

    // This is the set accessor.
    set {
      if(ok(index)) {
        a[index] = value;
        ErrFlag = false;
      }
      else ErrFlag = true;
    }
  }

  // Return true if index is within bounds.
  private bool ok(int index) {
   if(index >= 0 & index < Length) return true;
   return false;
  }
}
```

```
// Demonstrate the improved fail-soft array.
class ImprovedFSDemo {
  static void Main() {
    FailSoftArray fs = new FailSoftArray(5);
    int x;

    for(int i=0; i < fs.Length; i++)
      fs[i] = i*10;

    for(int i=0; i < fs.Length; i++) {
      x = fs[i];
      if(x != -1) Console.Write(x + " ");
    }
    Console.WriteLine();
  }
}
```

8. A struct **defines a value type. A** class **defines a reference type.**

9. enum Planets {Mercury, Venus, Earth, Mars, Jupiter, Saturn, Uranus, Neptune };

Chapter 10: Exception Handling

1. System.Exception **is at the top of the exception hierarchy.**

2. The try **and** catch **work together. Program statements that you want to monitor for exceptions are contained within a** try **block. An exception is caught using** catch.

3. There is no try **block preceding the** catch **clause.**

4. If an exception is not caught, abnormal program termination results.

5. In the fragment, a base class catch **precedes a derived class** catch. **Since the base class** catch **will catch all derived classes too, unreachable code is created.**

6. Yes, an exception can be rethrown.

7. False. The finally **block is the code executed when a** try **block ends.**

8. Here is one way to add exception handling to the Stack **class:**

```
// An exception for stack-full errors.
using System;

class StackFullException : Exception {
  // Create standard constructors.
  public StackFullException() : base() { }
  public StackFullException(string str) : base(str) { }
  public StackFullException(string str, Exception inner) :
    base(str, inner) { }
```

```
    protected StackFullException(
      System.Runtime.Serialization.SerializationInfo si,
      System.Runtime.Serialization.StreamingContext sc) :
        base(si, sc) { }
}

// An exception for stack-empty errors.
class StackEmptyException : Exception {
  // Create standard constructors.
  public StackEmptyException() : base() { }
  public StackEmptyException(string str) : base(str) { }
  public StackEmptyException(string str, Exception inner) :
    base(str, inner) { }
  protected StackEmptyException(
    System.Runtime.Serialization.SerializationInfo si,
    System.Runtime.Serialization.StreamingContext sc) :
      base(si, sc) { }
}

// A stack class for characters.
class Stack {
  char[] stck; // this array holds the stack
  int tos;  // top of stack

  // Construct an empty Stack given its size.
  public Stack(int size) {
    stck = new char[size]; // allocate memory for stack
    tos = 0;
  }

  // Construct a Stack from a Stack.
  public Stack(Stack ob) {
    tos = ob.tos;
    stck = new char[ob.stck.Length];

    // Copy elements.
    for(int i=0; i < tos; i++)
      stck[i] = ob.stck[i];
  }

  // Construct a stack with initial values.
  public Stack(char[] a) {
    stck = new char[a.Length];

    for(int i = 0; i < a.Length; i++) {
      try {
        Push(a[i]);
      }
```

```
      catch(StackFullException exc) {
        Console.WriteLine(exc);
      }
    }
  }

  // Push characters onto the stack.
  public void Push(char ch) {
    if(tos==stck.Length)
      throw new StackFullException();

    stck[tos] = ch;
    tos++;
  }

  // Pop a character from the stack.
  public char Pop() {
    if(tos==0)
      throw new StackEmptyException();

    tos--;
    return stck[tos];
  }
}
```

9. checked **and** unchecked **determine whether or not arithmetic overflow causes an exception. To avoid an exception, mark the related code as** unchecked. **To raise an exception on overflow, mark the related code as** checked.

10. **All exceptions can be caught using one of these forms of** catch:

    catch { }

    catch(Exception exc) { }

    catch(Exception) { }

Chapter 11: Using I/O

1. **Byte streams are useful for file I/O, especially binary file I/O, and they support random access files. The character streams are optimized for Unicode.**

2. **The class at the top of the stream hierarchy is** Stream.

3. **Here is one way to open a file for byte input:**

    ```
    FileStream fin = new FileStream("myfile", FileMode.Open);
    ```

4. **Here is one way to open a file for reading characters:**

    ```
    StreamReader frdr_in = new StreamReader(new FileStream("myfile",
                                        FileMode.Open));
    ```

5. Seek( ) sets the current file position.

6. Binary I/O for the C# built-in types is supported by BinaryReader and BinaryWriter.

7. I/O is redirected by calling SetIn( ), SetOut( ), and SetError( ).

8. A numeric string can be converted into its internal representation by using the Parse( ) method defined by the .NET structure aliases.

9.
```
/* Copy a text file, substituting hyphens for spaces.

   This version uses byte streams.

   To use this program, specify the name
   of the source file and the destination file.
   For example:

   Hyphen source target
*/

using System;
using System.IO;

class Hyphen {
  static void Main(string[] args) {
    int i;
    FileStream fin;
    FileStream fout;

    if(args.Length != 2) {
      Console.WriteLine("Usage: Hyphen From To");
      return;
    }

    // Open the input file.
    try {
      fin = new FileStream(args[0], FileMode.Open);
    } catch(IOException exc) {
      Console.WriteLine(exc.Message);
      return;
    }

    // Open the output file.
    try {
      fout = new FileStream(args[1], FileMode.Create);
    } catch(IOException exc) {
      Console.WriteLine(exc.Message);
      fin.Close();
      return;
    }
```

```
      // Copy the file.
      try {
        do {
          i = fin.ReadByte();
          if((char)i == ' ') i = '-';
          if(i != -1) fout.WriteByte((byte) i);
        } while(i != -1);
      } catch(IOException exc) {
        Console.WriteLine(exc.Message);
      }

      fin.Close();
      fout.Close();
    }
  }
```

10.
```
/* Copy a text file, substituting hyphens for spaces.

   This version uses character streams.

   To use this program, specify the name
   of the source file and the destination file.
   For example:

   Hyphen source target
*/

using System;
using System.IO;

class Hyphen {
  static void Main(string[] args) {
    int i;
    StreamReader fin;
    StreamWriter fout;

    if(args.Length != 2) {
      Console.WriteLine("Usage: Hyphen From To");
      return;
    }

    // Open the input file.
    try {
      fin = new StreamReader(args[0]);
    } catch(IOException exc) {
      Console.WriteLine(exc.Message);
      return;
    }
```

```
      // Open the output file.
      try {
        fout = new StreamWriter(args[1]);
      } catch(IOException exc) {
        Console.WriteLine(exc.Message);
        fin.Close();
        return;
      }

      // Copy the file.
      try {
        do {
          i = fin.Read();
          if((char)i == ' ') i = '-';
          if(i != -1) fout.Write((char) i);
        } while(i != -1);
      } catch(IOException exc) {
        Console.WriteLine(exc.Message);
      }

      fin.Close();
      fout.Close();
    }
  }
```

Chapter 12: Delegates, Events, and Namespaces

1. `delegate double Filter(int i);`

2. **A multicast is created by adding methods to a delegate chain using the += operator. A method can be removed by use of − =.**

3. **An anonymous method is a block of code that is passed to a delegate constructor.**

4. **Yes. Yes.**

5. **An event requires the use of a delegate.**

6. event

7. **Yes, events can be multicast.**

8. **An event is always sent to a specific instance.**

9. **A namespace defines a declarative region, which prevents name collisions.**

10. using *alias* = *name*;

11. ```
namespace X.Y {
    // ...
}
```
```

Chapter 13: Generics

1. True.

2. A type parameter is a placeholder for an actual type. The actual type will be specified when an object of a generic class or delegate is instantiated, or when a generic method is called.

3. A type argument is an actual data type that is passed to a type parameter.

4. When operating through object references, the compiler won't catch type-mismatch errors between the type of data supplied and the type of data required. This causes those errors to occur at runtime.

5. A base class constraint on a type parameter requires that any type argument specified for that parameter be derived from or identical to the specified base class. The value-type constraint requires that a type argument be of a value type, not a reference type.

6. Yes.

7. To obtain a default value for a type, use the default operator.

8. The type parameter list for a generic method immediately follows the name of the method. Thus, it goes between the method name and the opening parenthesis of the method's parameter list.

9. Yes.

10. Here is one approach. It uses auto-implemented properties for X and Y.

```csharp
public interface ITwoDCoord<T> {

  T X { get; set; }
  T Y { get; set; }
}


class XYCoord<T> : ITwoDCoord<T> {

  public XYCoord(T x, T y) {
    X = x;
    Y = y;
  }

  public T  X { get; set; }
  public T  Y { get; set; }

}
```

Chapter 14: Introducing LINQ

1. LINQ stands for Language Integrated Query. It is used to retrieve information from a data source.

2. IEnumerable in either its generic or non-generic form.

3. The query keywords are from, group, where, join, let, orderby, **and** select.

4. `var allData = from info in myDataList`
`select info;`

5. `var heightData = from info in myDataList`
`select info.Height;`

6. where

```
var allData = from info in myDataList
where info.Height < 100
select info.Height;
```

7. orderby

```
var allData = from info in myDataList
where info.Height < 100
orderby info.Height descending
select info.Height;
```

8. group
group *range-variable* by *key*

9. join
from *range-varA* in *data-sourceA*
　join *range-varB* in *data-sourceB*
　　on *range-varA*.*property* equals *range-varB*.*property*.

10. into

11. let

12. `new { Author = "Knuth", Title = "The Art of Computer Programming" }`

13. `=>`

14. True.

15. Where( )

16. An extension method adds functionality to a class, but without using inheritance. The first parameter defines the type that is being extended. It must be modified by this. **The first parameter is automatically passed the object on which the extension method is called.**

17. Extension methods are important to LINQ because the query methods are implemented as extension methods for IEnumerable<T>.

Chapter 15: The Preprocessor, RTTI, Nullable Types, and Other Advanced Topics

1. The conditional compilation directives are #if, #elif, #else, **and** #endif.

2. The #elif **means "else if." It lets you create an if-else-if chain for multiple compilation options.**

3. To obtain a System.Type **object at runtime, use the** typeof **operator.**

4. **The** is **keyword determines if an object is of a specified type.**

5. **The** as **operator converts one type into another if the conversion is a legal boxing, unboxing, identity, or reference conversion. Its benefit is that it does not throw an exception if the conversion is not allowed.**

6. `int? count = null;`

7. **True.**

8. **The** ?? **is called the null coalescing operator. It returns the value of a nullable instance if that instance contains a value. Otherwise, it returns a specified default value.**

9. **Unsafe code is code that executes outside the managed context.**

10. `double* ptr;`

11. **Attributes are enclosed between square brackets, as shown here:**

    [*attribute*]

12. **There are implicit and explicit conversion operators. Their general forms are shown here:**

    public static operator implicit *target-type*(*source-type v*) { return *value*; }

    public static operator explicit *target-type*(*source-type v*) { return *value*; }

13. **A collection is a group of objects. The generic collections are in the** System.Collections.Generic **namespace.**

14. ICollection<T>

15. **The** partial **keyword is used in both cases.**

Index

T